Uwe Petersen

Blessings and Victims of Globalization

Economic and social development, relative impoverishment, unemployment, economic crises, right-wing and left-wing radicalism, religious wars, refugee flows and the responsibility of Europe

Author: Uwe Petersen

Blessings and Victims of Globalization
Economic and social development, relative
impoverishment, unemployment, economic crises,
right-wing and left-wing radicalism, religious wars,
refugee flows and the responsibility of Europe

Translated and updated

Original German Title:
Segen und Opfer der Globalisierung
Wirtschaftliche und gesellschaftliche Entwicklung,
relative Verarmung, Arbeitslosigkeit, Wirtschaftskrisen,
Links- und Rechtsradikalismus, Religionskriege,
Flüchtlingsströme und die Verantwortung Europas

Published 2017

Book cover design:
TomJay - bookcover4everyone / www.tomjay.de
Cover photo: © ginae014 - Fotolia.com

Date of publication: 2018

ISBN: 978-3-7469-1105-2 (Paperback)
ISBN: 978-3-7469-1106-9 (Hardcover)
ISBN: 978-3-7469-1107-6 (e-Book)

Publisher: tredition GmbH, Hamburg

Contents

Introduction

The fact that we must deal with the problems of the whole world today is a result of globalization. We must be aware of the fact that globalization is a globalization of our European spirit, our way of life, our technology, including the atomic bomb, our economy and society, and so we are responsible for what is happening worldwide.

As a result of globalization, we cannot only observe a growing standard of living and a faster population growth due to improved health care and medicines, but we also have to complain about relative impoverishment, unemployment, economic crises, left-wing and right-wing extremism, religious wars and huge refugee flows.

To the extent that the negative consequences of globalization affect the Western world, they lead to general uncertainty, which then manifests itself in a loss of confidence in political institutions. Even the greatest achievements of the post-war period, the overcoming of nationalism and the unification of Europe, are questioned and disproved, and salvation is sought in foreclosure and national autonomous regions.

A possible interim climax has been this aversion to established institutions and powers in the election of US President Donald Trump who, and this is already the questionable nature of his programmed policy, promises, along with other billionaires and, with the promotion of capital market games, to lead the mass of the economically backward to new prosperity and new greatness. To this end, he wants to decouple the US from the world market and return lost industries to the country.

All the small Trumps: Victor Orbán, Jaroslav Kaczyinski, Gerd Wilders, Marine le Pen, Beppe Grillo, and the leaders of the PEGIDA and the AfD and their followers in Germany, cheer him and also proclaim their independence and their intention to leave the Eurozone or even the European Union. In doing so, they forget that the US can afford to foreclose and be self-sufficient because they have such a large domestic market that they can force foreign manufacturers to produce in the USA if they want to sell there. But who else wants to invest in smaller European countries?

From purely economic market perspectives, these nationalists would lead their country to the outside and without the backing of the other European countries and without the European Central Bank defending them against the growing monetary and economic turbulences. What a withdrawal from the European Union means can be clearly seen in Great Britain according to BREXIT, if Great Britain can still be called "great" after a loss of Scotland.

Their ray of hope is that Donald Trump would help countries leaving the EU. He only thinks of America and only recognizes strength. Of course, he is interested in the fact that the power factor of Europe is disintegrating. Since the European Trumps do not recognize the need for a strengthening of Europe, in order to be able to confront America and other great powers, they also prove to be political twits.

The increasing dissatisfaction with the given circumstances is not unfounded. It is the result of an inadequate development of the economic and social theories and ideals and the policy determined by them. Disharmonies developed in this

9

way. In particular, there was an increasingly unequal development of wealth and income. Apart from the social injustice involved, an ever-growing economic demand gap arose as a result of the too high savings in relation to the promising investment opportunities and innovations. The demand gap could only be compensated by increasing government expenditures or by the fact that, as in Germany, excess demand is shifted abroad by export surpluses. Thus, the growth rates remained lean and favored almost only the already wealthy. Only the capital market games flourish and celebrate the breakthrough of ever higher stock index brands.

In order to understand economic development and globalization, we must analyze the underlying motivations. It will be shown that the driving forces and objectives of economic development and globalization are based on the special intellectual development of Europe, as it grew out of an antique and Jewish / Christian heritage.

The naivety of the assessment of contemporary history, society, and thus economic development also means that a man's image is expressed according to how he has always been more or less structured and assessed as in the modern Western world. This also makes it unclear why civilizations and cultures have developed differently and why it is not possible to introduce Western democracy into any social order. It must be realized that the spirit of people, their feelings, their willingness, their behavior, their self-confidence have only developed over many thousand years and the development has been different in the individual countries. Many things are common to all men, but many things are also different, and if these differences are not heeded, no reasonable interpretation of social, economic and political conditions is possible.

The analysis of the economic, social and political conditions of the world also shows that it is not enough simply to compare power relations, economic development and raw material reserves, but that spiritual and, in particular, religious motivations can be much more important drives for political and social actions. The failure of the US in Vietnam, the Iranian revolution, the quick growth of the IS, and its assertion cannot be explained otherwise.

It may come as a surprise to the contemporary reader that we trace the discussion of the problems of globalization back to religion. But if one considers how far other religious denominations, especially Islam, determine the social ideals of Muslim countries and international politics, then it should really be possible to understand that Europeans should also refer to their intellectual heritage and the resulting behavior, especially in order to meet other religious demands and to understand their own position. Thus it should be allowed, since *Europeanism* has as its roots in antiquity and, Christianity, to reflect on their essence.

In the discussion of *Europeanism*, it must not be overlooked that it is divided into a western and an eastern component, both of which have been globalized. The leading countries for Western *Europeanism* were Great Britain and later the Anglo-Saxon world, dominated by the United States. The Eastern *Europeanism* is represented by the Eastern European countries, initially most notably by Poland, but then more and more by Russia with its expansion to the Black Sea and to Vladivostok.

These two *Europeanisms* and their globalization became antipodes since the founding of the British and the Russian Empire. In particular, Russia's efforts to become a sea power since Peter the Great, and his urge for the Black Sea, the Persian Gulf and the Indian Ocean, were felt by the British to be threats to their route to India. The resulting East-West opposition continued to determine nearly all conflicts in the Near and Middle East caused by the East-West divide after the Russian October Revolution and superimposes the current conflicts in Ukraine and the Middle East.

In order to understand current political problems, the essence of the East-West opposition and the position of Europe must therefore also be discussed. The lessons to be gained from this can help to understand the responsibility and task of Europe and, as the strongest economic power of Central Europe, of Germany in overcoming and mediating the East-West opposition. This results in an outline of this elaboration:

A. Europeanism as the source of Globalization.

B. Western and Eastern Europeanism as the origin of the East-West Opposition and their Globalization

C. The crisis and the further development of Europeanism in the globalized world.

In order to make the importance of East-West opposition clearer to Western readers, the intellectual, social and political motives of Russia as bringer of Christian salvation, Third Rome, and Eurasia, which are now increasingly determining the Russian politics, and also Poland's antagonism against Russia, is discussed in more detail.

To understand the impact of the globalization of Europeanism on countries outside Europe, their development has been described in more detail. Every country has its own problems and can influence world peace. Anyone who knows the history of colonization and the movements of independency in the tension relationship of the East-West antagonism can skip these reports. They are identified by special letters.

A. Europeanism as the source of globalization

Globalization is understood as the union of individual people into a world community. The motives for globalization were and are:
1. Domination and exploitation
2. Trade
3. The mission and development of nan.

I. Domination and exploitation as motives for globalization

Already the behavior of nomadic cattle breeders was relatable in terms of production conditions. Grazing land is used and tolerates only a certain amount of humans, so that the stronger nomad tribes destroy others and take over only their cattle.

Tribes who settled down as farmers and later as city dwellers and founded a society with a flourishing economy and culture gained an intrinsic value for conquerors, so that the latter did not expel the population anymore and kill them, but made them subjects and slaves, and frequently even adopted the culture of the subordinates. There are transitions. Thus, the Vikings not only operated extensive maritime trade, but also undertook the exploitation of prey and reduced cities such as Paris and Hamburg to rubble. Later, especially with the takeover of Christianity, the Vikings began to found empires.

Since in Asia, Egypt and South and Central America much higher cultures had already developed and much earlier than in Europe, very early large empires were there already established. The first great European empire was that of the Romans. All these empires were land masses, unless the countries were grouped around the Mediterranean, as in the Roman Empire.

For this reason, the first approaches to globalization can already be seen in the formation of great empires. There, a tribal emperor ruled over other people, who often kept a limited independence, and only a tributary, or kingdom god, represented by the ruler, was imposed on the cults of families and clans. Thus, came the well-known god kings, like the emperor in China, the Pharaohs in Egypt, the Incas in South America.

As far as these empires could create a protected, legally-regulated economic space, they also promoted the division of labor, a key factor in economic growth. Trade and economy flourished in these empires and provided the conditions for a flourishing cultural and social life.

Since the technical revolution, pressure to create larger economic areas has been increased by new production facilities. In Great Britain, where the industrial revolution began, sales markets for industrial products were very small. British companies were forced to conquer foreign markets. Even other industrialized European countries sooner or later had to offer their products abroad, in order to utilize the capacity of their industries.

The increased production facilities required more raw materials. It was a good idea to import these from overseas areas. Development of sales markets and raw material requirements were therefore a decisive driving force for globalization.

II. Trade as a form of globalization

The primary form of globalization was trade. Even thousands of years ago, amber from the Baltic Sea, furs from Russia, gold and artifacts from the Mediterranean countries, exotic products from East Asia and incense from Ethiopia were traded across continents, to name but a few examples.

Traders are primary forms of individualists. They emerge from their local production conditions and try to make profit from buying and reselling goods. The more adventurous they are, the more travel they make and thus connect economically distant countries with each other.

Traditional producers, that is, early craftsmen in particular, are subject to social conditions which, for example, do not allow them to produce something for the sake of profit only if this profit is used not only to lead a way of life appropriate to their station.

For traders, there were no such limits. That's why they couldn't become very rich. They also had no emotional relationship with their goods, but only looked at which profit was achievable by what exchange. As far as international trade was later institutionalized, for example, between Greek trade branches or the Hanseatic League, traders also imposed certain rules of conduct, for example those of a *royal merchant*. Yet, in their minds, they were always much freer than craftsmen. Traders were therefore also regarded by decent society and people as a dubious and traveling people.

III. Religious missionary work for the further development of mankind

The third motive for globalization, the spread of one's own religion as a mandate to God, and to eternal salvation of humanity, have existed only since Buddhism, Christianity and Islam, as far as cults and philosophical doctrines were concerned, which were directed not at communities but at individual humans.

Primitive religions are the link of communities that define individual human beings and in which traditional people have their own ego. The further we go back in history, the less we find that the individual man as his own ego – he is a member of a community. This can also be seen in the development of language. In earlier cultures, the individual person spoke like a child in the third person. For example, today the Vietnamese prefer to call themselves in their role, which they play in the family, and they are also so called. They call themselves "older brother," "younger sister," "child," "grandfather," etc. The word "*I*" was created in Vietnam only during the colonization of Indochina by the French and is referred to in its original meaning as well as "the most devoted servant of the Emperor". I deal with this in more detail in my book *Language as a Scientific Object, Philosophical Phenomenon and Act*[1].

---

[1] Uwe Petersen: *Sprache als wissenschaftlicher er Gegenstand, philosophisches Phänomen und Tat.*

Genuine communities are families with an ancestral cult and tribes and peoples who each have their gods. The Jewish God Jehovah is also the tribal god of the Jews.

In Christianity and Islam, the missionary mission is an essential part of religion. Christianity and Islam turn to the individual to save him or to secure his soul. Family, tribal or ethnic status are not important. Everyone is regarded as a self-sufficient individual who is to be honored, loved and promoted in his peculiarity, regardless of his or her affiliation with a race or nation.

1. Christian missionary work

With the emergence of Christianity, a new impulse came into the dying Roman-antique world. While in pre-and non-Christian religions, the god-world was experienced or presented beyond man in nature or beyond the terrestrial world, the particularity of Christianity was that its supreme God in his Son was linked to the individual man, and the individual thus deified, or the prospect of personal deification was opened up to him.

Christianity emerged from Judaism. Jehovah made the Jews his own people, and, according to their understanding, concluded with them a treaty by which they were led by him. The direct relationship the Jew had to his God was extended in Christianity to all men. In addition, everyone was given the opportunity to receive Christ in themselves and thus become divine. This possibility meant calling for free, self-responsible action.

Gerald Kruhöffer writes: 'Paul takes the word "freedom" out of the Greek-Hellenistic context and gives it a new meaning within the framework of his theology. The new aspect of Christian interpretation lies primarily in the fact that freedom is linked to a historical event: Jesus Christ is the origin of freedom. In its history, liberty has become an event. For this reason, freedom is understood and experienced as liberation.

Paul pointedly put it: "For freedom Christ set us free. So be firm and do not let the yoke of slavery lay on you again!"(Galatians 5: 1) The liberating God experience, which originates in the history of Jesus Christ, is essential.'[2]

The merging of Christianity with the traditional Caesar's domination led to true Christianity being to a certain extent perverted and spread with fire and sword.

Islamic missionary work

Islam is, in a simplified way, a submission to the otherworldly God Allah. Islampedia writes: 'ALLAH, the creator of all being, tells us in His last book of revelation to all mankind, the Quran, the following:

"And I created the jinn (immaterial creatures)
and the people only to serve Me. "(Quran 51:56)

The true meaning of the life of all men is therefore solely to serve ALLAH, in the way that He gave man over the way of revelation through His messengers (last,

---

[2] Gerald Kruhöffer: *Was heißt christliche Freiheit heute?*, Text published in: Loccumer Pelikan 3/2003.

in the Quran and in the Sunnah / the model of the last Envoy of Muhammad). This kind of way of life is called "Islam" or in German "god-givenness". In this sense, Islam is the name of a way of life of all devout people and all the prophets of God.'[3]

According to this, in Islam the souls' blessing and the long-term happiness of men depend solely on whether they submit to their God completely. Allah is described as a despotic God, who promises Paradise only to men submissive to him, and is merciful, compassionate and forgiving, only until the time of repentance, which he established, has elapsed and who, after that deadline and without mercy, is sent into eternal damnation and the cruelest fires. Allah takes the same position as in early Judaism Jehovah.

According to the original doctrine, Allah is also the ruler of the world, or the world is governed in his name by the Caliph, who is the representative of Allah, and because, according to Mohammed, there is no further divine inspiration, Sharia law is the only possible law book.

Since Islam already has a theocratic structure as a religion, the connection between politics and religion is already designed. This is why it is so difficult for Islamic states to develop democratic, secular forms of rule. This means that where more or less secular forms of government were formed in the Islamic world, they were either military dictatorships or already takeovers of European social orders.

The image of man in Islam is also determined by human sensual needs. Allah greatly reduces man to a sexual being and does not treat men and women alike. Women are treated in many places in the Koran as second-class people. There is therefore no place for a self-conscious, intellectually developing individual in Islam. Thus, it is not surprising that spiritual cultural, economic and social development has stagnated in Islamic states, while it is self-evident for a modern humanist social order that the individual is at first spirit and only differently *incorporated* as a man or woman.

The fact that in many Islamic states archaic tribes could be preserved is also the reason for the persistence of a strict patriarchal family principle with its hierarchy, also for the sons and daughters, and their integrity towards the patriarch. According to this, the individual human being is primarily responsible for his tribe, and only to the second degree to his leadership of the state.

Because of this tribal affinity, the Islamic world since Mohammed has been less concerned with the conviction of individuals than with the conversion of entire tribes. Accordingly, Islamic warriors were led by tribal leaders into the war, that is, the king or caliph was supported by the leaders in his campaigns. If the Sultan's religious recognition diminished, conflicts of loyalty could arise. In doubt, the authority of the tribal leader was more than that of the caliph or sultan.

Should a greater empire be conquered and preserved by war, then the Caliph or Sultan needed him unconditioned soldiers. He found them in the so-called slave soldiers. To this end, as *kriegsreisende.de* writes, 'The adolescents, torn away from their familiar surroundings, isolated and uprooted in the new culture, they were given a new identity. The long training was at the same time an imprint on her new master. As slaves, they were not only his possessions, but also belonged to his household, to his family. And the Caliphs, of course, were determined to increase

---

[3] http://www.islam-pedia.de/index.php5?title=Mensch.

this sense of affiliation by rich gifts, magnificent clothes, and other privileges. Slave soldiers were among the social elites in Islam. This system of privileged slaves, trained and educated with great effort, was then copied later in Egypt, Spain and even by the Turks themselves.'[4]

'To a fixed institution were slave soldiers ... around 830 under the caliph Al-Muetasim, who had Turkish slaves bought up in a very great style and formed a standing army from them. At the same time, he moved his government from Baghdad to nearby Samarra, where his military slaves - about 70,000 men lived in their own city districts.'[5]

' The military slaves then quickly became an integral part of the system, and in most Islamic states, they were the backbone of the armies, or at least the bodyguards of the rulers. There is no evidence of rebellions in which the slaves fought for their freedom, or even attempted to return to their homeland. When they rebelled, on the contrary, they were concerned with maintaining their position and the privileges they had. They then behaved more like the Praetorian Guard in the Roman Empire. In Samarra, too, the successors of Al-Muetasim were soon completely dependent on their Turkish guards, who the Caliphs used at their will. In Egypt, the Mamelukes themselves completely seized power around 1250 and founded their own dynasties, and in Turkey many Sultans were later overthrown by the Janissaries'[6]

In order to submit as many people as possible to the Islamic faith, Muhammad and his successors created great Muslim empires. The Islamic rule extended to Spain, across the Balkans, but also towards Persia, India, and far into Russia today. For a long time until Tsar *Ivan the Great* the Christian Russian rulers were haunted by Muslim Tartars.

However, Islamic beliefs did not provide any particular impulses for scientific, cultural and intellectual development. Mohammed had called for adopting all existing knowledge, and because of the richness of the Middle East in Hellenistic and other cultural heritage, the Islamic caliphs were first and foremost leading the cultural and civilizing world in the European and pre-Asian world. Through Muslim-domination, valuable science also came to Spain and cultural impulses to Europe. However, to the extent that the Koran dominated culture and the mind, the cultural prosperity of the Islamic world was ruined. In addition, the cultural heritage was destroyed by Mongols.

The present fanatical beliefs, which want to turn Islam into the ruling world religion, the dream of the medieval culture flourishes. However, they have overlooked the fact that Islam at that time established not only state framework, but its culture and civilization were fed by pre-Islamic sources. The Muslims' fervor of faith was the study of the Koran, and Islamic terrorists again claim the Koran to be the only standard in our time.

In 1299, Muslim countries in the Middle East were conquered by the Ottomans. They succeeded in founding a vast empire over the entire Middle East and

---

[4] http://www.kriegsreisende.de/mittelalter/sklaven.htm.
[5] Ibid.
[6] loc. cit.

North Africa, and to hold it for many centuries until their belligerent missionary formation of the empire had ceased.

In addition, the economy of the Ottoman Empire was decisively weakened as the lucrative trade via the Silk Road and from the south of Arabia ceased, because Europeans were directly involved in East Asia with their ships. The Ottoman Empire became a so-called "sick man on the Bosporus".

In contrast to the Islamic Near East and Africa, the tribal affinity of the people of Europe was overcome in the course of history. This development was promoted by the fact that individual tribes migrated across Europe in the course of the migration of people and intermarried with the subjugated people. The Ostrogoths, Visigoths, Vandals and other tribes who moved to the south have quasi-culturally disappeared in Italy and Spain. The Franks still exist in name in today's France.

In the empire established by Charles the Great, free knights developed, who were supported by land. The territories of the region overlaid a network of counties, in which the nobles formed a separate social class, who only intermarried.

The dominated areas were later inherited as property or were given other masters in the course of wars or inheritances or were connected with other areas. The individual fiefdoms were hierarchically related to the emperor. The originally free peasants turned into serfs. Correspondingly, the Russian Empire also developed, centralized on the Tsar.

Through the development of handicrafts and commerce, cities emerged, into which serfs could escape and thereby become free citizens.

While traditional Islam prescribes a rule of God, something which is also targeted by radical Muslims in the caliphate of the IS and mullahs in Iran, the kingdom of Christ was *not of this world*, so that in Europe there developed a secular rule that was more and more independent of the Church.

The Catholic Church attempted to establish the papacy over the whole of Christendom, and the Pope still dominates the small Vatican state. Corresponding tendencies also existed in the areas dominated by the Orthodox Church, especially in Russia. But this claim has been more and more defended over the course of European history, so that a separation of the state and the Church in the European world is regarded as self-evident.

Christianity also developed beyond Islam in that it was increasingly linked to the ancient heritage. Western Europe in particular was characterized by the Roman tradition, which manifested itself in particular in the self-understanding as a *Roman citizen*. In addition, Europe assimilated the Hellenistic heritage, which was conveyed to it especially by the Arabs through Spain. The result of the confluence of Christianity and ancient heritage is called *Europeanism*.

Their minds and attitudes of life are now regarded as so self-evident to Europeans, that all other forms of beliefs and societies differing from them are considered underdeveloped. The missionary commitment also continued in the secularized forms of Christianity, and as a result, natural rights of the people, democracy, free market economy, freedom of belief, free science and freedom of expression and socialism were promoted and demanded all over the world.

Recent developments of revitalization and mission of Islam, especially in response to *Europeanism*, are, on the other hand, reversed, and can lead to religiously motivated wars, terror and destruction, which are observable in various ways.

IV. Europeanism and its globalization

We find the origin of *Europeanism* in antiquity and in Christianity. In the Greek Polis, the free individual was born. The individual, as a self-sufficient actor, felt opposed to his gods, and was no longer merely the subject of a god or divinely legitimate ruler. He felt as a member of a society, but not only backed by it, but also backing it. Thus, as with the free individual, the *democratic form of government* arose.

Strengthened and legally founded, self-confidence as a free citizen was still established in the Roman Empire. As a *Roman Citizen*, the individual emancipated himself also from his archaic rootedness as a member of a tribe. The monopoly of power passed to the state. It was no longer the right of the blood-race and the archaic code of honor. This created the foundations for the economic and social life of free citizens, which, in principle, is possible worldwide.

While in ancient times the gods existed independent of men, although men depended on the work of the gods and they had to make them merciful with sacrifices and prayers, Jehovah made the Jews his own people and concluded according to their understanding with them a contract by which they were led by him.

The direct relationship the Jew had to his God was extended to all men in Christianity, which had emerged from Judaism. In addition, he was given the opportunity to take Christ into himself and thus become divine. This possibility meant a man's call for free, self-responsible action.

The self-realization of man requires that he can be detached from higher hierarchies, such as a family, clan or tribe. People who walked this way were, exclusively, either robbers, knights or warriors, or hermits, clergy or monks. Because Christianity in some way deified the individual and offered him the opportunity to develop his soul, monasteries were built wherever men were baptized. The monasteries were also the incubators for science and research.

The ideal of the Christian, however, is not only to develop his own self, but to turn it back into the world and society and thus to realize himself in the world.

Self-realization is work. Man is changing the world, so to speak, and thus continues the divine process of creation. With every conscious activity, the human being influences one's own world, the most striking in art. The artist is the sum of his works. But basically, all the actors are the sum of their deeds. Whoever does little is a simple light. Whoever has done a lot is a personality. By understanding work as self-realization, work is ennobled.

Work became the essence of man in Europe. This work ethos did not only overcome the antique disdain of work. Thus, the European work-related understanding still differs from that of other cultures. It is true that, in Europe too, the religious-based attitude, which originally underpinned the working ethos, has largely been lost, but it continues to exist as the basic intellectual formation of the Europeans. Work is not only a hassle in Europe, and no worker is seen in Europe as a second-class human being. For people of other cultures and civilizations, however, work was always a subordinate activity and luxurious idleness was the ideal. This makes it more difficult, for example, to promote practical vocational training in developing countries.

Accordingly, the value estimation of the work can be found in early Christianity. The work has already been ennobled in the monasteries. K. Simonyi wrote: 'So we read in the Rule of the Benedictine monasteries founded by St. Benedict of Nursia in addition to the requirement that monks read books, that is, they have to develop themselves mentally, and there is also a requirement that they have to do physical work for a certain part of the day. This rule of the first European monastic order has been the model for all later European monastic orders. The Benedictine Rule is important from two points of view. First, it gives mentally-working intellectuals physical work, thus promoting the development of new work methods and technologies, and on the other hand, the spiritual leadership of the feudal society contributed to the social recognition of this work through its direct involvement in physical work.'[7]

Eastern Orthodox Christianity also has this positive relationship to work. Thus, Berdiaiev (1874-1948) says: "No doubt man is called to work and activity; man must organize and declare the world, must continue the worldly deed".[8][9]

Such a relationship with work is not found in any outside European culture and civilization. In all foreign European cultures, the only thing that was economically feasible was to seek enjoyment as much as possible, and the work was regarded as an effort and drudgery necessary to maintain a livelihood. It was therefore, if possible, transferred to slaves and servants. Monks in non-Christian cultures were preferred begging monks. That is, they did not work, but only meditated and prayed. Even where asceticism was world-related work, it was not worship and self-realization but, at most, self-conquest.

Even today, foreign European people are generally only concerned about becoming rich when it comes to the acquisition of Western technology and its economy. They do not live to work, but work to live. This also has to be taken into account when the economic development in non-European countries is assessed.

In general, production methods and know-how are taken over by these countries at best. In the non-European emerging markets, the know-how will also be further developed. But fundamental innovations and fundamental new developmental impulses that bring humanity forward, as for example by Copernicus or Albert Einstein, and even such dynamic knowledge favors as Silicone Valley, are hardly to be expected in these countries. As long as non-Europeans are not already influenced by Europeanism, they do not know the ethos of sacrificing their lives to the realization of an idea with which one can also fail, where self-fulfillment is the primary goal, before possible economic exploitation.

Of course, the majority of people in Europe also wants to get rich. Nevertheless, in Europe, the work ethos has transcended so far into flesh and blood that a

---

[7] K. Simonyi: *Kulturgeschichte der Physik*, p.129f.
[8] N. Berdiajew: *Der Mensch und die Technik*, Sonderdruck Luzern 1943, p.28-30.
[9] p.640.

life without work is felt to be unsatisfactory and simply an enjoyable contemplative life is not enough as a primary goal.

From Judaism, Christians also took on the idea of a radically linear time. Traditionally in the pre-Hebrew era, time was experienced as a cyclical occurrence: *summer* and *winter*, *day* and *night*, *new moon* and *full moon*, *born* and *dying*.[10] By believing in the creation of the earth by God, the sinful fall of man and his subsequent salvation or condemnation in the Last Judgment, the Hebrews came to a temporal orientation from beginning to end.

This idea was also taken over by the Christians, and it then appears in its secularized form as *eternal progress*, an idea which has not existed in ancient cultures. Human beings could also develop in other cultures, become more moral, increase their abilities up to the idea of overcoming the world in nirvana. But the earth itself was excluded. A change in the conditions of life and the earth as a whole created by man in freedom was alien to other cultures.

In the visualization of natural phenomena, the European gained his self-consciousness and became himself. In the next step, he also faced his social environment and began emancipating himself from the natural communities, such as family, clan and tribe to the self-conscious individual.

The confession to the self-conscious, free individual includes the freedom of the other. The relationship to the other is the basis of Christian self-understanding. As Gerald Kruhoffer writes, Paul emphasizes that "the individual cannot have freedom alone: "You are called to freedom, brothers, only: make sure that freedom does not give space to your self-seeking, but serve one another in love" (Galatians 5, 13). The freedom given by Jesus Christ cannot be understood in an individualistic sense. Rather, it is related to human communion and therefore will be effective in love. With regard to tradition, Paul adds that the whole law (Torah) finds fulfillment in the commandment of charity (Galatians 5, 14).'[11]

The other ego is the same as I, and in this respect my relation to the other is in relation to myself. From this derives the life maxim: *Love your neighbor as yourself!* Freedom and universal love are the fundamental life-maxims of a true European. However, self-realization must precede, because only as long as a person has become a free self can he turn to others and love them.

The emancipation from the family, the clan and the people should, in the final analysis, make the individual a citizen of the world. This ideal is also contained in *all-love*, that is, of the individual's reference to other people

The relationship of a man emancipating from his family to the members of the family is different from that before emancipation. As a child, man does not yet feel as a single ego, but the younger the man is, the more so as a member of the family. The family is his own. In archaic Muslim families this self-understanding is still valid today.

---

[10] In more detail on the development of the modern concept of time, see: Uwe Petersen: *Raum, Zeit, Fortschritt. Kategorien des Handelns und der Globalisierung.*

[11] Gerald Kruhöffer: *Was heißt christliche Freiheit heute?*, Text published in:_ Loccumer Pelikan 3/2003.

As a rule, the adult remains related to his or her family of origin. However, he stands opposed to it, that is, he confesses to the family by his own will and not instinctively from biological attachment. If and so far as the self-realization of a man and his emancipation from the family are not successful or only imperfect, the most diverse mental disorders are manifested. Where is there such an emancipation of the young adult from the family in non-European cultures?

Man, however, is not only the product of his family, but also of his people and his intellectual heritage, his deeds and his fate. The more he identifies with his people, the richer the content of his soul. For man is the sum of his relations. But as far as the individual is identified with his people, he has his own self in the people, he is a nationalist, and as such is separated from men of other peoples.

From nationalism, as the history of Europe shows, wars can arise. It took two world wars to overcome nationalism in Europe and to develop to a certain extent a European consciousness. But even today many people are in danger of falling back into narrow-minded nationalism.

With the development of the cosmopolitan environment, the motivation is to make all other people into world citizens. The missionary attitude towards European mentality is already founded in Christianity, and from there on also transmits to secularized missionary efforts. These are reflected in the world-wide ideals of human rights, democracy and socialism.

The spread of Europeanism to the whole world is the real core of globalization. Naturally, these noble aims are mixed or even dominated by nationalist and exploitative interests. Moreover, with the adaptation of Europeanism in non-European countries nationalism is also a motive for the self-identification of people. Nationalist endeavors, as will be shown, promote the development of secular tendencies, that is, the emancipation of men from a narrow tribe, clan, or familial context. But they also lead to new forms of delimitation and conflict between people and can intensify or compete with other social tensions, especially in the Near East.

With the emancipation of women as socially equal independent people, the highest stage of the self-realization of men and society is achieved. It is well known that this stage is not even fully realized in Western societies. With the development of productive forces, women could or had to carry out more and more professions that were typically performed by men. This is also enriched by the fact that as a society becomes more complex, team spirit and empathy are increasingly demanded and thus the women supplement male unities.

Other cultures are also struggling with participation of women. Islamic societies are the most difficult because the woman is degraded too much to sexual beings, to the extent that she cannot show herself in public or only by covering her body in a veil. She cannot even be a fully-fledged conversation partner for her own husband, as for him, in Islam, his mother is the real female reference point.

Since men can develop only to the extent that women have their femininity, the oppression of women also means that the incomplete development of man and the exclusion of women from society and culture is a social impoverishment.

From the objectification of the phenomena of the world, the individual gains his self-consciousness. In the ideal of Europeanism, however, it is also the case that the ego reverts back to the world and realizes itself in it, developing the world further. Man is the master of the world, but is also responsible for it.

There was no such relationship in ancient cultures. Man, in earlier cultures, felt himself to be sustained by a great mother, still revered as a *Pachamama* among the Indios in America, or he saw as Hindus and Buddhists the incarnation into matter as an imprisonment, or he enjoyed simply the earthly fruits. All of these examples can also be found in the European world. But they are exaggerated from their religious spiritual motives by a loving relationship to the earth. Thus, the philosopher Ernst Bloch, during a discussion in Heidelberg in June 1960, asked the rhetorical question: "Why should not man's task be to salve the stones?"

These interpretations may also sound strange to modern Europeans. From their intellectual heritage, however, they are shaped and embedded in them, and for this reason the Europeans see and judge secular and societal tasks to a certain degree differently from representatives of other cultures.

If Europeanism and globalization are spoken of, Europeanism is equated with what emerged as the colonization and mission of Western Christianity, the Western image of mankind, its democratic forms of society, and especially its capitalist economy. What is overlooked in this interpretation is that Russia is also part of Europe. The Roman Catholic and the Orthodox Church had separated almost 1000 years ago. 'As a date for the Schism is assumed the year 1054, as Humbert de Silva Candida, the envoy of Pope Leo IX, and Patriarch Michael I of Constantinople, after failed union negotiations mutually excommunicated one another. ... The final separation took place on the Roman side only in 1729, when the Congregation of Propaganda Fide prohibited the sacramental communion with the Orthodox. In 1755, the Orthodox Patriarchs of Alexandria, Jerusalem and Constantinople declared the Catholics to heretics in return.'[12]

As for how to work this out, East and West differ in their basic understanding to this day, and this difference is also in the difference between Western and Eastern theology.

---

[12] https://de.wikipedia.org/wiki/Morgenl%C3%A4ndisches_Schisma..

B. Western and eastern Europeanism as the origin of the east-west-opposition and globalization

The intellectual and political center of Western Europeanism was Rome. With the founding of the *Holy Roman Empire of German Nation* by Charles the Great and his successors, the political power shifted increasingly to developing individual European countries. Western Europeanism reached its peak when Great Britain rose to become an industrial and world power. After the Second World War, it became more and more perverse to *Americanism*.

The original spiritual and political center of Eastern Europeanism was Constantinople and then became Moscow. Wikipedia writes: 'After the conquest of Byzantium by Ottoman Turks (1453), a large number of Orthodox church members had migrated to Russia. It was then the only Christian-Orthodox power that was not occupied by Islamic conquerors. For the sake of Ivan's favor, the immigrants accepted the already existing notion among Russians that Russia should take over the legacy of Byzantium as guardian of the orthodoxy. They even supplemented it with the gladly accepted thesis that Russia was the *Third Rome*.'[13]

Russia sees itself as the home of true Christianity. As Jörg Himmelreich wrote, the messianic salvation of the "Third Rome" also corresponds to the secular idea of freedom of *communist ideology*. As the "last Rome" of Christendom alone was in possession of the ultimate absolute truth, this points to the totalitarian claim of Soviet communism. Thus, the historical, orthodox rule of ideology today still forms the gold foundation for Putin's autocratic regime.'[14]

It is true that Eastern as well as Western Churches interpreted the human being to be the image of God, who can overcome earthly death through and in Christ. But a fundamental difference between the Eastern and Western worlds is crystallized in the relationship of the individual to the human community.

This is also due to the different cultural and civilization traditions. The West was more strongly marked than the East by the Romans and Roman heritage. Even Roman law and the Roman form of government were tailored toward free citizens. In the vastness of Russia, however, people lived in village communities. Among them was a strong sense of community and a more intense connection with the earth, and "the tsar was far". Where comradeship and love relations prevail between people, paragraphs disturb and lawfully regulated order act destructively to spontaneous action. So the Russians remained masters of improvisation.

Of course, in the East and West, individualism and community are related to one another. However, the emphasis in the West is on the freedom of the individual and in the East on the joint creation of a community that encompasses all human beings.

Westerners were concerned about freedom and self-realization. Rousseau suggests that the community is then formed as *a social contract* of individuals, or, as per the ideal of the market economy, there is, as it were, an *invisible hand*, which

---

[13] https://de.wikipedia.org/wiki/Iwan_III._(Russland).
[14] Jörg Himmelreich: *Putins Dienerin. Die russisch-orthodoxe Kirche und ihre Mission*, NZZ, 2. 5. 2015.

always ensures that by maximizing profits the market participants are at the same time raising everyone's welfare.

It is true that, as Ernst Benz puts it, the difference between Eastern and Western Christianity does not lie in the fact "'that the idea of dignity of man in the East had developed less than in the West, but that this dignity of man saved by Christ is so strongly emphasized there as opposed to anywhere else in the Christian world, for the mystery of the incarnation of God and the consequent deification of man are placed so much at the center of the doctrine of faith, as is the case in the Eastern Church. Nowhere is the dignity of man as high as in the thought of the deification of man as the goal of the incarnation of God - a thought which has been proclaimed by the Eastern Church since its beginnings, and nowhere is the dignity of man elevated so much as in the thought of the deification of man as the goal of the incarnation of God - a thought which has also been proclaimed by the Eastern Church since its beginnings."[[15]][16]

But the East sees the individual as always related to the community. The good of the community is also linked to welfare and, if the individual gives his best in accordance with his abilities for the community, he also promotes his own development.

The state is regarded as a necessary evil, as in the West. Nevertheless, the state as an institution, like the church, is bound to the spirit of communion and is, to this extent, *divine*.

Marxist socialism was a secularized form of orthodox community. The party, as a representative of true faith, had taken the place of the Orthodox Church.

East and West have their one-sidedness, and that is exactly the opposite of each other. With the economy, this contrast was so apparent that the individual self-realization of the individuals in the East was only directed mentally morally, but remained undeveloped in the transformation of the world and in the economic sphere. Therefore, the socialist central administration economy fell far behind that of the West. The West, on the other hand, tended to forget the consumer and to look only at the *maker*. In the prevailing *supply-side economic policy*, the entrepreneur is still today, not as a s*upplier* of things that are wanted, but as a *creator* of these things. So it is very much in the foreground that the economic policy is constantly trying to meet the structurally lagging demand - the cause of the current *secular stagnation* - by promoting the entrepreneurs.

Correspondingly, the secularized Christian social ideology in the *French Revolution* took the form of the liberation of the citizen from called feudal servitude, while the Russian Christian social ideology in the Russian revolution was the realization of a communist community. In relation to the activity of the people, the difference was formulated as striving to have equal producers in the West and equal consumers in the East.

After the disintegration of the Roman Empire, Europe formed a spiritual unity, which remained limited to geographical Europe until the 15th century, although

---

[15] Ernst Benz: *Die russische Kirche und das abendländische Christentum*, München 1966, P.77f.
[16] P.431.

the ancient and Christian heritage developed differently in Eastern and Western Europe.

After the conquest of Constantinople by the Turks in 1453, the then Grand Duke of Russia, Ivan III the Great, felt himself called upon to take over the succession of the Byzantine empire and to make Russia the Third Rome. Wikipedia writes: 'In order to reaffirm this theory, Ivan III. married 1472 Sofia (Zoe) Palaiologos, the niece of the last East Roman Basileus Constantine XI. Palaeologus. Under the pretext that the Patriarch of Constantinople, who was at the time in Turkish power, could not complete the coronation ceremony, he became the first Russian Grand Duke to accept the title of Tsar. He and his descendants henceforth bore the title, "Preservers of the Byzantine Throne." '[17]

Eastern Europeanism was born. Ivan III consolidated his empire, 'and liberated the country from the rule of the Golden Horde.'[18] With Ivan III. began the expansion of Russia to the Pacific and the Black Sea and thus its globalization.

Also in the 15th century, Western Europe expanded to America. Thus, Western and Eastern Europeanism became independent. The Western European countries, especially Great Britain, colonized the overseas territories. At the same time, it was understandable that breaches of interests between Russia and the UK in particular had to occur very early.

Britain became the center of Western Europeanism as a naval power. After the First and even more after the Second World War the USA advanced to become the clear leader over the West.

After the Second World War involving the Western world and the Soviet Union, the East-West opposition intensified into the so-called *Cold War*. In accordance with their respective missions, Western countries tried to make as many former colonies and dependent territories as possible into Western democracies and to involve them in the capitalist market economy, while the Soviet Union tried to convert the countries to socialism, using the motto: *Proletarians of all countries unite!* to form a community of socialist states.

After the United States and the Soviet Union called a halt to arms contest and the Eastern bloc collapsed at the end of the 1980s, the Cold War ended. The United States became the sole world power and have sought their form of Europeanism to spread worldwide and to become the benchmark for social and economic action.

Americanism also sought to further marginalize Russia's influence and even to submit it to Western Europeanism. In opposition, however, Russia has regained strength and returned to the world stage as a political force.

Let us follow the development of Western and Eastern Europeanism and its globalization.

---

[17] https://de.wikipedia.org/wiki/Iwan_III._(Russland).
[18] loc. cit.

I. Western Europeanism and its globalization

1. The individualization of man as the essence of Western Europeanism and globalization

The basis of the western European concept of life was the human being who became an individual. This fundamental understanding is also found in all secularized derivatives of Christianity, as in European legal opinion, freedom of expression, the pursuit of scientific knowledge and self-realization in economic success (capitalism).

As far as secularized Christianity goes, first of all, beside Italy, the countries most influenced by the cultural and civilizing heritage of Rome are Spain, Portugal and then France, who became the spiritual and political center of Europeanism. The spiritual and cultural development of Spain and Portugal was also promoted by the centuries-long rule of the Moors, which bore the legacy of Hellenism to Spain and Portugal. As the developing maritime powers emerged from them the first overseas globalizations. Wikipedia writes: 'In the 15th and 16th centuries, in the age of discovery, Spain and Portugal were the pioneers of the European exploration and conquest of the world. They formed enormous colonial empires, which brought them immense wealth.'[19]

In Germany and Northern Europe, the focus of intellectual development was on deepening developmental ideas and personalization. The idea of development, which then more and more secularized to the idea of progress and the pursuit of eternal economic growth, emerged from the one-dimensional time-conception of Judaism from the beginning of history to the Last Judgement, the individualism from a recourse of Luther and the other founders of Protestantism to the first Christian European missionary, Paul.

By the early Roman domination and later the conquest of England by the Normans on the one hand and the invasion of the Anglo-Saxons, coming from Central Europe, the Roman inheritance is synthesized with the motif of the self-developing individual originating from North and Central Europe. Thus, Great Britain became the cradle of science and technology, with a capitalist economy and globalization in the British world. The conquered territories became colonies and protectorates.

After the Second World War, the USA became the leader of the Western world. Co-motivated by the desire to stop Soviet expansion, the USA also propagated the Western form of life, its society and its economy. After the collapse of the Eastern bloc, the USA became the single world power.

The actual bearers of social development are self-confident and self-actualizing individuals. They gave impulses for social development as prophets, leaders, artists, scientists and entrepreneurs. What is developing the world and society beyond what has already been created by nature is the result of creative actions. People change the world and supplement the natural environment with artificial products.

An individualism that is not also related to nature and society can, however, destroy the economy and society, and these effects also affect developing societies

---

[19] https://de.wikipedia.org/wiki/Britisches_Weltreich.

of other cultures in a globalized world. It is therefore necessary to analyze the nature of individualism and its development more precisely, and also as a yardstick for assessing economic and social development.

1.1 The essence of individualization

Individualization takes place in two development stages:

1. Individuation and
2. Self-realization.

The most primordial mode of human being is similar to that of animals. They are instinctively controlled and this control is coordinated with the environment. An animal always feels how it has to behave, what it can eat, when it has to reproduce and how to bring up its offspring. In order to self-discover, man has to free himself from his instinctive embedding in the environment and confront it as an external world so that he can reflect on the impressions and stimuli emanating from the environment and experience it himself.

The most basic form of self-living is sensual pleasure. The animal also feels well when eating. But it does not generate enjoyment, so that it disappears after saturation. Man, on the other hand, can conceptualize the enjoyment conceptually and thus keep it intellectually. He can then want to eat something not only from hunger, but also because of the pleasure generated. An animal, on the other hand, will never engage with food, unless his instincts are lost in human captivity.

Under capitalism, there was a further possibility for people to accumulate wealth through the acquisition of financial capital, which would go beyond the consumption requirements, in order to reinvest it and to make the fortunes grow even further. This possibility exists, however, only since new technical products and new products can be produced as a result of modern natural sciences.

The theoretical objectification of natural phenomena is the most spiritual form of self-living. By recognizing the laws of nature, natural phenomena lose their mystery and magical horror and gain the power of man over them. As long as it remains with the theoretical analysis, it remains in the self-life. But if man uses this power to realize his own ideas, he comes to *self-realization*.

While in traditional high culture, essentially only a steady repetition of the same things takes place, the self-realization which is released in Europe is about the constant overcoming and further development of what is given. European history is full of constant development and revolution. Self-realization of as many individuals as possible is the dynamite of economic, cultural and social development.

Self-realization, of course, requires individuation. For whoever has not become an individual before cannot realize himself. This also applies to the material implementation of ideas in the economy. Those who do not have sufficient capital cannot invest and those who cannot dispose of property cannot act. This also includes the necessity of the legal institution of property. At the very least an entrepreneur must be able to dispose of his or her resources.

Individualism should always be completed with self-realization. Only experiencing self-*feeling* is not enough. Sensible comforts are destroyed, just as excessive eating leads to obesity or other health damage. As far as enjoyment enables or generates life, it also resurrects. This means, in an economic sense, that income must be re-spent for consumption and investment. If this does not happen, then commodities remain unused and the economy falls into depression.

The individualization of human beings is not a one-time act, but a progressive process. This process is connected with different states of consciousness and the corresponding self-understanding.

An example of self-understanding in ancient times may be the old Hebrews as described in the Old Testament. They are always portrayed and also felt themselves to be part of a genealogy, ultimately traced back to Abraham. For the lack of individual self-awareness, it is also typical that when someone died, as was always mentioned in the Old Testament: he laid himself down to his fathers. There is never any question of an individual fate. All that is done refers to people as a whole. What a Hebrew does is for his descendants "to the seventh limb," or, if he is a king, to the people as a whole.

The misdeeds of kings must also be disfigured by people and by their descendants, just as the king has to suffer under a life of the subjects which is not to be desired. So because the woman of King Ahab killed a citizen who did not want to sell his vineyard in the Old Testament God decreed: 'I will now bring disaster on you and will sweep you and will eradicate from Ahab's relatives what is of the male sex, immature, adult in Israel; and I will make it with your house as with the house of Jeroboam the son of Nebat, and with the house of Baashaz the son of Ahaz, because thou hast provoked me to anger, and have made Israel sinful: and unto the speech of God presented by the prophet Elijah Ahab humbled himself. That is why God modified his threat: "Because he humbled himself before me, I will not allow the misfortunes to break in during his lifetime; first under the reign of his son I will bring the evil upon his house.' [20] We would ask today from our related to the individual thinking: Why are the descendants punished for the crimes of their ancestors?

An archaic man is also obliged to face his people alone. Barbarians can, if necessary, be exterminated without moral concerns. There are also many examples from the Old Testament where even God himself demands the extermination of other people, and if this command is not executed in full, he punishes the responsible person. 'Thus God, the Lord of the Hebrews, said to Samuel, "I will punish the injustice that the Amalekites once added to the Israelites, when they set out on their way out of Egypt. Therefore, now go and slay the Amalekites and execute the spell upon them and on all that they possess; Do not be careful with them, but let them die, men like women, children like babies, cattle like small domestic animals, camels like donkeys".'[21]

Over the course of time, man increasingly consciously perceived his environment in clear contours. More and more, he saw things instead of *beings*. Accordingly, the immediate magical effect of phenomena disappeared. The Old Testament can also be representative for this purpose. While at the beginning of the Old Testament, Jehovah, their tribal god, spoke to them, gave them instructions, and led them, he revealed this later only to a few prophets, and finally to no-one. Then

---

[20] Altes Testament, 1. Könige 21, p. 467f., Die Heilige Schrift tranlated by D. Dr. Hermann Menge, 7. ed., Stuttgart, Privilegierte Württembergische Bibelanstalt.
[21] Altes Testament, 1. Könige 11, p. 364.

it could only be *believed* from what is *written* in the Old Testament. Accordingly, individualization initially increased in tribes. In addition, the Israelis did no longer want be led by God directly, but by a king[22].

In a monarchy, the instinctive/mythical self-elevation feeling is secularized in a comprehensive tribal or national spirit. The subjects of a king no longer feel themselves to be inspired by instinct, but by the will of a king. In the kingdom of God, for example, an Egyptian pharaoh, spiritual and secular authority form a unity. More and more, however, the King is only an institution of the grace of God, persecuting secular interests for himself and his people, and leaving priestly activities to priests.

The more a king satisfies his own needs and pursues interests of power, the more the subjects feel themselves to be *individual* servants of the ruler, and religion becomes more and more a private matter of the individual citizens. This also contributes to the fact that the more successful a king can enlarge his empire, the more different ethnic groups and corresponding faith groups will find themselves in the empire. In such empires men were less and less dominated by a common spirit and more and more by a martial aristocracy. Thus, the history of mankind took place over thousands of years as a history of the changing domination of the nobles and the rise and fall of the empires.

A new impulse for quality emerged from mankind in antiquity. Through the Greek schools of philosophy, the thinking of men was raised to a more abstract level, thus overcoming the perception of bewitching images, which was entrancing exact thinking. Not only individual phenomena but also mental connections are intellectually objectivized. Through this thinking, man increasingly experienced himself as an individual entity of society and nature. In the legal position of the *Roman Citizen*, the autonomy of the individual was also recognized by the state in the Roman Empire.

If man has driven individualization so far as to rise above his family, clan, and tribal affiliation, that is, he has emancipated himself as a self-conscious individual, he no longer feels at home in an ancestral cult or a tribal or a local God. He is no longer so much a member of a family, clan or tribe. He is an individual soul who is responsible for his actions and wants to keep his soul well.

---

[22] Old Testament, 1. Samuel 8., P.353f.: >>Then all the elders of the Israelites gathered and came to Samuel [prophet] to Rama, and said unto him," You are now old, and your sons do not enter into your ways; so now place a king over us, who is to govern us, as is the case with all peoplep." Samuel was dissatisfied with the fact that they demanded the establishment of a king to reign over them; but when he prayed to the Lord, the Lord gave him the answer: "Follow the demand of the people in everything they ask of you; for they have not rejected you, but have rejected me, that I shall no longer be their king over them. They are doing the same with you, as they have always done with me since the time when I took them out of Egypt, to this day, leaving me and serving other god. So, therefore, meet her demand; only she would seriously warn them and wise them on the rights of the king, who will reign over them.<<

1.2 Humanism as the authoritative philosophy of life in the European Western world

Humanism is the secularized form of European self-understanding. It is described by Wikipedia as follows: 'Humanism of the Renaissance was a broad educational movement, which was based on antique or as antique regarded ideas. The Renaissance humanists hoped for an optimal development of human abilities through the combination of knowledge and virtue. Humanist education should enable man to recognize his true destiny and to realize ideal humanity and to form a corresponding social form by imitating classical models. The humanistic design of life, which was based on the ancient Roman concept of *humanitas*, was an alternative to the traditional image of the human race, which was strongly orientated on God and the world beyond. ... The humanist concept of the existentialist philosophy, as well as Marxism and real socialism, has experienced novel forms, from completely new approaches to a sharp distinction from "classical" humanism. Anthropocentrism, the concentration of interest and effort on man and his uniqueness, as opposed to worldviews that place God or the nature of things in the center, or the human form of life as one among many, can be seen as the connecting element of old and new approaches.'[23]

In Europe, at least since the Greek philosophers, we have developed a spiritual individualization into a conscious self. However, humanism regards itself as a revival of the ancient attitude towards life and the Renaissance has been a counter-design to a Christian self-understanding, Christianity has also contributed significantly to European self-understanding.

1.3 The secularization of Jewish-Christian eschatology in strive after progress

The southern European countries were shaped by more than 1000 years of ancient and Catholic history in such a way that the people there could experience their individuation only in a return to the ideals of Greek antiquity. In the culturally less developed countries of Northern Europe, individualization and self-realization took place more radically. The ancient heritage had formed them less and the mental return to society and nature was more strongly based on Pauline Christianity.

Wikipedia writes: 'In the Middle Ages Christianity was regarded as a sacred ordinance, which assigned each person a fixed place determined by God. The Church as a whole, according to the Gospel, had the freedom to establish this order essentially according to its own discretion (as opposed to be bound to a detailed divine law, as Judaism knew it). But the individual man had to fit into this order. It was only through the insertion into the order and the fulfillment of many formal duties defined by the Church that the Christian was part of the salvation of Christ according to the hitherto binding doctrine of justification.'[24]

But Protestantism again renewed Christian self-understanding, already formulated by Paul. Luther, for example, postulated in his theses: "A Christian is a free master of all things and is not subject to anyone. A Christian is a servile servant of all things and subject to everyone."

---

[23] https://de.wikipedia.org/wiki/Humanismus.
[24] https://de.wikipedia.org/wiki/Von_der_Freiheit_eines_Christenmenschen.

Individualization and its return to the world as *self-realization* was most strongly developed in Protestant North-West Europe and then realized in its most extreme form in North America. The Protestant Christian rejects all spiritual tutelage and feels as an individual responsible only to God and called by him to develop the world further. As a Christian, the individual is still connected with all other Christians, but not in a hierarchical order with a pope and saints, but as a community shared by all members of the community. In many Protestant sects, each member can also function as a priest.

Tobias Becker writes: 'Theologians have called Protestantism a "religion of conscience" a "personal religious conviction and attitude," which places high ethical demands on the individual. Luther no longer saw the true worship service in ordinances, carried out by consecrated masters, but in the fulfillment of daily duties, especially in his profession. The whole life a worship. Luther, too, praised the work, and lamented the laziness: "No man dies of labor, but work stoppage and idleness make men loosing life and limb; for man is born to work like a bird to fly." [25]

This self-understanding then also determined all European secularized world views. The secularized result of the ancient Christian tradition, the humanist image of the free self-responsible individual, is, as it were, the divine Roman Citizen.

More than other religions, Jewish eschatology encompasses a linear time with a beginning and an end. Life is, as it were, a test of the end goal, and the life-content is thus supported by the ideal of developing itself. Secularization is the result of scientific, cultural, economic and social progress.

The development of science was the prerequisite for the technical revolution by which productive forces could be developed. The masters of the productive forces, that is, the technicians and entrepreneurs, were finally able to free themselves from the rule of nobility and to form a democratic society.

1.4 Work as a means of self-realization

As a peculiarity of Christianity, we pointed out, strikingly expressed, the *deification of man*, less in the form of a man becoming a saint because of his aspirations to live as a wise man – that you find as well in other cultures and civilizations - but in that man himself becomes the creator, who transforms the world and develops it further. This makes work a means of self-realization.

Such a self-understanding is a blasphemy for a Muslim. Only God can be creative, but it is also by its nature incomprehensible for Asians. East Asia goes for an eternal cosmos. His ideal is to resonate in the cosmic rhythm. For the ancient Indian, the material world is even a pseudo-world, Maya, into which he is constantly born and in which he must suffer, until he has overcome his individuality and has emerged in nirvana. The idea of the development of the world and society and self-realization through work in the material world is alien to them.

While man used to be a user of the fruits of the earth and work was a necessary evil, which was imposed as far as possible on slaves, work in Christianity became the actual content of life, to give oneself an existence. The first realization found this determination of man - first in the form of enlightenment by God, later under

---

[25] Tobias Becker: *Deutsche Protestantische Republik*, in: Der Spiegel 48/2016, P.141.

the adoption of the ancient inheritance also as knowledge of nature - in the monasteries.

Markus Clausen writes: In the Regula Sancti Benedicti, the work ethos 'has taken shape. While work, especially work for another person, was unworthy for real Roman and the true Greeks [of the upper class], it has a positive value for Benedict. He has overcome the old contempt for work and contributed to the modern up-to-date assessment of the work in which man can earn his livelihood himself and unfold his abilities. Benedict found examples in Egyptian desert monasticism, which flourished from the year 300 strongly.

The Anachorets saw in their work a means of asceticism, securing their own livelihood and not least the basis of their social-charitable activities. The monks, especially the younger one, forbid them to be idle. Zeal of the heart and progress in patience and humility they measure in working diligence.' [26]

' From the best traditions of desert monasticism and under the influence of Saint Augustine's writings: De opere monachorum (From the Handicrafts of the Monks), Benedict has formulated his work ethos. This should come to practical effect not only in monastic communities but throughout the whole of the West. The motto "pray and work," though it is nowhere else in the rule, has rightly become the hallmark of Benedictine monasticism.' [27]

Work as an inner-world asceticism was, in addition to striving for knowledge, the motive for the self-realization of the European man and, as Max Weber elaborated, the religiously founded philosophy of life of Protestantism and Calvinism and capitalism developing in the Anglo-Saxon world. Maximizing profit was not primarily a means for extended consumption, but a sign of a choice by God. Therefore, profits had to be invested as much as possible.

At the same time, however, in the seclusion of the monasteries a bustling intellectual life was cultivated. Thought was based on the logic of the ancient philosophers, especially Aristotle. In dealing with the cosmological and natural sciences of Aristotle, which penetrated through Spain and which were further developed by Arab philosophers, Catholic dogmatics was increasingly questioned critically. Thus, it is not surprising that theologians, such as Martin Luther, Calvin, Jan Hus, and others, also revived the ideal of free Christianity and introduced Protestantism. Through the translation of the Bible into German and the invention of book-writing, Luther made the content of the Bible widely known

This revival of the roots of Christianity and the increasing moral depravity of the Catholic Church in that time unfolded a great revolutionary potential for peasant uprisings. Ultimately, however, it was only the Northern European local princes who could benefit by increasing their sovereignty. They were able to shake off the spiritual tutelage through Rome and to advance themselves to church leaders in their respective countries.

---

[26] Markus Clausen: *Am Ursprung des Arbeitsethos*, Schweizer Monatshefte : Zeitschr. f. Politik, Wirtschaft, Kultur, Bd. (Jahr): 75 (1995), Heft 3, S.23, PDF establ. on: 30.05.2016. Persistenter Link: http://dx.doi.org/10.5169/seals-165423 .
[27] Clausen: loc. cit.

The importance of monasteries for the spiritual development of Europe went even further. Ultimately, they were the origin of universities. 'Before the 12th century the intellectual life of Europe had taken place at the monasteries.'"[28] Research and teaching got increasingly emancipated from the theological framework and the sciences could develop in Europe. Accordingly, the emerging European universities have a more positive view of the work. Thus, the respect for the manual work was expressed by HUGO DE SAINT-VICTOR (1097? -1141),' that he added to the seven liberal sciences (septem artes liberales) the seven mechanical sciences (septem artes mecanicae) (...). Among them are the science of weaving, the science of forging, the architecture, the shipping, the agriculture, the hunting, the science of art and the science of healing.'[29] [30]

Natural science and research, regarded as work, were the prerequisites for the industrial revolution and the capitalist economy.

2. Nationalism as an imperfect individualization of men

In the course of the development of the productive forces, the citizens gained such power that they could overthrow the nobility or were able to subdue to a constitutional monarchy. As scientists, artists and traders, they were, like the nobles, already world-citizens who traveled to other countries, did business there and / or changed their place of residence. The French Revolution was therefore less a national than a general bourgeois revolution and was thus celebrated as a humanitarian event.

Now the stratum of people who considered themselves world citizens was only thin. The masses of the population, as far as they had emancipated themselves from the authority of family patriarchy, sought a national identity and, if possible, a national emperor as a national father or leader.

The French Revolution with its ideology of the world was therefore an intellectual premature birth, which did not adequately take into account the real intellectual and mental development of the people. This means that the step to understand oneself not just as a member of a family or clan, but as a *world citizen* was too great. The French, too, wanted to continue being Frenchmen, though they also equated this *being French* with *being a citizen of the world* and so with the founding of the Napoleonic Empire they wanted the conquered countries to participate in that French world citizenship.

In fact, we owe Napoleon the rationalization of the bourgeois legal order, a secularized order of government, an adjustment of the time zones and other standards and much more. In addition to the independence and democratization of the United States, France was also a decisive source of inspiration for the ideal of the free citizen. But people from the other countries who emancipated themselves from their family and subject structures did not want to be "French", but rather to

---

[28]https://de.wikipedia.org/wiki/Mittelalterliche_Univer sit%C3%A4t.
[29] Simonyi, p.132.
[30] More details regarding the importance of work in Christianity see: Uwe Petersen: *Im Anfang war die Tat I. Die Geburt des Willens in der europäischen Philosophie*, p.361ff.

fill their own political order with their own folk traditions and their own popular feelings.

Nationalist tendencies developed everywhere. The positive element of their confession was the principle of *freedom, equality, fraternity*, and they allowed people to grow beyond their simple family and local ties and to become national citizens. Nationalists saw themselves as members of a people, for whom they also assumed responsibility right up to suffering heroic death. However, this was connected with distinction from members of other nations and representing national interests against others.

Thus, the individualization brought about by nationalism was imperfect. For a truly self-conscious man can no longer fix himself on a nation or religion, but must understand that he is a citizen of the world who bears responsibility not only for his nation, but for mankind as a whole.

The nationalism is thus twofold: as a nation-conscious people differ from other ethnic groups and can thus create antagonisms that can lead to conflicts, especially since every nationality tends to consider its own nation as superior to the nations of others. At the same time, self-awareness grows with the size of the state experienced as a higher self.

Conflicts develop when another country shall be subjugated or integrated into its own country or the other country is perceived as a threat. Both motifs usually go together. The countries militarily upgrade and the danger of the outbreak of warfare is growing.

Integration is usually strived for when it comes to neighboring countries and the ethnic and cultural differences are small. Distant areas are more likely to be tolerated or colonized if the ethnic and cultural differences are too large.

There have also been bloody conflicts in the pre-historic period. But these were carried out in the interest of princes. Their subjects were only financiers, cannon fodder and victims. This means that the people lived relatively peacefully with others and were united with other peoples or separated from them or themselves, depending on the inheritance and the success of the war. There were no wars between civilized subjects themselves, but only family feuds and, if necessary, tribal feuds, which, however, were no longer bloody because of the monopoly of power of the rulers.

The antagonisms arising from nationalism are its negative side. The positive side is that the awareness of one's own ethnic and cultural roots and the self-consciousness of the nation in the people at the same time arouse the will to develop and strengthen the nation, and that the antagonism to other nations, in particular, can release immense forces.

Upgrading times lead to scientific, technical and economic revival. Thus, the consequences of the global economic crisis of 1929 were overcome by rearmament, until which there were war disturbances. But even after the war, the economy remained under fire for as long as the rebuilding period lasted. The Korean War and other conflicts, indeed the Cold War as a whole, were also stimulating and then again, when America declared war on Islamic terrorism. On the other hand, the economy began to stagnate after the rebuilding phase in the 1960s and after the end of the Cold War, so that other government spending and impulses were needed to prevent the emerging secular stagnation from slipping into a depression.

3. The economic and social development of capitalist industrialized countries and their misdevelopments through the perversion of individualism in egoism

European countries and, in the context of globalization, the rest of the world, owe its economic and social development to the release of individual creativity. But capitalism also contains the germs of its perversion and self-dissolution. The characteristics of economic development in industrialized countries are:

1. the danger of the self-destruction of the capitalist economy by displacing the labor force by increasingly intelligent machines and the danger of monopolizing the world economy by a few global players,
2. the transition of the capitalist economy into a secular stagnation as a result of a high saving rate which is too high in relation to the real economic investment opportunities and the growing danger of economic crises,
3. increasing global public debt and the rising danger of state bankruptcies,
4. the perversion of the capital market to a gambling casino.

3.1 The danger of the self-destruction of the capitalist economy by the displacement of the workforce by increasingly intelligent machines and the danger of monopolizing the world economy by a few global players

With the invention of the steam engine and through further innovations up to digitalization and robotization production processes, this could be rationalized and workplaces replaced by machines.

Although due to the production of machines and plants, the development of new products and the expansion of production, new jobs have always been created. Also, production-related services: research and development, logistics, distribution and the transfer of capital created new jobs. But since the beginning of the Industrial Revolution, again and again there have been periods of underemployment and social hardship.

At first, only unqualified workers were being rationalized. According to the ideas of the *supply-side economic policy*, the decline in industrial employment was normal. According to their ideology, an industrial society must develop into a service society. This would allow industrial jobs to migrate to developing countries. Planning activities, such as research and development, logistics, marketing and other services, would replace the lost jobs.

In addition, it was believed that service jobs were less threatened by unemployment and the fact that the computerization and robotization of the economy also have made service workplaces redundant was not overlooked. The result of this development was the de-industrialization of the United States and Great Britain in particular, as well as huge industrial brownfield sites.

The expected further decline in the workplace will be dramatic as a result of increasing computerization, digitization and robot development. All sectors of the economy worldwide are affected, albeit to varying degrees, as the following forecast shows:

Highly skilled occupations	Less vulnerable occupations
Robotization of automating professions in the next 20 years of at least 70%	Robotization of automating professions in the next 20 years of at least 30%
currently employed in millions	currently employed in millions
• office secretary staff ....2,7 • sales................................1,1 • catering............................1,0 • business administration..........0,9 • post and delivery services.......0,7 • kitchen staff.......................0,7 • bankers.............................0,5 • warehousing ....0,4 • metalworking.....................0,4 • accounting........................0,3	• childcare, upbringing ....0,9 • health and nursing care ....0,7 • management......................... 0,5 • Machine construction, operating, technology ....0,4 • automobile technology............0,4 • procurement, purchasing, distribution ....0,3 • social work, social pedagogy... 0,3 • geriatric care ....0,3 • academic teaching and research...........................0,2 • construction, electric.............0,2
	Source: A. T. Kearney

Cited: Der Spiegel Nr.36,3.9.2016, p.14

Thomas Schulz writes: 'In the American oil and gas industry, between 50 and 80 thousand good, high-paid, skilled workers have been lost since 2014, energy experts estimate, although the shops are running again. Many oil delivery systems will then be operated externally from remote control centers full of monitors.' [31] Frank Chen, Airnb's politician, 'sees the new world like this: "A trucker is one of the most widespread jobs, and perhaps already in 5 years, at the latest 15 years, this job will no longer exist" because the robot will drive safer and more economically.' [32]

'Intelligent machines are already better in many routine jobs than humans. First, cashiers and accountants were replaced, then tax consultants and bankers. Banker? Goldman Sachs had until recently still 600 stock traders on the stock exchange, now it is 2. Algorithms make the work of the other 598. Half a million employees threaten to be replaced in the coming years alone in the British financial industry by software, estimates the consulting company Deloitte.

The examples are endless. Frank Chen quotes publicly the AI researcher Geoffray Hinton: "We should stop radiologists immediately." Because machines can better analyze X-ray images.' [33]

The ever-increasing digital networking of production, services and communication is increasingly linked to research and development, production, logistics

---

[31] Thomas Schulz: Zuckerbergs Zweifel, in Der Spiegel 14/2017, p.19.
[32] Thomas Schulz: loc. cit., p.18.
[33] Thomas Schulz: loc. cit., p.19.

and marketing. In Germany it is called the fourth industrial revolution after the mechanization, the electrical revolution and computerization, hence, *Industry 4.0*.

The driving force is the rationalization of communication technology, such as Google and Facebook, which allows an ever-better evaluation of customer data, more sophisticated advertising and computerized logistics and thus the possibility of Internet commerce. Anderson and other trade chains force production plants under their software networks and make them dependent on them, provided that the trade chains do not themselves include production sites.

Since the development of communication technology has its center in the USA, especially in Silicon Valley, and is also financed there, capital has flowed from other countries to the USA. The relevant Internet companies are located in the USA and even other industrialized countries are in danger of becoming more and more dominated by US companies.

This danger is seen even for the German industry, which is still leading in machinery and plant construction. How much greater is the danger for other industrialized countries or developing countries? The whole world, even the American economy, is at risk of being monopolized by globally-operating internet companies.

Developers in Silicon Valley, as well as elsewhere in the world's leading research and development centers, are less driven by expected profit than by the satisfaction of research and development, as well as their results and beliefs to advance humanity. The fact that digitization and computerization can also endanger the economic and social life is also recognized by the authoritative developers. Mark Zuckerberg is one of them. Thomas Schulz writes: '"Our job at Facebook is to help people to have the greatest positive impact and to minimize the pages where technology and social media contribute to division and isolation," Zuckerberg says. There were some doubts at least – Zuckerberg's doubts. Not everything is automatically good.'[34]

' "We are calling on legislators to deal with the future," says Frank Chen, the AI expert. But the prevailing sentiment is that nothing will happen or go wrong, and that is why the Californian advocates of progress are beginning to make their own political instruments: they are launching large-scale field trials on how a universal basic income could work. They are developing concepts for a new education system in which employees are always trained for new occupations in order to keep up with the machines.'[35]

' Not individual billionaires, but parliaments must decide how we live. However, politics must first recognize that change, progress and technological inequality change the playing rules and increase the necessary commitment. No society can afford to ignore the future, because in 5 years more will happen than in the past 20 years.'[36]

'Without the state it will not happen – that, meanwhile, is what the biggest pessimists guess. There must be political instruments to shape change, because it will not stop. Perhaps that way: Companies that replace people with people pay a

---

[34] loc. cit., p.13.
[35] loc. cit., p.21.
[36] loc. cit.

robotic tax so that the warp does not come in a single big wave. The idea comes from Bill Gates, who does not want to fight progress but secure it in the long term. He says, "If people are afraid of progress instead of rejoicing, then we've get a real problem."[37]

3.2 The transition of the capitalist economy into a secular stagnation as a result of a too high saving rate in respect to the real economic investment opportunities and the growing danger of economic crises[38]

The ideal of the free market economy is based on the assumption that free individuals offer products and services according to their abilities and possibilities, and acquire what they need as economically as possible in the market. The market is intended to ensure that prices of goods are formed according to their relative scarcity and suppliers expand production when they make profit and limit it when they suffer losses.

In the case of atomistic competition, i.e. when there are as many suppliers as possible, the ideal is achieved. If, however, companies are already established in the market, have acquired special know-how and are already producing large quantities and are therefore cheaper overall than the competition, it is hardly possible to produce these goods as newcomers. This is why it is so difficult to retrograde industrialized regions, and if so, only by making these regions dependent on established enterprises in industrialized countries. This difficulty also applies to the remaining regions in the industrialized countries themselves, as well as to developing countries.

A capitalist market economy should also be a service company. All participants should have the same start-up opportunities and be able to earn income and make a fortune depending on their performance. This ideal is, however, violated by inheriting property. The heirs of wealthy people have far better conditions than poor people, quite apart from the fact that they already have better conditions from their education as children and at higher schools. This marked the beginning of the industrial revolution, and laid the foundations for an increasingly unequal distribution of wealth and income.

As long as innovation provokes investments and they ask for the respective savings, an unequal income distribution and a high savings volume can stimulate economic development. Periods in which pioneering innovations are realized are called *Kondratiev Cycles*. Wikipedia writes: 'Kondratiev published in 1926 in the Berlin journal *Archiv für Sozialwissenschaft und Sozialpolitik* his article *The Long Waves of the Economy*. On the basis of empirical evidence from Germany, France, England and the USA he found that the short economic cycles were overlaid by long economic cycles.'[39]

Pioneering innovations are the invention of the steam engine at the beginning of the industrial revolution, the invention of electroenergy, computerization and

---

[37] Thomas Schulz: Zuckerbergs Zweifel, loc. cit., P.21.
[38] Further defined in: U. Petersen: *Säkulare Stagnation unser Schicksal? Grenzen der Angebotsorientierten Wirtschaftspolitik.*
[39] https://de.wikipedia.org/wiki/Kondratjew-Zyklus.

now digitalization and robotization. That is, the four types of industrial revolutions can be called the Kondratiev cycles.

If, however, the Kondratiev cycles were to expire, overproduction would come about as a result of a lack of demand. Then all savings would be no longer invested with the result of economic depression and high unemployment.

Over the course of the economic development of industrialized countries, however, the revitalizing effect of pioneering innovations is diminishing more and more. At the beginning of the Industrial Revolution, the investment requirements were at their highest due to the construction of heavy industry, the expansion of infrastructure, housing and urban development. However, after these investments were largely completed, less capital was needed.

The more the economy changes into a service and knowledge society, and the larger the markets and thus the sales become, the less capital is needed in relation to expected sales. Accordingly, the investment requirement per saved labor force is reduced. But capital gains increase with every saved labor force. This means that *wage costs become the company profits and the income of capital providers*.

Of course, this equation applies only to the extent that profits do not lead to further investment and to the production of new products and therefore additional labor was hired. Entrepreneurial and capital incomes would then also increase, but the previous wage volume, and thus the current economic demand for the economy, would only decline relatively.

Moreover, the gains do not grow to the extent of rationalization due to competition causing price reductions. On balance, however, inequality in the distribution of wealth and income is increasing and thus the economic volume of savings, for which real investment opportunities must be found.

The measures to prevent the outbreak of economic crises are:
1. the absorption of rationalization gains through wage increases,
2. export surpluses,
3. increase of government expenditures,

3.2.1 Possibilities and limits to stabilize the economic demand by wage increases

Through the formation of trade unions, which monopolize the supply of labor, higher wages could be achieved, depending on the progress of production, and the consumption demand could thus be stabilized. This possibility, however, exists only in closed economies and decreases as the labor market becomes globalized.

In the context of globalization, ever more relocation of production facilities and later service providers, such as call centers and programmers, weaken trade unions. This means that the wage level in competition with developing countries also decreases to that of unindustrialized countries or increases less than the company's profits and returns on capital and the salaries of the higher qualified.

This development is supported even more by general tariff reductions and the reduction of import barriers. In order to prevent and reverse the migration of companies, the new American President, Donald Trump, is again aiming for higher import taxes for sensitive products.

3.2.2 Export surpluses to fill the domestic demand gap

Powerful companies often have the problem that the national market is too small or has still too little purchasing power so that they cannot sell all goods in the domestic market. This is why modern industrialists have always tried to sell products that go beyond national requirements abroad. This export pressure is extreme in newly-industrialized countries. England, as the first leading European industrial power, first swept across the rest of the world with cloths and industrial products. Since the import requirements were not growing at the same rate – due to mass purchasing power still lacking, export surpluses for these countries arose, that is, goods which cannot be sold in the country are moved abroad.

In our time, a typical example of this is China. China's domestic demand is also developing with industrialization. But it lags behind and to the extent that more surplus products have to be exported abroad than are imported from abroad. This results in huge export surpluses for the PRC.

Similarly, the export surpluses of Germany and Japan show that the domestic demand is too low because of the excessive volume of savings due to economic saturation and the increasingly uneven distribution of wealth and income.

We will see later on what problems arise from this for the global economy and the European Union and in particular the Eurozone.

3.2.3 The Importance of state expenditure for the economic balance of supply and demand

Armaments and luxury requirements of the noblemen were already in the preindustrial time substantial driving forces for the development of the economy. Even during the industrial revolution all industrially manufactured products could not have been sold without massive government expenditures, especially since the industrial development began in the heavy industry and these products did not meet the consumption requirements of individual citizens.

As the investment demand for pioneering innovations diminished, the importance of government expenditure to prevent economic crises grew. Accordingly, in times of war preparation and wars and in post-war reconstruction we have a rather overwhelming economic demand. If, after the rebuilding phases, saturation phenomena turn up again, there are economic crises, such as 1929, or, according to public opinion for *cyclical reasons*, government expenditures have to be extended, as has been the case since the end of the sixties though also at that time several international conflicts and the Cold War required high government expenditures. After the collapse of the Eastern bloc, deflationary threats arose, which provoked additional government spending. A substantial portion of state expenditure is also the result of necessary social transfers for the benefit of the disadvantaged in the economic process.

As long as capital was scarce and had to be saved in order to be able to be invested, unequal distribution of income increased investment possibilities and thus also general economic prosperity. But at the moment when economic savings exceed profitable investment possibilities, saving becomes a poison, for savings which do not become investments leave offered goods unsold on the market and the economy shrinks.

In the end, the global economic crisis in 1929 could ultimately only be overcome by additional government expenditure – in the USA, by public investment in the New Deal policy and in Hitler's Germany, through public investment and armaments.

At least since 1929 it could have been seen that the outbreak of economic crises can only be prevented by the fact that the public sector is increasingly using more government spending. From the purely social point of view, lower income earners and the unemployed become relatively impoverished, so social intervention and thus additional government expenditures become necessary.

Since the 1960s, depression, due to the lack of economic demand because of the high economic savings, has been prevented by a sufficient increase in government expenditure. However, the importance of government expenditure for balancing the gap between supply and demand is hardly discussed. Therefore, the causes of rampant *Secular stagnation* are generally not recognized.

3.3. The increasing global public debt and the rising
   danger of state bankruptcies

Unfortunately, the extra government expenditure was not financed by taking excess purchasing power from upper income earners, but by giving the upper income earners the opportunity to draw government bonds for their funds. The result was rising public debt worldwide, not least because more and more funds were needed for social transfers. Wikipedia writes: While in the Federal Republic of Germany 1960 only 18.3% of GDP accounted for social benefits, social benefits amounted to 30.7% of GDP in 1975. [40] [41] Public social expenditures (state expenditure including social insurance) amounted to 45.2% of GDP in Germany according to calculations by the Federal Statistical Office in 2012 in order to mitigate the relative impoverishment of lower income earners'[42]

Sovereign debt securities differ from industrial bonds and equities in that they are not based on real value. The money taken is spent by the state.

In order to be able to allocate a debt value to state debts it is repeatedly argued that only public investments can be financed with loans. But first that affects only a small part of government expenditure. On the other hand, public investment can only be liquidated under certain circumstances and used to reduce debt. Just think about the discussions about the privatization of infrastructures, such as roads, water companies, etc. Debt can only be repaid to a certain extent. After all, if the *markets* are no longer able to invest their current savings in a sensible way, what are they to do with repaid debts?

This means that in the amount of debt repayments the gap between national demand and national supply increases because the state can spend less. For this reason, the circulating state debt can be described as *scrap papers*, which can only be refinanced by means of *new* loans, which means that they can only be *prolonged*. Whether the state securities represent an intrinsic value and, if so, whether

---

[40] Universität Duisburg Essen: *Sozialpolitik aktuell, Entwicklung der Sozialleistungssysteme 1960-2012.*
[41] https://de.wikipedia.org/wiki/Sozialleistungsquote.
[42] https://de.wikipedia.org/wiki/Staatsausgaben.

the current government debt is 60%, 100% or even 250% of the gross domestic product as in Japan, is not of any interest to the buyers of state securities as long as they are sure that the *markets* will provide the state with sufficient new loans at maturity to meet the debt which is due.

In the case of the USA and Japan it is regularly expected that repayments can be refinanced through new acquisitions. For smaller countries, such as Greece and Spain, this question can be answered in the negative and the result may be state bankruptcy. But since *no* state can repay its debts net, they are basically all bankrupt and need to be rehabilitated by debt cuts as would be the case in the private sector with such a debt burden. In the first place, those would be affected who are also the main believers of the government's debts and who, in the case of repayments, would also have to bear the tax burden. To this extent, debt cuts are *zero-sum games*.

Now the perishing of the enormous and steadily rising public debt is not without danger to the world economy. Depending on the situation, the securities may suffer more or less price increases and price reductions and thus also lead to bankruptcies or through inflows or outflows to international currency fluctuations and thus to economic crises. This brings us to the capital market, which is perverted to a gambling casino.

3.4 The perversion of the capital market to a gambling casino

The real market is about goods and services. When a production period is complete, all manufactured goods and services should be sold. If goods and services remain unsold, their production is restricted and unemployment occurs if there are not enough other possibilities for production.

For the real economy, the capital market is only needed insofar as savings are sought to finance investments. In contrast, investors and speculators in the capital market, however, tend to lose interest in investment financing. For them, purchases and disposals of financial assets and their market increases as the number of government bonds, shares, industrial bonds and invented derivatives which pervade the market are much more important.

Over the last few decades, companies have been calculated less and less according to their net asset value but to the most short-term value. Speculators buy companies whose income value is low and their earnings value is high with borrowed money, sell the unused real estate and assets and pay back with the proceeds as far as possible the credit for the purchase. So, it is possible that Porsche could have bought its much larger sister, Volkswagen AG, with speculative funds and repay the credit taken from the bar reserves of VW-AG.

In the Anglo-Saxon world, and particularly in the USA, it was very early on that economic morality went to ruin, reducing interest only to *make money*. The difference in the working attitude between Europeans and especially Germans, who are said to be not working to live, but living to work, and the Americans is illustrated by a quotation from Carl Martin Welcker (head of the Cologne Machine Tool Manufacturer *Schütte* and elected President of the German Engineering Federation (VDMA) in November 2016). In an interview, Alfons Frese asked him: 'German machine-builders are the world's best, the distance to other countries has grown even bigger. Is that solely due to German engineering? "Welcker replied:"

Of course not. It also depends on the prices. The Americans no longer enter the market, which is determined by the low yields of the Germans and the Japanese. They say, "let the German mid-size companies make it, they are such blithering idiots and are satisfied with a 2% return". Anyone who wants to make a profit is not on the road in German mechanical engineering. We are an industry that is characterized by family businesses and not by the logic of the capital markets.'[43] Typically, in the USA, a person is assessed by how many dollars he has. Before the financial crisis, financial service providers in the USA should have earned 40% of all company profits. If, however, one is not pleased with the property of things and corporations, but only in all its *monetary value*, then all things owned become *chips* with a certain value.

For the Americans, the doctrine that all corporate activity should only serve the *shareholder value principle* was then created in the 1980s. Executives were sworn to this principle through bonuses, especially in equities. As a result, managers were furthermore only little interested that their employers could survive and realize their potential in their jobs.

Although real investment plays only a subordinate role for capital market games, they can have a massive impact on the real economy. If purchases and sales of goods and services alone were to determine international economic relations, there could be no unbalanced current account. How is it possible for the USA to suffer enormous deficit losses on an annual basis? From the beginning of 2006 to the end of 2015, the USA's trade deficit averaged 720.1 billion dollars per year[44].. In the USA, because of the import surplus, the dollar's price would have to fall to an extent until the foreign goods became too expensive and / or the American export goods were cheap enough for foreign buyers.

Unbalanced performance balances have become possible through *capital market transactions*. For foreign capital flows into the country within the scope of American import surpluses. The US is considered a safe haven for all the rich in the world to invest their money. Since the Americans also have disproportionately low savings and the state is always sufficiently indebted, depression is prevented. However, the fragility of crises is increasing.

Capital market transactions were also the cause for the Asian crisis in 1997/98, which brought many Asian countries into economic turmoil. The rating decreases of individual euro countries led to the euro crisis affecting the entire global economy. Even if the US central bank FED increases the interest rate, capitals move additionally into the USA and let the dollar rate rise. Although international economic crises always have real economic causes, capital market transactions have the effect of expanding economic problems into global economic crises.

The importance of today's capital market in the global economy can also be seen in the volume of capital transactions. Already in 2006 Klaus Stocker, referring to the *Bank for International Settlements (BIS)* and the *IMF* wrote: 'Payments from trading transactions, i.e. imports and exports, are now only about 1.3% (!) of

---

[43] Alfons Frese: „*Protektionismus würde uns böse treffen*", in: Der Tagesspiegel Nr. 23 060/18.3.2017, p.10.
[44] http://de.statista.com, zitiert: https://de.wikipedia.org/wiki/Handelsbilanzdefizit.

the IMF global capital movements.'[45] "Accordingly, liquidity needs are also far higher than those for real economy sales.

3.5 The money flooding of the capital market by the central banks to avoid depression

In order to stimulate the economy, central banks have for a number of years been creating more money than the real economic turnover has grown. Correspondingly economic theorists constantly warned against inflation. What they disregarded was the much greater need for capital market transactions. For real economy companies it makes no sense to hold excessive liquidity. For the capital market on the other hand, money has a chip function and facilitates speculation.

For banks, the investment on the capital market is more attractive than lending to the real economy. As a result, the real economic need for credit will only be financed if the wishes of the capital market are satisfied. If the central banks do not have sufficient liquidity, there is a fear that the economy will stall due to insufficient credit. That is why the central banks have been throwing more and more money at the market to raise the speculative fire, hoping that enough money will flow to the real economy and real investment will be made.

A real economic effect has not yet been felt and is not to be expected, unless, without the flood of money, investments would become even lower. But the capital market has already begun to cope with the flood of money and expects further price increases.

In the perverted capital market, a *monster* has evolved that has to be continually *fed up* with money and monetary values in the current global economic system so that the global economy does not break.

3.6 Summary of economic and social Development of capitalist industrialized countries

The factors for the dynamic economic and social development of Europe can be summarized as follows:
1. creative free self-actualizing individuals, to whom labor is not only labor, but life purpose,
2. the necessary social framework in the form of a market economy and the formation of democratic will without religious pre-eminence.

Over the course of economic development, there are imbalances in the form of
1. unequal income and wealth development,
2. a dangerously high national debt in all countries, which at any time can become a threat to the capital market and thus also to the real economy,
3. the perversion of capitalism into a Casinocapitalism.

---

[45] Klaus Stocker: *Management internationaler Finanz-und Währungsrisiken*, Gabler Verlag, Aufl. 2006, p.3.

4. The Globalization of Western Europeanism

4.1 The globalization of Western Europeanism by colonization of the Third World

The countries of Europe had a common history and were at the same level of cultural and civilization development as in their military skills, although the scientific, technical and economic development of northern European countries, and especially Great Britain, lay ahead. As Max Weber pointed out, the Puritan faith, according to which the selectivity of a person through God manifests itself in its economic success, was particularly conducive to capitalist development. European countries have always had close economic relations and have been able to intensify their division of labor in the course of the technical revolution.

The actual globalization thus begins with the domination of the outer European countries through Europe. In the east, Russia was extended to Vladivostok. The West forced non-European countries to establish trade relations, then exploited and colonized them. This was connected with the missionary mission to the Christian faith and later to the humanistic human image and the European social system.

In the following, the spread of Western Europeanism and the colonization of overseas territories which it initiated are summarized. At the same time, it is important to make it clear how people have embraced the traditional societal conditions of countries outside Europe and which responsibility for Europe is derived from them. Any experts in colonial history may skip these remarks. They are written in different fonts for this purpose.

4.1.1 The development of international trade relations, imperialism and colonization up to the First World War

Thousands of years ago, merchandising merchants were transporting goods all over the world. In most cases they were goods which did not exist in other countries, such as amber from the Baltic Sea, ivory and spices from Africa and Asia, or special objects of art according to the nature of the people.

H. Schumacher writes: 'The maritime Phoenician traders are generally regarded as the first transatalogists. Around 1100 BC, they started colonies on the coasts of the Mediterranean. Since the 8th century BC, Many Greek cities followed this example and established trading centers in the Mediterranean. The city of Carthage, founded as a Phoenician colony, itself became a major colonial power: the Carthaginians built a trading empire based on the control of the shipping of the Mediterranean, including colonies in Spain and Sicily. The empire of the Carthaginians was destroyed by the Romans in the Punic Wars (3rd to 2nd century BC). In the centuries that followed, the Romans continued to expand their domination, and ruled over large parts of Europe and the Near East as a colonial power'[46]

As *Die Zeit* writes, the desire to open up foreign countries for commerce was developed in Western Europe 'with capitalist economic systems ... from the 16th century onwards. The demand for raw materials, gold, spices and dyes was high in Europe and no longer covered by local resources. Buying goods from intermediaries like the Ottoman Empire was expensive. Population growth and the growing demand for food also led the Europeans to build colonies. Industrialization also promoted movement.

Merchants joined together in trading companies and, like kings and nobles, financed sea travels into the new world. Thus, a world-wide trading network emerged. The rulers of Europe gained control over by colonies sending military forces to the colonies and building civilian administrations. This was justified

---

[46] http://www.hschumacher.de/html/kolonialismus.html.

by the fact that they declared the population in the colonial possessions to be inferior. The so-called savages were seen as racially subdued, uncivilized and unable to manage themselves. It was therefore considered legitimate to force them to work in the colonies or to export them as slaves.

However, colonial powers did not only want to dominate and exploit colonies, but also to impress upon them their cultures and religions. The churches sent missionaries to Christianize people in the colonies. The colonial administrations forced the population into the language of the colonial masters and tried to abolish regional traditions. At the same time, scientists used the colonial population as a research subject.'[47]

H. Schumacher describes the further development of the colonial history: 'With the conquest of the Moroccan Ceuta in 1415 and the establishment of bases on the African coast for the purpose of gold and slave trade, Portugal began a European expansion. However, the discovery of America by Columbus from Spain (1492) and the development of the sea route to India by the Portuguese Vasco da Gama (1498) were the starting point of the epoch of modern colonialism. In the Treaty of Tordesillas (...), Spain and Portugal, the first two colonial powers of the modern era, agreed on the division of the still undeveloped parts of the earth.

Spain and Portugal pursued different colonial strategies in their zones of influence. Within a few decades, the Spaniards conquered large parts of South and Central America as well as the Caribbean; the conquistadors built huge viceroys (New Spain 1535, Peru 1543), systematically built overseas territorial administrations, drove economic development and subjugated the native population to a drastic system of exploitation (Encomienda). The territories and the gold wealth of the colonies secured, for a time, the claim of the Spanish crown on the pre-domination in Europe and across the world.

The Portuguese took possession of Brazil in 1500 and integrated it as an integral part of their monarchy, colonized it on the basis of sugar cane cultivation and extensively used their monopoly on the transatlantic trade with slaves, with which they were supplied through their African bases. In addition, since the Portuguese were predominantly supreme in the spice trade, for which they built fortresses and trading posts on the coast of West Africa (including Mozambique, Zanzibar), India (Goa, Kalikut) and China (Macao), they renounced a vast conquest of the country, especially as they were hardly able to do so due to significantly lower capacities compared to Spain. At the end of the 16th century, Englishmen and Dutchmen challenged their monopoly in long-distance trade with Eastern Asia and the Portuguese edged out them bit by bit from their bases; At the beginning of the 17th century, the English East India Company established itself in India and began the conquest of the subcontinent in 1757 and by around 1800, the Dutch had begun rule over Java and Ceylon (now Sri Lanka) .'[48]

' At the end of the 16th century, the Netherlands joined the circle of colonial powers through the activities of the privileged private company. In 1619, Batavia (Jakarta) was conquered on Java, which became the center of the Dutch colonial empire. The founding of Cape Town as a supply station in 1652 on the route to Southeast Asia enabled the immigration of settlers, who soon developed a life separated from the Motherland as a Boer. They advanced on treks to the interior of the country and founded several republics in the nineteenth century, such as the Orange Free State and the South African Republic (Transvaal).'[49]

'The arrival and settlement of English colonists who emigrated for religious reasons in America in the first half of the 17th century laid the foundations for the formation of the 13 English colonies on the east coast of North America. On the basis of a massive immigration from Europe the colonies gradually expanded their settlements to the west, and they were repeatedly in conflict with the French, who had founded Quebec in 1608 and expanded in the same direction. Despite some minor violent opposition in

---

[47] Zeit-Online 30. 3. 2012: *Europäischer Kolonialismus*, http://blog.zeit.de/schueler/2012/03/30/kolonialismus/.
[48] http://www.hschumacher.de/html/kolonialismus.html.
[49] http://www.hschumacher.de/html/kolonialismus.html.

India, British settlers formed an uncompromising expulsion and extermination policy. The common practice of England was to leave the colonies largely to self-administration, and by avoiding danger, they would emancipate themselves quickly from the mother country, that they would rather rebel when the policies of the motherland were contrary to the interests of the colony. Such a conflict in 1776 resulted in the declaration of independence of the British colonies in North America and in the independence war, from which the USA was victorious and became a sovereign state.

Despite this defeat, England, which had defeated France during the Seven Years' War (1756-1763) in the struggle for colonial domination, remained a leading colonial power. At the core of the British empire, the Indian subcontinent developed in the 18th century, which became accessible by the East India Company, which was founded in 1600 after it had edged out the French colonizers until 1761. In 1858, the company had to transfer its rule over the subcontinent to the British government after a broad insurrection movement in the north of India.'[50]

' Since 1608, France has been building trade and military stations in Canada, extending its sphere of influence further into the West and South. In the conflict with Great Britain it had to withdraw from the southern parts of its conquests, which stretched all the way to the Gulf of Mexico (Louisiana), after the Seven Years War.'[51]

'In the wake of the industrial revolution, which intensified Europeans' urge for raw materials and at the same time expanded their weapon technology advantages, the 19th century in the intention and form of colonialism changed. With the intention of building a new colonial empire, France seized Algeria (1830-1847), expanded its colonies in Senegal and began the conquest of Indo-China. Great Britain expanded into the Indian subcontinent, including the Cape Colony (1815), Australia and New Zealand (1840), Natal (South Africa, 1843), Burma (1852) and Lagos (Nigeria, 1861). At the same time, new regions were opened up for trade and the influence of European nations as the Ottoman Empire and Egypt, Persia, parts of China and Japan.'[52]

' After the opening of the Suez Canal in 1869 and, above all, the occupation of Egypt by Great Britain in 1882, European colonialism developed a new dynamic. The rivalry among European powers for the areas which had not yet been colonized, and geostrategic advantages, increased to a race of colonial expansion, in which Germany also participated after the German empire in 1871 (...). In order to reduce skirmishes, the great powers agreed on the mutual delimitation of their interests; at the most important of these conferences, the African Conference of Africa (Congo) in 1885, the colonial powers of Africa shared everything between each other. France took over the regions north and south of the Sahara (French West Africa and French Equatorial Africa), while the British took over most of the East (British East Africa) and the South, and the claim of the German Reich on Central African territories was recognized, Portugal extended its coasts of Angola and Mozambique into the interior of the country, Belgium's King Leopold was awarded the Congo region as a private Congo free state. The colonization of the continent (with the exception of Liberia and Ethiopia) took place without any consideration for the interests of the people of Africa and was concluded in 1900 practically. Besides, in regions in which the interests of colonial powers overlapped, e.g., in Sudan and in Morocco, conflicts (Fashoda Crisis between France and Great Britain in 1898, Morocco's crises in 1905 and 1911 between Germany and France) which contributed to the deterioration of the international climate and an increased focus on the arms race, in particular toward naval construction.

For the politically-weakened China, the great powers, some of which already controlled important areas in China, agreed on an open-door policy in 1899/1900. The USA had opposed a regional division of China in the model of Africa to ensure that all countries had unimpeded access to the potentially huge

---

[50] loc. cit.
[51] loc. cit.
[52] loc. cit.

Chinese market. They formed a joint expeditionary corps to the downfall of the Boxer Rebellion (1900), which ensured the unconditional assertion of their imperialist interests'[53]

'Only since the eighties of the 19th century as a "belated nation", Germany, after the first hesitation of the Reichskanzler, Otto von Bismarck, asserted expansionist interests overseas. Colonial societies, especially the Deutsche Kolonialverein and the Society for German Colonization under the leadership of Carl Peters, who joined the German colonial society in 1887, were champions and the first bearers of colonial policy. In 1884/85, Bismarck placed the first territorial acquisitions - in South West Africa (Namibia), Togo, Cameroon, East Africa and the Pacific - under the "protection" of the empire. It was true that Bismarck publicly recognized these colonies merely as insignificant trade bases, but with them Germany joined the circle of the colonial powers. The Berlin Africa Conference, conducted by Bismarck in 1885, confirmed the German colonial claims in Africa and the Pacific. ... In the second wave of colonial applications (1897-1899) only relatively insignificant areas were added: Kiaochou in China as a naval base, Nauru, the Caroline, Mariana, Palau and Western Samoa islands in the Pacific.'[54]

In non-European countries, there were no conditions comparable to European countries for industrialization. They were thus at the mercy of the trade interests of more developed industrial countries and could not resist militarily. However, there were differences between the developing countries depending on cultural and civilizational development. East Asian high cultures, such as Japan and China, were, as a trade partner for European industrialized countries, not only more interesting than culturally less developed countries because of their cultural and civilizational development. They were also able to preserve their sovereignty accordingly, but they had to grant trade concessions to European countries.

As long as they could not protect their own markets and their own industries, they were at the mercy of the dictates of European trade interests, so much so that China even had to import opium. However, Japan and China have been able to open up mentally to Western thinking and economics and therefore could also industrialize themselves.

Japan also had to submit to unequal trade agreements. Marcus Kunath writes: 'When the warships of Admiral Perry finally forced the opening of the country, Japan had to grant to the Western nations in the trade treaties of 1858 a series of concessions which gave them a considerable advantage:

Thus, the treaties defined extraterritorial jurisdiction for Western nationals through their respective consuls, until finally, in 1899, Japan was able to fully enforce its own legal power.

Japan also lost its autonomy and had to submit to the single-customs tariff of 5% set unilaterally in 1866.

Finally, an extremely damaging effect on the state budget was the establishment of an external exchange rate for gold and silver coins, which, by its nonconformity with the international exchange rate, offered the possibility of arbitrage transactions and, up to its revision in 1860, caused a substantial loss of Japanese gold reserves[55].'[56]

In contrast to Japan, China had to abandon territories for trade branches, such as Hong Kong, Macau, Tsingtau and further suffer from unequal contracts.

Far more than in all the other colonies and dependent areas, emigrants who had left Europe for unemployment reasons or as persecuted Christian sects, had settled in America. They formed not only the social elites, but also felt themselves as citizens of America and thus even suppressed by the colonial powers. There were independence struggles in which the United States of America had already declared itself an independent republic in the eighteenth century.

---

[53] http://www.hschumacher.de/html/kolonialismus.html.

[54] loc. cit.

[55] Baba, Masao/Tatemoto, Masahiro: *Foreign Trade and Economic Growth in Japan: 1858-1937.* p.162f.

[56] Marcus Kunath: *Japans Industrielle Revolution im 19. Jahrhundert,* TU Dresden 2005, p.7f. http://www.qucosa.de/fileadmin/data/qucosa/documents/1458/1140508799041-4763.pdf.

' In the first third of the nineteenth century 'the growing self-esteem of the Spanish citizens in South America, also fueled by the independence struggle of British settlers in North America,' as H. Schumacher writes, 'led to a relatively rapid replacement of Spanish Overseas territories from the motherland. In 1822, Brazil also declared itself an independent constitutional monarchy, as a result of the growing contradictions between the Portuguese class in the colony and the headquarters in Europe.'[57]

Particularly unfavorable was the market position of African countries against industrialized countries. Africans lived in tribal associations as animal breeders and farmers who lived off their own fields. Originally, Africa had hardly any products which were of interest to industrialized countries and, accordingly little purchasing power. For example, African potentates could only sell slaves, who had been captured in fighting with other tribes.

In order to gain a financial benefit from Africa, these regions had to be colonized and, as Sören Utermark writes with regard to the German African colonies, 'certain conditions had to be fulfilled, These included, in particular, the establishment of the German power apparatus, i.e. the complete seizure of the country, the subjugation of the people living there, the construction of an administration and infrastructure, and the settling of settlers, merchants and economic enterprises.'[58] The colonization allowed white settlers to come to Africa to take away most of the land from the locals and plantations on which exportable products were grown.

But there were problems with the employment of domestic workers. Sören Utermark: 'A fundamental circumstance which led to an insufficient supply of labor was the subsistence economy of the autochthonous population, so many tribes lived by hunting, fishing or exclusively from cattle-raising. In many places, the locals were firmly involved in the traditional structure of this economic form, so that for many of them there was initially no need to enter into paid employment with Europeans. A further problem arose from the fact that the African workers had to be fetched over long distances. This was made even more difficult by the fact that many workers could only be employed on the plantations on a seasonal basis, which in turn led to problems for the rest of their lives. It was also unthinkable for many Africans to leave their families for a longer period of time and to work on a plantation far from their homeland. This disinclination was reinforced by the fact that Africans must have remembered their kidnapping and abduction from the time of slavery. [59]

Considering the nature of the events and the actions of the colonial men it is not surprising that the native population did not have much interest in wage labor for German companies. German colonizers came as a foreign power into African countries, subjugated the primitive population in a relatively short time and destroyed indigenous structures. By way of landlifting, expropriation, the rigorous use of force and expulsion, accompanied by a racist and extremely derogatory sense of superiority, a German system of values and work should have been introduced from the beginning of colonialization.'[60]

Utermark distinguishes between the time up to 1906, where problems were criticized in Germany, and the so-called reformatory period in which the new Colonial Commissioner Dernburg was responsible for the African colonies, and writes: 'In the pre-reform era, the German colonial administration tried to use compulsory methods, to meet the ever-growing need for indigenous workers. The methods of compulsion can be divided into three forms:

- "Proper compulsory labor". Under regulations, Africans could be used for free-of-charge work (for example, road construction). Officially, compulsory labor was lawful when ordered

---

[57] http://www.hschumacher.de/html/kolonialismus.html.
[58] Sören Utermark: „Schwarzer Untertan versus schwarzer Bruder". Bernhard Dernburgs Reformen in den Kolonien Deutsch-Ostafrika, Deutsch-Südwestafrika, Togo und Kamerun, Dissertation, p.61.
[59] Vgl. Gründer, Horst: Geschichte der deutschen Kolonien, p.151.
[60] Sören Utermark: loc. cit.

by the colonial administration in the public interest. [61]. With the approval of governments, male natives were also "used to other work", mostly on European plantations [62]. Also, by carrying out unpaid government work, the readiness of Africans to be encouraged to perform better, using paid labor on private plantations. Thus, the Africans were not only used to unpaid forced labor to serve the public welfare, but also to being indirectly turned into paid employees with private employers. A general labor force consisted for all Portuguese-East African colonies for all Africans able to work; as well as in the French, British and Belgian colonies.[63]

- Unlawful compulsory labor. Above all in Cameroon and German East Africa the Africans were forced illegally, and by the use of force, onto paid working on European plantations[64].
- There was an indirect work constraint. Indirectly, the Africans were to be induced to work on wages by taxes, expropriations, or, as in the case of German-South-West Africa, by laws against vagabondage. [65] However, tax legislation as an indirect compulsion to take up wage labor was only of limited use, as it was generally concerned only with Africans who were not involved in native production in the poorly developed state of the country. With the development of railway lines, however, Dernburg's entrance to the city continued to increase the possibility of producing agricultural products for the market and selling them for cash. In the era of Dernburg, therefore, the development of the colonies reduced the effectiveness of the tax legislation as a compulsory measure for the labor market [66].'[67]

The same is reported from the colonies of other countries.

'The Portuguese had replaced serfdom with so-called contract work. Blacks who could not prove that they had volunteered for half a year had to do free compulsory labor in the fields. Most of the workers even had to bring their food and equipment. The forced laborers were as lawless as Gulag convicts. They could be brought anywhere from one colony to another. Still in the early fifties [19. Century], several hundred thousand contract workers were moved back and forth between Portuguese colonies or to Rhodesia and South Africa'.[68]

' When the American adventurer Henry Morton Stanley bought the Congo colony for the Belgian King Leopold II in the 1870s, more than 20 million people lived there. Until the First World War the population had decreased by about 10 million. It was the result of the genocide, which entered history as Congo-Grail.'[69]

Reports of the scandalous, inhumane behavior of Europeans towards the indigenous people are available from all colonies.

61 Claß, Paul: *Die Rechtsverhältnisse der freien farbigen Arbeiter in den deutschen Schutzgebieten Afrikas und der Südsee*, p.73.
62 See: § 2 of the instruction for the implementation of the ordinance, concerning the attraction of the natives to public works. In: Zimmermann, Alfred (Hg.): Die deutsche Kolonial-Gesetzgebung, Bd. 9/10, p.108.
63 Claß, Paul: Die Rechtsverhältnisse der freien farbigen Arbeiter ..., p.73.
64 Schröder, Peter: *Gesetzgebung und Arbeiterfrage in den Kolonien*, p.366-370.
65 Claß, Paul: loc. cit, p.74ff.
66 Schröder, Peter: *Gesetzgebung und Arbeiterfrage in den Kolonien*, p.593.
67 Sören Utermark: *„Schwarzer Untertan versus schwarzer Bruder",* p.61f.
68 Erich Wiedemann: DAS ZEITALTER DER KOLONIEN ZWIESPÄLTIGES ERBE, in: SPIEGEL SPECIAL Geschichte 2/2007, p.40.
69 Erich Wiedemann: p.41.

4.1.2 The colonization of the Near East and North Africa by the establishment of French and British mandated territories after the First World War

The Ottoman Sultanate, which dominated the Middle East and North Africa, had become the so-called "sick man on the Bosporus," and was broken by the First World War. This created a new situation for the European colonial powers of Great Britain and France.

Persia and the Ottoman Empire were a bulwark against Russia's potential threat to the sea routes to India and were thus natural allies of Great Britain against Russia. The Near East and Persia also gained increasingly strategic importance due to the discovery of oil deposits, which they wanted to prevent the Russians exploiting. As long as the Ottoman Empire existed, oil sources could be exploited through concession agreements with France and Turkey.

However, England had to interfere with the benevolent policy towards the Ottoman Empire when, before the First World War, the Turks' relations with the German Empire intensified and Turkey became a German alliance in the First World War.

Georg Brunold writes: "The British were compelled to revise their Near East policy within a few weeks, which have kept them loyal throughout the nineteenth century. Their imperative was the preservation of the great empire. Even during the Crimean War between 1853 and 1856, the British and the French joined the Turks against Russia. Tsar Nicholas I, in a conversation with the British Ambassador, had sarcastically designated the Sultan of the High Porte, the governor in Constantinople, as a "sick man on the Bosporus", a title that passed over the entire Ottoman Empire overnight , But until then, the rotten colossus on the British routes to India, the crown jewel of the Victorian Empire, was worrying the British less than the visions of chaos after its collapse."[70]

Thus, Great Britain began not only to support, but even to provoke the independence efforts of the Arab countries controlled by Turkey. Wikipedia writes: 'In 1916, Emir Faisal I united the Bedouin tribes against Ottoman rule and played a decisive role in the guerrilla campaigns during the First World War. Together with the British officer T. E. Lawrence he stood in the struggle for the independence of the Arabian Peninsula. He fought successfully in Palestine and Syria. The Arab troops of Damascus arrived in Damascus in 1918.'[71] 'Faisal was proclaimed King of Syria by the Syrian National Congress on March 7, 1920.'[72]

France and England did not fulfill the Arabians' previously promulgated independence, but enforced their own claims to power. Georg Brunold writes: The secret 'Sykes-Picot agreement of May 16, 1916 divided the Arabian Ottoman provinces into British and French influence zones. The territory of today's Lebanon and Syria, as well as the Vilâyet Mosul, should go to France. The United Kingdom claims Palestine for itself, and also the Ottoman Vilâyets Baghdad and Basra. Russia too [which was a coalition partner in the First World War] is not forgotten in the treaty: Constantinople with the sea-mountains and Armenia are now to be part of the tsarist - a plan which will be lost when, the following year, the Bolsheviks take power and publish the secret agreement.'[73]

'On the basis of the Sykes-Picot agreement, however, at the San Remo conference in April 1920, France was given the League of Nations for Syria and Lebanon. Faisal I was then expelled by the French after the battle of Maysalun on July 24, 1920 and went to exile in Great Britain.[[74]]'[75]

Great Britain received the trusteeship on Palestine and Mesopotamia. The British territory of Mesopotamia was comprised of three distinct territories: the Turkish territories, the Basque, Baghdad, and,

---

[70] Georg Brunold: *Die Erfindung des Iraks*, in: http://www.zeit.de/2015/03/osmanisches-reich-entstehung-irak-winston-churchill.

[71] https://de.wikipedia.org/wiki/Faisal_I.

[72] https://de.wikipedia.org/wiki/Faisal_I.

[73] Georg Brunold: *Die Erfindung des Iraks*.

[74] Al-Massad Joseph: Colonial Effectp. *The Making of National Jordan*, P.102ff.

[75] https://de.wikipedia.org/wiki/Faisal_I.

ceded by France, Mosul, three different regions with different populations and religious affiliation. Apart from the fact that these three provinces with their respective different populations and differences already formed the conflict potential that still dominates Iraq, they also rebelliously opposed the British mandate.

4.1.3 What has the colonization and domination of protectorate areas brought about for Europeans and for the colonies and protectorate areas?

The original motivation of industrialized countries to extend trade to the developing countries was to find additional sales markets and import more and cheaper raw materials. If we ask whether this goal has been achieved, the answer is usually at least negative for the time of colonization.

An extreme example of this is the use, or better, of the loss which the German Empire drew from its colonies. Sören Utermark reports: 'In order to clarify the question of the value of the colonies as raw material suppliers, it is necessary to consider imports from the colonies into the Reich as well as the share of colonial imports in the German economy. The following data is exclusively for the German-African colonies[76]'[77]

Year	Import from Col. In The Reich (in million marks)	German Total Import (in million marks)	Share of Imports from Colonies of the Total Import of the Reich
1895	3.37	4566	0.07%
1900	5.76	6406	0.09%
1910	41.52	9535	0.44%
1913	42.51	11638	0.37%

German exports to German colonies were correspondingly low:

Year	Export of the Reich in the Colonies (in million marks)	German Total Export (in million marks)	Share of Export in the Colonies of the Total Export of the Reich
1895	4.90	4132	0.13%
1900	17,54	5101	0,34%
1910	43,78	8080	0,54%
1913	52,02	10892	0,48%

[78]

For the German taxpayer, the maintenance of the colonies was a minuscule business. 'The revenues of the colonies consisted chiefly of duties, taxes and charges [...]. The tariffs formed the main source of income [...]. Each colony formed a customs territory with its own import and export duties in respect to the

---

[76] Compiled by Sören Utermark aus: Stat..s Jahrbuch für das Deutsche Reich, Bd. 1895-1914 in: Sören Utermark: „Schwarzer Untertan versus schwarzer Bruder", S.332.f
[77] Sören Utermark: S.110f.
[78] Compiled by Sören Utermark aus: Stat. Jb. für das Deutsche Reich, Bd., loc.cit. p.333.

German Reich. Accordingly, the colonial goods were cleared for import into the German Reich. This was also true for the colonies [...].' [79]

However, the revenue was not enough to finance government expenditure. That is why during the colonial period, that is, from 1894-1913, grants of the Reich had to be given. They accounted for 58.1% for Cameroon, 330.4% for German South West Africa and 73.5% for German East Africa. For Togo, only 5.4% of the revenue were needed as grants of the Reich.

According to Horst Gründer, the national colonial loss business was, 'however, from the outset associated with the private enrichment of individual soil specula-tors, large-sized companies and colonial entrepreneurs or colonial council mem-bers, Woermann, Scharlach, von der Heydt, Hofmann, Douglas and their trading companies. Likewise, the banks, which are connected with the trading and ship-ping companies, were able to gain huge profits thanks to the colonies, most of which were obtained from state subsidies and only through the Reich's role as administrator and guarantor[80]. All in all, the development of the colonies re-mained far behind initial expectations, so that among the German public, criticism of the many shortcomings of the German colonial policy was growing[81]'[82]

Speaking of this disproportion, Bebel declared in 1899, 'in the German Reichs-tag: "Whenever we look at the history of colonial policy in the last three centuries, we encounter violence and the oppression of the peoples concerned, which often end with their complete extermination. ... And in order to be able to operate the exploitation of the African population to the full extent possible and as undisturbed as possible, millions are to be used from the pockets of the Reich, from the pockets of the taxpayers.... That we, as opponents of any oppression, do not give our con-sent to these expenditures, you will understand."'[83]

By and large, this negative balance is likely to apply to other European coun-tries as well. Erich Wiedemann writes: 'Certainly, the slave trade was a great busi-ness for the Europeans in the sixteenth to eighteenth centuries. But no land-based resorts were needed. Locals were supplying the slaves for free on board. But at the latest after the southern states of the USA abolished slavery after the American Civil War (1861 to 1865), this exploitation model was finally overtaken.

It is true, some colonies have helped to make some colonialists rich. But these were exceptions. There are even indications for the assumption that the prosperity of the European powers was inversely related to the expansion of their colonial wealth.

Adam Smith, the world economist, predicted in 1776 that the cost of maintain-ing British possessions in North America, illusion-adjusted, was in sharp contrast to the economic output. If these colonies could not be made more profitable, he advised that they should be given up. "Our men of government finally have to realize the golden dream which they and probably the people have dreamed or

---

[79] Sören Utermark: p.99.
[80] Vgl. Gründer, Horst: *Geschichte der deutschen Kolonien*, p.240.
[81] In particular, the mismanagement and the assessorism and bureaucracy of the colonial administration were criticized. See: Laak van, Dirk: *Über alles in der Welt*, p.84.
[82] Utermark: p.110f.
[83] Erich Wiedemann: Das Zeitalter der Kolonien *zwiespältiges Erbe*, loc.cit.. p.45.

awaken." England would be well advised to adapt its policy of mediocrity to its economic situation.'[84]

' For French imperialism, Morocco and Algeria were two welcome fields of experimentation that were certainly also useful to the French economy. But what are Mali, Mauritania, Senegal, Chad and Ubangi-Shari good for? It was only the lust of the military might game that caused them to seize foreign territories.

In the private sector, the cost-benefit accounting was more favorable. A handful of ship-owners, merchants and plantation owners became rich with the trade of coffee, cocoa, ivory and minerals. But overall, these yields were not of great significance.

Colonial Africa has enormous mineral resources. But the resources already developed were not very significant. Ghana's Mining Industry produced 1949 diamonds worth 6.4 million pounds sterling. That was the equivalent of a good three percent of the Ghanaian foreign reserves. Super returns from gold and diamond mining were made in South Africa. But the colonialists had no access to this. And the oil age had not yet begun in Black Africa.'[85]

The protectorate areas also soon proved to be cost traps and problem areas, with the exception of the oil production areas in Iraq, the Arab Emirates and the influence on Iran, which gained huge profits. In order to save costs, Great Britain nevertheless denounced protection treaties with the United Arab Emirates against their will in 1971, so that these countries were forced to build up their own forces. The domination over Egypt secured the royalties for the Suez Canal.

What is the result of colonization for the developing countries concerned? Their traditional society was destroyed. They were oppressed, humbled and exploited.

On the other hand, the traditional high cultures in Asia and Latin America have not experienced any significant economic and social development over a thousands of years, and the people of Africa, North America and other areas were still at the level of collectors and hunters or at most cattle breeders and were only, to a small extent, self-procurers of agricultural products.

As far as Africa is concerned, Sören Utermark writes: 'The conditions of life on the Black Continent were anything but paradise in the pre-colonial phase. Africa was not a natural *Garden of Eden* in which noble savages lived from the fruits of their honest work and practiced in charity. Africa was a predominantly dark place, dominated by tyranny, slavery, and partly by cannibalism.'[86] The population of Africa was also repeatedly decimated by armed conflicts. That is why, in order to secure internal peace, many territories were also ready to join together to protected areas guaranteed by European states.

It is also recognized by representatives of the former colonies that the colonized have also profited from individual elements of colonialism. The Indian Prime Minister, Manmohan Singh, has praised his home country of India as the "most brilliant jewel in the British crown" in a speech to the students of the University of Oxford. India, he said, was the country with the lowest per capita income

---

[84] Wiedemann: loc.cit.
[85] Wiedemann: p.46.
[86] loc. cit., p.37.

on the earth at the beginning of the 20th century. British civilization was to be blamed for this. However, the rule over India also had some " beneficial components". They would have given India a free press, an exemplary administration and a "good idea of the constitutional state." In principle, this also applies to the former British possessions in Africa.'[87]

' James Feyrer and Bruce Sacerdote of Dartmouth College in New Hampshire have quantified the utility. They calculated a plus of 40 per cent of social product per century of colonialism.'[88]

'The subjugation to the language of the colonialists also proved useful. Without the colonial languages of English, French and Portuguese, the largest part of Black Africa would remain Babylonia. Above all, the English and French are today the cultural bridge to the rest of the world. African literature, because the great cultures knew no script, would be nothing without the languages of their former occupiers.'[89]

Without the compulsory opening up of the markets and the provoked initiatives to industrialize as in Japan, or without colonization, the developing countries would not have been able to develop into independent states that are partners in the globalized world. To this end, the traditional behavioral patterns and social conditions had to be broken and the people developed into self-sufficient individuals. The more they succeeded or succeed in the individual countries, the more they can develop their economy and society further.

4.1.4 The end of the colonies

After the Second World War, European countries were able to separate themselves from the colonies because of the relatively small advantages or even the high costs and in face of the independence movements. The European powers were also so severely weakened by the Second World War that they could barely control their colonies. The movements of independence were also fostered by the intensifying East-West antagonism, which forced the colonial powers to hold the colonies in their sphere of influence by means of concessions. Nevertheless, this process has often been bloody, as the examples in Indo-China and Algeria, demonstrated also the disputes with the Mau-Mau movement in Kenya.

Contrary to the rest of the colonial powers, France, even if its colonies wanted to be politically sovereign, has even compelled them to pay for compensation and to grant France privileges, of which France still benefits at the expense of the former colonies. France 'in return for the recognition of Haiti's independence in 1825, compensation for former plant owners was demanded. Over many decades, Haiti paid a total of 90 million gold francs to France.'[90] The former colonies remained dependent on treaties and capital relations in many ways from the industrial powers.

---

[87] loc. cit., p.42.
[88] loc. cit.
[89] loc. cit.
[90] https://de.wikipedia.org/wiki/Haiti#Geschichte.

As the Deutsche Wirtschaftsnachrichten wrote, the African colonies of France in the 1950s and '60s decided 'to make themselves independent. Although the government in Paris formally accepted declarations of independence, it demanded that the countries sign a so-called "pact to continue colonialization". They pledged to introduce the French Colonial Currency FCFA ("franc for the colonies of France in Africa"), to keep the French school system and military system and to establish French as an official language.

Under this law, 14 African countries are still obliged to store around 85% of their currency reserves in the French Central Bank in Paris. They are under the direct control of the French Treasury. The countries concerned have no access to this part of their reserves. If their remaining 15 percent reserves are insufficient, they must borrow the additional funds from the French finance ministry at market rates. Since 1961, Paris has been controlling the currency reserves of Benin, Burkina Faso, Guinea-Bissau, Ivory Coast, Mali, Niger, Senegal, Togo, Cameroon, Central African Republic, Chad, Congo, Equatorial Guinea and Gabon.'[91]

In addition, these countries have to pay their "colonial debts" to Paris for the infrastructure constructed by France, as Silicon Africa has reported extensively. 'The French state collects 440 billion euros of taxes annually from its former colonies. France is dependent on the revenue, so as not to sink into economic insignificance, warns former President Jacques Chirac. The case shows that a just world is difficult because the former colonial powers have become dependent on exploitation themselves.'[92]

' The government in Paris also has a right of pre-emption to all newly discovered raw mineral deposits in the African countries. Finally, French companies must be given preferential treatment when awarding contracts in ex-colonies. As a result, most assets in the areas of supply, finance, transport, energy and agriculture are in the hands of French corporations.'[93]

If a country refused to accept or abdicate France's conditions, the French opposed it by force. *Wirtschaftsnachrichten* writes: 'An example of this is the first president of the West African Togo, Sylvanus Olympio. He refused to sign the "pact to continue colonization". But France insisted that Togo paid compensation for the infrastructure that the French had built during the colonial period. The sum amounted to about 40 per cent of the budget of Togo in 1963 and brought the newly independent country quickly to its economic limits.

In addition, the new president of Togo decided to abolish the French colony currency FCFA and print its own national currency. Only three days after this decision, the new government was overthrown by a group of former foreign legionaries, and the President was killed. The leader of the legionaries, Gnassingbe Eyadema, received 550 euros from the local French embassy for the assassination, as the British telegraph reports. Four years later, Eyadema, with the support of Paris, became the new president of Togo. He established a tyrannical dictatorship in the West African country and remained in power until his death in 2005.

[91] https://deutsche-wirtschafts-nachrichten.de/autor/deutsche-wirtschafts-nachrichten/ published: 15.03.15 01:12 h.
[92] Loc.cit.
[93] loc. cit

In the following years, the government in Paris used to resort to former foreign-legionaries to overthrow unpleasant governments in its ex-colonies. Thus, the first president of the Central African Republic, David Dacko, was overthrown in 1966 by former members of the Foreign Legion. The same happened to the President of Burkina Faso, Maurice Yaméogo, and the President of Benin, Mathieu Kérékou. And the first president of the Republic of Mali, Modiba Keita, fell victim to a coup of former legionaries in 1968. Only a few years before he had decided to abolish the French colonial currency.'[94]

It is therefore understandable that in the French colonies there were only regiments which pursued a policy favorable to the French, but whose members also profited themselves. Thus, when French troops continually intervene in crisis situations in their former colonies and restore order, they do so also to preserve their own interests. However, in view of the chaotic situation in countries ruled by blacks, one can also get to the conviction that the normally relatively peaceful development in the former French African colonies is due to the interest of France in its revenues from these countries.

Regarding the end of the colonies of other European countries, it is said: 'In contrast, the other colonial powers have adopted such measures. Great Britain had to learn its lesson over the course of the American Revolution of 1763. The trigger was the decision of Great Britain to impose the cost of the recently-ended French and Indian war on the American colonies. The protest, on the other hand, resulted in the "Boston Tea Party" and finally in the independence war and the founding of the United States in 1776. In 1778, the British Parliament passed the "Taxation of Colonies Act". For the future, the UK waived tax and duties on sales in its "British America" and "British West Indies" colonies.

The same applies to the former colonies of Australia and Canada. Although they are still part of the "Commonwealth of Nations", they formally form part of the British royal house, but tax sovereignty has existed exclusively with the governments there since the Declaration of Independence of the countries at the beginning of the 20th century.

Even the former colonial power, the Netherlands does not raise any taxes on its former areas of influence in South America and Southeast Asia. In South-East Asia, finances were so disastrous at the beginning of the twentieth century due to devastating wars, that the Netherlands regularly had to support their colonies financially. The kingdom separated itself from a large part of its colonies as early as the beginning of the 19th century. Lastly, the Dutch Antilles left the kingdom in October 2010. Only the Caribbean islands of Aruba, Curaçao and Saint Maarten are still part of the Kingdom of the Netherlands.'[95] The former Belgian colony of Congo and its ending and the chaotic circumstances need no further explanation.

Franz Ansperger summarized: 'While the cost-benefit balance of the colonial powers was partly ambiguous and partly negative[96], the colonized were largely

---

[94] loc. cit.

[95] France can maintain its status only with exploitation of the former colonies loc.cit..

[96] Significant in this context is the word of D'Estournelles de Constant in the French Parliament: „Il y a deux choses dans la politique coloniale: d'abord la joie des conquêtes et ensuite la carte à payer." Franz Ansprenger: *Auflösung der Kolonialreiche*, p.22 f.

devoted to plundering. Thus the colonies and semi-colonies of the European powers in Asia and Africa remained poor and backward during the decades of intense economic relations with their mother countries as well as the semi-colonies of the USA in Latin America, while development in Europe and North America showed a rapid increase in social prosperity. In 1914, approximately one-quarter of the French investment went to Russia, but only 9 per cent to the French colonies. Germany's foreign investment before the outbreak of the First World War was only 2 percent compared to colonial protected areas.[97][98]

4.2 The development of nationalism in Europe and developing countries after the Second World War

4.2.1 The demise of ancient European nationalism and the independence of the colonies and protectorate territories after the Second World War

In the contest of the great national states, Great Britain and France were relatively saturated by their colonies and their capacities were exhausted. Germany and Italy, however, were striving for a larger empire.

In 1871, the German Empire was dreaming of also getting a "place in the sun", which meant to match the colonial possessions of other West European countries. After the colonies had been lost in the Versailles peace treaty (or rather: dictate), the Nazis proclaimed Germany to be a "people without space" and pursued an extension of Germany to the East. Italy wanted to revive the Roman Empire and extended itself to Libya, Eritrea, Ethiopia and Somalia and tried, in the Second World War, to conquer the Balkans and Greece. As these world *Empire Dreams* destroyed national frameworks, the self-confidence of the people was based not only on the nation, but on the Germanic-respected Roman race.

A nation still contains the entire spiritual and cultural heritage of a people. Whoever identifies with his nation can still develop mentally and humanely. *Race*, however, was a subhuman concept and accordingly made the behavior of the Nazis and the Italian fascists bestial. It is understandable that nationalism had to collide and unleash wars.

The First World War has already been guided by a nationalist goal. In the Versailles peace treaty, the pure nationalism of the Western countries lived on and was also raised by the then American President, Woodrow Wilson, to a *Principle of Peace*. The result was that oppressed nations, such as the Poles, Czechs and Slovaks, were free, but then also lived under their own nationalism. Thus, the newly-created Polish state under Pilsudzki began to submit to Baltic states. Józef Piłsudski pursued 'the goal of restoring borders from the time before the divisions of Poland also far beyond the borders of the Polish settlement area. This policy led first of all to the integration of Great Poland as defined by the Treaty of Versailles, the war with Soviet Russia and the war with Lithuania on account of the area claimed by both sides around Wilna / Vilnius (Central Lithuania).'[99]

---

[97] Franz Ansprenger: loc. cit., p.22 f. and 26.
[98] https://de.wikipedia.org/wiki/Kolonialismus.
[99] https://de.wikipedia.org/wiki/J%C3%B3zef_Pi%C5%82sudski.

The new states also received a German population. Parts of Silesia fell to Poland, the Sudetenland region to Czechoslovakia and South Tyrol to Italy. This encouraged new nationalist tendencies. In addition, the central powers, especially Germany, were given the sole war blame and they were so burdened with war charges that they were in danger of falling apart.

In addition, there was the socialist revolution in Russia that created an antithesis to Western capitalism, which then competed with the Western economic and social order, and the collapse of the capitalist economy in the world economic crisis in 1929. From this mixture emerged extreme reactionary nationalism in Italy, Spain and Portugal, but in the most extreme form in national-socialist Germany.

In addition, a similarly extreme racist-based nationalism developed in Japan. Germany and Japan triggered the Second World War, which brought enormous destruction and misery, but in which, too, realization matured over the dangers of nationalism. This gave rise to the idea of a Unification of Europe. It was still furthered by the intensifying East-West antagonism to the Cold War, and by the fact that the European colonial powers were too weak to hold onto their colonial world and tended to lean against each other.

4.2.2 Nationalism in developing countries as the driving force for the development of a secular society and its tense relationship with religion, theocracy and tribalism

In non-European countries, nationalism also became the driving force for the individualization and emancipation of man from traditional forms of life and the secularization of society. This development was driven by the European-trained intellectuals and the military.

As far as nationalist efforts came into conflict with other groups of the population, bloody wars were and are being waged. In Turkey, the nationalist aspirations of the Turks, the Armenians and the Kurds met, even leading to the genocide of the Armenians.

The division of the British Indian Crown Colony into India and Pakistan led to the most bloody feuds and expulsions, since Pakistani nationalism at the same time was Muslim-motivated. But while during pre-colonial and colonial times religious groups lived together relatively peacefully, the influence of nationalist aspirations resulted in conflicts that, with regard to Kashmir, continued to smolder.

Nationalism dissolves people from traditional relationships and they no longer understand themselves as members of the tribe, but as citizens, nationalism promotes the globalization of human beings and thus, economic and social development. However, Europeanism usually only affects the thin layer of the intellectuals and the military, which can then become a foreign body for the mass of the population living in traditional relations. In addition, secular dominations are relatively prone to corruption. Muslim groups are bound to the social commandments of Islam, while religious anchoring in secular actions is comparatively less. This is different from the situation in Christian countries, especially in Protestant countries - consider Prussian official morals and the puritan roots of capitalism as described by Max Weber.

Among other reasons, because of the greater corruption potential of secular power structures, the Hamas, which are based on religious beliefs, could secede from the secular PLO. The corruption of the Egyptian military rule was always scourged by the Islamic Mujahid. They also obtained their consent through their social behavior. This is the reason why secular regimes in Muslim countries are always in danger of being swept away by the populace spurred on by Muslim clergy, as was the case in Iran and was tried in Egypt.

Secular regimes therefore also have difficulties in democratization and are, therefore, subsequently rather autocratic dominations, which prevail in almost all Muslim states in the Near and Middle East and in Africa. Extreme examples were Saddam Hussein in Iraq, Gaddafi in Libya and also, in a weaker form, the autocratic rule in Algeria and Egypt as well as the Assad regime in Syria.

By eliminating dictators with Western help and not immediately providing alternative secular structures that would naturally have to be adapted to countries, the West has contributed to the chaoticization of the situation in these countries and the resulting refugee movements.

4.3 The impact of Europeanism on Third World Countries

4.3.1 The destruction of traditional forms of life by Europeanism

Secular social relations are disturbed by secular economic and social forms. Economically, this means that people have to become wage and salary dependent or even have to start a business themselves. People no longer work in a hierarchical family union, but instead work together with totally unknown other workers and are not evaluated there as a member of a family, but according to their individual achievements.

The qualification itself also affects the relationship between the boys and the elderly in the family, because modern knowledge is first acquired by the boys and thus the knowledge pyramid is reversed to a certain extent. Who is not dependent on their grandchildren when problems arise with their smartphone? Thus the individualization of society is encouraged. In a traditional and still religiously-founded family this can lead to shocks in the self-understanding of all family members and destroy traditional societies.

Parallel to the first stages of industrialization or even ahead of development, colonies and later-developing countries were flooded with goods from industrialized countries, and since the agrarian revolution, agricultural products are also included. As a result, traditional economic enterprises and many farms were destroyed and the people involved in them became unemployed. The main problem why many developing countries were not able to develop into industrialized countries by adopting industrial know-how, is the lack of adequate research and dynamic entrepreneurs.

In over 2000 years, as described, individualized and creative researchers and entrepreneurs in Europe have evolved – those who invested money in research and development and machinery and equipment to develop, produce and market new products. In developing countries as well, there were always people with extreme wealth and property. They did not, and even today, come up with the idea of using their means for their own research and development and the establishment of production sites, unless production processes are already established and promise quick profit. In these countries, self-employment is actually only motivated by the trader's mentality. Otherwise the capital is exported and invested in industrialized countries. Thus, a country cannot become a progressively industrial.

Countries with valuable raw material reserves can indeed achieve an elevated standard of living. The profits from the mineral resources are, however, generally only distributed to the elite, which they then tend to invest in industrialized countries. Only in the case of extreme profits from, for example, oil deposits and in countries with small populations, are the revenues shared with the broad domestic population to a certain extent. That is to say, in the Gulf States, but also in Iran and the rather socialist Venezuela. But if revenue then falls because of a reduction in commodity prices, then, as is the case at the present time in Venezuela in particular, mass poverty and the collapse of supply to the population can occur.

Most unfavorable is the economic situation in the countries in which people still regard themselves as members of the family rather than as a national citizen, as in black Africa, but also more or less strongly in Muslim countries, especially in Libya and Afghanistan.

As far as economic and social development is concerned, these countries will always remain dependent on European countries. European countries, whether they like it or not, will have to ensure that these countries develop so that the impoverished and unemployed do not make their way to Europe.

In many countries, especially Muslim ones, many qualified engineers are also trained. However, since these people do not work as developers and / or entrepreneurs and do not find employment in the country, an academic proletariat is formed in these countries, who often only envisage their future in emigration.

In contrast to the incapacity of Black African states and the unwillingness of Muslim states to open themselves up completely to Europeanism, the Taoist, Hindu and Buddhist religions of East Asia hardly offer any resistance to the adoption of Western thought and will. The most striking examples are Japan and China, if, in China's case, we look away from the perhaps necessary adherence to an autocratic party dictatorship.

4.3.2 Faster population increase through better medical care as an additional reason for conflicts in developing countries and emigration to Europe

Europeanization also improved the health of the population and the mortality rate decreased dramatically, particularly as a result of lower infant and child mortality rates. Thus, the population could grow more strongly. In industrialized countries, the birth rate decreased. But in non-European countries, it grew all the more.

Since all people, if they have not already been born rich, have to earn their livelihood and seek jobs that are not created in countries lagging behind industrially to the extent that jobs are needed, so unemployment increases. This also leads to migration into industrialized countries. In part, these migratory movements are still fueled by tribal or religious conflicts, which are also triggered or exacerbated by population growth.

In itself, the improvement of the health situation is an advancement, just as only the Europeanism has made the development of the economy, society and man to individuals possible. It must be noted, however, that some countries cannot cope with the consequences of these developments alone without the support of industrialized countries, and also because they are not able to "inhale" the European mentality quickly enough so that they themselves become inventors and investing entrepreneurs. If Europeans fail to provide this support, more and more people will emerge and seek their salvation in industrialized countries.

4.4. The economic development of developing countries and the development policy after the Second World War

Franz Ansperger writes: 'From an economic point of view, colonial-political switches ... were re-established after the First World War. While colonialism for France and Great Britain before 1914 had been an unprofitable business because of the cost of military and administrative bureaucracy in the colonies, despite partial high profits of individual firms and speculators, it began to pay off for the mother countries to invest in colonial infrastructure, especially for France. [100] Large railway constructions were followed by the development of highways, which also opened up remote areas for trucking and helped the local transport entrepreneurship. At the same time, the foundations were laid for a new logistics of colonial domination by being able to transport armed forces faster and more easily to trouble spots. Added to this were the new possibilities of air monitoring and air attacks. The fact that the export production from the coastal regions extended further and further into the interior through new transport routes led to an increasingly profitable upturn in the colonial export economy[101]]' [102]

As already pointed out, the triggers for globalization were the economic interests as well as the missionary intentions of European countries. The missionary intention was originally the spread of Christianity for the benefit of all human beings. This also included of course that the standard of living of all people should be increased. To this extent, the entire colonization was already connected with the goal of the development of the countries. This goal was of course also maintained after the colonies had become independent, especially because of the political as well as economic commitment in these countries. This development was also in the interest of European countries.

The commitment of the West as well as the communist world was accelerated by the East-West opposition. Both sides were interested in attracting as many countries as possible. Developing countries were wooed and this wooing triggered development aid payments and military aid for the former colonies.

An interest in the sales markets and the raw materials remained, of course, whereas the raw materials gained increasing importance over the course of the

---

[100] Boris Barth: *Die Zäsur des Ersten Weltkriegp.Hochzeit und Dekolonisation der Koloni alreiche*, p.115.

[101] Jürgen Osterhammel: *Vom Umgang mit dem „Anderen". Zivilisierungsmissionen – in Europa und darüber hinaup.* In: Boris Barth et al.: Das Zeitalter des Kolonialismus. Stuttgart 2007, p.43.

[102] Sören Utermark: „Schwarzer Untertan versus schwarzer Bruder", p.61f..

contest, and thus the raw material reserves were opened up, which they had been relatively little before the colonial period. This required more investment in developing countries, especially since they had neither the capital nor the know-how to use their resources.

The trade competition in the least creditworthy developing countries then led countries to provide public guarantees (in Germany, the so-called *Hermes Guarantees*) for goods delivered on payment terms and guarantees for investments. But these guarantees also allowed developing countries to borrow and to commit themselves more than they would have been possible without these guarantees. As a result, debt relief and rescheduling agreements were necessary over and over again.

Except in lucrative raw material development, no major investments were made in developing countries. The reasons for this are not only the often nonexistent legal conditions and the lack of security of investments as well as an insufficient infrastructure, but also an insufficiently trained workforce and the necessity to train them.

This changed when larger developing countries made it difficult for those industries to access their markets, which did not even invest in the country. Thus, industrialized countries were compelled, if they wanted to maintain the market, to establish at least minimum production in the developing countries themselves. For the pharmaceutical industry, this was the final stage of the production process, the so-called *finishing*, that is the pressing of pills and the packaging.

But even for these production steps, workers had to be trained and the more this happened, the more interesting it was to use this cheap labor for more qualified activities and thus to produce things in developing countries not only for the market itself, but also for the world market. In developing countries, the so-called *contract manufacturing* was created. In so doing, unless production processes were specific to certain industries, the risk of production was passed on to local companies. As a result, independent companies in developing countries could emerge in certain areas, such as the textile industry.

However, contract manufacturing has the disadvantage that it can be transferred to other countries at any time if even cheaper labor can be used there. Sustainable development therefore requires the creation of self-employed enterprises in the country, which also participate sufficiently in entrepreneurial profits, so that they can invest themselves and not direct almost all profits to foreign investors and capital providers.

In order to achieve this, it is often necessary to request foreign investors to make a joint venture with a local partner for investments. In smaller developing countries, this is more difficult to achieve than in large economies, which represent a non-negligible sales market for foreign companies. Thus, for example, in China, a Chinese entrepreneurship and wealthy capital provider could emerge, providing the basis for rapid industrial development and making China into one of the largest economies in the world.

Less developed, smaller developing countries, on the other hand, are dominated by increasingly powerful global players. To be of interest as an investment location, smaller developing countries must accept that Western countries flood them with their products, including agricultural products from the vast US and

Canadian farms and agricultural products from modern agribusiness in Europe. The result is that one's own industries are all the less able to develop, and even traditional agriculture is endangered.

4.4.1 The increased globalization of trade through the conclusion of the General Agreement on Tariffs and Trade (GATT)

In order to intensify international trade relations, the General Agreement on Tariffs and Trade (GATT) was established in 1947. Wikipedia writes: GATT 'is an international agreement on world trade. Until 1994, tariffs and other trade barriers were gradually reduced in eight rounds of negotiations. GATT has laid the foundation for the establishment of the World Trade Organization (WTO 1995), into which it is still integrated today. At that time, the agreement included 123 equal member countries. In order to distinguish between the original and current WTO agreements, the year 1947 and 1994 are added as a rule.[103][104] '105

Members undertake to continue lowering tariffs and reduce other import barriers and switch to the so-called *Most-Favored-Nation Treatment*, which means that import concessions granted by one country to another country must also be granted to all other countries.

If one considers that the barriers to imports of individual products in their respective height for individual products also have a protective function, that domestic industries are not ousted and so destroyed by foreign products or that they can develop better, it is understandable that tariffs differ in each country and also in relation to different products and it takes a very lengthy process to lower tariffs so that the countries concerned have greater benefits from the cuts than if they kept the barriers.

The strength of industrialized countries in relation to developing countries is that, because of their higher level of development, they can produce more efficiently and in many cases, through their know-how, they can even produce those products more cheaply than can normally be produced more favorably by natural geographic conditions in developing countries, That is why developing countries need more import barriers than developed countries and these are made possible, if not always high enough, by the GATT.

However, with developing countries still lagging well behind developed economies in terms of diversified economic development, further liberalization of general trade relations will become increasingly difficult with lower tariffs and barriers.

A particular problem is agriculture. As a result of the industrialization of agriculture and land reform, productivity is also generally higher in industrialized countries than in developing countries. In particular, the huge wheat plantations of the USA and Canada are superior in productivity to other countries and push their products onto the world market.

---

[103] Allgemeines Zoll- und Handelsabkommen (GATT). BMZ, 7. August 2010, downlopaded 20. 10. 2010.
[104] Welthandelsorganisation und allgemeines Zoll- und Handelsabkommen. BMZ, 29.12.2009downloaded 20. 10. 2010.
[105] https://de.wikipedia.org/wiki/Allgemeines_Zoll-_und_Handelsabkommen.

Nevertheless, the productivity of agriculture in industrialized countries generally lags behind that of the rest of the industry. In order to ensure that agricultural incomes do not fall behind urban incomes and farms are abandoned, agriculture in industrialized countries receives a variety of subsidies. This removes import opportunities from other countries and, if the agricultural economy in industrialized countries produces more than it consumes in its own country and the excess products can otherwise not be exported, the prices of agriculture fall too far so that the United States also support their agriculture through export subsidies.

Due to the more productive production options, plus export subsidies, agricultural products are then offered on world markets at such a low price that they can destroy agriculture in developing countries. Of course no country can afford that, and as a result, the GATT negotiations on further liberalization of world trade often fail because developing countries demand that export subsidies for agricultural products from industrialized countries be discontinued, but industrialized countries are not prepared to do so. Developing countries then have to give in to the pressure of industrialized countries because they are economically dependent or their elite earn money that way, so the agriculture in the affected country comes under the greatest stress.

Harald Schumann writes: 'Because many African countries are dependent on the development funds of industrialized countries, they have given in to the demands of their creditors and lowered their tariffs for years. The consequences have been devastating. European agricultural exporters flooded African markets with cheap chicken wings, subsidized milk powder or canned vegetables, killing domestic producers.

In Ghana, for example, tomatoes are a staple food. The red paradise fruit is used in almost every dish and its production was once offered to many thousands of peasants. But then, at the behest of their donors, the government lowered the canned goods tariff. The farmers were impoverished and their sons were on their way to Europe. There, as described by Matthias Krupa and Caterina Lobenstein in an award-winning reportage for "Die Zeit", thousands of Ghanaians are now working for starvation wages on Italian plantations to do just the same they used to do at home: picking tomatoes '[106]

A particular danger for the global economy, and especially for developing countries, arises from the strengthening of international corporations and so-called global players. For today, it is not primarily other states with which individual economies are involved. The economic power lies more and more with globally operating companies, which have values that can be larger than the national product or the budget of a country.

These companies are less and less able to be controlled by states, but they can even force the states to serve their interests. As the latest economic crisis showed, states felt compelled to support hedge funds and banks when they stumbled, and important companies were saved with state funds and the auto industry was backed by scrapping premiums.

---

[106] Harald Schumann: *Fluchtursache Handelspoltik*, in Der Tagesspiegel Nr. 22925, 31.10.2016, S.6.

Global players enjoy the support of their home countries in which where they are based, because these countries participate in global corporate profits, as long as international corporations and potential investors do not escape the tax sovereignty of their home country by shifting their profits into tax havens. For the other countries are vying for investments by global companies. Internationally operating companies are even trying to deprive states of jurisdiction by demanding international economic agreements that disputes between companies and states should be decided by international arbitration tribunals.

They refer to the legal protection provisions concluded with developing countries. The purpose of these agreements, however, was to make investment in a developing state possible in the first place, provided that there was no adequate legal system and no investment security. Today, however, there are usually sufficient national protection provisions, so that disputes can also be settled before national courts. Incidentally, global players have so much capital power that they are far less vulnerable than the people of the countries concerned, for which the states are responsible.

It is therefore important in international economic agreements and customs and economic unions, to ensure that states' rights to protect a diversified economy are not undermined. Otherwise, globalization can become a curse.

4.4.2 The merger of individual countries into free trade zones and economic unions

In order to avoid the disadvantages of a general reduction in tariffs and barriers to imports, and yet to exploit the division of labor over a larger economic area, countries comparable to other countries in their economic power combine to form economic unions.

On the one hand, the founding of regional free trade zones and economic unions is a step towards further globalization as they reduce trade barriers and possibly investment barriers for the treaty area. On the other hand, they are also a safeguard against too comprehensive globality, because the countries participating in the Union can set up protective tariffs and barriers against third parties. Because it must not be forgotten that the established industrialized countries have a natural advantage over developing countries in the form of know-how, capital, global trade organization, logistics companies, etc., whereby a small country, which exposes itself defenseless to these powers, could become their plaything.

Undoubtedly, the unification of European countries into the *European Economic Union* set an example for the aspirations of other countries, even though European countries are developed economies. To be sure, individual countries in the European Union complement one another to some extent. The southern countries can prefer to sell their agricultural products in the European Community, while industrialized countries have a competitive advantage for their products. Nevertheless, economic power is diversified and therefore the European Union can only flourish if the less developed countries are supported by the industrialized countries and their economies are promoted.

European countries have gone one step further and created a common currency with the euro. However, a monetary union can only work if there is a single economic and financial policy that also gives the nation states the framework for their economic and financial policy.

Since the framework conditions were inadequate and there was no uniform policy, wages and salaries in individual countries could develop differently. As a result, many European countries also lost their competitiveness against Germany and therefore had negative foreign trade balances.

Following the example of the European Union, free trade zones and approaches to economic unions also developed in other regions. But even there, those responsible had to make sure that, as far as possible, countries at the same level of development unite and no economy dominates the others.

Since there are different strengths among individual partners even in less developed countries, better division of labor, which is made possible by merging, can bring benefits to all partners. It should be noted, however, that in free trade zones and economic unions, which do not yet have a common economic policy and, if possible, a common currency, it may also be dangerous for individual countries to give up production capabilities in favor of other countries.

It is true that all countries benefit from exchanging the goods that everyone can produce more cheaply. But the purchasing power parities between two countries can change for a variety of reasons. The exchange rate of one country may fall or rise for whatever reason, and so do the relations in purchasing power parities. For example, problems with the merging of Brazil and Argentina into the Mercosur Economic Union may be cited:

Helio Jaguaribe writes: "Integration processes inevitably bring 'each member state to give up its own non-competitive sectors in favor of the more competitive ones of the other country. The Brazilian wheat and the Argentine sugar are typical examples of such a situation. Indeed integration processes are created with the express purpose of giving space to the more competitive sectors of the other participants in their own market, which in turn benefits all parties, provided that global exchange has reached a satisfactory balance. South Brazilian wheat is advantageously substituted by Argentine sugar with the consequence that the Brazilian producers have to move to other products such as e.g. soy. Sugar from Tucumán, in turn, is advantageously replaced by Brazilian produce, so that the Argentine producers should consider producing other products, e.g. citrus fruits.'[107]

If the exchange rates between Brazil and Argentina change, other competitive conditions may arise, and this is particularly problematic in the cultivation of agricultural products, which also require special marketing.

Even more difficult is to merge into an economic union, if the different production conditions are based on a different use of know-how and a different capital power. Then trade does not necessarily have to be beneficial to the country which has less know-how or less capital. Rather, then there is the danger that the weaker country will be flooded by products of companies from the stronger country.

---

[107] Helio Jaguaribe: *Mercosur: faktische und institutionelle Probleme*, p.29ff.
  http://www.kas.de/wf/doc/kas_297-544-1-30.pdf?020319150939.

In such a situation, it may be better for the weaker economy to shield itself and only open its market, if at the same time it brings with it the opportunity of developing know-how, skilled labor and capital in one's own country. For this, as is the case in Europe, it will usually be necessary for the stronger partners to contribute to the economic development of the backward ones through financial means.

In the light of the above, free trade zones between industrialized countries and developing countries must be strongly discouraged. An impressive example of this is the North American Free Trade Agreement NAFTA of the United States, Canada and Mexico, which came into force on January 1, 1994. 'Already on the occasion of the ten-year review of the agreement, the World Bank had admitted in a study that in Mexico too, the "development since the NAFTA launch was not exactly remarkable". Although exports had increased, the wage level was even below the level of 1994 and the number of Mexicans living below the poverty line is steadily rising.'[108]

On the results of this agreement after 20 years, that is, until the end of 2013, Wikipedia writes: 'The economic and social consequences of the agreement are judged rather negatively than the main beneficiaries: Mexico, formerly self-sufficient in their main food, maize, the market was flooded with heavily subsidized American agricultural products and meat, whose price was 20 percent below production costs. The expected specialization of Mexican agriculture did not materialize: Millions of corn farmers had to give up, according to the USA Trade Union Umbrella, but many rural and unemployed people could not be absorbed into the newly created supply industries. Crime increased. Today, Mexico has to import 60 percent of its wheat and 70 percent of its rice needs. Canada has once again become an exporter of raw materials and is increasingly struggling with environmental problems, while the international oil industry is putting pressure on environmental regulations. Overall, incomes stagnated in member countries, while income inequality increased. [109],110

As a result of relocating operations to Mexico, the USA also lost jobs itself. The TAZ writes: 'In the run-up to the founding of NAFTA, the promises about new jobs that would have come about automatically through free trade were as full-bodied as they were unsubstantiated - .... In fact, two years ago the Washington-based think-tank Economic Policy Institute estimated the number of jobs lost by NAFTA in the USA to be around 700,000.'[111]

Since the lost jobs in Mexican agriculture were greater than the newly created industrial jobs, there was pressure to reduce jobs and wages fell. As an economic result of the NAFTA, one can therefore speak only of an income shift from workers to capital owners achieved through rationalization. 'In the meantime, even the so-called maquiladoras, where Mexicans produce goods for the American market

[108] BERLIN taz 1. 1. 2014: *Weniger Jobs, weniger Kleinbauern. 20 Jahre Nafta,* http://www.taz.de/!5051711/

[109] Barbara Eisenmann: *Das Netz des Geldep.* In: Der Tagesspiegel, 6. Dezember 2014, online:

[110] Wikipedia: *Das Nordamerikanische Freihandelsabkommen,* https://de.wikiped ia.org/wiki/Nordamerikanisches_Freihandelsabkommen#Folgen

[111] BERLIN taz 1. 1. 2014: *Weniger Jobs, weniger Kleinbauern. 20 Jahre Nafta.*

at starvation wages, are no longer employment creators, because even cheaper factories in China and other East Asian countries have long outstripped them.' [112]

With the TAZ, one can only say: 'So, has anyone gained anything through NAFTA? The answer is yes, investors and corporations. The aim of the agreement in addition to the reduction of tariffs and other trade barriers is also the protection of foreign investors against expropriations and other arbitrariness of the respective host country. The Ethyl Corporation first showed what that leads to: The American company had sued the Canadian government in 1997 before a NAFTA court of arbitration for damages because the Canadian import ban on gasoline with the toxic additive MMT is equivalent to an expropriation. Canada then lifted the ban and paid a million in compensation.' [113]

'Stephen Gill of York University in Toronto, one of the "Fifty Key Thinkers of International Relations," speaks of privatizing commercial law and of the "legalization of neoliberal dogmas". In 2014, according to a study conducted by the NGO *Public Citizen's Trade Watch*, NAFTA proceedings against governments (especially the Canadian government), amounting to $12.4 billion, were pending before the arbitral tribunals. [114] According to the study, states were sentenced to pay damages totaling $360 million. [115],116

4.4.3 Growth spurt for developing countries due to rising raw material requirements

Over the course of the Cold War and the associated arms race as well past wars, such as the Korean War and the Vietnam War, general economic development in industrialized countries increased the demand for raw materials and developing countries benefited as far as they could supply raw materials. When the East-West conflict came to an end and states began to consolidate their budgets, the raw material demand collapsed. As a result, raw material-producing developing countries were not only able to export less, but commodity prices also collapsed, leaving developing countries with much less revenue.

It would have made sense if raw material exporting countries had used their profits from exports to diversify their economies in order to become less dependent on raw material exports. In that case, they would have suffered less from the decline in exports and commodity prices, or even from their own growth, they would have contributed to a higher demand for raw materials.

Due to the rapid economic development in emerging countries with their additional demand for raw materials, in particular China, the export opportunities of raw material exporting countries and the prices of the raw materials rose again substantially and gave these countries increasing revenue. In particular, China's high demand yet lack of raw materials in relation to its industrial development has

---

[112] loc. cit.

[113] loc. cit.

[114] NAFTA's 20-Year Legacy and the Fate of the Trans-Pacific Partnership, Public Citizen, Februar 2014.

[115] NAFTA's 20-Year Legacy loc. cit.

[116] Wikipedia: *Das Nordamerikanische Freihandelsabkommen*, https://de.wikipedia.org/wiki/Nordamerikanis-ches_Freihandelsabkommen#Folgen.

led to a shortage of raw materials worldwide, thus providing developing countries with resource reserves with stronger economic growth and additional revenues.

Again, too little was done in most African countries, but also in Russia, to develop their own industry. It is significant that in the recent embargo due to the conflict in Ukraine, the Russian government even sees some advantage in providing an incentive to better develop domestic production capacity.

In addition, China in particular has invested in the development of raw materials in Black Africa and other regions and has also improved the infrastructure there. However, China's investments in African countries have barely given these countries the opportunity to train and employ their own professionals, as the skilled workers were often brought from China. The less developed countries are also flooded with products from China, and this is felt more and more painfully. Despite their independence, many developing countries are largely dominated not only by the old industrialized countries, but now also by China.

In this case too, the fatal situation arises that the elites of the developing countries in sub-Saharan Africa do not develop their own economic entrepreneurial initiative, but allow themselves to be financed and corrupted by the new investors from China.

The hunger for energy in the world has made oil-exporting countries rich. In addition, most of the oil-exporting countries had joined forces to form the OPEC cartel and pushed up energy prices extremely quickly.

The dependence of the industrialized countries on oil-exporting countries enabled them to reduce the oil volume in order to achieve political goals and thus trigger the first oil crisis. Wikipedia writes: 'The first and most consequential oil crisis was triggered in autumn 1973 on the occasion of the Yom Kippur War (October 6- 26, 1973). The Organization of Petroleum Exporting Countries (OPEC) deliberately reduced oil production by about five percent in order to pressure western countries not to support Israel. On October 17, 1973, the price of oil rose from about three US dollars per barrel (159 liters) to over five dollars. This corresponds to an increase of about 70 percent. Over the next year, the price of oil rose to over twelve US dollars worldwide.' [117]

The second oil crisis was triggered in 1979/80, 'mainly caused by production failures and uncertainty after the Islamic Revolution in Iran and the subsequent Iraqi attack on Iran (First Gulf War). The price increase at that time found its maximum at about $38 per barrel (159 liters). At the end of the 1980s, the oil price fell back below $20 a barrel.'[118]

In respect of what the first oil crisis meant for Germany, Wikipedia writes: 'In 1974, the Federal Republic had to pay about 17 billion DM more for its oil imports than the year before. This aggravated the economic crisis and led to a significant increase in short-time work, unemployment, social expenditure and bankruptcy of companies.'[119]

It is understood that the higher energy prices make all products using energy more expensive according to their energy consumption. In the longer term, such

---

[117] Wikipedia: Ölpreiskrise, https://de.wikipedia.org/wiki/%C3%96lpreiskrise.
[118] Ibid.
[119] Ibid.

price increases may be passed on to customers. But in the short term, companies can break into it.

Of course, such an increase in the price of raw materials and price increases for other products that result from them lead to a significant redistribution of world economic income. In industrialized countries, it is particularly affecting consumer spending, which means what is lacking in the household of consumers must be spent instead on heating, gasoline and the price increase of the other products, unless they save less, but this is only possible to a limited extent.

In oil-exporting countries, on the other hand, this purchasing power, which is lost in industrialized countries, is an additional income. Since these countries are initially not used to spending these revenues, these funds are initially saved on a larger scale and so far are lacking in world economic demand. Accordingly, fewer products can be sold. This requires a restriction of production and unemployment. In other words, the already existing secular stagnation turns into depression.

To the extent that the oil-exporting countries used their wealth again as purchasing power, that is to say, consumed and invested, the global demand for the world rose again and the depressive tendencies subsided. Of course, spending by oil-exporting countries became an integral part of world economic demand.

The oil market shows that in a globalized world, individual countries can gain such power that they can almost paralyze the global economy. As a result of the oil crisis, industrialized countries were anxious to be as independent as possible from oil and gas supplies. For this reason, additional nuclear power plants were initially built and the development of renewable energies was driven forward under the influence of the expected climate catastrophe.

The US went one step further by increasing its oil and gas production through so-called fracking to the extent that it relies less and less on world market supplies and even aspires to become an energy exporter in 2020 itself.

In addition, the slowdown in growth rates in China will also result in lower energy demand growth and, in addition, after the nuclear deal, Iran will push for market with its huge oil reserves. However, it is conceivable that oil-exporting countries will reduce their export volume and thus stabilize prices. But no country wants to lose revenue from energy exports. Saudi Arabia also fears that the USA will no longer be its protector to the same extent or pursue Saudi Arabia's interests because of their lower dependence on oil imports from them. Saudi Arabia believes that maintaining its existing production flows and the resulting continuation of low energy prices will also be a means of making US fracking uneconomic and thus increasing American dependence on Saudi Arabia. It appears that, in the foreseeable future, a further reduction in oil and gas prices is more likely.

Of course, low energy prices have a significant impact on oil-exporting countries, because raw material exports and income derived from them make up the largest part of exports and budget revenues in many countries. According to *VOV*: 'Forecasts by the International Monetary Fund, IMF, say that Russia is hit hardest by oil, which accounts for up to 80 percent of Russia's total export value and contributes about 50 percent of its gross domestic product. Since the oil price crisis, the Russian government budget has suffered a loss of more than 100 billion US dollars. The depreciation of the Russian currency has accelerated dramatically. ...

Iran, Venezuela and Nigeria are also hit hard by the fall in oil prices. They can only balance your household if the price of oil is at least $120 per barrel.[120]

While the purchasing power from industrialized countries was transferred to the oil-exporting countries as a result of the oil price increases at that time, this of course, with the reduction in energy prices, flows back into industrialized countries and favors consumer spending. However, the resulting increase in revenue in developed countries only partially benefits the lower strata of the population, who spend most of their income on consumer spending. The biggest part is likely to go to entrepreneurs and lenders, who do not know what to do with excess savings anyway, so on balance, secular stagnation can be expected to intensify.

It is clear from the above that the possession of raw material resources can be a significant source of wealth for an economy. However, long-term resource abundance leads to blessing only if

1. it benefits all citizens of the national economy and does not just get stuck with more of the less corrupt elites and
2. it does not mislead the economy into not refining itself spiritually and industrially.

Otherwise, resource wealth can become a curse. The elites, when earning on their own, are often not even committed to eliminating the environmental damage caused by resource exploitation and if the population participates in commodity revenues, a price erosion can impact the whole economy significantly. Overcoming the energy shortage caused by the development of renewable energies and also fracking once again shows that research and development and the resulting know-how are more important in the longer term than raw material reserves.

4.4.4. The emergence of Emerging Markets and their impact on the economic development of industrialized countries

As already stated, the size of a potential sales market is one of the most important investment motives for industrialized countries. The major economies outside the Western world are China, Russia, Brazil, India and South Africa. These countries, however, are also those who, like China, India and Russia and, to some extent, Brazil, have a very long tradition of their own or have many European immigrants, such as South Africa and Brazil, who decisively influence economic and social development.

Because of their size and developed society, they have also prevented Western investors from dominating their own economies too strongly or by flooding the market with their products. Thus, these so-called BRIC countries had an extraordinarily dynamic development, especially China, which at the same time revived the global economy as a whole. Indeed, one could say that they prevented the global economy from falling into depression.

Due to the enormous growth in emerging markets, in China it rose in 2007 by more than 14% and 10.6% in 2010, a tremendous pull for highly industrialized goods emerged giving industries in the industrialized countries additional sales opportunities. Without this demand, the economies of industrialized countries

---

[120]http://vovworld.vn/de-DE/Politische-Aktualit%C3%A4t/Einfl%C3%BCsse-der-%C3%96lpreissenkung-auf-die-Weltwirtschaft/295081.vov

would probably be in a depression. Today's fears of a slump in growth in the industrialized countries are correspondingly high, because growth rates in China are falling.

Of course, it must also be taken into account that as a result of lower wages in developing countries, many productions have been transferred there from industrialized countries and thus developing countries now supply textiles, shoes, mass electronic devices, etc. in return for the machines and equipment they are purchasing in industrialized countries. But the supply of bulk consumer goods to industrialized countries is reaching saturation limits. China is therefore forced to sell its products more in the domestic market. Of course, the Chinese economy will continue to grow, but not to the same extent as before and the question arises for industrialized countries, where to deliver their products. On balance, this increases the risk that secular stagnation will turn into depression.

4.4.5 The globalization of the capital market

When investing in industrial plants, capital usually comes from industrialized countries. It is true that there are considerable differences in wealth in the developing countries and wealthy people too. However, their assets remain marginal relative to the profits generated in industrialized countries. Also, the elite in developing countries often lack the Western entrepreneur mentality, so if they invest their money at all, they invest in Western companies. The capital can then flow back into their country when the Western company sets up production sites in the country of the capital providers. But the country of the capital providers remains dependent on corporate decisions in industrialized countries.

The dependence on industrialized countries also exists for the borrowing of developing countries from industrialized countries. Investors from industrialized countries are also trying to acquire attractive real estate in developing countries. They are then in competition with domestic investors. Domestic wealthy people prefer to invest in real estate. Thus, real estate prices can rise more strongly due to the influence of speculative capital and that can lead to speculative bubbles.

If a country is heavily indebted to other countries or if the economic conditions in the developing country or in the industrialized country deteriorate, funds from developing countries can be quickly withdrawn. When economic conditions deteriorate in developing countries, the reasons are worse returns and as the economy deteriorates in developed countries, companies may need capital to finance losses and therefore deduct money from developing countries.

An example of a crisis triggered by the capital market is the Asian crisis in the late 1990s. Wikipedia writes: 'As a result of the liberalization of the financial sectors of Asian countries, a credit boom arose in Asia in the 1990s. Credit growth in this period was on average 8 to 10 percent higher than GDP growth. It was not just industrial overcapacities like in South Korea, but more and more of the credit was used to buy stocks and real estate. The consequences were a rise in the stock markets and a strong increase in real estate prices up to four times. With rising real estate and stock prices, Asian banks believed they had good securities, which would allow further lending. This capital, in turn, flowed into equities and real estate. The out of it resulting price increases created a speculative bubble in some areas. This "vicious circle" of lending and increased collateral value has resulted in a highly one-sided alignment of lending. By the end of 1997, the share of mortgage backed loans in Thailand, Indonesia and Malaysia was between 25 and 40 percent.[121] This made banks vulnerable to price declines of equity and real estate.'122

' The main problem of this fiscal policy was that the short-term foreign currency loans that Asian banks had raised were relatively high in relation to the foreign reserve holdings. [123] With the onset of the crisis and maturity of previously borrowed loans, the crisis countries were unable to repay them on time with foreign currency. ...

Japan's relatively low interest rates at that time are considered a factor that led Asian banks to raise foreign currency loans in yen. Many investors wanted to be in the promising market of Southeast Asia and financed their commitments with a low equity ratio. In the West, too, it was believed that if there were problems, Asian governments would have the resources to deal with potential solvency problems. However, when the creditor banks ceased to "hold still" as Asian currencies and assets began to decline and their claims matured, there was a massive withdrawal of capital from these countries. This in turn led to a downgrade of the credit-worthiness of these Asian countries, which led to the further sale of assets held there by security-oriented institutional investors. This self-reinforcing capital flight from the crisis countries is considered a failure of coordination. For a single creditor, it was rational to collect claims as quickly as possible and thus limit losses. The fact that many creditors acted at the same time (herd behavior) contributed to the depreciation of their investments'124

Capital flows from other countries can also be triggered by a central bank deciding to limit the money supply or raising interest rates and this capital outflow can cause significant economic turbulence in the country concerned. Thus, it is also important how far the American interest rate level should be raised again, and whether this causes monetary flows from developing countries.

Substantial negative influences can also arise from a change in the exchange rates among currencies and these can have a variety of causes. During the euro crisis, there had been a significant run on the Swiss franc. Switzerland was forced to abandon the fixed exchange rate relative to the euro, which caused the value of the Swiss franc to rise sharply. This had significant consequences for countries that had borrowed Swiss francs. For example, what is reported about the consequences in Poland and other Eastern European countries:

' The end of the Swiss franc exchange rate triggered panic in Poland. The soaring price of the franc is expensive for around 700,000 households there, who have

---

121 For banks, the proportion of loans secured by real estate is usually 15% to 20% compared to total lending. In India, for example, real estate-backed loan bookings averaged between 8% and 17% on March 31, 2006. See: Weber, W.L., Devaney,M: Bank Efficiency, Risk-Based Capital, and Real Estate Exposure: The Credit Crunch Revisited. Real Estate Economics, Vol. March 27, 1999 und RBI to cap banks' home loan exposure.
122 Wikipadia: Asienkrise, https://de.wikipedia.org/wiki/Asienkrise
123 Vgl. McKinnon, Ronald; Pill, H (1996): *Credible Liberalizations and International Capital Flows: The "Overborrowing Syndrome*, in: Takatoshi Ito, Anne O. Krueger (Hrsg.): Financial Deregulation and Integration in East Asia, Chicago, London, P.7–42., 1996.
124Wikipadia: Asienkrise, https://de.wikipedia.org/wiki/Asienkrise.

to pay off real estate loans, which were concluded in Swiss francs. The Polish national currency Zloty lost almost 20 percent in value compared to the strong rise in the Swiss franc. The leading index on the Warsaw Stock Exchange lost about two percent at noon.

In total, around 40 percent of real estate loans in Poland were made in Swiss francs. According to the Polish Financial Supervisory Authority they amount to around 31 billion euros.

The trend had come at the beginning of the millennium in Poland, Croatia and Hungary. In Croatia around 60,000 borrowers are affected who have to pay off loans taken out in Swiss francs, as their advocacy organization Franak announced.'[125]

Rising public debt, once it reaches a level no longer tolerated by the capital markets, can also trigger currency turmoil, which can affect global trade. An example of this was the euro crisis, which can flare up again.

4.4.6 The globalization of secular stagnation

It has already been stated that the economies of the western industrialized countries are in a state of secular stagnation because the sum of their savings is higher than the lucrative investment opportunities. An eloquent sign of this is the one-time low level of interest rates and that the central banks cannot stimulate enough investment by further artificial interest rate cuts.

Developing countries have been stagnating for millennia, because the economic elite have, at best, accumulated treasures, but have not invested their money in production facilities. The tremendous growth, especially in emerging markets, has created new investment opportunities for investors both in developing countries themselves and as well as in industries supplying developing countries. Now it is clear that the high growth rates in China and certainly also in other countries cannot be sustained and sink more and more to the level of the old industrialized countries. For investors from industrialized countries, but also for investors from China and other developing countries, even this valve for additional investment falls away.

As there are also considerable differences in wealth and income in developing countries, there is also a discrepancy between savings and investment opportunities in these countries with the result that secular stagnation is also likely to be exacerbated by developing countries.

4.4.7 Tendency for decreasing employment by rationalization, especially as a result of increasing digitization and robotization

The more skilled jobs are more likely to be situated in industrialized countries and the less skilled ones in developing countries. Due to the expected rationalization, the latter will lose their jobs more and more, and try to make a living in Europe.

The previous rationalization of production was essentially about mass production. If mass production is based on assembly line production, which requires a large number of skilled workers, it is worth outsourcing production to low-wage

---

[125]http://www.t-online.de/wirtschaft/boerse/devisen/id_72511678/nach-aufwertung-des-schweizer-franken- die-folgen-fuer-verbraucher.html.

countries. Since the workforce can be replaced by machines, computers and robots and only a handful of highly skilled workers are needed, it may be interesting to relocate manufacturing to developed countries.

Many technically manufactured products consist of parts, which in turn are themselves subject to rationing possibilities in their production. The more these parts are standardized and the processors are encouraged to use these standard products, they can be made in even greater numbers - think of screws, computer chips, elements robotics, controls and much more -. So, it made sense to buy parts from a few factories located anywhere in the world. This resulted in a networking of industrial production worldwide and correspondingly large international transport movements. It goes without saying that these parts are also produced where the necessary specialists are the cheapest.

The more partial production is distributed at mass production facilities, the greater the international goods movements. On the other hand, fewer and fewer mass production companies are left and most countries lose their production capabilities.

Neoliberals, of course, object to such dangers, arguing that through innovation and investment in expansion, released workers will come back into paid employment. In times of secular stagnation, however, that does not happen at all, because the demand from wealthy consumers who are also willing to buy products lags behind the production possibilities and savers lack sufficient investment opportunities.

The latest possibilities of digital production, the so-called *fractal* factories, make it possible to reunite separate production processes, because the different parts are programmed in production steps and can be called up when needed. As a result, transport costs and the associated logistical processes are eliminated, which means that means of transport, as well as the workforce involved, can be released.

If one's own market is large enough, the markets can be closed down and the international know-how carriers can be forced to manufacture the quantities used in each country in the country itself. It has already been shown what enormous rationalization possibilities the increasing digitization and robotization of the economy entail. The resulting exemption from labor also affects developing countries in particular. The expected increase in unemployment may be better spread across the world by foreclosure of the markets. On balance, however, it will increase and with it, the impoverishment of the vast majority of the workforce. Accordingly, the demand previously made by them will decrease. If politicians do not solve the problem of vastly unequal distribution of wealth and thus income distribution, secular stagnation will continue to increase.

4.5 Globalization and the environment
The industrial revolution intervened ever deeper into the natural conditions. As long as the technical and economic development concerned Europe alone, then the negative impact on the environment was manageable. With globalization, however, environmental pollution is becoming a problem, primarily for air, water and climate and then for plants, animals and humans as is repeatedly and more urgently described.

This development is favored, albeit unintentionally, by development aid. Instead of supporting smallholder farms and conserving the environment in developing countries, it rather encourages large-scale farming companies to export their products such as soya, palm oil and other commodities to industrialized countries.

Agricultural and pharmaceutical companies from industrialized countries export genetically modified seeds, fertilizers and pesticides and destroy the environment. The profit goes mainly to foreign suppliers and recipients of the products. Since the interests of the largely corrupt elite of developing countries meet foreign capital interests, it cannot be prevented that large-scale jungle is cleared and small farmers are displaced and become unemployed.

As Philipp Lichterbeck from Rio de Janeiro writes: 'After three years of stagnation, the Brazilian economy has risen again: one percent growth in the first quarter of 2017. A closer look revealed that the growth was due solely to a soybean bumper harvest. 20% more beans than what farmers reaped in 2016/17. The harvest now amounts to 114 million tons. Soy makes up more than half of the cereals harvested in Brazil, followed by feed maize with 94 million tons.

The figures outline a looming environmental catastrophe. Because the bumper harvest is primarily due to an expansion of soybean acreage. They grew by seven percent within a year - soy in Brazil flourishes in an area that is almost as large as Germany. ... More than half of soya goes directly to export to China, Europe and the USA. There, the beans are fed to fattening animals, especially pigs and poultry.

The ecological consequences are devastating. In Brazil, soy monocultures today cover soils that once had rainforests or the tropical forest of Cerrado. Little known outside of Brazil, the Cerrado is the second largest ecosystem of South America.

Just as destructive is the production method. 100 percent of Brazilian soy is genetically engineered to withstand all-round pesticides that kill every other plant and every pest. The best known of these pesticides is glyphosate. It is suspected to trigger serious illnesses. It could also be responsible for the worldwide bee mortality. Without all-round pesticides and gene modification, however, massive soy cultivation would no longer be possible.'[126]

The negative effects of major agribusinesses, especially factory farming, are also affecting the environment in industrialized countries. Nevertheless, not even the government of the Federal Republic of Germany can make up its mind to fight the nitrate pollution of the soil, which has already been demanded by the European Union.

Now, technical and economic progress does not automatically cause natural destruction. This is because technical progress can also develop the means and ways to avoid or remedy natural damage. To do so, however, people must commit to observing the rules, not only by setting aside selfish motives, but also by the willingness of the more developed countries to help the less developed. Global environmental protection requires worldwide solidarity.

---

[126] Philipp Lichterbeck: *Der Fluch des Sojas*, in: Der Tagesspiegel, Nr. 23 161/ 2.7.2017, p.32.

II. Eastern Europeanism and its globalization

Russia, but also other Eastern European countries, especially Poland, are the bearers of Eastern Europeanism. Post-Byzantine East Europeanism began with the founding of Kievan Rus, when in 882, the capital of the Old Russian state of Novgorod, which had been founded a few years before, was transferred to Kiev and in 988, Greek Orthodox Christianization began[127].

' The Duchy of Poland, whose name derives from the West Slavic Polan tribe, was founded in the early 10th century originating in Poznań and Gniezno. It was ruled from 960 to 992 by Duke Mieszko I of the Piast dynasty, who gradually subjugated the other West Slavic tribes between Oder and Bug.

In 966, Mieszko I was baptized in a Roman Catholic rite. Through conquests under Mieszko I and his son Bolesław the Brave, the territory reached borders that came very close to the present state borders'.[128]

'Today's Ukraine has its origin, just like Russia and Belarus, in the first East Slavic state, Kievan Rus. From the 8th century, Vikings sailed the Eastern European rivers and mingled with the Slavic majority population. These warrior merchants, also called Varangians or Rus, contribute significantly to the founding of Kievan Rus with centers in Kiev and Novgorod.'[129]

'Areas of modern-day Ukraine came ... to the Polish territory from the 16th century. In the east, the Principality of Vladimir-Suzdal became the Grand Duchy of Moscow, gradually consolidating all the neighboring Russian principalities and eventually subjugating the Tatar Khanate Kazan. Ukraine came about by its extension to the Russian-Polish rivalry area and borderland.'[130]

Russians, Ukrainians and Poles are Slavs and thus have the same tradition and ideals. However, the Russians are Orthodox and the Poles are Catholic Christians and thus represent different Christian faiths.

According to the influence of Russia and Poland, Ukraine 'is a confessionally mixed country. Approximately 75% of Ukrainians belong to Orthodox churches. The highest number of believers belong to the internationally recognized Ukrainian Orthodox Church Moscow Patriarchate, [...] an autonomous part of the Russian Orthodox Church. There is also the internationally unrecognized, Ukrainian Orthodox Church of the Kiev Patriarchate, established after 1991 ... The Orthodox rite is also followed by the Ukrainian Greek Catholic Church founded in 1596, which, however, recognizes the supremacy of the Pope and is unified with Rome. It has about 5.5 million believers, mainly in the west of the country.

In addition, there are about 2 million Muslims in Ukraine (4%, of which 1.7% Tatars), 1.1 million Roman Catholic Christians (2.4%, especially Poles and Germans) and 1.2 million Protestant Christians (2.7%) and about 300,000 Jews[131].'[132]

---

[127] https://de.wikipedia.org/wiki/Ukraine#Geschichte.
[128] https://de.wikipedia.org/wiki/Polen#Fr.C3.BChgeschichte_und_Gr.C3.BCndung.
[129] https://de.wikipedia.org/wiki/Ukraine#Geschichte.
[130] loc.cit.
[131] http://www.worldjewishcongress.org/en/about/communities/UA.
[132] https://de.wikipedia.org/wiki/Ukraine#Religion.

Since the beginning of their state formation, the antagonism of their same ethnic origin and their different denominations has determined the relationship between Russians and Poles and remarkably ignites this antagonism with Ukraine to this day. To understand the political development and the current political situation, it makes sense to analyze both the self-understanding of the Russians and that of the Poles.

1. Russia

1.1 Russia's perceived mission

Russia's perceived mission can be made clear with quotations from Wilhelm Goerdt in his book *Russian Philosophy*: According to Louis J. Shein, the leitmotif of Russian philosophy is 'the question of the "nature of man", the "nature of freedom", "man's moral responsibility to society" and finally the "transcendence and immanence of God and the organic unity of the cosmos."' [133] The Trinitarian formula of Russian aspiration was: *orthodoxy, autocracy, ethnic values*. [134]

According to a thesis by M. Leo Russian, philosophy is accomplished in a complex process of convergence, as a syndrome of object-consciousness, self-consciousness and national consciousness. 'Objectivity creates self-consciousness. If you understand a thing, "can", you can work with it? Knowledge of the object and the task of philosophy implies the possibility of the consciousness of one's own competence in the matter, namely the ability to philosophize, to not only reproduce philosophy, but to produce it. ...

A special component of the connection of the consciousness of the general task of philosophy and the ability of the individual to it is formed by patriotism, the consciousness of national identity, in such a way that individuals, as Russians, as the offspring of the Russian country, of the fatherland, as it were to face the universal task of philosophy on its behalf. The "patriotic leadership" of Russian culture has been powerfully felt since Peter the Great [135]'. [136]

Radishchev starts 'from a conception of man "in himself", whose natural system must be formed by enlightenment, so that man can truly become himself – man.

The sequence of his chain of thought works via a conception of true philosophy that conveys the knowledge of "true duties," to the conception of the "true man," who acts on the basis of his good nature, pointed to the right way by the Spirit, that is, he acts virtuously ... "In eternal service to the human race, but especially to one's own compatriots" [137] ... Patriotism is the ultimate consequence, which can be derived from the general concept of humanity under concrete spatio-temporal circumstances. Radischtschew also sees himself as a patriot. He can act as

---

[133] Wilhelm Goerdt: *Russische Philosophie*, p.43.
[134] Wilhelm Goerdt: p.57.
[135] M. Leo: *Patriotische Färbung und Wirklichkeit in der rusp.Lit.im ersten Drittel des XVIII. Jahrhundertp.*
[136] Goerdt: p.180.
[137] A.N. Radischtschew: Ausgew. Werke ..., Berlin 1959, p.119: „Wer ist ein Sohn des Vaterlandes?";

the "Son of the Fatherland" only for reasons, and not in the "darkness of passions," [138] for reasons which must have been made intelligible by thought and by philosophy. This means that in Russia, Russians must philosophize creatively for their compatriots and the whole human race .... The general, philosophy is to be realized by individuals, by individuals in a historical peculiarity - on the other hand, the realization of philosophy in Russia is to do with the human race, the ecumenism, (...) meaningfulness for all people.'[139]

'Skoworoda's indisputable critique of them and their consequences, despite his insight into the positivity of the sciences, is based on his conviction that those like the historian, chemist, physicist, logician, grammarian, geometer, soldier, tenant, watchmaker, etc. and so on - "whose object is this material world", can bring neither happiness nor peace of mind to men. This was the task of the "enlightened Christian teachers," the "spiritual fathers" and apostles, to whom Christ's word "My peace I leave you" (John 14:27) has been awarded. Skoworoda's - L. Tolstoy's anticipatory sentence sounds like a call of contemplation to Lomonosov and all science optimists: "Your truth is on the earth, but the truth of the apostles is in us, as it is written, 'The kingdom of God is in you' (Luke 17:21). "[140].'[141]

'While Lomonosov uses the "sacred-fatherly" writings to justify the legitimacy of modern science, Skoworoda uses them to justify his criticism of science and as evidence of his conception of true science, as the "science of Christ," "Christian philosophy," self-knowledge and knowledge of God, which leads practically to self-becoming and God-becoming – deification.

Lomonosov, too, had spoken of "deification", where man participates in the knowledge and reconstruction of nature as its second lord and creator, while Skoworoda means the union of God with man and in him, the vision of God through ascetic-mystical "Theoria" and practice is reached. '[142]

Accordingly, Vladimir Solovyeff writes: "'The aim of labor, in relation to material nature, is not its use for the acquisition of property and money, but the perfection of this nature itself - the animation of what is dead in it, the spiritualization of it, what is material in it "- that is "right to our help "(...), [143] our "service" to it.[144]'[145]

1.2 Russia's ambivalent relationship with the West and the consequences for the development of Russia

In 1915, Rudolf Steiner described how the mission perceived as a task by the Russians is mixed up with imperial motives, and this is also recognized by Vladimir Solovyeff:

---

[138] Ibid., p.114.

[139] Wilhelm Goerdt: *Russische Philosophie*, P.182f.

[140] Grigorij Skoworoda: *Socinenija v dvuch tomach* (Werke in zwei Bänden), Moskau 1973 T. 1, p.354f. ...

[141] Goerdt: p.208.

[142] Goerdt: p.208f.

[143] Wl. Solowjew: *Deutsche Gesamtausgabe der Werke*, Bd. V, Freiburg i.Br. 1957, p.498;

[144] Ibid. p.498;.

[145] Goerdt: p.500.

In the idea of the special mission of the Russian people 'lives the belief that Western European intellectual life had entered the state of old age and decline and that the Russian national spirit is called upon to put into effect a complete renewal and rejuvenation of this spiritual life. This idea of rejuvenation grows into the opinion that all historical development of the future coincides with the mission of the Russian people.

As early as the first half of the nineteenth century, Khomiakov developed this idea into a comprehensive teaching building. ... It is supported by the belief that Western European spiritual development was basically never designed to find the way to right humanity, and that the Russian people must first find this way.

Khomiakov sees in his way this Western European mental development. Into this, according to this mode of intuition, the Roman essence first flows. This has never been able to reveal inner humanity in the deeds of the world. On the contrary, it imposed on the human inwardly the forms of outward man's decrees and it conceived intellectually and materialistically what was to be grasped in the inner weaving of the soul. According to Khomiakov, this externality in grasping life continued in the Christianity of Western European people. Their Christianity lives in the head, not in the core of the soul.

What Western Europe believes to be an intellectual life, according to the belief of Khomiakov, the modern "barbarians" - in their own way again externalizing what ought to live internally – is what they have made of Romanism and Christianity. Internalization will have to be supported by the Russian people, after the higher mission has been incorporated into it by the spiritual world. ...

If, on the one hand, one can say of the amiable, poetically intelligent Khomiakov that he expected the fulfillment of the Russian mission from a peaceful intellectual current, it must on the other hand also be remembered that in his soul this expectation coincided with that Russia as a warrior want of Europe intended to reach. For it will certainly not do him any harm to say that in 1829 he took part in the Turkish war as a volunteer hussar, because he believed in what Russia was doing at that time as a first glimpse of his historical mission. What the amiable Khomiakov often rumbled in poetic transfiguration, rumbled on; and in a book by Danilewsky, "Russia and Europe," which at the end of the nineteenth century was regarded by a number of personalities as a gospel of the task of Russia, expressing the driving forces which merged the "spiritual task of the Russian people" with a far-reaching conqueror's will.

... Particularly characteristic is the position which the subtle Russian philosopher, Vladimir Solowieff, has taken with regard to these ways of thinking and feeling. Solowieff can be regarded as one of the most important embodiments of Russian spirituality. In his works lives beautiful philosophical power, noble spiritual outlook and mystical depth. But he also was long steeped in the idea of the Russian mission festering in the minds of his fellow countrymen. With him, too, this idea together with another of the abandonment of Western Europeanism was found. For him, the reason why Western Europe could not help the world to reveal the full innermost humanity was that this Western Europe had expected salvation from the development of the inherent powers of man. But with such striving for man's own powers, Solovieff could see only a foolish aberration from which mankind must be redeemed, without human intervention, by a miracle pouring spiritual power upon the earth from other worlds and that Folk, chosen to receive this power, become the savior of the lost humanity. In the nature of the Russian people, he saw that which was prepared to receive such an extra-human force and therefore the savior of true humanity.'[146]

However, he made 'the discovery that many others do not even speak of – the ideals that the Russian people are seeking for their own salvation, but that they make the Russian people an idol, as they are today. And by this discovery, Solovieff became the harshest critic of those who, under the auspice of a mission of the Russian people, introduced into the will of the nation the attacking instincts directed against Western Europe, as the salutary driving forces of further mental development. ...

Solovieff, who saw the Russian attacking instincts dressed up as ideas to do with the historical mission of Russia, specially declared in Danilewsky's book, found in a critique of this book (1888), the answer to this question. Danilewsky had said, "Europe fears us as the new and higher type of culture, which is called to replace the senility of Romance-Germanic civilization". Solovieff cites this as the faith of Danilewsky. And he replies: "Nevertheless, the content of Danilewsky's book, as well as his later concessions and those of his like-minded friend", Strachov, who advocated Danilewsky's ideas after his death, "lead to another answer: Europe looks at us with fear and adversity, because inside the Russian people, dark and unclear elementary powers are living, because its mental and cultural powers are poor and insufficient, but its claims appear clearly and sharply determined. These are the cries of what the Russian people wanted as a nation – that they wanted to annihilate Turkey and Austria, to beat Germany, to conquer Constantinople and, if possible, India.'[147]

The Russian missionary will also respect the West, prompted with the desire to open up to the West and make use of its achievements.

The essential difference between Eastern and Western Europeanism was, as we found out, the form of relationship to the individual and to society and nature. The Western man wants to develop his individuality and to realize himself in nature in accordance with the original Old Testament divine mandate: "Populate the earth, subjugate it and rule over the fish of the sea, the birds of the sky and all the animals that live on the Land"(Gen 1:28). The Eastern man, on the other hand, is primarily concerned with perfecting himself together with his fellow man, so he rather followed Christ's request: "Where two or three are gathered in my name, there am I am in the midst of them"(Matthew 18:20).

Accordingly, the Western man wants to push back the state as much as possible in favor of the possible free development of the personality. The underlying egoism is rather suspicious for the Eastern people. He sees this as a threat to interpersonal relationships and the danger of social chaos. Although the eastern man would also like to see the state die, he would like people to maintain a loving community. According to K. S. Aksakowa, however, their history has taught Russians to recognize the state as a necessary institution, and to integrate it as part of

---

[146]Copyright Rudolf Steiner Nachlass-Verwaltung Buch: 24 p.310ff.
http://fvn-archiv.net/PDF/ GA/GA024.pdf.
[147] Ibid.

their loving community. Accordingly, Wilhelm Goerdt interprets Russian history as follows: 'At times, the Slavs lived for themselves and without compulsion, full of hatred for every foreign yoke in the community (..., Obshchina), peaceful and independent, united in customs, faith and way of life.

"Thus, the Slavic community was a covenant of people based on moral principles, guided by internal law and thus by communal custom." But in AD 862, the Slavic communities came under the yoke of foreign peoples invading them. The northern Slavs were soon able to drive them away. The times of subjugation, however, showed them on the one hand "the impossibility of living on earth in a purely moral community-based organization", and on the other a path "giving them security from their neighbors, crucially, and order in the internal turmoil so far from moral principles". So the Slavs themselves began to reign. But these deviations from their inner moral principle led to inner quarrels and turmoil, "for they could not run an organization of external justice – it was alien to them." Their own experience showed them the "wrong side" of state institutions, while on the other hand their "benefits and necessity were evident".

"In this paradoxical-aporetic situation, which pushed for a solution, the state was "appointed". So the Slavic community recognized the "necessity" of the state, but "preserves itself, does not mingle with the state, separates the state from itself and appoints it from foreign soil."

Thus, the foundations of Russian history have been laid: the country as a multitude of morally free communities and the state as a unity of law-based organization" in the bond of love. Nowhere does the state mingle with the land ..."[148]

This *ordo naturaliter christianus* was finally sanctified by the acceptance of Christianity; [149] Axakov sees the deduction of the state, considered empirical and historical, embedded in religious substance: The external law, the state is necessary because of human weakness and economic efficiency that does not allow the kingdom of God on earth, which necessitates the state[150], and that also attacks the church, the land, from within. [151],152

To repel enemies but also because of the weakness of man, especially because of his egoism, the need of the state is recognized. Social development is also expected by the state rather than by individuals. It overlooks the fact that creativity can only come from individuals and that the state also acts through individuals. That is why a state is all the more creative, the more democratic and accordingly, the less creative the more centralized it is. Even the most dynamic ruler cannot develop as much creativity as millions of free citizens. But a dynamic autocratic ruler can change social conditions through his power and thereby stimulate dynamics in society.

Significantly, the developers of Russian society also came from the West or opened Russia to the West and received its new impetus from there. The very first founding of the empire goes back to the Waräger, a Viking tribe from Sweden.

---

[148] K. P.Aksakowa: *Socinenija istriceskija*, Moskva 1861, p.53-56.
[149] K. P.Aksakowa: Zapiska, p.N.L. Brodskij: *Rannie slavjanofily*, Moskva 1910, p.73.
[150] N.L. Brodskij: *Rannie slavjanofily*, Moskva 1910, p.76.
[151] K. P.Aksakowa: *Socinenija istriceskija*, Moskva 1861, p.54.
[152] Goerdt: P.307ff.

Peter the Great opened his land to Western ideas and brought Western intellectuals, artists, entrepreneurs and farmers into the country. He documented the opening to the west with the founding of St. Petersburg as the new capital. The subsequent tsars followed him in this way, especially the tsars imported from Germany: Peter III. and Catherine the Great.

The traditional Russian social order and the self-image of the nobility and serfs was thereby undermined. In the traditional society of Russia, the nobility was obliged to serve under the crown and therefore had to be made exempt from the peasantry by its own breadwinning. This is how serfdom in Europe had developed. Through the window to the West and modern war technology, the service nobility was no longer needed and the nobility was therefore released from the Tsar's service.

Wilhelm Goerdt writes: 'In 1762, Tsar Peter III issued his decree "On the Freedom of the Nobility" (...). The nobility was thus freed from the civil service – he no longer needed to serve in the military or civil administration, although the decree pointed to the moral obligation to serve. The nobleman was even allowed to leave the country. The nobility had thus won the privileges he had long struggled for. But that was just one side of this decree. For with the liberation from the civil service, the nobility was not at the same time stripped of those rights which derived from the former duty of service: the aristocracy, who were for the most part service nobility, and were allowed to keep their possessions, and this meant that the peasant was still obliged to serve their landlords, and, moreover, in many cases to give them the possibility of enjoyable and comfortable lives in the capitals of Russia and Europe.

This new order of things completely contradicted the tasks assigned to the peasants within the fabric of the medieval Russian service state. As the nobility served the tsar in the army and state administration, the peasant found his dignity in enabling the nobility's service to the tsar through his work in the country. But now that the nobility was no longer obliged to serve, the free movement of the farmer would have to be consistently restored. This did not happen. On the contrary, the more the nobility consolidated their freedoms before the crown and their new status, the more the peasants sank into the shadow of the nobility. In 1785, Catherine II had issued the "certificate of mercy" (...) for the nobility which confirmed the decree of Peter III., introduced the self-government of the nobility and made property, together with peasants, hereditary.

But soon afterwards, the same enlightened monarch had ordered that the nobleman was allowed to send his peasants to Siberia for forced labor and that any action brought by the peasant against his master was forbidden. Thus, the peasant had become an object, an object of arbitrariness standing outside any reasonable order and a universal right, while the nobility basked in the enjoyment of a hitherto little-known, securitized subjectivity. Here one usually used to speak of the capacity for suffering of the Russian peasantry, of suffering Mutschíg - and there was this power of toleration of unspeakable proportions really - but there were also and very much continuing riots, revolts and rebellions of the peasants, whose greatest, the Pugatschów uprising (1773-1775), unmistakably carried a social touch and caused the Russian Empire to tremble to its very foundations.'[153]

But even the nobility had lost their task and degenerated to celebrate festive swarming and suffering and idleness, if it did not itself rebel against the tsarist rule.

'After the Decembrist uprising of 1825, the success of which might have created a lot of change, the Russian aristocratic society sinks in lethargy under the pressure of the III Department of the Registry of His Majesty, Tsar Nicholas I, the public-secret mind and thought police. The mood of not being able to alter anything is taking hold. Here and there, one tries to soften the situation of the peasants, to meet them personally, but that basically does not matter [[154]]. It is the social nullity of Russia which almost obliged to contain the sophistry of doing and thinking in the as if, of illusionary planning and acting beneath every reality.

This is the birth of the *Oblomoving*: The social and political crisis of Russia, which was going on to its climax until the middle of the nineteenth century and the associated and at the same time rising disruption of intellectual order and consistency, as well as emotional well-being, the inadequacy of all and of oneself, the disgust, the paralysis, the inner chaos, the boredom and the escape into the fleeting aesthetic enjoyment, which, evaporating, lets the boredom condense again.' [155]

In simplified terms, individualism imported from the West was met with Russian community affiliation. The Russian soul and society were thereby split into Westerners and Slavophiles. The Slavophiles, and among them the mass of simple subjects in the vast empire, wished to see a return of the capital to Moscow. The Westerners were the Western-oriented elites who determined social life. Nevertheless, the elites were split themselves. The Western spirit, as it were, laid itself over the textured Russian soul. As the Russian elites, too, were guided by the ideal of perfect communion, they were open to socialist ideas. So, it does not come as a surprise that a transformation into a communist society was sought for Russia.

By the Industrial Revolution, in the West also, workers had become unleashed from traditional manufacturing facilities and were in need. The developing modern class society was addressed in particular by Karl Marx and Friedrich Engels, describing economic development no longer as the work of creative entrepreneurs and scientists, but as crystallized work and thus work of the working class. The community of workers was declared the subject of economic and social development.

In the West, because of its pronounced individualism, socialism could not become the prevailing social doctrine. Socialist ideals are synthesized in the West either with individualistic ideals, as in Social Democracy, but also in the ideal of the social market economy, or merely end up a political niche existence.

In the East, the revaluation of individual entrepreneurial activity into collaborative work as the engine of history was met with enthusiasm. Thus, in Russia, Marxism became the prevailing doctrine and justification for the October Revolu-

---

[153] Wilhelm Goerdt, p.254ff.
[154] See: V. Gitermann: *Geschichte Rußlandp.*Bd. 1-3, Hamburg 1949, …
[155] Goerdt: p.256f.

tion. But Marxism is only a development utopia for an increasingly saturated industrial society, in which capitalists throw each other out of the market and in the end only the last ex-propriate ones have to be expropriated.

As an instruction for a social and economic development, especially in an industrially underdeveloped country like Russia, Marxism had to be supplemented by Leninism. Leninism can be understood as a manual according to the administrative principles of the Deutsche Reichsbahn, as Lenin formulated it. For him, referring to the economy, communism is: *Soviet Power plus Electrification of the whole Country*. Realized in the vast Russian Empire and based on the tsarist administration, the Soviet Union became a modified socialist tsarist rule.

The founding of the Soviet Union was a provocation to the Western world. It was also seen as a political danger with its missionary claim to make the world socialist. Therefore, until the Soviet Union consolidated in the 1920s, all counterrevolutionary actions in Russia were supported militarily by Western countries.

Contrary to their own ideology, economic development in the Soviet Union and throughout the Eastern bloc continued to decline against the West. Therefore, it is understandable that the Soviet regime finally collapsed.

1.3 Russia's Globalization

Regarding the globalization of Russia, it started with the Russian Tsar, Ivan III., who shook off the Islamic Tatar yoke in 1480. Afterwards, Russia continued to penetrate 'to Siberia and Central Asia, where it conquered the culturally highly developed khanates of Kazakhstan, Turkestan, Turkmenia, Kokand, Khiva and Bukhara and came to the British sphere of influence on the border with Persia and Afghanistan. In the east, it extended its colonial activities to Manchuria and North Korea, where it eventually violated Japan's expansionist interests, from which it was pushed back in 1904-05 in the Russo-Japanese War.'[156]

Wikipedia writes: 'Russia became a multinational state for the first time after the conquest of the Tatar khanates Kazan and Astrakhan in 1552 and 1556. Subsequently, the conquest of Siberia began, where, after the fall of the Khanate Siberia, the Russian Cossacks advanced further and further east, founded fortifications and forced the indigenous population to Tribute payments to the Tsars. A major driver for development and settlement was the fur trade and freedom from serfdom. At the end of the 17th century, the Treaty of Nertzhinsk was concluded with China, which set the limits of the spheres of influence of the two states on the Amur. During the 18th century, Russia brought all of Siberia up to the Bering Strait under control and began expanding on the North American continent (Alaska, Fort Ross). In the second half of the 19th century, Russia, fearing it was overstretching, got rid of ist American possessions (sale of Alaska), but expanded its influence in the Far East at the expense of China (Treaty of Aigun). Further Russian penetration into Manchuria and the founding of ports Port Arthur and Dalian triggered tensions with Japan and led to the loss of influence in Korea and Manchuria.'[157]

---

[156] http://www.hschumacher.de/html/kolonialismus.html.
[157] https://de.wikipedia.org/wiki/Russische_Kolonisation.

The Russian expansion was understood to be an internal colonization. But since Peter the Great, Russia has also sought to become a naval power and to get access to the Black Sea, the Persian Gulf and the Indian Ocean. Russia managed to take the Ottoman Empire areas towards the Black Sea more and more. It was even Russia's goal, if possible, to conquer Istanbul and thereby control access to the Black Sea.

Since Constantinople is the place of origin of the Orthodox Church, Russia even saw in this endeavor a kind of crusade for the reclamation of conquered lands of Islam and this crusade lay in the conscientiousness of Russia as the *Third Rome*.

In Persia, Russia also tried to gain influence. In order to 'extend the Russian influence on the Caspian region and the South Caucasus at the expense of Persia and to prevent the rival Ottoman Empire from territorial gains'[158], Peter the Great waged a war against Persia from 1722 to 1723. 'On the eve of the Russo-Turkish War of 1735-1739 Tsarina Anna Ioannovna [however] returned all the conquered territories to the Persians to enter into an alliance against the Ottoman Empire.'[159]

During the Russian-Persian War of 1804-1813, Russia was able to expand its territory to the Kura and Aras Rivers ... In the aftermath the khans of Azerbaijan gradually deposed or died, so that the territories became Russian provinces.'[160].

In another war of 1826-1828, Persia lost the 'Khanate of Yerevan and Naxcivan, which now belonged to Russia. In addition, the Shah had to pay 20,000,000 silver roubles and allow the migration of Armenians to Russia. Moreover, the Russians were assured the naval supremacy over the Caspian Sea and free trade.'[161]

The clash of Eastern and Western Europeanism and concentration on commercial interests and Christian missionaries culminated in the globalization of China. From the north east, Europeanism tried to incorporate parts of China, Mongolia and Korea's Russia. However, Russian territorial extensions did not meet with Western trade interests, so that Western and Eastern Europeanism went hand in hand in controlling China.

At the end of the 19th century, however, the Asian model pupil of Western Europeanism, Japan, began to expand its sphere of influence and to colonize Korea and parts of China. This led to the Russo-Japanese War of 1895-1905, which Russia lost not least because of its underdeveloped industry. The self-confidence of the Tsarist Empire suffered from this defeat, and that also contributed to its disintegration in the Russian Revolution of 1905 and finally in the October Revolution of 1917.

The expansion of Russia to the east, south and west of course was largely determined by imperialist ambitions, but was, as we have seen, supported by the perceived Russian mission.

After the October Revolution, Russian politics changed into a globalization of communism with the battle cry "Proletarians of all countries unite!" Until the beginning of the Second World War, however, the Soviets were fully occupied with

---

[158] https://de.wikipedia.org/wiki/Russisch-Persischer_Krieg_(1722%E2%80%931723).
[159] https://de.wikipedia.org/wiki/Russisch-Persischer_Krieg.
[160] Ibid.
[161] Ibid.

consolidating their power in the area of the former Tsarist empire and to consolidate the country. During the Second World War, all forces were used for to defend against and then defeat Germany.

The increasing weakness of the former colonial powers in Asia, combined with the destabilization of their societies by the Japanese invasion, then fostered socialist developments in China, Korea, and Indo-China. Japan was the common enemy of East and West. Only after the Second World War with the beginning of the Cold War was there an increased front position against the West.

2. Poland

Although Russians are the most important East European people, even if its Europe reaches only to the Urals. Nevertheless, it is, of course, a constriction of Eastern Europeanism to refer only to Russia, especially since in the Middle Ages, other Eastern European people had a greater importance.

We want to analyze the Eastern Europeanism of Poland as the largest Eastern European country after Russia. It also largely represents other Eastern European countries.

Poland is therefore dealt with in more detail because together with other smaller Eastern European countries, it forms the border with Russia and because of its history, and in particular because between 1772 and 1918, it was divided between Russia, Austria and Prussia, between 1939-1945 between Russia and Germany, and indeed occupied by Germany and from 1945 to 1989 was part of the Eastern bloc determined by Russia. This therefore aggravated its antagonism in particular toward the partitioning powers.

Poland's national character is as Slavic and Catholic people, albeit modified in a nationalistic way, and this still lives on somehow and makes the understanding of Poland for the other Europeans more difficult, because Poland was hardly taken seriously as a political power factor until 1989, when large changes occurred. But today, as a member of the European Union, Poland's peculiarities assert themselves especially among the voters of the current ruling party PiS Law and Justice.

In the interests of the harmonious integration of Europe, which has already been urgently demanded in world politics, Poland needs to be better understood in its motives and fears by other European countries. This also goes hand in hand with a better understanding of other smaller Eastern European countries – indeed, up to a certain extent, also with a better understanding of East Germans.

For this purpose, the following points should be analyzed:
1. The Eastern Europeanism of Poland as a Slavic country.
2. The self-image of Catholic Poland as the guardian of true Europeanism.
3. The decline of Poland as a noble republic and its rebirth as a nationalist state.

Essentially, I refer to the book by Alix Landgrebe: "*If Poland did not exist, then it would have to be invented*", in which the development of Polish national consciousness in a European context is presented in great detail over 294 pages.

2.1 The Eastern Europeanism of Poland as a Slavic country

Axil Landgrebe writes: 'The attitude to the Slavic element of Poland is very different for Democrats and Conservatives in the sense that there is disagreement about how much being Slavic can be considered as an important category of Poland's national destiny.

At the beginning of the 19th century, there were some Slavophiles among the Polish aristocracy, who were oriented towards Russia and recognized Russian hegemony. But as early as the 1820s, they had deviated from this position and professed to be a Polish leader within the Slavs, also because they did regard the Russian system of power as despotic, and was thus not adequate to be Slavic as well Polish, according to the Rzeczpospolita traditions. ...

Pro-Slavic attitudes, but rejections towards Russia, have been a reaction particularly since the mid-nineteenth century to the increasingly pan-Slavism in Russia, which, ... has its roots in Slavophile Russian ideology and evolves into an expansive, aggressive ideology, which is seen as a special danger in Poland.'[162] 'According to Polish thinkers, Poland, as a leader in slavery, is not about establishing hegemony like Russia, but first and foremost about protecting smaller Slavic people against the Tsarist empire and other imperialist powers (especially the Teutons).'[163]

Alix Landgrebe refers to Joachim Lelewel's romantic historiography of Poland, 'one of the most important Polish historians of the 19th century. His view of Polish history, especially in the period between the two uprisings (1831-1863), is of decisive importance and characterizes the Polish romantic picture of history.'[164]

After that, the Poles in their self-image also invoke 'Herder's famous chapter on slaves in the "*Ideas for the History of Humanity*," in which he emphasizes that, despite its historical age, this tribe has received an unusual youth that has its significance in the future as the most important and leading element in the future of Europe, with Poland being the main reference point. [165] The Slaven's particular youth is interpreted as having remained faithful to the simplicity of their lives and preserving non-corruption, as opposed to the rational nature of the West among the people, that is, among the peasants. ... Among the Slavic tribes the Poles are considered by most thinkers to be the people who best preserved Slavic traditions, and whose history makes them the most faithful followers of the ancient Slavic world and the representative of Slavic civilization.'[166]

The Slavs 'are portrayed in some accounts as one of the first people on Earth, either of which is already reported in the Genesis or it is believed that the Slavs should at least as well as the Romans, Greeks or Gauls call themselves ancient glorious people, who already settled in Europe many centuries before the birth of

---

[162] Alix Landgrebe: *loc. cit*, p.156.
[163] Landgrebe, p.156.
[164] Landgrebe, p.64.
[165] See also: Kuk, Leszek: *Orientacja slowianska w mysli politycznejWielki Emigracji. (do wybuchu wojny krymskiej). Geneza uwarunkowania, podstawowe koncepcje*. Thorn 1996: 101. Zur Herder Rezeption im allgemeinen: Drews, Peter: *Herder und die Slawen. ...*
[166] Alix Landgrebe, p.65f.

Christ. The Slavs are also referred to as the "oldest prehistoric European colony of the Indo-European tribe"[167].[168]

According to this self-image, the Slavs 'were always a good tribe who lived unnoticed and self-sufficiently without attracting much attention and who were oppressed and enslaved by other people because of their good nature. Also, they are seen as a tribe, who lived in complete closeness to nature and "pure virtue" and because of their emotions, knew how to organize their life and needed no written form. Thus, the Slaven's intuitive way of life is interpreted in a more moral sense than that of other societies that developed writing, precisely because the lack of written language is attributed to the natural harmony and morality of the Slavs. ... The spirit of the Slavs "turned to the righteous, beautiful, holy and divine, distinguishing them from all other people in Europe." [169] ...

The principle of civilization of the Slavs is consistently regarded as a village (*wiejska cywilizacja*) in contrast to the foreign Roman or Western European principle of the city '[170]

'The gmina myth is to be regarded as an integral part of the pro-Slavian picture of history, as it is one of the foundations in the ideological application of the "Slavic principle". [171] The virginity and remoteness of the early village community from the other cultures is seen from the pro-Slavian point of view, not as a shortage, but as an opportunity for the Slavs, because only through this particular situation, is the tribe granted to take up a special position. It had not, like other people, absorbed the influence of numerous other cultures, but remained in his organism (ustroj), and had already realized the true process of living together in prehistoric times. The salient features of Slavic primitive society were its patriarchal and just structure and its democratic organization, which were named after the principles of equality and freedom. The village community (*gmina*) and the coexistence or their form of government (*gminowladztwo*) is seen as the principle to which the entire society was subjected in the ideal state and that at the same time, was regarded as the main principle of Polish predestination [172].[173]

Compare that with what has already been said about the Russians. What the Poles also have in common with the Russians is their perceived mission and their capacity for suffering, through which they, like the Jews, experience themselves as a chosen people. At the same time, the ethnic capacity for the suffering of the primitive peasant is exaggerated by Christian motives.

'The history of Poland seeks to prove that this nation is chosen to be the savior of true Christianity and humanity. In this context, Poland, as the pillar of civilization, has the position of a savior of humanity. ...

---

[167] See: Mickiewicz, Dziela 1875:250ff. ... The quote is from the newspaper *Gmina* 1866 Ner.1: 1. This idea also holds in the history of the second half of the 19th century and is frequently represented. ...

[168] Landgrebe, p.66.

[169] See: Mickiewicz, Dziela. 875:233 und 242.

[170] Landgrebe, p.67.

[171] See: Bronowski, Franciszek: *Idea gminowladztwa w polskiej histografii*. Lodz 1969.

[172] See: Lelewel, Uw.agi: In: *Polska*. Dzieje i rzeczy jej. Posen 1855: p.278ff. ...

[173] Landgrebe, p.68

The hypostasis of Poland as a chosen people is based on the course of its history and in its "martyrdom". In part, the idea of Poland was taken from the Polish Messianicus, as Christ of the people is included in the Theory of Falling, thus attributing a meaning to the suffering of the Poles in the context of world history. Mickiewicz expresses this idea in his account of history. He sees its meaning in the fact that Poland made mistakes over the course of its development, because it had left its actual *ustroj* and will resurrect after its repentance in "purity" and then at the same time will redeem the other nations, thus emphasizing the moment of one redeemed world community '[174]

Like the Russians, Poland has reservations about any form of hierarchy and was thus against a hierarchical state. That is why in Poland there was only a nobility democracy – the so-called *szlachta*, in which each member has a "liberum veto", that is, can prevent joint decisions. Decisions require unanimity.

The members of the *szlachta* understand themselves as being closer to the people as the Germanic nobility is subordinated by a much larger proportion of the population. Nevertheless, for Radicals, the *szlachta* is an impairment of the equal coexistence of all citizens in a village community.

'The emergence of the nobility is seen in the context of a raid theory on the Slavs. The ancestors of the *szlachta* were therefore invaders and not slaves, but one supposes that the Normans had corrupted the principles of the Slavic primitive society. [175] Partly it is also emphasized that the alienation of the Knights of the Slavs should finally have been introduced because the Slavs were constantly harassed by foreign powers. However, the *szlachta* is seen by many thinkers, even in the times of the earlier *Rzeczpospolita*, as a representative of Slavic democratic ideals, [...] so that in principle it is very different, partly from the ideological view of romantic historiography, resulting in contradictory interpretations made about the Slavic element in connection with Poles.

The emergence of a monarchy with feudal elements is also interpreted by some historians as a foreign, Slavic contradictory element, which was taken as a disaster for the Slavic-Polish from the Germans, whose social systems in world history represented Poland's opposite principle of sole rule [176]. This form of society has always been tied to Latin and Western religion, while Poland has borrowed its most important traditions from the Slavs and had long known the positive values inherent in Christianity.' [177]

The Russians, on the other hand, in many representations are not considered to be Slavs either, but Mongolians, that is, as an Asiatic people that has nothing in common with European people. Many authors, however, do not deny the Slavic origin of the Russians, but they are seen as a people in which Slavic virtues were

---

[174] Landgrebe, p.82.

[175] Representative of this raid theory is for example Waclaw A. Maciejowski. Other historians also regard the nobility as something foreign in Poland, such as historians of the Warsaw School Koronowicz, Wroblewski or the historian Karol Szajnocha, see: the same: *Nowe szice historyczne*. Lemberg 1857: 265,269. Moraczewski, Jedrzej, *Dzieje Rzeczypospolitej Polskiej do pietnastego wieku*. Posen 1843: 2f.

[176] Lelewel, Joachim: *Historyczny rozbior prawodawstwa polskiego* (1828) In: Polska wiekow srednich, 3. Bd. Posen 1859, p. 1ff.

[177] Landgrebe, p.69f.

first undermined by the Vikings or Varangians and the Tatar yoke, centuries ago. The Russians are therefore regarded as Asianized, barbarized, or Germanized Slavs, who, under Tatar and Yaric rule, became despotic and thus fated to be Oriental and not European.' [178]

'Orthodoxy is also seen as an expression of the dark, backward, superstitious state of the Russian people. It is often referred to as heresy or superstition, but not recognized as a Christian religion, the Catholic Poland is compared to a heretical Russia. Russia's church is a kind of hostile pseudo-church with barbaric content.' [179]

The Poles are the haven of pure Slavicism and thus deserve the leadership of the Slavic people. Poland feels obliged to return the Slavs to their own true Slavonic heritage.

'Other Slavic people, including the Southern Slavs, are usually considered "friends", but the Czechs are held by some thinkers as being Germanized or too Russian-oriented. ... The Rusins (later Ukrainians) are usually judged positively, often in contrast to Russia, they are not portrayed as barbarians, but appear in a positive light. Thus they are considered by Slavophiles as the "purest Slavs" who, protected by Poland, could best preserve the ancient principles of the *gmina*. [[180].'[181]

However, in Poland there are also critics of the romanticization of Poland, so that the Poles, like the Russians, are divided into Westerners and Austrians. The Westerners see the cause of the economic, social and political backwardness of Poland in the romanticization of Polishness and want Poland to adopt the Western attitude to life, social structure and economy. Here are some examples:

Karol Boromeusz Hoffmann 'is one of the harshest critics of the glorification of the Rzeczpopolita propagated by the Lelewel school. Above all, Hoffmann's criticism of Polish history is based on the fact that in his view Poland did not have a sufficiently strong state and this was the reason for the negative development of Polish history. He stresses that anarchy has arisen throughout history that made it completely impossible to make good use of the rich resources of the country; that explains the economic downfall of Poland [[182]. ...

The liberties glorified by Lelewel and other representatives of the romantic school are thus seen here as negative and interpreted as a depravation of a state formerly characterized by meaningful reforms. Hoffmann describes the behavior of the *szlachta* as patriotic individualism that harmed the community and thus the entire nation. [[183] ... Hoffmann criticizes the lack of feudal development in Poland, as there was no absolutism in Poland that Hoffmann regards this as necessary for the modernization of the state. Therefore, Hoffmann does not insist on the reinforcement of the *rodzimosc* demanded by the Romantics, but, on the contrary, sees

---

[178] Landgrebe, p.145.

[179] Landgrebe, p.146f.

[180] Siehe *Gmina* 1866, (August) Nr. 1: 3f.

[181] Landgrebe, p.144.

[182] See for example the term *nierzad*, Hoffmann, Skarb 1839, p.111. The worst phase is dated by Hoffmann 1365-1717. So here the entire "golden age" is seen negatively.

[183] Vgl. Hoffmann, Karol Boromeusz: *Historya reform politycznych w dawnej Polsce*, Leipzig 1867, p.71.

too weak a realization of Western European principles as a reason for the weakness of Poland. For him, the specific positive element of Poland is not the *rodzimosc*, but rather the elements that Poland adopted from Western Europe and then further developed in its own way, that is, revaluated in nationally. For Hoffmann, Poland clearly belongs to Western culture, has nothing in common with Asia, which makes the development of Poland even more pathological in Hoffmann's view.[184]

Accordingly, the monarchy is considered positive by many Western-oriented Poles. Thus, Karol Sienkewicz assumes 'that the *narod* [people] need a strong king for guidance and that there was no *concordia* in Poland when the weak elected-kings ruled in Poland. The weakness of the state, according to Sienkewicz, led to the fact that the formerly virtuous *szlachta*, when it still had a king to orient, suc-cumbed to decadence and cultivated an egoism that plunged the state into misfor-tune. [185] Sienkewicz sees this as all the more fatal, as the *szlachta* at the beginning of Polish history from his point of view had played a positive role in the develop-ment of Poland.' [186]

Josef Szujski, one of the most authoritative representatives of the Krakow school, expresses similar criticism and also sees weaknesses in the Polish national character. 'Thus he states that the Slavs had been fatalists from primeval times, from which the other negative qualities also resulted: "From the fatalism [of the Slavic AL] stirs his total carefreeness over the future, therefore his lively reckless cheerfulness comes on eve of the misfortune [...]; he is contentious, quarrelsome and suspicious when general discipline and unity are required. He likes the cur-rents of the simple people (*rucho ludowe*), but he rarely acknowledges the success of organization, [...] for a long time he was unable to govern. "[187]. However Szujski admits that "the Slav" compensates for these weaknesses with other good points, such as the fact that he has a particularly good heart and true national tra-ditions (*narodowe tradycje*). The fact that "the Slav and Pole" have good souls does not help them, because this does not suffice for a functioning state. [188]'[189]

2.2 The self-image of Catholic Poland as the guardian of the true Europeanism

Wikipedia writes about the religion of Poles: Poland was 'never homogeneous in the Middle Ages. Even before the Christian faith finally prevailed in the centuries to come, favored by the Edict of Tolerance of Kalisz, 1,265 Jews from Western Europe and Hussites from Bohemia immigrated to Poland. Through the union with Lithuania in 1386 and 1569, many Belorussian and Ukrainian-speaking Orthodox Christians came under the rule of the Polish kings. Since the 16th century, Luther-anism has had many followers, especially among the German population in the north Polish cities, while Calvinism has been popular with the nobility, Szlachta.

---

[184] Landgrebe, p.87f.
[185] See: *Kronika Emigracyi Polskiej* Bd. 5 1837, p.113ff.
[186] Landgrebe, p.89.
[187] See: Szujski, Josef: *History polskiej trasciwie opowiedzianej -Ksiag dwanascie.* Warschau 1880: II.
[188] See: ibid.
[189] Landgrebe, p.73.

The Reformed Church was the birth of the Unitarian Church of the Polish Brothers in 1565, which had its own academy in Raków .... The Sejm of 1555 debated the introduction of a Protestant national church in Poland. Although this was not introduced, but the Warsaw Confederation and the Articuli Henriciani of 1573 secured the individual freedom of belief in the Polish Constitution, therefore there were never in Poland war of religion. In 1596, the Greek Catholic Church was founded in the Church Union of Brest. In the 17th century, however, the Counter-Reformation was able to draw most "dissenters" to the Catholic side.

At the end of the 17th century, the Polish king Jan Sobieski settled Muslim Tatars in Podlaskie. A relatively large Muslim minority also lived around Kamieniec Podolski in Podolia, which belonged to the Ottoman Empire between 1672 and 1699.' [190]

'Since the Second World War and the western shift of Poland, the country is mostly Catholic. 87% of the total Polish population is Roman Catholic (percentage of Catholic baptized people out of total population, 2011) [[191]], whereas before 1939 it was only 66%. [[192]] Of these, 54% say that they also practice their faith.[[193]]'[194] As Catholics, the Poles feel that they belong to Europe. Russia, on the other hand, belongs to Asia.

'The world view of the Poles is almost exclusively euro-centralistic, so it is argued consistently: It is self-evident in Polish thinking that positive values are European, whereas all threatening and negative ones are Asian.' [195]

Poland sees itself as a bulwark against Asia. 'Buoyancy theory gained popularity in the 17th century during the Turkish wars, [...] especially through the success of Jan Sobieski in Vienna. Finally, in the eighteenth century, it continues in the context of a pre-missionary idea, in the sense that the Poles are the wall of Europe and serve to defend the sacred faith.' [196] As the next enemy of Poland in the East, Russia embodies Asia. 'The bastion myth is also supported by non-Polish thinkers. ... such as Napoleon's statement about Poland as the *clef de voute de L'Europe* (capstone) or Victor Hugo's view that Poland is the border guard of Europe.'[197]

Russia is 'stylized in numerous portrayals as Europe's most dangerous representative of Asia and the enemy of Europe and described under the name of Moscovia as a Tatar-Mongol entity, which has its first purpose and its mission and destiny as the destruction of Europe and finally to take over and achieve world domination. Asia is thus equated with the principle of expansion, with an unstoppable barbaric urge for conquest.' [198]

Correspondingly, the geographical dimensions of Europe and Asia are seen as displaceable in the representations of the Polish thinkers and thus in ideological

[190] https://de.wikipedia.org/wiki/Polen#Mittelalter_und_Neuzeit.
[191] Główny Urząd Statystyczny: Mały rocznik statystyczny Polski 2012. Zakład Wydawnictw Statystycznych, Warszawa 2012, p.117, 134–135 (PDF [downloaded 15. 1.2013]).
[192] Dieter Bringen, Krzysztof Ruchniewicz (Hrsg.): *Länderbericht Polen*, p.373.
[193] Ibid.
[194] https://de.wikipedia.org/wiki/Polen#Mittelalter_und_Neuzeit.
[195] Landgrebe, p.115.
[196] Landgrebe, p.123.
[197] Landgrebe, p.124.
[198] Landgrebe, p.117.

dimensions: Europe's original borders were the eastern borders of Poland in 1772, after which Ukraine (Rus) belonged to Europe. Also, on the other side of the Dniepr was the Asian border, and not just behind the Urals, Poland has been so geographically outposted of Europe.' Alix Landgrebe cites Ks. Wojciech z Medyki: 'The barbaric nudity of Asian civilization immediately manifested itself on the borders of the two continents. The wildness and savagery of Asia caught the eye. If you crossed the Dnieper, you saw the nakedness and cruelty of Asia.'[199]

Poland sees itself as a representative of Western civilization, which is committed to the civilization of Asia. Kasimierz Kazimierzewicz writes: 'Poland's beautiful, yet extremely difficult and dangerous, unenviable mission was, is and always will be to spread the culture, humanity, freedom and civilization of the Occident ever further to the Orient and North of Europe and Asia and by claiming its own independence to protect and preserve the independence and culture of the West from the outbreak of the Eastern Barbarians.'[200]

Within Europe, the Polish self-image is clearly marked by the idea that Slavic is not considered a foreign element to Europe, but that despite all views that still regard Poles as barbaric in the nineteenth century, they even give it a special position in Europe. This means that in their historical versions, too, the pro-Slavian positions can be interpreted as an attempt to make the Slavic element in Europe more popular, more natural and at the same time to emphasize that it is indispensable as an element of Europe and also for the future of Europe and that its progress could be harnessed.'[201]

Jedrzej Moraczewski even distinguishes between 'the good Europe, which is represented by Rome, and the negative Europe of the Teutons. Therefore, he sees Poland as a double bulwark protecting the Slavs from Western German civilization on the one hand and Eastern Asian on the other hand. [[202]][203]

Josef Ordega writes: 'Among the people of Europe, Poland is the country that has done the most, except France, to realize the Word of God as the principle of humanity. Poland, like France, is the daughter of the Church through the influence of Catholicism.'[204]

Julian Klaczko writes: 'The Slav is the true democrat, for Slavs, democracy is the voice of conscience, immanent custom and morality, not like in Germany, where there is only a paragraph adopted by votes, which is why the Slav also fights against the Teutons and for the freedom of all nations.'[205]

---

[199] Kp.Wojciech z Medyki: *Poglad na wschopdnia Europe i Azya i wyjasnienie stosunkow, jakie miala Moskwa z ludami slowianskiemi od pierwocia bytu do czasow naszych.* Przemysl 1864: 7ff. cit. after Landgrebe loc. cit. p.117.

[200] Kazimierzewicz, Kasimierz: *Europa wird es kosakisch oder republikanisch?* p.140. cit. after Landgrebe p.172.

[201] Landgrebe, p.93.

[202] See for example Zbyszewski, Leon: *La Pologne*, Paris 1863, p.158.

[203] Landgrebe, p.126f.

[204] Ordega, Josef: *O narodowosci polskkiej z punktu widzenia kotolicyzmu i postepu.* Paris 1840, P.65. zit. nach Landgrebe loc. cit. p.241.

[205] Vgl. dazu Klaczko, Julian: *Die Deutschen Hegemoden.* Offenes Sendschreiben an Herrn Georg Ger Venus, Berlin 1849: 22. cit. after Landgrebe loc. cit. p.233.

For Poles, Slavic and Germanic principles are 'antagonists insofar as the Germans, throughout history, are considered to be an aggressive imperialist people, always having a desire to conquer the Slavs. As proof of this, the catchphrase "Spread to the East " is cited. At the same time, they represent the typical Germanic principle of individualism, while the Slavs embody the principle of altruism and brotherhood. Examples of this are what the German empire created after Charlemagne and the Order of Knights, which are cited in order to prove that the German craze for destruction runs throughout history.'[206]

In terms of their original social attitude, Poles are anti-capitalist and advocate Catholic-inspired socialism. At present this Slavic-Catholic attitude is represented in particular by the Polish majority party and the current ruling party *PiS Law and Justice.*

Jan Puhl writes: Ideologically Jarosław Kaczyński 'stands for the basically leftist vision of a generous welfare state, which he refines with "national-catholic sauce", as the liberal politician Leszek Balcerowicz once said. Kaczyński defends himself as the protector of the needy, who keeps them from the supposedly "pathological" consequences of postwar economic liberalism.

Since the beginning of his political career, he has argued that the economic boom after 1989 did not benefit the masses, but former communists and the dissidents. These people would have torn down, after Kaczyński, the best pieces from the Polish bankruptcy estate and taken the most important posts and companies and then unleashed a predatory form of capitalism. The simple Poles had been excluded. A strong state had to fight the "networks" of that time and contain the worst excesses of the cold new economic order.'[207]

'PiS addresses Poles who are frustrated that economic progress is slower than they hoped. It is not the poorest people who elected PiS, but middle-class people: families who find dilapidated schools and kindergartens, but also small business owners or shopkeepers who see themselves in danger as a result of international chains. For these voters, it is particularly important that PiS introduced a child allowance of 500 zlotys from the second child and lowered the retirement age from 67 back to 65 years for men and 60 years for women.'[208]

' Kaczyński "loves Poland, believes in God and in the state," says Michal Kamiński. ... Kaczyński was deeply convinced that he himself knew best what was good for Poles and their country. He is not against democracy in principle, but does not want to be stopped by annoying checks and balances such as a constitutional court. "PiS is more like an internal sect than a political party," says Kamiński.'[209]

2.3 The fall of Poland as a noble republic and its rebirth as nationalist state

Wikipedia writes: 'After the Battle of Tannenberg (1410) and the associated heavy defeat of the Teutonic Order in Prussia against the dual state of Poland-Lithuania, the great empire that emerged from Poland and Lithuania rose to become one of

---

[206] Landgrebe, p.151.
[207] Jan Puhl: *Herrscher im Hinterzimmer*, in: Der Spiegel 30/22.7.2017, p.90.
[208] Jan Puhl: p.90.
[209] Ibid.

the leading continental powers and was, for a long time, Europe's largest state, with spheres of influence from the Baltic to the Black Sea and from the Adriatic Sea to the gates of Moscow. At the instigation of the last Polish king of the Jagiellonian dynasty, Zygmunt August, the personal union between Poland and Lithuania in Lublin in 1569 was transformed into a real union. Poland and Lithuania have formed, since 1569, the so-called aristocratic republic and thus the first modern state of Europe with a system of republican nobility and a separation of power.'[210] During this time, Russia also felt endangered by Poland and there were repeated wars that the Poles allowed to reach Moscow.

Since the Poles did not develop further economically and socially, and in addition they also glorified the undeveloped primitive state of the country as being particularly high, they could not assert themselves as a state and were divided by Russia, Austria and Prussia.

A key reason for the weakness of Poland was the grassroots democracy of the aristocrats, in which each member could prevent joint decisions. Sienkiewicz sees *the liberum veto* as a '"political monster" that has destroyed the Sejme and its laws. [[211]]'[212] Thus, political life in Poland was largely paralyzed long before the division. In addition, the later powers of division over individual aristocrats were able to prevent political decisions, which were not in their interest, by vetoing them.

Poland claims from its basic democratic attitude that it adopted a French equivalent constitution even before the French Revolution. 'The principles of equality (*rownosc*), freedom (*wolnosc*) and fraternity (*braterstwo*) have always been the principles of the Slavic-Polish primitive society, with which the Slavs, much earlier, have peacefully adopted the principles that prevailed in Western Europe only through the French Revolution and had to be fought there with so many losses. [[213]]'[214]

Tragically, however, this constitution was also a reason for the last political division, because the divisionist powers, which continued to be governed by absolutist rule, wanted to suppress the revolutionary dynamics within these principles.

' One of the most important stereotypes of nineteenth-century, Polish historiography is the injurious influence of the Jesuits and the resulting internal weakness of the country. It is taken up by representatives of all kinds of different political directions, is therefore the most widely used explanatory model and goes back to Joachim Lelewel. ...

In the polemic against the Jesuits, it is argued that their ideas were not Polish but, on the contrary, completely opposed to the Polish nature. The Jesuits represent all the negatives of Western societies and invaded a system which they rejected and therefore knowingly, and with all means at their disposal, destroyed it. The

---

[210] https://de.wikipedia.org/wiki/Polen#Mittelalter_und_Neuzeit
[211] Vgl. Sienkiewsicz, Karol: *Skarbiec historii polskiej*. Paris 1839: XIV.
[212] Landgrebe, p.89.
[213] See: Widman, Karol: *Narodowosc a rewolucja. Studjum plityczne*. Lemberg 1864, p.12. ...
[214] Landgrebe, p.68.

invasion of the Jesuits was again the fault of foreign kings; With the ever-advancing establishment of the Order that ended the golden age, the glory of Poland faded [...].

The Jesuits are held responsible for the inhibition of progress and the prevention of all positive political ideas in Poland, just as many thinkers assume that until the time of the Jesuits, the *szlachta* did not become ideologically aberrant. They regarded themselves as a privileged caste and acted that way. Thus, the Jesuits were accused of infiltrating the just Slavic democratic society, the basis of which was so important to Poland that it could no longer justify its existence without it. It is argued that they weakened the monarchy by corrupting the kings and the entire court with their "pagan organizational principles" contrary to Catholicism. [215]'[216]

As pure Polish destructive forces next to the Jesuits, Teutons and Jews are considered, 'the Polish trade in the hands of Germans and Jews happened according to the fact that the Poles were constantly deceived by these foreign elements and thus neither imported nor exported anything from the land [217] ... The typical Pole is juxtaposed with the so-described Jewish being, and the good folk-soul of the Polish peasant is oppressed or spoiled by the Jewish population from this point of view. [218]'[219]

Polish positivists opposed this interpretation. 'Among the "diseases" of Polish society, the Polish positivists reckoned that the *lud* was in a dark and sorrowful state. The romantic idea of the *lud* and its democratic power is completely abandoned. The writer Boleslaw Prus sees the *lud* and its customs as primitive: through the feudal structures of society, it is still "wild" and has a medieval mentality. [220] The old social structures, against which the positivists also polemicize, are thus to a great extent blamed for the misery of the nation. Prus draws the conclusion that one must educate the *chlop* (peasant) in order to be able to use him within the framework of a national policy. That is, to educate him as a modern citizen. [221] This was similarly formulated by the historian Josef Szujski, who wants to solve these social grievances with educational reforms.' [222]

'The verdict of the positivists, that the common people have no national consciousness [...], is the basis for a conscious promotion of this group. The positivists imagine in this context that they themselves as a spiritual elite could shape the nation. The intention is to dissuade the peasants from thinking in dynastic and traditional categories and to feel themselves to be subjects of the respective rulers of the divided areas. If activity is required from them, then it is in the national interest.'[223]

---

[215] See Jablonowfski, Waclav: *Do emigracyi polskiej*. Paris 1843, p.8f.

[216] Landgrebe, p.105f.

[217] See: Zebrowski: *Polska*. Paris 1847, p.35f.

[218] Zukowski, Jan Ludwik: *O panszczyznie z dolaczeniem uwag nad moralnym i fizycznym stanem ludu naszego*. Warschau 1830,. S.6, 26 und 96. ...

[219] Landgrebe, P.108.

[220] Prus, Boleslaw: *Wybor publicystyki*. Hrgp.V.F. Przylubski 1957, p.106.

[221] Ibid.

[222] Landgrebe, p.252.

[223] Landgrebe, p.254.

However 'despite all criticism and utilitarian arguments, positivist thinkers are not lacking in national pathos. With reference to memory, they also insist on orienting one's own *zywiol* (Polentum) and preserving, with all progression, what is important to traditions in order to preserve the unity of all.[224]' [225]

In *szlachta*, nobles, like all the nobility of Europe, were not primarily Germans, Russians, Poles, but simply distinguished people. That's why aristocrats of other ethnicities could become king. In burgeoning nationalism, citizens emancipated themselves from family and tribal ties, but did not simply become world citizens, but members of a national community.

We characterized nationalism as a group egoism. Nationalism contains a socio-Darwinian component that has led to many conflicts in Europe and the world, but is ultimately of Western European origin.

By capturing the Eastern European people, nationalism already corrupted the true Slavic ideal of the peaceful coexistence of all human beings. Poland was only able to re-establish itself as a state on a nationalistic basis, but, like other Eastern European countries that were reforming, created nationalist conflict zones. Thus, after 1918, there were many minorities in Poland and the strongman of Poland, Józef Piłsudski, tried to conquer Lithuania and other former Polish territories immediately after independence.

In Czechoslovakia, the Sudeten-Germans, but also the Slovaks, felt disadvantaged, which is why the latter parted from the Czechs. Similar problems existed in Hungary, Romania, Tyrol and elsewhere.

International as well as social tensions arise when, as in Poland, Slavic-Catholic self-understanding is to be lived out in a nationalistic manner. Then it can lead to the split of one's own society into secular and traditionalists and to boundaries and egoistic behavior towards neighboring countries.

As shown, nationalism has two sides. On the one hand it individualizes man so much that he no longer ties himself to the family and the tribe, but to the nation. We have portrayed the Slavic and Catholic roots of Poland. These also resulted in a return to a brotherly coexistence of the people. This return can contribute to overcoming perverted capitalism in Europe.

On the other hand, nationalism also includes the freedom of the citizens and thus a constitutional separation of powers and independence of the judiciary. These are being abolished with recourse to primitive Polity by the ruling PiS. In addition, the narrowness of the self to the nation in Europe must be overcome.

By contrast, the actual leader of the PiS, Jarosław Kaczyński, cultivates the old prejudices of Poles against Russians and Germans with a brutal mystification of his twin brother, who died in a plane crash in Smolensk. Jan Puhl writes: Kaczyński 'believes like many in his party, that his brother did not fall victim to a misfortune, but was killed by an assassination attempt launched by Russia - and the then liberal government in Warsaw approved it. "The surviving twin, Jaroslav, has become part of the national myth, which is so identity-creating for Polish rights: Poles are the eternal heroes and repeatedly victims of Russians and Germans.

---

[224] Prus: *Wybor*. Warschau 1957, p.7.
[225] Landgrebe, p.255.

This basic understanding also shapes Kaczyński's foreign policy. "He does not understand the EU principle," says a former PiS member. History is, for Kaczyński, a single competition between nations. Consequently, he also does not consider the European Union a project to secure peace and prosperity together. For him, the EU is first and foremost an instrument of power for the Germans.' [226]

III. The development of East-West antagonism and its impact on the Third World

Nationalism in Europe had led to the two devastating world wars. These disasters have roused people and called them to unite European countries.

These aspirations were reinforced by the developing *Cold War*. As a result of the Second World War, the Soviet Union was able to extend its communist social order to all Eastern European countries. It also supported the development of the so-called *People's Democracies* in Asia, Africa and Latin America.

According to Soviet ideology, there is only a *formal* democracy in the West, since power lies with the capitalist, who also controls the media. Thus, the masses do not recognize their own interests and cannot enforce their interests due to the given power relations. So, under Western democracy, a minority – the capitalists – would dominate over the majority – the working people. Under socialism, on the other hand, the working class, represented by the Communist Party, would rule over the capitalists and thus the majority rules the minority. What the interests of the majority are for the communists comes from Marxist analysis of social development. This analysis is considered scientific.

The Soviet Union also hoped that the plight of the Europeans, and especially the Germans and Austrians as the losers of the war, would make them join Socialism after the Second World War.

Fearing that the growing misery in Germany would fuel socialist aspirations, but also due to Western powers not coming to an agreement with the Soviet Union on how to stabilize Germany's economy, they carried out a currency reform in the western zones of occupation and created the *Federal Republic of Germany*. In response, the Soviet occupation zone became the *GDR German Democratic Republic* and the Soviets attempted, by way of a blockade, to involve West-Berlin in the GDR.

In the West, for military defense, *NATO*, the *North Atlantic Treaty Organization,* and in the East, the *Warsaw Pact* were founded. Germany and its capital Berlin were divided, and was thus the most visible part of the sharpening east-west opposition.

1. The effects of the Cold War on Third World countries

Between East and West, a contest arose to draw Third World countries into the western or eastern sphere of power. The East-West opposition therefore favored

---

[226] Puhl: p.90.

the independence efforts of the colonies held by western industrialized countries. With military and development aid, these countries were also lured to join the West or East.

In this tug of war, the Soviet Union succeeded in making China, Vietnam and Cuba communist. In Korea, as in Europe, the country was divided. In particular with the help of the CIA, the USA had been able to stifle socialist aspirations in Iran, at the time of Mohammad Mossadegh, and in Chile under Allende.

Preceding connection to the east or west were left revolutionaries such as the Maoists in China and in the West, autocratic rulers, as well as *Mobutu Sese Seko* in the Congo. However, it was not clear to all countries which camp they would join. *Ho Chi Minh*, for example, first hoped to unify Vietnam with the help of the USA and only joined the Eastern bloc when the USA followed in the footsteps of the former colonial power, France, and sided with South Vietnamese Emperor, Bao Dai. Even *Fidel Castro* only joined the Eastern bloc because of the resistance of the United States against his takeover and social changes.

Apart from the Cuban missile crisis, the conflict between East and West was most pronounced at the border of the Eastern Bloc, that is, in Europe and the Near, Middle and Far East.

From the Western point of view, in order to contain the Soviet Union, like NATO in Europe, and, in 1954 in East Asia, SEATO (Southeast Asia Treaty Organization), as well as in 1955 in the Near and Middle East, CENTO (Central Treaty Organization), also called Baghdadpakt, were founded. SEATO included the countries: Australia, France, New Zealand, Pakistan, Philippines, Thailand, the United Kingdom and the United States. The contracting states of CENTO 'were Great Britain, Iraq, Iran, Pakistan and Turkey. The USA had observer status. [227].'228

Egypt and Syria resisted the Western powers' bid to become members of anti-Soviet pacts. Markus Eckelt writes: 'In the 1950s, a plan was announced by the CIA to finance an invasion of Turkey, in order to end the cooperation of the Syrian state with the Soviet Union. The invasion of the US Marines in Lebanon in 1958 increased the fear of US interference in the region. US diplomatic pressure to force Syria and Egypt to join the anti-Soviet Baghdad Pact failed and only intensified their rapprochement with the Soviet Union. [229]'230

The wrestling of the West and East for states that became independent only after the Second World War, is represented on the Russian Television Station, RT, using the example of Syria, as follows: 'Even before the international community of states had recognized the independence of Syria, the then Soviet Union, in 1944, established diplomatic relations with Damascus. A few months after the expiration of the French Mandate in October 1945, Syria concluded the first important agreement with the USSR. On February 1, 1946, they signed a secret treaty stating that

---

[227] Guy Hadley: CENTO: The Forgotten Alliance. ISIO Monographs, University of Sussex, UK 1971, p.2.

[228] https://de.wikipedia.org/wiki/Central_Treaty_Organization.

[229] Vgl. Stäbeli 2001, 32.

[230] Markus Eckelt: *Syrien im internationalen System. Die Politische Ökonomie des Ba'th-Regimes vor und nach der doppellten Zäsur 1990, Demokratie und Entwicklung* Bd.64, LIT Verlag. p.34.

the USSR would support Syria in foreign affairs and in building its armed forces. In the 1950s, the Kremlin sought improved relations with Arab states to stem the growing influence of the USA.

At the turn of the year 1954/55, a war loomed between the Baghdad Pact countries (Britain, Iraq, Iran, Pakistan and Turkey) and Syria, which refused to join the pact. The Soviets rushed to Syria's help, guaranteeing that they would defend Syria against similar threats in the future. Against the backdrop of this threat, in 1955, Damascus agreed to a major arms purchase and trade agreement with the Soviet Union. In the following years, Syria signed further economic agreements with the Soviet Union and other socialist states. Trade rose sharply. In 1957, the USSR again supported Damascus against Turkish aggression. The Kremlin sent a small aviation squadron to Syria.

The phase of the United Arab Republic (1958-1961), when Egypt and Syria merged into one state, resulted in a brief breakdown in relations. After the withdrawal of Syria from the state network, both states re-established close contacts. They reconciled arms supplies, an agricultural aid program and other agreements. Although the Syrian government took anti-communist measures internally, Moscow maintained its contact with Syria, as it was an important ally against Western influence in the Middle East.

After the left-wing faction of the ruling Ba'ath Party took power in 1966, the Soviet-Syrian partnership continued to improve. Since the new Syrian government pursued a left-wing course, it was dependent on the support of the USSR. The Soviet influence on Syrian domestic politics increased. Moscow now regarded Syria as a country on a non-capitalist path. The perspective of a socialist development opened up.

A further rapprochement of both states took place in 1967 after the Six-Day War between Israel and Egypt, Jordan, Syria and other Arab states. For the Syrian military, the war ended in ruinous defeat. From then on, the West no longer sold weapons to Syria. Syria covered this gap by buying large quantities of Soviet weapons. Moscow sent military advisers. Contacts with the USSR became more and more important to the Syrian leadership as the country was politically isolated internally and externally. The states of the Eastern bloc issued loans to strengthen the state sector in Syria.

Hafiz Al-Assad's takeover in November 1970 put the Soviet-Syrian partnership to the test. He was, in contrast to the left-wing faction of the Ba'ath Party, politically independent and Moscow-critical. However, Soviet-Syrian relations survived this crisis. Damascus promised the USSR its cooperation. Assad traveled to Moscow in February 1971. Both states relied on each other to achieve their regional strategic goals.

Although the influence of the Soviet leadership on Syrian domestic policy diminished, cooperation in other areas strengthened. From 1971, the economic activities and arms deliveries of the Eastern Bloc countries increased rapidly. Between 1971 and 1980, the volume of Soviet economic and technical promotion tripled. In the early 1970s, a quarter of Soviet military aid to developing countries went to Syria. The stability assured by Assad became more important to Moscow than the establishment of a socialist Soviet-style regime. He put an end to the political instability that plagued Syria in the 1950s and 1960s.

During the October war of 1973, which was waged between Israel and Egypt as well as Syria, the USSR greatly supported Damascus. By the end of the war, 42,500 tons of military equipment had been delivered. Military advisers and engineers from the Soviet Union helped the Syrian armed forces. After the war, the Syrian leadership once again relied on the USSR to rebuild its armed forces.

When Egypt distanced itself from the socialist camp in the mid-1970s, Moscow was left with Syria as the only reliable ally in the Middle East. They worked closely together to stem the "shuttle diplomacy" of Henry Kissinger. Kissinger sought bilateral US-mediated peace negotiations. By contrast, the Soviet Union insisted on a major international peace conference in which it also played an important role.

Assad's intervention in the first Lebanon conflict in 1976 caused a crisis in relations between Moscow and Damascus. Syrian troops occasionally attacked Palestinian and left forces with which the USSR was allied. The Kremlin then reduced its support of Syria. However, the Soviet Union eventually had to accept Syria's Lebanon policy as it relied on the Syrian leadership to effectively influence developments in the Near East. The fact that more military advisers from the Eastern Bloc countries were stationed in Syria in 1978 than in any other developing country shows how important the country was for the Kremlin.

Against the background of increasing domestic and foreign policy problems, for the second half of the 1970s, Damascus sought even closer relations with the Soviet Union. This effort culminated in 1980 in a treaty of friendship between the USSR and Syria. The Syrians tried to impress Moscow. Syria was one of the few Muslim countries that did not condemn the Soviet intervention in Afghanistan. The Soviets were granted greater access to Syrian port facilities. Moscow was able to fend off several Western and Israeli diplomatic initiatives in the Lebanon conflict. Damascus made this possible through its great influence in Lebanon.'[231]

As countries in the Middle East became independent or their regimes changed, they often changed their position in the East-West relationship, as the example of Syria shows. In addition, the East-West relationship in Asia changed after the end of the Vietnam War and the rapprochement between the USA and China. The result was that SEATO and CENTO disbanded in the 1970s.

'At the initiative of Indian Prime Minister Nehru and Yugoslav Prime Minister Tito, 1955 envoys from 23 Asian and six African countries met in Bandung, Indonesia. These were states which belonged neither to the western nor the eastern alliance system.

As a result of the conference, the 29 states passed several resolutions. In one, they condemned "any form of colonialism and racial discrimination" and called for "respect for the United Nations Charter". In another resolution, they spoke out in favor of "reducing the tensions between the blocks of power, universal disarmament and a ban on nuclear weapons." For the first time, the Bandung Conference also called for Third World demands for equal rights and equal treatment with the

---

[231]rt on 6.08.2016: *Historischer Überblick der russisch-syrischen Beziehungen seit 1946*, https://deutsch.rt.com/der-nahe-osten/39826-historischer-uberblick-russisch-syrischen-beziehungen/..

former colonial powers. The spirit of Bandung contributed significantly to the process of decolonization.' [232] '120 states were members of the Non-Aligned Movement in 2012'[233] The Independents also used the East-West tensions to gain maximum support from both sides, as did Egypt for the financing and construction of the Aswan Dam. ...

2. The development of the Muslim world and its resistance to Europeanization

The people in the ancient civilizations of Central and East Asia were so highly developed spiritually and civilizationally that they were able to open themselves up to Europeanism and even develop themselves into industrial powers, especially Japan, China and India, or are still on their way to doing so.

Muslim countries, on the other hand, had and still have great difficulties in opening themselves up to Europeanism. It is well known that Islam came about 500 years after Christianity. It was a development of Judaism and Christianity and Muhammad called himself the last prophet. Christianity was thus a backward religion for Muslims, but ultimately also of the devil. Because, as Wikipedia writes: 'The lawyer and theologian Bin Qayyim al-Ğauziyya († 1350) lists five non-Islamic communities: the Jews, the Christians, the Zoroastrians, the Sabians and the polytheists. Accordingly Bin'Abbās is said: "There are six religions: one (i.e., Islam) is for the merciful (God), the other five for the devil."

Sura 2, verse 42: "And do not obscure the truth with deceit and delusion ..." is already interpreted by the earliest Koran exegetes like Yaḥyā bin Salām († 815) [[234]], citing Qatāda bin Di'āma as follows: "do not mix up Islam with Judaism and Christianity. "With the later exegete Al-Qurṭubī († 1275), the tendency to give Islam the absolute priority over other religions becomes even clearer: "Do not confuse Judaism and Christianity with Islam, for you know that the religion of God is Islam, in whose stead nothing else is acceptable and replaceable. Judaism and Christianity (on the other hand) are heresy (Bid'a); they are not from God."[[235]]'[236]

As a result, a Christian like a Jew or a Gentile may become a Muslim, but the conversion of a Muslim to Christianity is considered a deathly crime. In addition, the early Caliphates based on Hellenism had a higher cultural and civilizational rank than the then Christian lands. Therefore, it was an impossibility for Muslims to be ruled by Christians.

Muslims have generally become so absorbed in their submission myths under their Allah that there is nothing higher for them than to delve into the Koran. Western education and Western individualism are an abomination and a sin to them.

Man by its very nature is a pleasurable and sexual being that can only fully live its life in paradise. Correspondingly sensual, the paradisiacal pleasures are sung. On earth, however, Allah requires that enjoyment and sex life be subject to strict

---

[232] https://de.wikipedia.org/wiki/Bewegung_der_Blockfreien_Staaten.
[233] Ibid.
[234] Fuat Sezgin: *Geschichte des arabischen Schrifttump.*Brill, 1967. Band 1, p.39.
[235] M. J. Kister: „*Do not assimilate yourselves...*" Lā tashabbahū. In: Jerusalem Studies in Arabic and Islam (JSAI) 12 (1989), p.321. Anm. 2.
[236] https://de.wikipedia.org/wiki/Dhimma.

food laws and laws for gender relations. In particular, women are considered notorious tempters of men. They must be dominated by their father or husband and otherwise locked away as much as possible and veiled from third parties.

Apart from the fact that according to the Islamic view, only God can be creative and can limit one's own creative action on presumption and sin, in such a society, in which men and women are not considered to be free individuals, hardly any creative dynamic can be expected. In this religiously-based image of mankind, people could not even emancipate themselves from their families, so that they continued to live in a pre-medieval, tribal society and their loyalty to tribal chieftains or elders was greater than to the state or king.

The tribal affiliation of most Muslims in the Near and Middle East and North Africa has survived to this day. Wikipedia writes: 'The power of the tribes can go so far that they have reduced within their territory the influence of the state to a minimum and the state cooperates with the tribal elders according to the principle of indirect rule. The Pakistani province of Balochistan is a prime example of tribal rule. [237] In the Kurdish areas of Turkey and Iraq, the influence of the tribal leaders has increased despite the simultaneous urbanization since the 1980s. [238]'239

'In North Africa and the Middle East, with a predominantly Islamic population, Muslims identify with tribal units in most cases, while Christian minorities are fragmented into numerous sects that create social cohesion for their members. The universal religious and political leadership claim raised by Islam is ideologically incompatible with the striving of the tribes for political self-determination.'240 The ancient archaic tribal orientation underlying the Islamic states additionally complicates the development of the individual into a self-confident and creative individual and thus also democratic societies.

In order to have loyal followers, Islamic rulers bought or robbed boys as early as the Middle Ages, turning them into soldiers loyal only to them. Therefore, private armies such as the Mamelukes in Egypt and later the Janissaries of the Ottoman sultans emerged. The boys were preferably robbed or bought from Christian parents from the Balkans.

So it is not surprising that Western ideas and ideals in Islamic countries, which also apply to other colonies, were taken over primarily by military personnel who were initially recruited as auxiliary troops by colonial powers. The military were then those who fought for independence and tried to modernize and industrialize their countries. They also adopted democratic forms of government, but always fell back into military dictatorships when their progressive secular social ideals were endangered. This development can be clearly seen in Turkey after Kemal Atatürk, but also in other Islamic states.

Accordingly, the relatively secular-minded military was inspired not by religious, but by nationalist ideals. The reforms were particularly supported by traders, industrialists and an emerging middle class.

---

237 Boris Wilke: *Governance und Gewalt. Eine Untersuchung zur Krise des Regierens in Pakistan am Fall Belutschistan*, p.20.
238 Martin van Bruinessen: *Innerkurdische Herrschaftsverhältnisse: Stämme und religiöse Brüderschaften*. epd-Dokumentation, Evangelischer Pressedienst, Juli 2003, p.9–14.
239 https://de.wikipedia.org/wiki/Volksstamm
240 Ibid.

For the majority of the Muslim population, the military and the supportive strata were perceived as a foreign body because of their secular attitude, especially because they intervened in the way of life of the population, with the enforcement of secular institutions and behaviors. An example of this is the headscarf ban in Turkey after Kemal Atatürk. Thus, there was a split in Islamic society: on the one hand there was the military, developing intelligence, cross-border merchants and industrialists, all living predominantly in the cities, whereas on the other hand, there were the masses, especially Muslim rural residents.

Added to this were social tensions between the various religious groups themselves. For the Christians, Druze and others, but also Islamic sects, some of which still contained Zoroastrian elements from the pre-Islamic period, such as the Alawites, the Alevis, Yazidis, but also the Kurds, they were the mentally more open minded to modern ideas than the orthodox Sunnis and Shiites.

Before globalization, the different religious groups lived together peacefully. The majority religion was the one supporting the state and the followers of other religions had to pay special taxes to Mohammed, but were also exempt from military service.

In addition, the military in individual countries were still supported by religious minorities. The majority in the Syrian army constituted the Alawites previously despised by the Sunni majority. In Iraq, on the other hand, a Shiite majority was dominated by Sunni-controlled military.

The tensions between the two main Islamic currents were strongest: the Sunnis and the Shiites, whose age-old controversy about the true doctrine and rightful succession of Muhammad flared up again.

Probably the greatest impulse for the resurgence of political Islamism, which at first even united all Islamic tendencies, was the founding of Israel. According to the Islamic view, Israel founded a state based on an even more backward religion than Christianity and which was also committed to western social ideals and developed Israel into a modern industrialized country.

The founding of Israel not only meant the separation of a country understood to be Arabic. It was also a religious and social provocation. In addition, Israel proved to be far superior to Muslim states in terms of military and economic power and let the Muslim countries constantly feel their economic and social backwardness. But life frustration is the most effective ferment for political radicalization

As long as general prosperity was approximately guaranteed as a result of modernization, the secularized upper classes could hold their own in the Islamic states. However, as the distribution of income and wealth worsened to the detriment of the masses of the Muslim population, the ruling classes became corrupt, unemployment increased and there was social unrest. The Islamic masses, disadvantaged by economic development, tended to blame *Europeanism* for their social problems. Therefore, social motives mingled with Islamist ones, and as in Egypt, even social unrest for more freedom and democracy was infiltrated by Islamists. As a result, in elections, Islamists grew stronger and threatened to wrestle power away from secular elites. The secular powers defended themselves by banning Muslim parties, excluding them from elections or manipulating elections in their favor. But this radicalized Muslim forces even more.

Thus, in the Muslim world, a mix of social, ethnic, nationalistic and religious motivations developed, along with economic, political and military interventions of industrialized countries, who saw their interests to be endangered. This resulted in the economic, social and political chaos in the Near and Middle East and North Africa which still remains to this day.

In the following analysis, I will try to make the interaction of various political forces in individual regions perceptible. Anyone who is an expert in the development of the Islamic countries may skip this statement or use it for reference only for individual countries. They are written in a different font in order to show this.

2.1 Persia/Iran

The conflict potential of today's Iran to the rest of the world emerges from
1.   its position as the center of Shiite Islam to the majority of Sunni Islam and
2.   its radical Islamic defense against Europeanism.

'The Achaemenid Empire (also known as the Old Persian Empire) was the first Persian Empire. It extended from the late 6th century BC to the late 4th century BC over the modern states of Turkey, Cyprus, Iran, Iraq, Afghanistan, Uzbekistan, Tajikistan, Turkmenistan, Syria, Lebanon, Israel, Palestine and Egypt. The Achaemenid Empire expanded for the first time in 550 BC under Cyrus II by the annexation of the Empire of the Medes. Among the successors was the sequel to the later largest expansion, culminating in 500 BC. At that time, it also reached parts of the Libya, Greece, Bulgaria, Pakistan as well as areas in the Caucasus, Sudan and Central Asia. In the year 330 BC, Alexander the Great ended the reign of the Achaemenids'[241]

After an eventful history, 1000 years later in around 600 AD, Persia became Islamic after the split of Islam in the Shiite direction. After another almost 1000 years, from 1501 to 1722, the Safavids ruled 'a Persian prince dynasty from Ardabil', which "established Shiite Islam as the state religion.'[242]

'The era of the Safavids had fundamental consequences for today's Islamic state. Under Ismail I. not just a union of mostly Iranian populated areas succeeded, but also the foundation of Persian "national consciousness" was laid and thus created the basis for today's Iranian state.'[243] But Persia was also the great antagonist to the developing Ottoman Empire since the twelfth century.

' From 1514, for a century, the Ottoman Empire and the Safavid Empire were involved in an almost continuous war that revolved around the rule of the Caucasus and Mesopotamia. The two empires were the most powerful in the Middle East. This rivalry was deepened further by the dogmatic differences between the two kingdoms. The Ottomans were Sunnis, while the Safavids were fanatical Shia Muslims ... and were considered heretics by the Ottomans. [[244]]'[245]

' The Ottoman-Safavid War of 1623-1639 was the last in a series of military conflicts between the Ottoman Empire and the Persian Safavid Empire, which involved the occupation of Mesopotamia.'[246] 'The Treaty of Qasr-e Schirin, which was signed on May 17, 1639, ultimately clarified the Ottoman-Persian border.' [247]

---

[241] https://de.wikipedia.org/wiki/Ach%C3%A4menidenreich.

[242] https://de.wikipedia.org/wiki/Safawiden.

[243] https://de.wikipedia.org/wiki/Safawiden.

[244] Caroline Finkel: *Osman's Dream: The Story of the Ottoman Empire 1300-1923*, P.104-105.

[245] https://de.wikipedia.org/wiki/Osmanisch-Safawidischer_Krieg_(1623%E2%80%931639).

[246] Ibid.

[247] Ibid..

As for Persia's confrontation with globalization emanating from Europe, Persia suffered from Russian expansionist struggles against the Persian Gulf and Britain and later especially the USA, which, provoked by the Soviet expansionist aspirations, therefore interfered in the internal affairs of Persia.

How Muslim countries:

    1. were forced to become secularized in order to develop,

    2. had to defend themselves against the claims of European states,

    3. were opposed at the same time to the European East-West conflict and

    4. these challenges also led to uprisings of the Islamic population

can be seen also in the development of Persia, later known as Iran.

'Until 1828, the Caucasus was lost to Russia and Russia got a say in the Iranian succession. Great Britain ensured that large areas of eastern Iran became part of Afghanistan. [248] ...

The fact that the Shah's government was barely able to collect taxes opened the door for the economic influence of European states. This was mainly achieved through the granting of concessions, which gave foreigners parts of the economy against payment of small taxes, such as the construction of the telegraph network, fishing rights, the operation of banks or oil exploration from the 1860s onwards. The culmination of this development was reached with the Tobacco Monopoly for a British consortium leading to a complete tobacco boycott and the withdrawal of the concession - the first successful movement of traders, clergy and intellectuals against rulers. [249]

The clergy were able to distinguish themselves in this environment as guardians of national interests and developed under the influence of intellectuals like Jamal ad-Din al-Afghani into militant Islamists. When the Shah wanted to make further concessions to Russia in 1905 in the face of a state bankruptcy, there were months of unrest, the result of which Iran received its first parliament. On August 5, 1906, it adopted its first constitution, which was comprehensively extended in 1907. [250] It envisaged a separation of powers based on the Western model, but also the compatibility of all laws with the Sharia [251][252][253] and a control body of five clergies. This constitution remained in force on paper until 1979. Thus, the constitutional revolution ended the absolute monarchy in Iran. [254][255]'256

Mohammed Ali, who was crowned in Persia on January 19, 1907, was unwilling to share the absolute power of a Shah with a parliament ... and wanted to reconvert the constitutional monarchy, which had existed since 1906, into the old, absolutist form of government. He was supported by the conservative clergy, which rejected the newly introduced democratic institutions as too secular and too Western. For the clergy, nationalism was a foreign, Western idea and fundamentally incompatible with Islam. While some clerics supported the constitutional revolution, they did so mainly because of opposition to Western concessionaries [257]'258

' The reign of Mohammed Ali Shah should, however, include a treaty that represented a new level of interference in the state's integrity of Persia. The Treaty of Saint Petersburg, signed by the Foreign

248 Monika Gronke: *Geschichte Irans, Von der Islamisierung bis zur Gegenwart*, p.87.

249 Monika Gronke: p.92.

250 Wilhelm Litten: *Die neue persische Verfassung. Übersicht über die bisherige gesetzgeberische Arbeit des persischen Parlaments.*In: Beiträge zur Kenntnis des Orients: Jahrbuch der Münchener Orientalischen Gesellschaft. 6 (1908), p.1–51, (online auf archive.org).

251 Mahnaz Shirali: *The Mystery of Contemporary Iran*, P.23–25.

252 Monika Gronke: p.97.

253 Michael Axworthy: *Revolutionary Iran: A History of the Islamic Republic*, p.28.

254 Ervand Abrahamian: *A History of Modern Iran*, p.47–48.

255 Monika Gronke: p.97.

256 https://de.wikipedia.org/wiki/Iran.

257 Cyrus Ghani: *Iran and the Rise of Reza Shah. From Qajar Collapse to Pahlavi Rule*, p.8.

258 https://de.wikipedia.org/wiki/Mohammed_Ali_Schah.

Ministers of Russia and Great Britain on August 31, 1907, divided Persia into three zones, a Russian, a British and a neutral zone. The Russian zone was comprised of the area north of the (coarse) line – Kermanshah, Yazd and Sarakh, and the British held the south-eastern part of the country (now Iranian-Balochistan). After the treaty became known in Iran in September 1907, there were demonstrations and protests throughout the country.'[259]

' The dispute between the regent and the parliament over future policy widened into a power strug-gle, in which Britain and Russia intervened directly in June 1908. They pressured the government and parliament to yield to the wishes of the Shah. At the end of June 1908, open fighting broke out on the streets around the parliament building between parliamentary and government-loyal troops. A little later street fighting also broke out in Tabriz. The whole country was in turmoil.'[260]

'Part of the regular forces under the leadership of Mohammad Vali Khan denied the Shah and marched from Mazandaran to Tehran to support the constitutional movement.' As a result of the resulting riots, Mohammed Ali then had to renounce the throne in favor of his son and went into exile in Russia. 'The Pahlavi came to power in 1925 as successors to the Kajars. These had been discontinued following a parliamentary decision of October 31, 1925. On December 12, 1925, the parliament decided to raise Reza Khan to the Shah. He was named Reza Shah Pahlavi.'[261]

'The two monarchs of the Pahlavi dynasty pursued a policy of modernization and secularization, in parallel with the occupation of the country during World War I by Russian, British and Turkish troops and during the Second World War by British and Soviet troops. After that, there was repeated foreign influ-ence, such as the founding of an Autonomous Republic of Azerbaijan with Soviet aid or a coup d'état organized by the CIA in 1953'[262]

The background to this 1953 coup d'etat was the nationalization of BP-controlled oil production and refining facilities and fears that Iran would slip away from the West and fall within the power of the Eastern bloc. In the Iranian power struggle, the then Prime Minister Mossadegh and his supporters, in-cluding the Communist Party on the one hand, stood opposed to the Shah and the military, but there was also the clergy on the other hand. The ensuing 'repression of the liberal, communist and Islamist oppo-sition led to many-sided tensions culminating in the 1979 revolution and the overthrow of the Shah'[263]

'The Shi'ite clergy (Ulama) has always had a great influence on the part of the Iranian population that was religious, conservative and opposed Western influences in Iranian society.' In his writings, rev-olutionary leader Khomeini referred directly to 1909, when the Constitutionalists hanged Sheikh Fazlollah Nuri, and described him as a role model who had fought for the supremacy of religion in Iran's political system. Nuri had asserted in the Constituent Assembly that a commission of Shiite clergy should review every law passed by parliament to ensure that it did not contradict the laws of Islam; otherwise it would be vain.'[264]

'Decades later it came to the expected clashes between the clergy and Reza Shah Pahlavi, who re-placed hitherto valid Islamic laws and courts in 1927 by a modern Western legal system, banned the wearing of the hijab and introduced coeducational education in schools .'[265]

Thus, in 1963, the Shiite cleric, Ruhollah Khomeini, vehemently opposed the Shah's reform program, which would later be called the White Revolution .... Khomeini saw an attack on Islam in the program, which focused on land reform, women's empowerment and a literacy campaign.'[266]

---

[259] Ibid.
[260] Ibid.
[261] https://de.wikipedia.org/wiki/Pahlavi_(Dynastie).
[262] https://de.wikipedia.org/wiki/Iran.
[263] https://de.wikipedia.org/wiki/Iran.
[264] https://de.wikipedia.org/wiki/Islamische_Revolution.
[265] Ibid.
[266] Ibid.

Khomeini was placed under house arrest, was arrested and eventually forced to leave Iran. In exile 'emerged Khomeini's most important work: The Islamic State (1970). In this work, he developed the state principle of the Welayat-e-faghih ("rule of the supreme jurist"). In his agitation, he gradually succeeded in discrediting the idea of social progress through Western orientation, which was one of the basis of the Shah's reform program, and to develop his own Islamic ideology of progress. He recalled Jalal al-e Ahmad's critique of the Westernization of Iran. Al-e Ahmad spoke of Westernization (Gharbzadegi) as a plague that poisoned Iranian society. [267] Another important contribution to making the backward-looking Shiite Islam progress-oriented was the publication by Ali Schariati. For him, Islam showed the way to the liberation of the Third World from the yoke of colonialism, neocolonialism and capitalism. [268] Morteza Motahhari's popular sermons on the struggle of Shiite Islam against injustice in the succession to Mohammad did the rest to mobilize his hearers for the new fight against the alleged injustices of the Shah's regime.

One of Khomeini's central themes was that the revolt and especially the martyr's struggle against injustice and tyranny should be central to Shiite Islam, [269] and that Muslims should follow neither the Western path (liberalism and capitalism) nor the eastern path (communism).'[270]

The development of Iran reveals how the Muslim population, led by its clergy, turns not only against the West, but also against its own secular elites. As the revitalized political Islamism turns against *Europeanism* and especially against competing Islamic faiths and feels obliged to politically question the existence of Israel, Islamic-influenced states are a constant threat to world peace. However, it must not be overlooked that Israel is constantly provoking the Islamic world with its settlement policy and its expansionism.

After the Shiite revolution in Iran, social conditions in the sense of the Islamic sharia were rearranged and thus, of course, the free development of the people was restricted. It is indicative of the attitude towards the Western intelligentsia that the Revolutionary Council, upon receiving instructions from Khomeini on June 4, 1980, decided to "close all the universities in the country and start a cultural revolution." Khomeini was not sure about the students and faculty with the words: "We are not afraid of military attacks, we are afraid of colonial universities, [271]". Background was the disturbance of the speech of Alī Akbar Hashemi Rafsandschani in April 1980 in the medical school. The words "Universities are more dangerous than hand grenades" [272] of December 17, 1980 brought the concern of Khomeini to the forefront.'[273]

Technically, however, Iran was trying to catch up with the West and as it pursued a prestige goal, which was the development of nuclear energy, Iran was perceived by the rest of the world as threatening world peace.

The West was hostile to the new regime anyway, because Iran fell out of the phalanx of the Western containment forces against the Soviet Union, totally nationalized the oil industry and stopped Western influence on oil production. In addition the USA was Iran's main ideological enemy. Iran built its religiously based social order as an alternative to the American image of man and society.

Iraq under Saddam Hussein, who, with a Sunni minority, ruled a predominantly Shiite population in Iraq, feared that Iran would influence the Shiite majority in Iraq, which he had repressed. However, Saddam Hussein also wanted to incorporate the Iranian oil-producing areas. We will come back to this point when we look at the treatment of Iraq.

---

[267] Sandra Mackay: Iranianp.1996, P.215.

[268] Nikki R. Keddie: Modern Iran. 2003, P.201ff.

[269] *The Last Great Revolution Turmoil and Transformation in Iran*, von Robin WRIGHT.

[270] https://de.wikipedia.org/wiki/Islamische_Revolution.

[271] Bahman Nirumad, Keywan Daddjou. Chomeini. p.343.

[272] Bahman Nirumad, p.343.

[273] https://de.wikipedia.org/wiki/Ruhollah_Chomeini.

Saudi Arabia, which, with the main pilgrimage sites of the Islamic world, Mecca and Medina, sees itself as the very center of the Islamic world and represents Sunni as the true Islam, namely in its radical Wahhabi version, feels that a Shiite state with the same sole representation claim true Islam as a religious provocation and political danger.

The already existing religious opposition between Shiites and Sunnis was further aggravated to a clash between Iran and Saudi Arabia. Daniel Steinvorth writes about Abd al-Aziz bin Mohammed al-Saud: on April 21, 1802 the inhabitants and Shiite pilgrims, who on that day celebrated a feast in honor in the name of the martyr Ali, raided and ended the pilgrimage in a bloodbath. 'Al-Saud was not all about money and jewels, it was also about a religious mission.' He was committed to Wahhabism. 'Shiites in his eyes had deviated so far from the pure doctrine of Islam that they could no longer be considered Muslims, but apostates.'[274]

2.2 Afghanistan

In order to understand the social and political conditions in Afghanistan, the interaction of the following conditions must be considered:

1. ethnic diversity of Afghanistan,
2. political relations with neighboring countries,
3. Afghanistan as a plaything of eastern and western globalization and religious resistance against it and
4. the development of militias in Afghanistan as a result of the dissolution of the traditional social structure and state order.

2.2.1 Ethnic diversity of Afghanistan

Wikipedia writes: 'The country's population feels that it belongs to a multitude of ethnic groups and tribes and for historical reasons, the Pashtuns often consider themselves a state-bearing people. Often, several ethnic groups live mixed up within settlement areas whose population numbers could only be estimated. The categorization into ethnic groups is also not clear, because self-identification and impersonation often differ.

Data on the size and population of ethnic groups can therefore not be given as concrete values, but only in specific areas. The following information is extrapolated to the population of the year 2009. [[275]].'[276]

The 'Pashtuns, historically "Afghans", are the founders and namesake of the country. They make up about 42% of the population. [[277]] The largest subgroups in number are the Durrani (south and west) and the Ghilzai (east). [[278]] The Pashtuns are associated with several nomadic tribes, especially the Kuchi with about 5 million people.'[279] The Pashtuns are organized in tribes, 'clans that rely on common ancestors. Popular sentiment still does not exist in most rural Pashtuns. Rather, each tribe stands alone as an association and considers other tribes partly as foreign and hostile. Thus, by the late 19th century, (and in some cases to this day) the two largest Pashtun tribes, Durranis and Ghilzai, were enemies. Until the early 20th century, the Durranis and Ghilzai were considered to be two distinct ethnic groups.'[280]

[274] Daniel Steinvorth: *Quelle des Terrors*, in: Der Tagesspiegel Nr. 23 175/ 16.7.2017,Geschichte p. 2.
[275] Conrad Schetter: *II. Strukturen und Lebenswelten – Stammesstrukturen und ethnische Gruppen*, p.124.
[276] https://de.wikipedia.org/wiki/Afghanistan#Ethnien.
[277] https://www.cia.gov/library/publications/the-world-factbook/geos/af.html.
[278] Aghanistan – Provincial Overviews, Afghanistan Tribal Map (Memento vom 28. April 2015 im Internet Archive).
[279] https://de.wikipedia.org/wiki/Afghanistan#Ethnien.
[280] https://de.wikipedia.org/wiki/Paschtunen.

'The Pashtuns are predominantly Sunni Muslims.' Therefore, their society 'is mainly determined by the tribal system with its strict code of ethics called Pashtunwali, which is strongly influenced by Orthodox Islam.' [281] 'The Pashtunwali is a code of conduct and common law, but it is called a code of honor by European researchers or "way of the Pathans" (Spain). It is of pre-Islamic origin and shows, according to Enevoldsen, an ancient Indo-European origin, but some practices, such as the Badal (revenge), recall the characteristics of the Abrahamic religion.

The most important terms of the Pashtunwali include:

- hospitality (Melmastya)
- revenge (Badal), literally "exchange" (see also blood revenge)
- cohesion of the family
- the right to asylum (Pana).'[282]

' For the settlement of conflicts, the Jirga ("assembly") is convened, and at the national level, it is the Loya Jirga ("Great Assembly"). The contending parties (Gond) are reconciled by the Jirga. If necessary, the decisions of the Jirga are enforced by the Zalwechti, an executive group of 40 men. The decisions of the Jirga are binding.' [283]

The combination of extreme tribalism and orthodox Sunni religion makes it difficult to build a state with a secular society and these forms of behavior.

'Tajiks are, with about 27%, the second largest group in the country. "Tajik" is a general term for the Persian-speaking population in Afghanistan, often referred to as "Parsiwan" ("Persian spokesman") or, in the East and South, as "Dihgan" and "Dihwar" ("village owner", meaning "settled"). [284] The Tajiks do not form an ethnic group in the narrow sense, since there is no recognizable cultural, social or political demarcation with other groups. In the West, they are the direct continuation of the Persian-speaking population of Iran, to the North of the Persian-speaking population of Central Asia. They also form the majority in most cities. [285] ...

Hazara, also Persian-speaking but largely Shi'ite and of Mongolian descent make up about 9% of the population. Because of their ethnic and religious affiliation, they were persecuted and killed in Afghanistan.

Uzbeks, one of the many Turkic peoples of Central Asia, represent about 9% of the population.

In addition, there are several smaller groups of, among others, Aimaken (4%), Turkmen (3-4%), Baluch (2%), Nuristani and numerous other ethnic groups (4%).'[286]

Edda Schlager writes: 'Again and again, the instability of the Afghan state is traced back to having many different tribes. Conrad Schetter of the Center for Development Research in Bonn, however, opposes the concept of ethnic background as a factor for conflicts in Afghanistan. Schetter sees more of a "problem of ethnic demarcation and the passivity of many Afghans towards their ethnic group". For many Afghans, villages, valleys, extended families, tribes and religious groups are much more the basis of their political identity. '[287]

---

[281] Ibid..

[282] Ibid..

[283] https://de.wikipedia.org/wiki/Paschtunwali.

[284] R. Ghirshman: Afghanistan, (ii) ethnography, in The Encyclopaedia of Islam. New Edition, CD-ROM Edition v. 1.0 ed. , Leiden, Niederlande.

[285] R. Ghirshman: Afghanistan loc. cit.

[286] https://de.wikipedia.org/wiki/Afghanistan#Ethnien.

[287] Edda Schlager: *Paschtunen, Tadschiken, Nuristani. Wer sind die Afghanen?*, http://www.scinexx.de/dossier-detail - 408-11.html.

2.2.2 Political relations with neighboring countries

Afghanistan is 'a landlocked country in South Asia at the crossroads of South and Central Asia, bordering on Iran, Turkmenistan, Uzbekistan, Tajikistan, the People's Republic of China and Pakistan.' [288] For more than 2000 years, Afghanistan has belonged to the great empires, which were alternately dominated by Persians, by Greeks at the time of Alexander the Great, by Mongols, Indian moguls and others. For the longest time, Afghanistan belonged to Persia.

Pashto, the Pashtun language, is the "official language" by royal decree since 1936, but Persian is the language of the majority, [289] and since the Middle Ages, has been the dominant administrative and cultural language of the region. The literary written language of Persian has been the official and administrative language since the founding of Afghanistan. More than half of the population of Afghanistan ... speaks a dialect of Persian as a mother tongue. ...[290]'[291]

Ethnically, the Afghans are close to the Iranians. In Afghanistan, over 99.9% of the population are Muslims, of which 'about four-fifth are mostly Hanafi Sunnis and one-fifth imamitic Shiites.' [292] By contrast, according to the 2011 census, '99.4% of Iran's citizens are Muslims. ...[293]. It is estimated that 89% to 95% of Iranians profess themselves to follow the state religion of the Twelver Shia and the remaining 4% to 10% to follow Sunni Islam[294].'[295]

Iran, as the center of Shiite Islam, seeks to influence the Shiites and to act as missionaries in neighboring Afghanistan, and, in particular, to prevent a government determined by the strictly Sunni Taliban. In order to eliminate Western and especially American influence on Afghanistan, Iran has also helped to destabilize Afghanistan by supporting the Taliban. While Afghanistan is opposed to religious missionaries by Iran, it needs Iran as a counterbalance to Pakistan, which long supported the Taliban in order to gain political influence over Afghanistan.

The largest population in Afghanistan are Pashtuns (about 12 million Pashtuns), which have significantly shaped Afghanistan's political development. In 1747, the Pashtu Ahmad Shah Durrani founded 'an independent, Pashtun kingdom that can be regarded as the predecessor of the modern state of Afghanistan.'[296] His empire ranged from the east of modern Iran to northern India at times. [297] From the history of Afghanistan, there is thus also a close association with Pakistan and India.

'All the linguistic analyzes say that Pashtuns date back to today's Pakistan, which took advantage of the conflicts between the Mughals and the Safavids to become completely independent, on the one hand, and to become rulers themselves on the other hand. In addition, about 23 million Pashtuns [298] that is, almost twice as many Pashtuns, live in Pakistan. [299]

After the first two British-Afghan wars, in 1893, Britain succeeded in setting out the Durand Line to demarcate its colonial possessions in British India (now Pakistan) against the Emirate of Afghanistan. ... The demarcation line was deliberately laid through the settlement areas of the Pashtuns, causing some

---

[288] https://de.wikipedia.org/wiki/Afghanistan.

[289] CIA World Factbook: Afghanistan.

[290] Ch. M. Kieffer: *Languages of Afghanistan*. In: Ehsan Yarshater (Hrsg.): Encyclopædia Iranica, Stand: 2009,einges ehen am 20. 9 2015 (engl., inkl. Literaturangaben.)

[291] https://de.wikipedia.org/wiki/Afghanistan#Sprachen.

[292] https://de.wikipedia.org/wiki/Afghanistan#Religion.

[293] Ervand Abrahamian: *A History of Modern Iran*, p77.

[294] Jacques Leclerc: *L'aménagement linguistique dans le monde – Iran*, Université Laval Québec, 1. März 2015, downloaded 8. 7. 2015.

[295] https://de.wikipedia.org/wiki/Iran#Religion.

[296] https://de.wikipedia.org/wiki/Afghanistan.

[297] https://de.wikipedia.org/wiki/Ahmad_Schah_Durrani.

[298] Jörg Mittelsten Scheid: *Pulverfass Pakistan.*.

[299] https://de.wikipedia.org/wiki/Paschtunen.

Pashtun tribes, such as the Kharoti, to split, and hundreds of Afghan villages to be separated. About a third of the Afghan territory fell to the British. The British colonial power also aimed to better protect the northwestern border of its territory, then-British India, from the expanding Tsarist Russia by establishing a strategic buffer zone. [300]'[301]The rupture of the Pashtun habitat has never been overcome and is also the cause of the current political problems between Pakistan and Afghanistan and the military problems in the unexplored border area.

' In 1947, the state of Pakistan was founded, including Pashtun areas. The Afghani Loja Jirga of 1949 then declared the Durand Line invalid, as the original agreement with the British and not with the Pakistani government had been agreed; The Vienna Convention on the Law of Treaties, according to which a bilateral treaty cannot be challenged by unilateral opposition, has not been ratified by either Afghanistan or Pakistan. [302].'[303] So Afghanistan expressed that it no longer recognized the fact that it was parting with the Pashtun areas of Afghanistan and thus actually reclaiming it.

In support of his claim, Afghanistan leaned more towards India and the then Soviet Union. This put Pakistan in a two-front position, on the one hand against India, with which it still had to fight the never-ending conflict over Kashmir, and on the other hand against Afghanistan. That is why Pakistan has always sought to bind Afghanistan more closely and has thus also counteracted secular tendencies in Afghanistan, firstly because of Afghanistan's attachment to the Soviet Union, and later because of its Western influence, while also supporting intra-Afghan militias and, later, the Taliban.

'After 1992, ethnic conflicts marked the clashes between the mujahedeen. The traditional rulers of Afghanistan were the Pashtuns, and they also form the vast majority of the Taliban movement. The fall of the Taliban regime in 2001 gave an alliance of Tajiks, Hazaras and Uzbeks the opportunity to enforce an agreement on the division of power. The Pashtuns have since been subjected to retaliatory attacks. There were also conflicts between Sunnis and Shiites under the Taliban.'[304]

'The barely-monitored demarcation line regained public awareness as a result of the anti-terror struggle following the 9/11 attacks. Taliban fighters and Al-Qaeda supporters were relatively unhindered in the area, finding protection in the Pashtun Autonomous Region in Pakistan. Thus, establishing an official borderline for the further peace and stability of both countries was of enormous importance and played a key role in peace negotiations.' [305]

Syed Irfan Ashraf writes: 'When the USA attacked Afghanistan in 2001, a motley crowd of thousands of foreign fighters fled across the Durand Line ... and spread to the seven districts of the Federally Administered Tribal Areas (FATA). Over the next few years, the newcomers networked with local radical groups from Pashtuns, and together they took control of the semi-autonomous FATA territories. Since then, the Pashtun areas have become (...) the most important recruitment area for terrorists and unsophisticated youth from all over Pakistan flock here to be trained by local "divine warriors" in armed struggle and then, after crossing the border, the "unbelievers" attack foreign troops in Afghanistan. The Taliban have succeeded in turning the tribal belt of Pakistan into a training center for radicals.

At the beginning of their reign of terror, the militants first broke the political and social order in the mountainous tribal areas and murdered over 8,000 Taliban leaders and so-called tribal elders. In 2007, violence in FATA areas continued to increase. The first units of unemployed youths were trained enough to carry the terror into the adjacent areas of Pakhtunkhwa and assist the Afghan Taliban across the

---

[300] Habibo Brechna: *Die Geschichte Afghanistans.*

[301] https://de.wikipedia.org/wiki/Durand-Linie.

[302] http://afghanic.de/images/Docs/Durand%20Line%20Agreement.pdf Durand Line Agreement 12 1.1893, downloaded 11. 12. 2014.

[303] https://de.wikipedia.org/wiki/Durand-Linie.

[304] https://de.wikipedia.org/wiki/Afghanistan#Ethnien.

[305] https://de.wikipedia.org/wiki/Durand-Linie.

border. The terrorists had five years to conquer all the Pashtun areas of Pakistan and Afghanistan from remote tribal lands, while the rulers of Islamabad looked away.'[306]

It was not until the riots in June 2007, as a result of a rebellion in the Red Mosque (Lal Masjid), which paralyzed the capital, Islamabad, that people were shaken awake. Finally, the military besieged the Red Mosque and ended the student riots that had lasted for 18 months. Armed students who resisted were shot at and the storming killed the hundred occupants in the mosque. In response, radicals from other Koran schools and jihadists attacked the Pakistani state. Al Qaeda-supported radicals within tribal areas had been waiting for such an opportunity.

After the security forces launched a total of nine military operations, all in predominantly Pashtun territory, Pakistan became a battleground. The attempt by the state to end violence with counter-violence led to even more violence. One thing, however, made this tragic episode clear – religious extremism was not a Pashtun culture (as previously believed in Pakistan). Rather, the years of official toleration of jihadism had led to the spread of religious academies and groups of "divine warriors" and widespread radicalization in Pakistan and Afghanistan.'[307]

'When, after 2001, Al Qaeda cadres arrived in the tribal areas, Pashtun nationalists and tribal elders feared that the specter of war could return. In addition, the Taliban represented a very strict interpretation of Islam, which is incompatible with Pashtun culture. For these reasons, nationalist and progressive Pashtuns resisted the Taliban and Al Qaeda in the vast tribal areas. However, they had to go through a lot before security forces beat the Taliban in the Swat Valley in early 2009.'[308]

2.2.3 Afghanistan as a plaything of eastern and western globalization and the religious Resistance against it

Wikipedia writes: 'In Afghanistan, Russian and British colonial interests (The Great Game) collided. Since the establishment of the Imperial Russian Navy by Tsar Peter the Great, Russia's policy of expansion has been to advance to the Indian Ocean and build an ice-free port there. In order to forestall Russia, the British tried in vain to defend Afghanistan from 1839-1842. When they retreated, 'they were attacked at the Khyber Pass and killed all the soldiers, including 690 British and 2840 Indian, but also 12,000 civilians.'[309] It was only in another 1878-80 war that the British succeeded in asserting themselves in Afghanistan.

A puppet was installed 'as king. At the same time, the British took over Afghan foreign policy for the next 40 years. Due to many uprisings in Afghanistan, the country was divided by the Durand Line in 1893 by the British and the south-eastern area (the present-day Pakistani provinces NWFP, FATA and a small part of Balochistan) were incorporated into the Indian Crown Colony'[310]

In May 1919, Afghanistan attempted to free itself from British colonial aspirations and finally by threatening to move closer to Russia on August 8, 1919, it succeeded in 'recognizing Afghanistan as a sovereign and independent state through Britain.' However, a large part of the areas was lost, which was awarded the Indian Crown Colony or today, the State of Pakistan. 'Independent Afghanistan was a buffer between Russian and British interests.'[311]

' Since 1933 a constitutional kingdom led by Sahir Shah Mohammed (Mohammedzai) existed. But Sahir Shah caused a democratic turnaround in Afghanistan. However, Shah's progressive and Western

---

[306] Syed Irfan Ashraf: *Paschtunen in Pakistan: Warum der Krieg gegen den Terror verloren geht,* https://www.boell.de/de/navigation/asien-Pakistan-Warum-der-Krieg-gegen-den-Terror-verloren-geht-DSAFGHANISTAN11-13515.html.

[307] Syed Irfan: Ashraf: Paschtunen in Pakistan ... I

[308] Ibid.

[309] https://de.wikipedia.org/wiki/Afghanistan.

[310] Ibid.

[311] Ibid.

policies were not uncontroversial among the Afghan population. [312] Following Daoud's fall in the Saur Revolution of 1978, the communist-oriented People's Democratic Party of Afghanistan, led by Nur Muhammad Taraki, seized power in Kabul, declared the Democratic Republic of Afghanistan [DVPA], and with Soviet support, sought a social transformation, such as rural literacy.'313 'Strengthening the secular government of Afghanistan should prevent the spread of radical Islam to the Central Asian Soviet republics (Turkmenistan, Uzbekistan, Tajikistan, and Kyrgyzstan). [314]'315

'In particular, the forced secularization, disempowerment and partial expulsion of previously privileged groups quickly led to widespread resistance, which was soon supported and financed by the CIA. Around 30 mujahedin groups were founded during this time. There were also political disputes and power struggles within the DVPA. With the assassination of Tarakis in September 1979, Hafizullah Amin took over power and tried to quell the resistance. As a result, the civil war escalated.'316

' Taraki had repeatedly and urgently requested Soviet military assistance since the end of 1978 to combat internal civil unrest. At that time, the Soviet Union rejected military aid because of the high foreign policy risk among other things. However, as the KGB now feared that Amin might look in the direction of the West and call in NATO forces to secure his power, voices within the USSR's leadership calling for temporary military intervention increased. When relations with the West reached a new low after the NATO double decree of December 12, 1979, this position prevailed and Leonid Ilyich Brezhnev gave the order. The aim of this invasion was to establish a pro-Soviet, Moscow-aligned regime in Kabul and to forcibly pacify the country and thereby also secure the southern flank of the Soviet Union.'317

' With the invasion of Soviet troops in December 1979, the Civil War developed into a 10-year proxy war between the Soviet occupying power and the Islamic guerillas (mujahed-din), supported by the United States, Saudi Arabia and Pakistan.' 318 'This finally ended with the withdrawal of Soviet troops in 1989. The Soviet-backed government under President Mohammed Najibullah was able to hold on until the inauguration of Kabul by the mujahedin in 1992. [319] In April 1992, the Islamic State of Afghanistan was founded by the Peshawar Agreement. After that, there were various battles between different tribal militias with and against the government residing in Kabul.' 320

' On September 27, 1996, the Taliban invaded Kabul and established the Islamic Emirate of Afghanistan, which was only recognized by Pakistan, Saudi Arabia and the United Arab Emirates. However, the government of the Islamic State of Afghanistan, to which Defense Minister Massoud belonged, remained the internationally recognized government of Afghanistan (based at the United Nations).' 321

Because the United States identifies 'Al Qaeda members of Saudi Arabian-born Osama bin Laden, who was based in the Taliban emirate and allied with the Taliban, as perpetrators of the terrorist attacks of September 11, 2001' 'in October 2001, the United States launched an invasion of Afghanistan through a military alliance under its leadership.' 'At the end of 2003, a constituent, Loja Jirga, was convened to ratify the new Afghan constitution in January 2004.'322

312 Sophie Mühlmann: *"Vater der Nation" Sahir Schah begraben*. In: Welt Online. 24. Juli 2007 (welt.de [downloaded 1. 6. 2016).
313 https://de.wikipedia.org/wiki/Afghanistan
314 Joseph J. Collins: *Understanding War in Afghanistan*.
315 https://de.wikipedia.org/wiki/Sowjetische_Intervention_in_Afghanistan.
316 Ibid..
317 Ibid..
318 https://de.wikipedia.org/wiki/Afghanistan.
319 Nikolas K. Gvosdev: *The Soviet Victory That Never Wap*.Foreign Affairs 10. December 2009.
320 https://de.wikipedia.org/wiki/Afghanistan.
321 Ibid..
322 Ibid..

The Taliban and the religious adversaries of every secularization went underground. For reconstruction, overcoming backwardness and protection against attacks by various militias, the democratic secular government in Afghanistan was politically economically and militarily supported by the western states.

It is clear from the above how Afghanistan came into the midst of Russian and British globalization and the traditional and especially religious forces rebelled and are still rebelling against it.

2.2.4 The development and role of militias in Afghanistan

Militias are armed groups that spontaneously form for criminal, political, national, but also religious motives or common defense. Often, it is also a combination of these motifs or the motifs change.

Militias finance themselves, recruit militants and often pursue their goals through criminal activities, such as blackmail, compulsory levies, robbery and acts of violence, and even terror. The transition to criminal gangs is fluid. However, their actions are only illegal as long as they do not yet dominate an area and are recognized as a state authority by other countries.

Militias arise when the state order fails or cannot be enforced everywhere due to ineffectiveness. This was also the case in Afghanistan. As shown, the secularization favored by Russia and Britain met with the strongly patriarchal-orientated rural population of Afghanistan living in religious tribes and clans. When the People's Democratic government was supported by Soviet troops, the fight against the Russian occupiers even became a national task. Innumerable militia formed, which, although there were no legal combatants, were enormously militarily strengthened by many different countries and for many different motives.

Claudia Hangen quotes Sayed Yaqub Ibrahimi, who has been working for the *Institute for War and Peace Reporting (IWPR)*, headquartered in London, since March 2004: '"Warlords, like the Taliban, are fundamentalists. They think in a similar way but wear different clothes. There are 20 warlords throughout Afghanistan, some of whom even hold key positions in the Hamid Karzai government", says Sayed Yaqub Ibrahimi. ... As one of the few independent journalists in the multi-ethnic state, he has contacts with all political and ethnic groups in the country.'[323]

The militias were mostly supported by Pakistan because Pakistan wanted to have an acceptable government in Kabul that did not cooperate with either the Russians or the Indians. The Western powers, and especially the USA, did not want a socialist Afghanistan dependent on the Soviet Union. Saudi Arabia was primarily concerned with stifling secular development and, if possible, a radically Sunni-oriented state.

As is known, it was possible to expel the Soviets from Afghanistan and overthrow the left-wing government as well. But the militias had become so strong and, in order to consolidate their power, had entrusted the tribes or murdered the tribal elders, so that the traditional tribal order was largely destroyed and only the radical Taliban remained as the only traditional power of order, who, in mountainous and rugged areas, are difficult to combat.

The role of the militia leaders in Afghanistan's development and politics shows very impressively the role of Abdul Rashid Dostum. Wikipedia writes: 'Abdul Rashid Dostum (...) is a former Afghan militia leader. Dostum is considered to be a representative of the Uzbek minority and attributed to it. During the Soviet occupation, he became a general in the Afghan government army. After the withdrawal of the Soviets, he built his own militia, with which he fought in changing alliances and gained control of several provinces in the north of the country. After the conquest of its northern strongholds by the Taliban in 1997 and 1998, he fled into exile in Turkey. In 2001, he returned to Afghanistan. Since the fall of the Taliban in the

---

[323] Claudia Hangen: *Die Macht der afghanischen Warlords*, http://www.heise.de/tp/artikel/28/28370/1.html.

same year, he has been a member of the government led by Hamid Karzai and has been able to regain part of his former position of power in the north of the country.' [324]

' Dostum is one of the most contentious individuals in recent Afghan history. [[325]] Human rights organizations blame him for numerous serious war crimes and his rule over the northern provinces he controls is considered brutal. His Chuvian-i Melli forces are accused of looting and ill-treatment of civilians in the Kabul area in the 1992-1995 period. [[326]] In addition, during the two re-conquests of Masar-e-Sharif and the surrounding areas in 1997 and 2001, the militias were charged with the targeted expulsion, ill-treatment and murder of thousands of ethnic Pashtuns and massacres of captured Taliban members. [[327]] He was also infamous for his frequent change in allies: between 1979 and 2000, he had used virtually every major group in Afghanistan both as an ally and an opponent.

At the same time, however, Dostum is also credited with the establishment of an efficient administrative system in the areas he controls. He succeeded in creating the framework for a nationally flourishing economy and, until the Taliban's conquest of Masar-e Sharif in 1997, staved off the battles that had been widespread throughout country since the Soviet invasion. The city of Masar-e-Sharif was generally considered the last island of peace and prosperity in Afghanistan in the 1990s. This was also helped by the fact that Dostum was the only one of the militia leaders that was not Islamist: despite his authoritarian rule, his secular politics enabled people in the areas he controlled to achieve personal freedom unrivaled in the rest of the country. In the rest of Afghanistan, under the Taliban, women were forcibly denied any paid work and girls were forbidden to attend school. In Dostum's territory, about 1,800 women studied at the Balch University in Masar-e-Sharif, most of them without any form of concealment. At the same time, famous musicians and dancers, who were no longer allowed to perform in Kabul, sought refuge in Dostum territory. [[328]][[329]]'[330]

This militia leader then served under President Hamid Karzai Minister, and after the last election on April 5, 2014, under the new President, Ashraf Ghani, as Vice President. But Dostum is still a militia leader and also plays with military targets that he cannot enforce in the government to do with his own militia. *Orf.at* reports: Dostum 'has spent months trying to persuade the government to launch an offensive against extremists in the north of the country, the New York Times wrote this week [20.08.2015]. However, after apparently not being heard by the National Security Council of his country, he has now taken the book into his own hands - according to the motto "back to the roots". He had already called his militias to arms in July, turned his palace in the province of Jowzjan on the border with Turkmenistan into a command center and announced his fight against the Taliban in the neighboring provinces of Faryab and Sar-i Pul. Numerous local militias, many of them with heavy weapons, had joined his cause "despite an expensive disarmament campaign," wrote an American newspaper.'[331]

The unstable political situation in Afghanistan cannot be summed up better than the fact that in one country, the vice-president is, at the same time, a militia leader.

2.3 Ottoman Empire
The most representative country, both for early globalization and as an example of

---
[324] https://de.wikipedia.org/wiki/Abdul_Raschid_Dostum.

[325] Frank Clements: *Conflict in Afghanistan*, p.74 ff.

[326] Human Rights Watch: Blood-Stained Hands: Past Atrocities in Kabul and Afghanistan's Legacy of Impunity Human Rightp.2005.

[327] Human Rights Watch: World Report, 2003: Events of 2002 (November 2001 – November 2002). HRW 2003. ISBN 1-56432-285-8. p.189 f.

[328] Achmed Raschid: Taliban: *Islam, Oil and the New Great Game in Central Asia,*, p.57.

[329] Angelo Rasanayagam: *Afghanistan: A Modern History*, p.154.

[330] https://de.wikipedia.org/wiki/Abdul_Raschid_Dostum.

[331] http://orf.at/stories/2294465/2294466/.

1. the difficulties of secularization of a Muslim country,
2. increasing internal social tensions of a multi-ethnic country with increasing nationalism,
    is the development of the Ottoman Empire to the Republic of Turkey.

2.3.1 Development of the Ottoman Empire.

Wikipedia writes: '1299 is traditionally considered the founding year of the Ottoman Empire. ... On July 27, 1302, the Ottomans led their first battle against a Byzantine army (Battle of Bapheus / Battle of Koyun-hisar), which ended with a victory for the Ottomans. According to the Byzantine scholar, Georgios Pachymeres, it was this victory over the Byzantine army that earned Osman fame in much of Anatolia. Thus, July 27, 1302 is regarded as the day of the founding of the dynasty. [332]'[333] 'The Ottoman Empire emerged from the remnants of the Rum-Seljuk Sultanate, and for several centuries was the decisive power in Asia Minor, the Near East, on the Balkans, North Africa and Crimea.'[334]

'The era of Suleiman I (1520-1566) is usually considered the culmination of the power of the Ottoman Empire. In Ottoman and Turkish historiography, he was nicknamed "Kānūnī" ("lawmakers") because under his rule, a number of laws were created, which should fill in the gaps in the provisions of the Sharia and consolidate and codify the positive law. [335] In the Western world, he is called "the Magnificent." He is also considered one of the greatest art patrons of the Ottoman rulers. His reign includes the architectural masterpieces of Mimar Sinan. Through many campaigns, Suleiman extended the empire to the west, east and southeast.'[336]

2.3.2 Decline of the Ottoman Empire, especially because of backwardness in relation to Europe and insufficient willingness to reform

'Even during the reign of Suleiman, there were the first symptoms of a crisis, which increased over time and initiated the decline of the Ottoman Empire. Thus, the Tımare, non-hereditary fiefs, with which the Spahi riders financed their livelihood and their equipment, were increasingly awarded to unauthorized persons, which led to a weakening of this core troop of the army. Because hardly any new territories were conquered, there was a lack of land that could be integrated into the Tımare system. The Tımare were therefore awarded in ever smaller denominations, which also weakened the Spahis.

The fewer troops that could finance themselves through Tımare, the more had to be paid, which put the High Gate before financial tasks that they could not cope with. The methods used by the Grand Viziers and the Diwan to remedy the empire's chronic financial woes, which had been going on since the sixteenth century, aggravated the crisis. On the one hand, a tax lease was introduced. The so-called "malikâne": the right to collect a certain tax, was auctioned off, which gave the taxpayers the sum immediately. The taxpayers named "Mültezim" were now trying to squeeze out a lot more tax from their assigned area than they paid at the auction, which made them hateful of the taxable rural population.

As a result, there was widespread corruption across the Ottoman Empire - without "gifts" or bribes nothing worked any more with the authorities. The widespread saleability of offices had contributed to this since the 17th century. On the one hand, this filled the treasury and especially the pockets of Grand Viziers and Beylerbeys responsible for the occupation of vacant jobs and posts with considerable sums. On the other hand, it also brought many incompetent and untrained staff for the respective tasks in office, who tried, in the shortest possible time, to amortize the amount invested for the purchase of the office. The consequence was the intensified exploitation of the common people.

---

[332] Devlet-i Aliyye – Osmanlı İmparatorluğu Üzerine Araştırmalar I – Klasik Dönem (1302-1606), p.17.
[333] https://de.wikipedia.org/wiki/Osmanisches_Reich.
[334] Ibid.
[335] Özay Mehmet: *Fundamentalismus und Nationalstaat*, p.95.
[336] https://de.wikipedia.org/wiki/Osmanisches_Reich.

Another means of restoring public finances was repeated coin deterioration by reducing the silver content of the Akçe, the currency of the Ottoman Empire, by reducing the coins or by adding base metals. The result was a significant inflation. The prices rose, among which especially the simple population suffered. Another reason for the decline in value of the coins came from the West: Because the Atlantic trade poured large quantities of silver from the Spanish colonial empire into Europe, its value fell. [337]'338

'The expansion of the Christian states overseas had further negative consequences for the Ottoman Empire. With the discovery of the sea route around Africa, the Ottomans lost their monopoly on the India trade. Although the caravans brought valuable luxury goods to the ports of the Levant in the sixteenth and seventeenth centuries via Spice Street and Frankincense Street, their share of world trade continued to decline in comparison with the Atlantic trade.' 339

' Also, in the Mediterranean maritime trade, the Ottomans lost more and more importance.'340 'In 1536, the first so-called Capitulation [Privileges of the Sultan] was signed with France, which agreed free trade and transferred to France the jurisdiction over its subjects on the soil of the Ottoman Empire. .' 341

'Later, more Capitulationss followed in France and also in other European countries. They granted considerable advantages to European merchants in the Ottoman Empire vis-à-vis local merchants, especially with regard to tariffs. For trading rights in the Ottoman Empire, European states awarded tribute or military aid. However, the form of the treaties meant that the Ottoman merchants in the European states had no commercial advantages. This led in the long run to the fact that the economic position of the Ottoman Empire deteriorated compared to the European competition. [342]

The economic and military development backlog led to the fact that in the 18th and especially 19th century, the agreements, which were still partly described as Capitulations, had negative consequences for the Ottoman Empire. In the 18th century, for example, the commercial disadvantages of Ottoman merchants led to more and more native Christian merchants being formally designated as translators and placed under the protection of a European state. They benefited from the commercial rights, but were also partially deprived of the influence of the state. [343] Only the Russian Empire had around 180,000 Orthodox Greeks in 1808, known as "Protegees"."[344]'345 'With the Tanzimat reforms, the Ottomans tried to stop the slow decline of their empire, especially in comparison to the emerging, industrializing powers of Europe.' 346 'But also during the Tanzimatära, the weakness of the Ottoman Empire led to the conclusion of unequal trade agreements. This applies, in particular, to the Ottoman-English Treaty of 1838. In the Paris Peace Treaty of 1856, although the High Gate was included in the European system of power, the state was supported by a conditional modernization, but the capitulations remained. [347]'348

'The Ottoman ships were soon technically inferior to those of the Europeans, who invested their trading profits in technical innovations such as the Galeasse. In other areas, too, there was a technical lag between the Ottomans and Christian Europe. The Sultans were not very innovative - Bayezid II had banned book printing with movable type, for example, in 1483, on pain of death. Therefore, in their soon-to-be-created factories, Christians were able to manufacture products significantly more cheaply and

337 Halil İnalçık und Donald Quataert (Hrsg.): *An economic and social history of the Ottoman Empire*, p.XIX.
338 https://de.wikipedia.org/wiki/Osmanisches_Reich.
339 Ibid.
340 Ibid.
341 Ibid.
342 Neumann: *Ein besonderes Imperium (1512-1596)*. In: Kleine Geschichte der Türkei, p.134.
343 Neumann: *Das kurze 18. Jahrhundert*. In: Kleine Geschichte der Türkei, P.280.
344 Neumann: *Das Osmanische Reich in seiner Existenzkrise*. In: Kleine Geschichte der Türkei, p.303 f.
345 https://de.wikipedia.org/wiki/Kapitulationen_des_Osmanischen_Reiches.
346 https://de.wikipedia.org/wiki/Tanzimat.
347 Schölch: *Wirtschaftliche Durchdringung und politische Kontrolle*, p.409, p.411.
348 https://de.wikipedia.org/wiki/Kapitulationen_des_Osmanischen_Reiches.

flooded the empire with their manufactured goods. The result was unemployment among artisans and manufacturing workers in the cities and a passive trade balance under which the Ottoman Empire suffered permanently since the 17th century. Exports of food, such as grain, which could have balanced the balance, were banned in order to secure the supply of bread for the population. However, they were smuggled to an extent that was sufficient for repeated supply crises.

The growing dissatisfaction of large sections of the ordinary population was reflected in a series of uprisings, such as the Celali uprisings, that barely allowed Anatolia to settle down between 1519 and 1598. Because the rural population suffered particularly from increasing tax pressures, inflation and corruption, many farmers left their homesteads. They moved into the cities, into inaccessible mountain areas or joined the insurgents or marauding robber gangs, the so-called Levent, who were often led by former Spahis whose Timare were no longer sufficient for a decent living. The rural exodus, the consequences of which can still be felt today in the structural problems of Anatolian agriculture, aggravated the problems, since without the peasants, the Timare no longer made any profit, the food supply of the population became more difficult and escaped the fiscal taxpayers.

The state was largely helpless against these manifold and mutually reinforcing symptoms of crisis. After the death of Suleiman I, unsuitable personalities repeatedly sat on the sultan throne, such as the alcoholic Selim II, the mentally retarded Mustafa I, Murad IV, who on his accession to the throne, was only eleven years old, and there was also İbrahim the Crazy. They were mostly under the influence of their wives or mothers, the Valide Sultan, who had no educational background to the government of a large empire and were not allowed to leave the harem, but still ruled the kingdom de facto. It is therefore called, in the late 16th and the first half of the 17th century, the period of the petticoat government ("kadınlar saltanatı"). The Grand Viziers were also powerless against the women of the harem, who were appointed and dismissed at the discretion of the harem dwellers. During the rule of the wives, the average term of office of a Grand Vizier was only a little more than a year, too short to initiate the necessary reform measures.' [349]

The so-called petticoat government at the court of the Sultan explains itself also from the Islamic sex relations. The woman is, for the man, primarily a sex partner and mother of his children. The father has a godlike position in Islamic families for children as well, and according to the Koran, the mother has a special role for the children so that they are emotionally more concerned with the mother than with the father. Incidentally, when a new sultan takes office, his father has already died. The mother is, for the sons, thus a closer counselor and interlocutor than the wives. 'The respect and esteem in favor of Walide is evident in the Islamic proverb: "Paradise lies under the feet of the mother".' [350]

'In 1783, Russia annexed the Crimea and began its economic development.' In 1792, at the Peace of Jassy, the Ottoman Empire suffered further 'territorial losses, including the Dnepr-Bug area.' [351]

'In Egypt, governor Muhammad Ali Pasha gradually took power and liquidated the influential Mamluk emirs. Through a series of reforms Egypt was soon superior in many respects to the headquarters in Constantinople. Muhammad Ali founded a dynasty, whose rule over Egypt came to an end only in the middle of the 20th century.' [352]

The Ottoman Empire became more and more the plaything of the European powers. 'Russia saw it as a chance to increase its influence in Europe and, in particular, to gain access to the Mediterranean and the Balkans. Ottoman rule in the Balkans seemed threatened and Russia was pressing for control of the important straits of the Bosporus and Dardanelles. In the Balkans, Russia came into play as the

---

[349] https://de.wikipedia.org/wiki/Osmanisches_Reich.
[350] Esmeray: "*Das Reich der Osmanen*".
[351] https://de.wikipedia.org/wiki/Osmanisches_Reich.
[352] Ibid.

protector of Orthodox Christians there. Earlier, the Russian Tsar had tried in vain to win over the governments of Austria and the United Kingdom for a partition of the Ottoman Empire. Britain and France, however, locked themselves against this Russian expansion. They did not want the key positions to fall into Russian hands and supported the Ottomans in order to maintain the status quo and thereby secure their own sovereignty in Southeastern Europe on the Ottoman borders.'[353]

2.3.3 The collapse of the Ottoman Empire due to increasing national aspirations of its different ethnicities.

As long as nationalism did not capture the people of the Ottoman Empire, the various ethnic groups and religious groups lived peacefully in the Ottoman Empire. The non-Sunnis had a legally lower status. They had to pay a special poll tax, but were exempt from military service. With Western influence came nationalism. 'Inside the awakening national consciousness of its people and ethnic groups came an increasing disturbance of the "delicate balance between official inequality and relative tolerance." [[354]]'[355]

'For the multinational Ottoman state nationalism, which increasingly made groups of peoples in the territories occupied by them' feel as nations, was therefore an ever-growing problem. 'First, the Serbs rose in 1804; By 1830, they were granted extensive autonomy. In 1830 'Greece was given independence.'[356]

'The Sultan, as well as conservative and liberal elites of the empire, saw, with increasing suspicion, that a small section of the Armenian ruling class sought reforms and sought protection from European powers. The independence efforts of the Armenians 'intensified, also supported by the political parties that emerged in the 1880s. In 1890, the Dashnak Party formed, which propagated a people's war against the Ottoman government. [[357]] In 1890, Armenian terrorists also began to target and murder Ottoman officials. [[358]]

...In return, from 1891, the sultan created irregular cavalry units after the model of the Cossacks and in the tradition of Akıncı [[359]] and Deli [[360]], which were named *Hamidiye* in his honor. They were mainly recruited from loyal Kurdish tribes and were rewarded with tax exemption and the right to plunder. Officially, they were supposed to protect the border with Russia, but in fact served as a domestic fighting force against the Armenians.[[361]] ....

Growing nationalism intensified the already longstanding tensions between Armenians and Kurds. These had a cause in the dispute over the so-called kischlak (winter pastures) of the Kurdish shepherd nomads in Armenian villages. In addition, the Kurds, sometimes by force, levied irregular taxes in the form of money, natural resources or fringe services from the Armenians, who, like all Ottoman nationals, were under enormous tax pressure. The Ottoman authorities were often unable or unwilling to protect

[353] Ibid.

[354] Norman M. Naimark: *Flammender Haß. Ethnische Säuberungen im 20. Jahrhundert*, p.32.

[355] https://de.wikipedia.org/wiki/V%C3%B6lkermord_an_den_Armeniern.

[356] https://de.wikipedia.org/wiki/Osmanisches_Reich.

[357] Yves Ternon: *Tabu Armenien: Geschichte eines Völkermordes*, p.61ff.

[358] Arnold Hottinger: *Sieben Mal Naher Osten. München 1972*, p.40.

[359] >>a member of irregular - so mostly unpaid and dependent on robbery and slave trade - equestrian troops of the Ottomans.<< https://de.wikipedia.org/wiki/Ak%C4%B1nc%C4%B1.

[360] >>Brave, heroic, daring, reckless, insane, madman ... the name of a single rider or mounted federation of Ottoman provincial troops who fought felicitously on the enemy in battle. It should have been the deli mostly intoxicated by opium.<< https://de.wikipedia.org/wiki/Deli_%28Soldat%29.

[361] Tessa Hofmann: *Annäherung an Armenien. Geschichte und Gegenwart*, P.85f.

the Armenians from such arbitrariness. [362] In the years 1894-1896, the tensions finally erupted in numerous pogroms against the Armenians.' [363]

In response to a tax rebellion, Turkish military and irregular Hamidiye units stormed the unruly villages in August 'after more than two weeks of bloody fighting. They killed between 900 and 4000 Armenians [364] and destroyed 32 of the 40 Armenian villages in the region.[365].'366. The nationalist aspirations of the Armenians are also the reason why the Turks, after the rise of Turkish nationalism, expelled Armenians from the territory of modern day Turkey and made them prey to destruction.

Uwe Becker writes: 'Over the course of its 600 years of existence in south-eastern Europe and the Middle East, the Ottoman Empire has developed into a multiconfessional community. It was crucial for the legal status and political identity of the subjects belonging to a recognized and autonomous religious community (Millet system).'367 'The majority of non-Muslims worked as peasants. Within the cities, non-Muslims worked as craftsmen, traders or money lenders, as well as in the classical disciplines: medicine, science, theology and diplomacy.'368

' The triumphal procession of the territorial state in Western Europe since the 16th century and the new conception of the nation state since the beginning of the 19th century, however, fundamentally called this system into question. In the field of conflict of competing interests, economic protection of influence, ethnic-cultural assimilation as well as national identification the foundations of political loyalty became obsolete and the multinational empire lost its raison d'être, as it were. In the context of these political, economic and cultural developments, the conditions of coexistence between Jews, Christians and Muslims in the Ottoman Empire changed [369].'370

Nationalist aspirations of Arabs in the Ottoman Empire were then fueled by the English and French in the First World War and led to the Ottoman Empire losing all areas south and east of modern day Turkey. Let's take a look at the development of the individual countries belonging to the former Ottoman Empire and then Turkey, which dreams of the rebirth of a Neo-Ottoman Empire.

2.4 Saudi-Arabia

The nomadic tribal leaders in the desert regions further away from Istanbul were independent of the Ottoman Empire, and even more so as the Ottoman Empire disintegrated. The most important desert tribes were the Hijaz, in the area around Mecca and the Saudis, who lived in the Hajj around Riyadh.

'The rule of the Hashimites in Mecca began in the 10th century.[371]'372 'Hussain I bin Ali, who, since 1908, had been Meerka's Great Sheriff, began the uprising against the Ottomans in 1916 during the First World War, led by Lawrence and supported by Arabia and the United Kingdom. However, Britain's promises of establishing an Arab kingdom after the war were not respected.' [373]

---

362 Tessa Hofmann: p.85f.

363 https://de.wikipedia.org/wiki/V%C3%B6lkermord_an_den_Armeniern.

364 Stefanos Yerasimos: Azgelişmişlik Sürecinde Türkiye. Istanbul 1977, p.554f.

365 Tessa Hofmann: 85f.

366 https://de.wikipedia.org/wiki/V%C3%B6lkermord_an_den_Armeniern.

367 http://www.osmanischesreich.de/kunst-kultur-1/recht-glaube/religi%C3%B6se-koexistens/.

368 http://www.osmanischesreich.de/geschichte/provinzen/milletsystem/.

369 Salem Kamel Isam: *Islam und Völkerrecht. Das Völkerrecht der islamischen Weltanschauung*, p.149 ff.

370 http://www.osmanischesreich.de/kunst-kultur-1/recht-glaube/religi%C3%B6se-koexistens/.

371 G. Rentz: *Hāshimidp*.In: Encyclopaedia of Islam. 2. Ausgabe, Bd. III, p.262.

372 https://de.wikipedia.org/wiki/Hussein_bin_Ali_(Hedschas).

373 https://de.wikipedia.org/wiki/Hedschas.

After the victory of the Saudis over the Hashemites in 1926, 'the kingdom of Hejaz was united with the Najd, and in 1932, part of the kingdom of Saudi Arabia.'[374] Thus, the Islamic sanctuaries of Mecca and Medina came within the sphere of power of the Saudis.

'As early as 1500, the Saudis governed one of the most important principalities in central Arabia. Muhammad bin Saud, who reigned from 1735-1765 made an alliance with Muhammad bin'Abd al-Wahhāb, the founder of the Wahhabis in 1744 in Diriyya (now a suburb of Riyadh). Bin Saud promised in his future kingdom that the Wahhabi interpretation of the Koran and Sunnah would be enforced as the only valid one, while Bin Abd al-Wahhab on the other hand pledged to religiously legitimize the claim to power of the Saudi ruler.'[375]

Daniel Steinvorth writes: 'Mohammed bin'Abd al-Wahhāb was born in 1703 in Uyaina, the son of a judge. Uyaina was located in Najd, home to nomads and sedentary tribes.' 'Two thinkers should inspire Abd al-Wahhab during his studies. One of them was the founder of the most conservative and smallest of four Sunni law schools, Bin Hanbal (780-855). He lived in a time when some Muslims tried to look at religion more realistically, for example, to distinguish between God and His Word. Bin Hanbal ran aground against this far-flung intellectualism. He was convinced of the "unfashionability" of the Koran. He rigorously rejected a metaphorical, non-literal interpretation of Scripture. Among the scholars in Najdd, his law school probably also dominated because it accommodated a simple view of religion and thus most closely responded to the needs of the people.

The second thinker whose writings Abd al-Wahhab read was Bin Taimiya (1268-1328). Influenced by chaotic times (the invasion of the Mongols, the plundering of Baghdad), this grim man calculated with all the innovations that he believed threatened Islam. All Greek philosophy and all forms of unorthodox Sufism were nothing but idolatry. Even visiting the tomb of the Prophet or celebrating his birthday is forbidden. Only the return to primitive Islam, as had been lived by the Prophet and his companions, could "cleanse" the religion. To achieve this goal, Muslims should not hesitate to go to war with their warriors against their enemies.'[376]

'For the hot young Abd al-Wahhab, it was clear that his countrymen had also betrayed Islam. Believing truly critical historians, superstition in his time was widespread. Bedouins and city dwellers not only worshiped dead, saints or angels, but even trees or stones. In his Kitab-al-Tauhid (Book of Unity of God), Abd al-Wahhab condemned these practices as worthy of death. Even those who doubted that deserved death. The idea of "takfir," that is, the excommunication of other religious brothers, became one of the preacher's main tenets. Inevitably, it had to lead to confrontation with all non-Wahhabis.'[377]

In 1744, the preacher was banished from his hometown and 'fled to an oasis further south, to Diryya. Here, he found refuge with the tribal leader Mohammed bin Saud. This equally ambitious and unscrupulous ruler of a hitherto insignificant small emirate quickly realized that he could use the immense explosive power of the teachings of Abd al-Wahhab for his military purposes. The Takfir doctrine allowed him to ruthlessly strike at enemies, ambush and rob neighboring villages at will, always under the banner of jihad.

Bin Saud and Abd al-Wahhab concluded a pact in the same year that was as simple as it was ingenious: while the Emir declared his willingness to enforce the doctrine in his domain, the preacher provided him with religious legitimacy. The conquerors had to choose between conversion and death and they also had to swear blind obedience to the new emir; this was also a religious maxim of Abd al-Wahhab, which is still valid today and explains why Saudi Arabia will remain an absolute monarchy for the foreseeable future.

---

[374] https://de.wikipedia.org/wiki/Saudi-Arabien.
[375] https://de.wikipedia.org/wiki/Saudi-Arabien.
[376] Daniel Steinvorth: *Quelle des Terrors*, in: Der Tagesspiegel Nr. 23 175/ 16.7.2017,Geschichte p. 2-3.
[377] Daniel Steinvorth: p 3.

While initially bin Saud's troops only attacked villages in the vicinity of the Diriyya, his successor in the second half of the eighteenth century succeeded in subjugating the whole of the Najd and parts of the neighboring area. For the first time since the 7th century, much of central Arabia now followed a single authority and a single interpretation of Islam. Before his death in 1792, Abd al-Wahhab made sure that his descendants, who from then on should be called the Family of the Sheikh ("Al Ash-Sheikh"), decided on religious questions. '[378]

' The Ottoman Empire had long watched the hustle and bustle along its borders, for the steppes and deserts in the interior of the Arabian Peninsula were of no economic or strategic importance to the Ottomans. It was only when the Wahhabis approached the birthplace of Prophet Muhammad that the sultan became nervous. News that the "Imam" al Saud not only expanded his reign in 1803, but also carried out destructive work there, finally roused the entire Islamic world ... Seven years, from 1811-1918, were needed by the Sultan Troops of the Egyptian Viceroy Mohammed Ali Pasha and his son Ibrahim Pasha to tame the spook from the desert.'[379]

The re-emergence of Saudi Arabia began with the return of Sheikh Abd al-Aziz 'from Kuwaiti exile and the conquest of Riyadh in 1902. In addition bin Saud was to prove himself master, in order to take advantage in his favor of the rivalry between the weakening Ottoman Empire and the expansionist Great Britain. When the Ottoman Empire collapsed after the First World War ... the playing field was freer for bin Saud.' He conquered the holy places of Mecca and Medina 'on December 5, 1925. Since then, and to this day, the Wahhabis are still setting the tone there. A day later, he proclaimed himself king, was immediately recognized by European colonial powers and continued to build his power on the Arabian Peninsula until in September 1932, when he established the new united Kingdom of Saudi Arabia.

The Wahhabi clergy, in reward for faithful service, ensured that the country was largely free from foreign cultural influences, secular science and anything that ran counter to the archaic view of the world and the humanity of scholars.'[380]

After much hesitation, bin Saud allowed 'the California Standard Oil Company to pay $25,000 a year and $1 per ton of drilling on the Persian Gulf. It was the beginning of a friendship that was as profitable as it was problematic.

During the Cold War, the House of Saudi in Washington was transfigured as the supposedly most important pro-American voice in an otherwise hostile region. With rapidly increasing oil revenues (...), which soon made Riyadh one of the most affluent customers of American weapons, the alliance solidified from year to year. The Americans saw the Saudis as a bulwark against communism.

Together with Pakistan, the Saudis supported the deployment of mujahedeen, fanatical religious fighters, in Afghanistan, which had been occupied by Soviet troops since 1980. Their plan to give the Soviets an "Afghan Vietnam" situation. According to the former US security adviser, Zbigniew Brzezinski, it even initiated the collapse of the Soviet empire.

But apparently, no-one knew what fatal long-term consequences this policy would have, namely the propagation of thousands of radical Islamists, among them the al-Qaeda leader-to-be, Osama bin Laden, a dissident descendant of the Saudi upper class. In addition to money, above all else, Saudi Arabia had given the jihadists ideological armaments on the way.

The Wahhabi ideology legitimized the fight against the "unbelieving" communists and also promised suicide bombers salvation. Through mosques and preachers, schools, colleges, hospitals and orphanages, Saudi petro-capitalism began exporting an Islamic model to every corner of the world since the 1960s. Thanks to satellite dishes and the Internet, today, the Wahhabi mission is easier than ever.'[381]

---

[378] Daniel Steinvorth: *Quelle des Terrors*, p 3.
[379] Ibid.
[380] Ibid.
[381] Daniel Steinvorth: loc. cit.

The Wahhabi form of Sunni Islam is its most archaic form, with floggings, public minds, hand-chipping, and extreme oppression of women, to the extent that women are not allowed to drive cars themselves.

By unlocking enormous oil reserves, Saudi Arabia became an extremely rich country. With only a small domestic population relative to its oil revenues, the Sunni elite could afford to provide basic services to every Saudi without having to sacrifice their luxury lives.

With their fanatical understanding of religion validated to all, the Wahhabis also felt called to proselytize the world and fight other interpretations of Islam. The Wahhabis support radical Sunni movements throughout the Islamic world and finance mosques, madrasas, and holy warriors. Bin Laden and Al Qaeda also have their origins in Saudi Arabia and the Taliban and the IS and Salafists around the world were funded by Saudis, albeit less by the ruling dynasty. Because along with the wealth in general comes the urge for political and military adventures, although this is waning and it is now more and more about ownership and power.

Governed by such interests, the ruling powers work together with foreign powers to secure their own state integrity and political position and there may also be changing alliances. In particular, Saudi Arabia has close military and political ties with the USA, even though the USA is actually the center of evil after Israel and when it comes to preventing the predominance of Shiite Iran, and it also works with Israel.

For Wahhabi hotspurs on the other hand, there is an ever-increasing number of princes who lose their religious zeal and are more likely to run a lottery, a thorn in the side of cooperation with the West, and especially with the USA, even if they also have bases in Saudi Arabia. This creates domestic tensions.

In addition to more than 29 million people in Saudi Arabia, 'more than six million people are legally residing foreigners'[382] who mostly work in the most difficult circumstances and do not enjoy the social benefits of the local Saudis. About 10 to 15% are Shiites. 'Over the past decades, and especially since the tensions of 2009, relations between the Sunni majority and the Shiite minority have intensified.'[383] There are, of course, secular Saudis who oppose religious oppression.

These various factions endanger royal power. The state therefore takes action against revolutionary groups in the country, but also financially supports militarily revolutionary authoritarian neighbors and therefore Al Sissi in Egypt.

The Saudis could not declare themselves Caliphs because they are not of Muhammad's family, but they call themselves *Guardians of the Holy Places*. Ideologically, the IS is ideologically close to Wahhabism. However, when the leader of the IS, Abu Bakr al-Baghdadi, declared himself to be the Caliph, that is, the leader of all Sunnis, he challenges the role of the Saudi king as *Guardian of the Holy Places* and Wahhabi religious leaders in their self-image as interpreters of the true faith. Thus, the IS became the common enemy of the royal family and Wahhabism. That is why both Sunni and Shiite regimes agree in the fight against ISIS. However, since ISIS loses its statehood in Iraq and Syria, only Turkey, with its Ottoman ambitions, remains a rival in leading the Sunni supremacy. The real antagonist of Saudi Arabia, however, is Iran, with which Saudi Arabia already leads proxy wars in Yemen, but also in Syria over religious and political dominance.

The Nuclear Agreement and the joint war against the IS had once again liberated Iran from its political and economic aftertaste. As the new American President, Donald Trump, wants to re-enforce sanctions on Iran, Saudi Arabia can lean back again on the USA, even though American-Saudi relations have been called into question by Trump's earlier rejection of Islam.

---

[382] https://de.wikipedia.org/wiki/Saudi-Arabien.
[383] Ibid.

2.5 Palestine and Jordan

Palestine and present-day Jordan had become British trust territories after the collapse of the Ottoman Empire. 'The British government took control of Palestine as a Mandate Territory with the intention of creating a buffer zone to the Suez Canal, [384] even though many politicians and officers were not convinced of strategic value of Palestine.[385]'386

In 1923, there were separate united areas to the east of Jordan and also 'under British protectorate, the emirate of Transjordan, with Abdallah bin Husain as head of state. He was assisted by the British general, John Bagot Glubb (Glubb Pasha), who, in 1939, established the Arab Legion as guardian of the royal family. On May 25, 1946 (National Day), the British mandate expired and Transjordan received its full independence. Abdallah I accepted the title of king'387

The obligation to give the Jews in Palestine their own state was associated with the fiduciary contract. This created the origin of the Israeli-Muslim conflict.

Jews who recognized that they were not recognized as equal citizens in other countries, especially in Eastern Europe, but even more because of the persecution of Jews in Nazi Germany, flocked to Palestine. Palestine was, for them, a land given to them by God. Jewish immigrants roused the resistance of non-Jews living there, especially Muslims, not only in Palestine, but also in the rest of the Islamic world.

After the partition of Palestine into a Jewish section, which then became Israel and an Arab part, it came immediately to violent confrontations and wars, in which Israel was able to extend beyond the area awarded to him at the expense of the Palestinians.

It was already the first post-partition war 'which ended with separate cease-fire agreements between Israel and its Arab neighbors under the auspices of the United Nations in 1949. They established strong borders for Israel, which included about 75 percent of Palestine. A strip on the south coast, stretching from Gaza to the Egyptian border, came under Egyptian administration, while the rest was incorporated into Jordan. Jerusalem was shared between Israel and Jordan. Many states did not recognize the division of Jerusalem.'388

The Palestinians, who previously lived in Israel, had largely fled or were expelled, and subsequently lived in large UN-subsidized refugee camps in the surrounding Arab countries.

'In the Six-Day War between Israel and the Arab States in 1967, Jordan lost all of its territory west of Jordan to Israel.' 389 In 1988, King Hussein renounced all claims to the Israeli-occupied West Bank for the benefit of the PLO Palestinian Liberation Organization. In fact, in 1980, Israel had already annexed East Jerusalem with the Old City. In addition, Israel also settled Jewish citizens in the remaining occupied Palestinian territories.

Accordingly, the administration of the Gaza Strip also moved from Egypt to Israel. 'The Israeli government approved the construction of Jewish settlements along the Gaza Strip. 8,000 settlers lived on 40% of the Gaza Strip in the Gush Katif settlement bloc in the southern Gaza Strip. These settlements were inaccessible to Arab residents of the Gaza Strip and cut them off from beaches and fields. For this purpose, a separate road system was built for settlers, separate from the Palestinian ones. '390

'Since the Gaza-Jericho Agreement (also known as the Cairo Agreement) in 1994, the Gaza Strip was under Palestinian Authority (Palestinian Autonomous Territories)' 391, but remained occupied by Israel.

---

384 Benny Morris: *1948 – A History of the First Arab-Israeli War*. New Haven 2008, p.9–11.

385 Tom Segev: *Es war einmal ein Palästina – Juden und Araber vor der Staatsgründung Israels*, p.216 f.

386 https://de.wikipedia.org/wiki/Pal%C3%A4stinakrieg.

387https://de.wikipedia.org/wiki/Jordanien.

388 https://de.wikipedia.org/wiki/Pal%C3%A4stinakrieg.

389 https://de.wikipedia.org/wiki/Jordanien.

390 https://de.wikipedia.org/wiki/Gazastreifen.

391 Ibid.

As a result of this development, the hatred of the Palestinians increased immeasurably and continued to be fueled by the expansive settlement of the Jews in occupied territories. Due to the incessant unrest and acts of violence, and 'after long domestic conflicts in 2005, Israeli Prime Minister, Ariel Sharon, enforced the withdrawal of Israelis from the Gaza Strip, and this is linked to the dismantling of all Israeli settlements.'[392] This withdrawal is probably the only thing the Palestinians could achieve in their fight against Israel.

The Palestinian resistance were

1. The secular Palestinian Liberation Organization (PLO), which is the authority of Fatah, a rather socialist party. It 'is a full member of Socialist International [393] and has observer status in the Social Democratic Party of Europe.'[394] and

2. the Islamic Mujahedin, from which Hamas emerged.

After the 1967 six-day war, that turned the Gaza Strip from Egyptian to Israeli, the Muslim Brotherhood in the Gaza Strip 'focused on the Islamization of its own society, including the construction of numerous mosques and madrasas. In doing so, it distinguished itself against secular, left-wing ideas, understood to be Western influences, as represented by the Palestinian Liberation Organization (PLO), founded in 1964. [395] For this purpose, in 1967, Yasin founded the Al-Mujama organization in the Schati refugee camp, which achieved its revenues from new Islamic-propagated fashion - headscarves and full-body veils for women and suits for men. It promoted the feeling of belonging to Muslims dressed in this way.'[396]

'In 1976, the Palestinian Muslim Brotherhood, under Yasin in Gaza City, founded the Islamist Center, which, in the following decade, became the center of power for all Islamist groups and institutions in the Gaza Strip. [397] Candidates from this center gradually gained leadership positions in professional organizations, Gaza University and other institutions previously dominated by leftist nationalists. Through moral and social aid, the fight against corruption and community projects, the Muslim Brotherhood in the Gaza Strip has gained a broad and solid base in the population. [398]'[399]

This makes it clear that, as is the case with Iran's development, tensions not only increased to the Jews and the Western world, but also to the secularized forces, and, in other words, to the PLO and Fatah, which played a major role in it. Tensions between the Islamists and Fatah led to Hamas being founded in December 1987. 'On August 18, 1988, Hamas published its founding charter. [400] This unites ideology and strategic considerations. [401][402]'[403]

Reading the charter makes it easy to see how little hope one can have for a cosmopolitan and secular development in the Muslim world. Here are some relevant excerpts from the charter:

---

[392] Ibid..

[393] List of members of the Socialist International, downloaded by Wikipedia 18. August 2013.
http://www.socialistinternational.org/viewArticle.cfm?ArticlePageID=931.

[394] https://de.wikipedia.org/wiki/Fatah.

[395] Beverley Milton-Edwards, Stephen Farrell: *Hamas: The Islamic Resistance Movement*, p.32-34.

[396] https://de.wikipedia.org/wiki/Hamas.

[397] Henrik Meyer: *Hamas und Hizbollah. Eine Analyse ihres Politischen Denkens*, p.86.-88.

[398] Muriel Asseburg: *Die palästinensische Hamas zwischen Widerstandsbewegung und Reformregierung*. In: Moderate Islamisten als Reformateure. Stiftung Wissenschaft und Politik, Berlin Februar 2007, P.38 (SWP-Studie [PDF; downloaded 25. November 2011].

[399] https://de.wikipedia.org/wiki/Hamas.

[400] Henrik Meyer: *Hamas und Hizbollah*, p.91.

[401] Englische Übersetzung der Hamas-Gründungscharta, The Middle East Media Research Institute (MEMRI).

[402] Hamas Charter (1988), kommentarlos, dokumentiert von palestinecenter.org.

[403] https://de.wikipedia.org/wiki/Hamas.

- ' Article 7 of the Charter states the killing of Jews, not just Jewish citizens of Israel or Zionists, as an absolute obligation for every Muslim by declaring it to be the precondition for the coming of the Last Judgment: "The hour of judgment will not come, before Muslims fight and kill the Jews so that the Jews hide behind trees and stones and every tree and stone will say: 'Oh Muslim, O servant of Allah, a Jew is behind me, come and kill him!"

- In Article 22, the Charter adopts the European anti-Semitic conspiracy theory of World Judaism as a fact: the Protocols of the Elders of Zion are real, the Freemasons, the Lions Club and the Rotary Club secretly worked "in the interest of the Zionists". The Jews are responsible for the French Revolution, "Western colonialism", communism and the world wars: "There is no war where they do not have their hands on the game ..." [404]

- From this, Article 32 concludes: "To leave the circle of conflict with Zionism is high treason. Everyone who does that should be cursed. 'Whoever turns his back on them [...] draws the wrath of Allah and his dwelling shall be hell ... (Quran, 8:16)'"[405]

Hamas pushed Fatah further and further out of the Gaza Strip. In 2007, a factional division of the Palestinian territories took place, which continues until recently. But nevertheless, we have to face a nearly insolvable conflict in Palestine.

Jordan, as the original part of the British Mandate, was affected in many ways by the conflicts in the Holy Land. We saw that Jordan was first awarded the later Palestinian anatomy area. It took in so many Palestinian refugees that they even became a threat to the Hashemite royal house and therefore, PLO-dependent Palestinians had to be expelled from Jordan. Nevertheless Jordan remained a socially stable country, and, as such, was able to live in peace with its neighbors.

'Jordan's foreign policy has been Western-oriented for decades. The kingdom is allied with the United States and belongs to its official category of being the most important ally outside of NATO. Jordan also has an association agreement with the EU.'[406]

Jordan is said to owe its inner stability to the fact that it has a 93% Sunni population and Sunni Islam is the state religion. In addition, 79% of the population lives in the cities[407], so they are more remote to traditional ways of life.

In general, it can be stated that Muslim states in which a religion predominates and whose representatives prevail, as well as in Saudi Arabia, Morocco, Indonesia and Iran, have relatively stable internal orders and, if they do not threaten other states, then they also play a balancing role internationally.

2.6 Syria, Iraq, IS Islamic State

The secularization of the image of man and of the social order based on the European model began in all countries liberated from European domination or supremacy by the military, supported by the young intelligentsia trained in Europe.

As we have already seen, the military, as far as they were not simply tribal militias, formed a foreign body in the Middle Ages in all Muslim societies. Like the Janissary or Mamelukes, they were often recruited from child slaves alienated from their families and loyal only to the ruler.

The colonial powers, too, could control their overseas territories only if they created military units of a European design from local people, who, though commanded by European generals, had a military hierarchy of natives. The members of the traditional elite did not like to become soldiers of the colonial powers. For the Alavites, a minority sect belonging to the lower strata in Syria, a military career was even a way to rise to become upper class.

---

[404] Auszug der Charta auf Deutsch in einer Rezension zu Jeffrey Herf.
[405] https://de.wikipedia.org/wiki/Hamas.
[406] https://de.wikipedia.org/wiki/Jordanien.
[407] Vgl. https://de.wikipedia.org/wiki/Jordanien.

The military also preferred to adopt the already decadent nationalism that had sparked two world wars in Europe. The military became the germ cells for independence aspirations. The intellectual armaments for their national ideals were given to the military by the intellectuals trained in Europe, who laid the ideological foundations for the Baath Party, which determined both Syria and Iraq.

Wikipedia writes: 'The Baath Party is formally based on the doctrine of a single undivided Arab nation and a nationwide Arab fatherland. Basic principles are unity, freedom and socialism. In essence, it is … secular.'[408] 'The party was founded in 1940 by the Syrian, Michel Aflaq, who comes from a Greek Orthodox Christian family and the Sunni Muslim, Salah al-Din al-Bitar, in Damascus. The date of the official unification and founding of the Arab Rebirth Party is dated April 7, 1947, and from July 1947, the newspaper A-ba'th appeared regularly. The predominantly intellectual followers at first united petty-bourgeois (non-Marxist, French) ideas of socialism and nationalist ideas (e.g., by Antun Sa'ada) instead of religious orientations.'[409]

'According to their nationalist-secular program, the Ba'ath Party preached unity (of the Arab fatherland), freedom (and independence from the colonial powers) and (an Arab) socialism of the "third kind". Because of the first point, the Ba'ath Party was a driving force for the unification of Syria with Egypt to the United Arab Republic (1958-1961) and upon its reissue of 1963, achieved the latter two goals, leading both to the adoption of Western conceptions of life and the Eastern bloc-originating conceptions of a modern socialist society.'[410]

'Instead of religious unity for all (Sunni) Muslims across national borders, Baathism demands national unity for all Arabs across religious boundaries; including Shiite, Christian Arabs, etc., and with no involvement of Turks and Persians. The Baath ideology is therefore basically secularist and implicates Islam as a religion of the Arabs. It defines them in her doctrine after "Art. 10: Arab is one whose language is Arabic and who seeks to live on Arab soil and believes in his connection with the Arab nation. "[411]'[412]

'The Baath party was organized strictly hierarchically, according to the principle of Democratic Centralism borrowed from the Eastern Bloc. For a career in the military, the bureaucracy or the unions a party membership was essential. In addition, non-party members were disadvantaged in admission to higher education. [413] The party tried to penetrate society through its sub-organizations for work, leisure, culture and education. Special attention to, according to the American historian, Ibrahim al-Marashi, the totalitarian state concept the party used, there was a penetration and so-called Baatherization of the armed forces, in order to receive the political power of the party. On the one hand, this was done through direct monitoring as well as through the formation of party-owned military structures parallel to regular armed forces. [414]'[415]

The centralism used by the eastern model came naturally close to the principles of a military hierarchy, but at the same time, had to promote further development into military dictatorships.

2.6.1 Syria

In Syria, on November 16, 1970, after the years of power struggles within the Baath Party, 'Hafiz al-Assad finally emerged as the winner. Assad, still Minister of Defense under Salah Jadid, had the former president and some of his supporters arrested in this so-called correctional movement, after he himself had spent some time in jail for political reasons. In 1971, he was elected with 99.2% of the votes (without

[408] https://de.wikipedia.org/wiki/Baath-Patei_%28Syrien%29.
[409] https://de.wikipedia.org/wiki/Baath-Partei.
[410] https://de.wikipedia.org/wiki/Baath-Partei.
[411] Andreas Meier: *Der politische Auftrag des Islam*, p.135.
[412] https://de.wikipedia.org/wiki/Baath-Partei.
[413] Efraim Karsh, Inari Rautsi: *Saddam Hussein - A political biography*, p.175-178.
[414] Ibrahim Al-Marashi, Sammy Salama: *Iraq's Armed Forces: An Analytical History*, p.8, p.124.
[415] https://de.wikipedia.org/wiki/Baath-Partei.

opposing candidates) to the presidency; in the same year, he became Secretary-General of the Baath Party.'[416]

'Many political parties in Syria have existed since the French Mandate. From 1963, however, the Ba'ath Party ruled in a one-party system: Article 8 of the constitution stipulates that "the Arab-Socialist Ba'ath Party directs society and the state." Since 1972, parties that accept the Ba'athist leadership and the Arab-Socialist as well as nationalist orientation have been allowed to act as members of the National Progressive Front (Unified List).'[417]

When the French assembled military auxiliaries in their protectorate territory, predominantly Alawites came forward. It should be remembered, and I quote from Wikipedia Syria, that 74% of the Syrian population were Sunnis [418] and only 12% were Alawites, [419][420] a little more than the Christians, who made up about 10% of the population. [421] In 1920 there were still 30% Christians.[422]

Ulrike Putz writes about the Alawites: 'About twelve percent of Syrians belong to the mysterious sect: on the one hand, their followers use the Koran, but on the other hand, they do not fast during Ramadan, but instead celebrate Christmas and believe in reincarnation. Alawites see their religious community as a secession of Shiite Islam. For centuries, the cohesive community lived in isolation from the outside world in the rugged Syrian mountains and along the shores of the Mediterranean. There they found shelter from their enemies.

But the seclusion that was part of the survival strategy of the religious minority came to an abrupt end in 1970. In the winter of this year, with Hafis al-Assad, an Alawite pushed seized power in a coup in Damascus. From then on, whoever belonged to the formerly persecuted minority were considered privileged.

To what extent the Assads hoisted their fellow believers to the top ranks of their regime is unclear. After the death of Hafez, his son Bashar took power and became president in 2000. It is proven that in the army and secret service, above average numbers of Alawites can be found among the officers. Also, the hard core of the regime's Shabiha thugs is interspersed with Alawites. For many Syrians, the repressive apparatus of the regime therefore has an Alawite face.'[423]

'In order to secure the support of the Sunnis, who were extremely suspicious of him as an Alawite, after taking power, Assad Snr pursued a two-pronged strategy. On the one hand, he sought the support of Shiite clerics. With Musa al-Sadr, one of the leaders of the Lebanese Shiites, he found a high-ranking imam who certified the Alawites by means of a fatwa to be Muslims. This was vital to Assad's survival, as the Syrian constitution requires the president to be a Muslim.

On the other hand, Assad sought to pacify the Sunnis by disadvantaging rather than promoting the Alawite religion. Where every other Faith Community in pluralistic Syria regulates its family affairs according to its own code, the Alawites are subject to Sunni law. The public exercise of Alawite practices is prohibited and there is no religious leader. Many Alawites who have not made it to the upper ranks of the regime still live in the poor rural areas along the Mediterranean coast.

Regime-critical Alawites complain that, on the one hand, they were disenfranchised by the regime, while on the other hand, they are seen by non-Alawite Syrians as the beneficiaries of the system and are hated accordingly.'[424]

[416] https://de.wikipedia.org/wiki/Syrien.

[417] https://de.wikipedia.org/wiki/Liste_der_politischen_Parteien_in_Syrien.

[418] CIA World Fact Book. downloaded 18. September 2013.

[419] Eva Berié (Hrsg.): Fischer Weltalmanach 2012. Frankfurt/Main 2011. p.467.

[420] Time Almanac 2010 – Powered by Encyclopaedia Britannica. Chicago 2009. p.441.

[421] Datenblatt zu SyrienCIA World Fact Book. downloaded 18. September 2013.

[422] Syria: Religionp.In: LookLex encyclopaedia.

[423] http://www.spiegel.de/politik/ausland/syriens-alawiten-minderheit-in-todesangst-a-816735.html.

[424] Ibid.

Almost simultaneously with the precursors of the Ba'ath secular party, the Sunni Muslim Brotherhood was founded in 1928. In Syria, the Muslim Brotherhood[425] has become the dominant Sunni adversary of the Baathist government, which is largely Alawite.

Seculars and military dictatorships are much more likely to lose their ideals and become self-serving, as opposed to religious movements. As we have seen, Hamas in the Gaza Strip displaced Fatah because corruption was flourishing in Fatah, while Hamas supporters were committed to social welfare. So, how much faster did the hatred of the Muslim Brotherhood against the Assad regime have to ignite, which was also perceived by the Sunnis as a foreign rule.

'There were inter alia terrorist attacks, which were on account of the Muslim Brotherhood. After a further attack in the military academy in 1979, in which 50 Alawit cadets were killed, the government took actions against the Muslim Brotherhood.

A momentous uprising, again initiated by Muslim Brothers, came in February 1982 in the Middle Syrian city of Hama. The army intervened with tanks and the air force, and it came down to fierce fighting, in the course of which large parts of the old town were destroyed. About 1,000 soldiers and between 10,000 and 30,000 civilians lost their lives. The suppression of the uprising, which became known as the Hama Massacre, was followed by a major arrest wave that broke the backbone of the fundamentalist opposition. As a result, Assad's power position was very strong and hardly endangered.' [426] But in the Syrian *Arab Spring* in 2011, there were demonstrations that developed into well-known chaos.

The civil war in Syria was a multilateral military conflict with international intervention due to religious, ethnic, economic, political and geostrategic conflicts of interest. It is an impressive example of what kind of chaos can arise when different national and religious objectives overlap. The relatively secular, albeit brutal, Assad regime supported by Iran, Hezbollah of Lebanon and Russia fights against:

- the archaic warriors of the self-appointed caliphate of the IS,
- the Free Syrian Army. The FSA is the original insurgency movement against the dictatorial Assad regime and is largely supported by the majority Sunnis in Syria, who feel that they are being set back by the Alawites, who are determining the political and military structure. They are supported by the USA and other countries.
- the Jabbat Fatah al-Sham (Al-Nusra Front). It also fights against the Assad regime, but for the same archaic religious reasons as the IS. It emerged from Al Qaeda just like ISIS. The Jabbah Fatah al-Sham is apparently receiving massive military support from Saudi Arabia and other Gulf states. It is therefore militarily stronger than the FSA and is therefore only forcibly accepted as a cooperation partner of the FSA.
- the Kurds. They pursue nationalistic goals: the merger of all Kurds into a single Kurdistan. In Iraq, they have already achieved autonomous status with their own armed forces. In northern Syria, Kurds have liberated themselves from the rule of the Assad regime and are fighting ISIS. They are supported by the USA, Russia, France and the Federal Republic. However, the Kurds do not form a single bloc. There are political differences between the more conservative Kurds in Iraq and the more socialist Kurds of the PKK and the PYD.
- The Turks, who, at the same time, want to prevent the creation of Kurdistan and therefore, for a long time, regard the IS and, even today, the Jabbat Fatah al-Sham (Al-Nusra Front) as a secret ally. Turkey has been involved in the fight against the IS only since the IS attacks in Turkey.

The Assad regime is supported by Hezbollah from Lebanon and Iran, who want to maintain or develop a Shiite bulwark between the Sunni countries in Syria, even if the Assad regime's dominant Alawites are, according to religious criteria, rather problematic Shiites.

[425] https://de.wikipedia.org/wiki/Muslimbr%C3%BCder.
[426] https://de.wikipedia.org/wiki/Syrien.

For religious reasons, Saudi Arabia and the Arab Gulf States have sympathy for the archaic Muslim ideology of the IS and the Jabbat Fatah al-Sham (Al-Nusra Front). But they want to ward off the Shiite influence of Iran. Since Saudi Arabia sees, in the ISIS Caliphate, a threat to its position as protector of the holy places of Islam, the Saudis also support the fight against the IS, but more the fight of the Jabbat Fatah al-Sham (Al -Nusra Front) against the Assad regime.

Russia supports the Assad regime because it wants to maintain and expand its bases in Syria and its influence in the Near East.

' The United Nations Special Envoy for Syria, Staffan de Mistura, estimates in April 2016 that 400,000 people have been killed since the beginning of the war. [427][428]Around 11.6 million Syrians are on the run: at least four million Syrians fled their country and 7.6 million were internally displaced within Syria. [429] The UN described the refugee crisis in February 2014 as the worst since the genocide in Rwanda in the 1990s. [430]'431

2.6.2 Iraq

Iraq is an artificial creation of Great Britain, which, after the First World War, placed the provinces of Mesopotamia that fell to it from Ottoman heritage under this name.

'The civilian government of post-war Iraq was originally led by High Commissioner Sir Percy Cox and his representative Colonel Arnold Wilson. After the murder of a British officer in Najaf, the British could not restore order despite reprisals. From the Hakkari Mountains north of Iraq and the plains of Urmia in Iran, thousands of Assyrians began to seek refuge from Turkish persecution in Iraq. The biggest problem, however, was the growing anger of Iraqi nationalists who felt cheated by their country's mandate status. The nationalists came early to the realization that the mandate was only a cover for the colonialism of the British '432

There were various riots. For the first time "Sunnis and Shiites, tribes and city dwellers came to-gether for a common cause." The country was in a state of anarchy for three months; the British only with difficulties could restore order with the help of Royal Air Force bombing.' 433

Britain recognized the difficulties of governing the Mandate and created the Kingdom of Iraq. 'At the 1921 Cairo Conference, the British set the parameters for Iraqi political life that lasted until the revolution of July 14, 1958. They chose the Hashemite Faisal bin Hussein, son of the former rifle of Mecca Hussein bin Ali, as the first king of Iraq [who had conquered Damascus and been proclaimed king there, but then expelled by the French and exiled in England], They built up a local Iraqi army and negotiated a new contract.' 434

'In Faisal, the British saw a leader who had enough nationalist and Islamic credibility for widespread recognition, but who was also reliable enough to depend on their support. Faisal traces his origins back to the family of the Prophet Muhammad.'435

The 20-year treaty, ratified in October 1922 and with Britain releasing Iraq into independence, said 'that the king should respect British advice in all matters affecting British interests and in fiscal policy,

---

427 https://deutsch.rt.com/der-nahe-osten/38027-un-sondergesandter-opferzahl-in-syrien/.

428 http://orf.at/#/stories/2336759/.

429 Total number of Syrian refugees exceeds four million for first time, UNCHR, vom 9. Juli 2015, downloaded 17. 7. 2015.

430 Uno-Bericht: Neun Millionen Syrer sind auf der Flucht vor dem Krieg, Spiegel Online, vom 1. 2 2014, downloaded 1. 2. 2014.

431 https://de.wikipedia.org/wiki/B%C3%BCrgerkrieg_in_Syrien#Nordkorea.

432 https://de.wikipedia.org/wiki/Britisches_Mandat_Mesopotamien.

433 Ibid.

434 Ibid.

435 Ibid.

as long as Iraq has a payment deficit with Britain, and says that British officials are being appointed to specific posts in all 18 ministries and they are acting as overseers and inspectors. A later financial deal, which markedly increased Iraq's financial burden, forced Iraq to pay half the cost of British officials. British commitments included various types of assistance under the new treaty, including military assistance and support for Iraq's early accession to the League of Nations. Ultimately, the treaty made Iraq politically and economically dependent on Britain. While unable to prevent the treaty, Faisal realized that the British went back on their promises to him.

On October 1, 1922, the Royal Air Force was reorganized in Iraq as the RAF Iraq Command, which had control of all British forces in the kingdom.[436]' 437

The explosive social situation in Iraq is largely determined by the relationship between different religious and ethnic groups, which are concentrated in different provinces, but have been joined together to form a common state by Great Britain and have a common capital in Baghdad.

Wikipedia writes: 'About 75-80% of the population living in Iraq today are Arabs, 15-20% are Kurds and 5% are Turkomans, Assyrians / Aramaeans or members of other ethnic groups..[438] From Turkoman sources, the proportion of their own is estimated to be about 10%. [439] Furthermore, 20,000 to 50,000 Marsh Arabs are to be found in the southeast.' 440 'Marsh Arabs inhabit the marshes and swamps of southern Iraq, the area around Shatt al-Arab, the confluence from the Euphrates and Tigris, south of the city of Amara and east of Nasiriyya. The (once) fertile land is often referred to as the "Garden of Eden."'441 Marsh Arabs are predominantly Shiite.

'About 97% of the population is Muslim. Over 60% are Shiites and between 32% and 37% Sunnis. The vast majority of Muslim Kurds are Sunni. Christians, Yazidis and other religions make up a minority of around 3% [442][443], compared to around 25% 100 years ago. In recent years, almost 2 million Christians have fled. Most Christians belong to the Oriental-Christian communities. ...

Until 1948, 150,000 Jews still lived in Iraq. Due to flight and expulsion in the 1940s and the subsequent establishment of the state of Israel, the number of Jews living in Iraq has greatly reduced and is currently estimated at fewer than 10 people. [444] Furthermore, there are Kurdish Yazidis, Shabaks and several thousand Mandaeans. Recently, there have been growing Zoroastrian communities in the Kurdish part of Iraq, especially in Sulaimaniyya. [445]' 446

From the composition of religions and ethnic groups, the potential social tensions in Mesopotamia are already becoming clear. In addition, the different ethnicities and religions have different emphases in the three provinces.

Basra 'is an Iraqi governorate located in the south of the country. The capital is Basra, which is the most important Shiite city in southern Iraq. The government borders Kuwait to the south and Iran to the north, where Shatt al-Arab forms the border. During the Ottoman rule, the government included Kuwait. After the First World War, Kuwait was separated as an independent British protectorate'447

436 Barker, A. J.: *The First Iraq War*, 1914-1918.
437 https://de.wikipedia.org/wiki/Britisches_Mandat_Mesopotamien.
438 CIA World Factbook: *Iraq: People and Society*. 20. 12. 2011, downloaded 6. 1. 2012 (englisch, ISSN 1553-8133).
439 H. Tarık Oğuzlu: *The Turkomans of Iraq as A Factor in Turkish Foreign Policy: Socio-Political and Demographic Perspectives*, p.7-12.
440 https://de.wikipedia.org/wiki/Irak.
441 https://de.wikipedia.org/wiki/Marsch-Araber.
442 CIA World Fact Book: CIA World Factbook Informationen über den Irak.
443 Otmar Oehring: *Zur gegenwärtigen Situation der Christen im Nahen Osten*.
444 jewishvirtuallibrary: The Jews of Iraq.
445 *Die Anti-IS-Religion*. In: FAZ.
446 https://de.wikipedia.org/wiki/Irak.
447 https://de.wikipedia.org/wiki/Basra_(Gouvernement).

The population of southern Iraq is almost exclusively Shiite and religiously closer to the Iranians. As Wikipedia writes, Basra 'wants to unite with the other governorates, Dhi Qar and Maisan, to form an autonomous region using the model of the Kurdistan Autonomous Region in northern Iraq'[448]

In **Baghdad** live about the same number of Sunnis and Shiites and a number of minorities. But there are massive religious tensions between these two groups. *Der Tagesanzeiger* writes: 'In the past, most Shiites and Sunnis lived side by side in most neighborhoods. Today, mixed districts are the exception. Meter-high walls separate one part of the population from the other with checkpoints at the entrance: it is always like entering another country.'[449]

'Mosul was a multi-ethnic and multi-religious city. In the division of the Ottoman Empire into the successor states, the Turkish Lausanne Commission submitted a demographic statistic in which the population was estimated at about 50% Kurds and 13% Arabs. The remaining 37% were distributed among Jews, Assyrians, Chaldeans and Turkmens. [450]

Since then, demography has changed in favor of the Arab population. Kurds make the Arabization policy of Saddam Hussein, and Christian Assyrians and Chaldeans responsible for the invasion of the Islamic State .... According to Archbishop Louis Raphaël I. Sako, 25,000 Christians still lived in Mosul when ISIS took power, [451] according to the BBC the figure is as much as 35,000.[452]'[453]

' In Iraq, as well as in other developing countries, the army was the most organized institution in an otherwise weak political system. As a result, the military gained more power and influence, while the political system was under great political and economic pressure for the duration of the monarchy. This is because as a consequence of the former Ottoman Rule, the officers in the new army were Sunnis and the lower ranks were largely occupied by Shiites, so Sunni supremacy could be maintained in the military.'[454]

' Under General Abdel Karim Qasim the so-called "Free Officers" teamed up to shake off British control. On July 14, 1958, they overthrew the pro-British monarchy (Faisal II. 1935-1958) with the help of the people. The last British soldiers left the country on March 24, 1959.[455]'[456]

As in Syria, the Baath Party in Iraq provided the spiritual foundations for politically-desired development. 'In the spring of 1963, the Baath Party seized power in Iraq through a bloody coup. Prime Minister Abd al-Karim Qasim was shot dead and his body displayed on national television. [457] The coup took place in coordination with the CIA. Following the successful seizure of power, there was a wave of repression with mass executions of true and alleged communists in cooperation with the US intelligence service. [458]'[459]

Kassem was a thorn in the side of American intelligence; he had quit the anti-Soviet Baghdad pact, legalized the Communist Party in Iraq and started to nationalize the Iraqi oil industry.

---

[448] Ibid.

[449] http://www.tagesanzeiger.ch/ausland/naher-osten-und-afrika/Bagdad-die-geteilte-Stadt/story/23122080.

[450] Yoanna Petros Mouché: *Verjagt aus Mossul,* http://www.zeit.de/gesellschaft/zeitgeschehen/2014-12/islamischer-staat-christen-vertreibung-irak.

[451] http://diepresse.com/home/politik/aussenpolitik/3841455/Nach-ISDrohung_ChristenExodus-aus-Mosul?from =gl.home_politik.

[452] http://www.bbc.com/news/world-middle-east-28381455.

[453] https://de.wikipedia.org/wiki/Mossul.

[454] https://de.wikipedia.org/wiki/Britisches_Mandat_Mesopotamien.

[455] Fürtig, Henner: *Kleine Geschichte des Irak: von der Gründung 1921 bis zur Gegenwart,* p.58 online.

[456] https://de.wikipedia.org/wiki/Irak.

[457] Phebe Marr: *The Modern History of Iraq,* p.115 - p.117.

[458] Shiva Balaghi: *Saddam Hussein - A Biography,* p.33f.

[459] https://de.wikipedia.org/wiki/Baath-Partei.

Even before the fall of Kassem, CIA agents including William McHale, a Beirut-escorted journalist, had assembled name lists of leftist intellectuals in Iraq with the help of Baath activists. Saddam is said to have contributed as well. Thousands were arrested and executed, and Saddam Hussein was placed in the security service of the new regime.'[460]

'When the Baath party came to power in Iraq in 1968, Saddam became deputy general secretary of the Revolutionary Command Council and head of the Ministry of State Security and Ministry of Propaganda in the new government. In 1969 he became vice president.

On June 1, 1972 he initiated the nationalization of Western oil companies that had an oil monopoly in Iraq. With the oil revenues, he developed the country into a regional military superpower. The revenue from oil sales, however, also ensured the prosperity of broader sections of the population. In 1972, Saddam signed a friendship treaty with the Soviet Union in Moscow. [461] ...

In 1979, President Ahmad Hasan appointed al-Bakr Saddam, at the age of 42, as chairman of the party and his successor. On July 11, 1979, he became Secretary-General of the Baath Party and on July 16, 1979, he took power as President and Prime Minister. In this position, Saddam publicly defamed members of the Baath Party, whereupon they were sentenced to death without trial and immediately liquidated. Other party members had been won over to the Saddam line by this example.

He saw himself as the actual successor to the King of Babylon and founder of the Neo-Babylonian Empire of Nebuchadnezzar II.'[462]

As "successor to Nebuchadnezzar II", Saddam Hussein wanted supremacy in the Middle East. Successful entry into Iran would make Iraq the dominant power in the Persian Gulf and the controller of a lucrative oil market. [463] This offered to wrest the Arabistan region from Iran, because there were significant oil and gas reserves. 'Shiite Arabs nearly represent the majority of the South in the Province'[464] 'In 1969, Saddam Hussein, then Vice President of Iraq, said: "Iraq's conflict with Iran refers to Arabistan [Chuzestan], which is part of the Iraqi soil and during foreign rule was annexed by Iran."'[465]

But not only Saddam Hussein had aggressive intentions towards Iran. The Ayatollah Khomeini, who had gained power in Iran, hated the regime in Iraq anyway. In addition, Saddam Hussein was Sunni. Sunnis did not recognize the Shiite followers of Muhammad over his kinsfolk and slayed the Shiite-recognized grandson of Mohammed Imam al-Husain bin'Alī at the Battle of Karbala.

Wikipedia says: 'In Kerbela, on October 10, 680, the Battle of Karbala took place, which is a pivotal event for the Twelfth Shiites or Imamites. In an uprising against the Umayyads [the Sunni caliphs residing in Damascus], almost all of the Shiite leadership was killed. The tomb of the martyred Shiite third Imam al-Husain bin'Alī is located in Karbala, making the city one of the most important Shiite and Alevi pilgrimage sites. The Imam Husain Shrine is the most important mosque in Iraq. The brother of Husain, Abbas, is buried in the Al-Abbas Mosque, which is within sight of the Imam Husain shrine. The Shiite Passion celebrations on the tenth of the Muslim month of Muharram recall these events with funerals, ritual narratives and processions. [466]'[467]

In addition, during the regime of the Baathist regime in Iraq, mass pilgrimages to Kerbela were banned.

Already in 1924, the Iranian province of Chusistan had risen unsuccessfully against the Iranian central government in Tehran. 'In 1979, after the Islamic revolution, the Arabs in Chusistan rebelled. They

[460] http://www.wingover.ch/Bush/Irak%20CIA.htm.
[461] George Black: *Genocide in Iraq: The Anfal Campaign Against the Kurds*, p.45.
[462] https://de.wikipedia.org/wiki/Saddam_Hussein.
[463] https://de.wikipedia.org/wiki/Erster_Golfkrieg.
[464] https://de.wikipedia.org/wiki/Chuzestan.
[465] https://de.wikipedia.org/wiki/Erster_Golfkrieg.
[466] Annemarie Schimmel: *Das islamische Jahr. Zeiten und Feste*, p.39 ff.
[467] https://de.wikipedia.org/wiki/Kerbela.

were supported by the Iraqi dictator, Saddam Hussein.'[468] Then it came to the Iraqi-Iranian war. The USA and other Western and Sunni countries not only gave Saddam Hussein the green light for an attack, but they also supported him with weapons, and the USA informed Iraqi troops about Iranian airborne troop movements.

The war lasted 8 years, required bloody sacrifices on both sides and ended with a ceasefire on July 18, 1988, ultimately under pressure from the UN Security Council.[469]

However, in order to ascend to the most important oil power of the Middle East, Saddam Hussein attacked Kuwait on August 2, 1990, that is, two years after the Iran war. The reasons he claimed for going to war were:

1. Kuwait's refusal to remit Iraq's $80 billion war debt. In order to finance the war against Iran, Iraq borrowed money from Kuwait, among others.
2. Kuwait is said to have gained oil on the Iraqi border that comes from adjacent Iraqi reserves.
3. Kuwait is said to have refused to reduce output to such an extent that the world oil price rose significantly.
4. The state territory of Kuwait belongs historically to the territory of Iraq.[470]

' Despite its size of more than 430,000 km², Iraq has only 58 km of coastline, which means that it is clearly at a disadvantage, both strategically and economically, compared to other Gulf countries. The much smaller Kuwait has a surface area of only 17,800 km², but 499 km of coastline. The final annexation of Kuwait would have increased the coastline almost tenfold. In addition, new ports would have been taken.'[471]

This power gain could not be permitted by the USA and the rest of the world. 'The United States, led by US Secretary of State, James Baker, formed a united military alliance against Iraq, eventually involving 34 countries: Afghanistan, Egypt, Argentina, Australia, Bahrain, Bangladesh, Denmark, France, Greece, Honduras, Italy, Canada, Qatar, Kuwait, Morocco, the Netherlands, Niger, Norway, Oman, Pakistan, Poland, Portugal, Saudi Arabia, Senegal, Spain, South Korea, Syria, Czechoslovakia, Turkey, Hungary, the United Arab Emirates, the United Kingdom and the United States itself. '

Therefore, starting in January 16, 1991, the 'Coalition, led by the United States and legitimized by the UN Security Council Resolution 678, began fighting to liberate Kuwait.' On February 27, Kuwait City was freed; 'The following night, on February 28, President Bush announced a ceasefire.' 'At the conference, Iraq negotiated the use of armed helicopters on its own side of the current border. Soon after, these helicopters and a large part of the Iraqi forces were on their way to fight a Shiite uprising in the south.

In the north, Kurdish leaders trusted American assurances that they would support a popular uprising and began fighting in the hope of provoking an attack. However, when American support failed to materialize, Iraqi generals brutally crushed the Kurdish units. Millions of Kurds then fled across the mountains to the Kurdish areas of Turkey and Iran.' 'On April 12, 1991, the ceasefire between Iraq and the coalition forces came into effect, signifying the official end of the war.'[472]

Economic sanctions immediately followed the war . Iraq has been allowed to import certain products under the Oil for Food program. A UNICEF report found in 1998 that the sanctions resulted in an increase of 90,000 deaths per year (IAC), especially in infants and babies. ...

---

[468] https://de.wikipedia.org/wiki/Chusistan.
[469] https://de.wikipedia.org/wiki/Erster_Golfkrieg.
[470] Siehe: https://de.wikipedia.org/wiki/Zweiter_Golfkrieg.
[471] See: https://de.wikipedia.org/wiki/Zweiter_Golfkrieg.
[472] https://de.wikipedia.org/wiki/Zweiter_Golfkrieg.

On May 15, 1991, under the terms of the ceasefire, the International Atomic Energy Agency (IAEA) began inspecting the facilities of the Iraqi Nuclear Program for the possible production of nuclear weapons.'[473]

The war in Iraq had consequences for the Middle East as well as for world politics as a whole. Because the Palestinians had stayed close to Saddam Hussein in the war, within a few days, about 450,000 Palestinians had to leave Kuwait, increasing the number of Palestinian refugees in the remaining areas.

Although Iraq had been severely weakened by the wars and also subjected to economic sanctions, Saddam Hussein was considered a cruel dictator and still unpredictable seeking biological, chemical and nuclear weapons. In addition, the anti-Iraqi attitude of the United States intensified after the Al Kaida-driven destruction of the New York World Trade Center and the attack on the Pentagon by suicide planes.

'In immediate response to the terrorist attacks of September 11, 2001, US Secretary of Defense Donald Rumsfeld, called for simultaneous attacks on Afghanistan and Iraq, if necessary, unilaterally and without evidence of their intentions to overthrow Saddam Hussein. [474]' 'On February 5, 2003, US Secretary of State, Colin Powell, made alleged evidence of Iraqi biological and chemical weapons as well as nuclear weapons components at the crucial UN Security Council meeting, which ultimately turned out to be false by mid-2004. In March 2003, US President Bush issued an ultimatum to Saddam Hussein to leave Iraq within 48 hours; otherwise Iraq would be attacked. On Hussein's refusal, the war coalition opened [without a mandate from the Security Council], on the night of March 19-20, with the bombing of Baghdad, known as Operation Iraqi Freedom.'[475] 'In May 2003, US President Bush declared that the larger combat actions had ended and Iraq was divided into occupation zones'[476]

' After the declared end of the war during the occupation of Iraq in 2003-2011, there were civil war-like conditions, thousands of terrorist attacks, acts of war and violent crime, both of different Iraqi groups against each other and against Western occupation forces. They claimed many victims among Iraqi civilians, an unknown death toll and injuries. Even after the withdrawal of foreign troops in 2011, there was no pacification in the country'[477]

'The Algerian UN Special Representative Lakhdar Brahimi mediated between various parties for an interim Iraqi government, which was created on June 1, 2004, to take power as of June 30. On January 30, 2005, Iraq's first free elections for over 40 years were held. On October 11, 2006, the Iraqi Parliament passed a new Federalism Act, envisaging the creation of the largely autonomous so-called "super-provinces". Critics of this law, notably the Sunni minority, see it as a threat to Iraqi unity. [478]'[479]

The tragedy of Iraq's development, as well as Iran's, was that a more secular society was breaking up into a society in which people have been made immature by traditional religion and even forced into archaic behaviors.

Iraq, ruled by Saddam Hussein, was a secular governmental system, albeit a bloody, inhuman dictatorship. Although the elites were mostly Sunnis, their understanding of society was secular. There were also ministers who belonged to other religions, such as the long-time Christian Foreign Minister and Vice President, Tariq Aziz, or the Shiites' Iyad Allawi. The connection was the Baath Party. The Baath Party was, as we have seen, a secular party, even though under Saddam Hussein it had degenerated into a cadre party and executor of his orders. In it there were also secular-thinking representatives of other religions.

---

[473] Ibid..

[474] Stephan Bierling: *Geschichte des Irakkriegep.Der Sturz Saddams und Amerikas Albtraum im Mittleren Osten*, p.62 and 96.

[475] https://de.wikipedia.org/wiki/Irakkrieg.

[476] https://de.wikipedia.org/wiki/Irak#Irakkrieg_2003.2C_Absetzung_Husseins_und_Besatzungszeit.

[477] https://de.wikipedia.org/wiki/Irakkrieg.

[478] Die Zeit: Irak: Parlament verabschiedet Förderalismusgesetz, 11. Oktober 2006.

[479] https://de.wikipedia.org/wiki/Geschichte_des_Irak#Politische_Neuordnung_seit_2003.

Instead of leaning on free-will and secular representatives of the Ba'ath Party after their victory over Iraq, the Americans destroyed it. Aliénor Carrière writes: 'The party also supports Saddam Hussein. The American authorities banned the Baath Party, which initially led to the dissolution of the public apparatus. It was not until 2008 that the Iraqi law allowed former members of the Baath Party to resume administration posts.'[480]

Wikipedia writes: 'Iyad Allawi described Iraq as a failed state. The country is heavily influenced by Iran and has a stagnant economy, high unemployment, high inflation, no functioning public sector and a security situation which is still poor. [481]'[482]

The only stable and relatively secular area of Iraq is the Kurdish Autonomous Region. As the Kurds strive for further independence, they are getting closer and closer to this goal as the rest of Iraq plunges into chaos.'[483]

2.6.3 The IS Islamic State

As a result of the crushing of the Baath Party and thus the elimination of Sunni leadership and religious discrimination against the Sunnis by the previously oppressed Shiite majority of Iraqis, the Sunnis were open to the radical terrorist ideology of Al-Qaeda. At the same time, they recalled their religious and cultural significance in the Middle Ages.

After the death of Mohammed, the Umayyad Caliphate dynasty was founded in Damascus. 'The Umayyads ... were a family clan of the Arab tribe of Quraysh from Mecca, the tribe of Mohammed, the founder of the religion. From 661 to 750 AD, members of the family ruled as caliphs from Damascus over the then-young Islamic empire ... and thus founded the first dynastic ruling order in Islamic history.'[484] It is therefore understandable that the Sunni al-Qaida Fighters did not want to be remotely controlled fighters of an al Qaeda leader on a permanent basis.

In 2004, their organization was still 'under al Qaeda in Iraq (AQI), from 2007 under the Islamic State in Iraq (ISI), from 2011 to June 2014 under the Islamic State in Iraq and Syria (ISIS), then under the name of the Islamic State in Iraq and the Levant (ISIL) and also under the transcribed Arabic acronym Daesch (Dā'isch / داعش). [485][486]

Following the military conquest of a contiguous area in north-western Iraq and eastern Syria, the organization announced, on June 29, 2014, the establishment of a Caliphate with Abu Bakr al-Baghdadi as the "Caliph Ibrahim - Commander of the Faithful"[487] - the succession of the Prophet Muhammad as a political and religious leader of all Muslims. [488][489]'[490] 'But there is no evidence for the descent of Ibrahim Awad Ibrahim al-Badris from the Quraysh tribe of the Prophet Muhammad.

---

[480] Aliénor Carrière: *Aufstieg und Fall der Baath-Partei*, http://irak.arte.tv/de/hintergrunde/aufstieg-und-fall-der-baath-partei/.

[481] *„Der Irak ist auf dem Weg in eine neue Diktatur"*. downloaded 5. November 2013.

[482] https://de.wikipedia.org/wiki/Geschichte_des_Irak#Politische_Neuordnung_seit_2003.

[483] https://de.wikipedia.org/wiki/Geschichte_des_Irak#Politische_Neuordnung_seit_2003.

[484] https://de.wikipedia.org/wiki/Umayyaden.

[485] Felicia Schwartz: *One More Name for Islamic State: Daesh*, The Wall Street Journal , 23. December 2014.

[486] Alice Guthrie: *Decoding Daesh: Why is the new name for ISIS so hard to understand?*, Free Word Centre vom 19. 2. 2015.

[487] Wilfried Buchta: *Terror vor Europas Toren*, p.19.

[488] Stephan Rosiny: „Des Kalifen neue Kleider": Der Islamische Staat in Irak und Syrien (PDF). In: GIGA Focus, Nr. 6/2014, downloaded 2.10. 2014.

[489] IS-Führer Baghdadi sieht sich als Nachfolger des Propheten. In: Rheinische Post, 29. Juni 2015.

[490] https://de.wikipedia.org/wiki/Islamischer_Staat_(Organisation).

One of his brothers died as a "martyr" for Saddam Hussein's army. For "medical reasons" he was not drafted for military service.[491] ... Originally he had applied for a law degree, but his graduation was not good enough for that. He initially studied at the University of Islamic Law at the Department of Islamic Jurisprudence and later moved to the Koranic Studies. In 1999, he completed his master's degree, after which he is said to have worked as a mosque administrator. Following the US invasion of Iraq in 2003, al-Baghdadi joined the Sunni resistance group, Ansar as-Sunna. [492] Arrested in February 2004, he was interned at Camp Bucca by US Armed Forces in Iraq until December 2004. [493] ... In the detention center, old companions of Saddam, generals and intelligence agents were interned with Islamists. ... [494] ...

On April 9, 2013, al-Baghdadi proclaimed the "Islamic State in Iraq and the Levant" (ISIS) and declared the Jabbat Fatah al-Sham (Al-Nusra Front) to be an offshoot of ISIS. Thus, the IS is in competition with al-Qaeda and its leader Aiman az-Zawahiri. . [495]'496

Because of the political and economic chaos in Syria and Iraq, the IS was able to expand very quickly. However, as a result of attacks by almost all the powers involved in the Syrian conflict, IS is being pushed back ever further and has already lost its important cities.

In Syria, of course, the Assad regime and its allies want all areas to remain in Syria. The FSA Free Syrian Army and other resistance groups would also agree to this if Syria becomes a democracy or if the Islamic resistance groups remove the IS, or if Syria becomes a theocracy. The Kurds, on the other hand, want to annex northern Syrian areas to the Kurdish region, which is close to the PKK. On the other hand, Turkey is changing.

In Iraq, of course, the government in Baghdad also wants to regain all formerly Iraqi territories. However, the Iraqi government is in conflict with the autonomous Kurdish region, which wants to annex the areas around Mosul, especially since Mosul was originally inhabited by Kurds and only through the Arabization policy of Saddam Hussein has lost the majority of the population. In addition, northern Iraqis are mostly Sunnis who fear repression by the Shi'ites, who rule the government of Baghdad and by their ally Iran. Thus, with every step made to weaken the IS, the potential for conflict with the opponents of the IS increases.

But even if the state structures in Syria and Iraq are destroyed, the IS is not yet defeated. It already has branches in many other Muslim countries, often in competition with Al-Qaeda and other Islamist groups.

The breeding ground for these Islamist terrorist groups is not only Islamic fanaticism but also social distress and a disturbed personality. For the latter reason, non-Muslims also convert to Islam and seek recognition, exaltation of their concepts of violence and paradise in the Islamic struggle.

2.7 "Kurdistan"

'The Kurds are an ethnic group with their own language with several dialects and their own customs. They profess predominantly to Sunni Islam. However, there are also Shiite Muslims, Yazidis, Alevis and Assyrian Christians among them.

There are no clear borders for the Kurdish settlement areas, including regions in the southeast of Turkey, in the north of Syria and Iraq as well as in western Iran, in which a total of about 30 million Kurds live. There are still a few tens of thousands of Kurds in Armenia.

---

491 Volkmar Kabisch, Amir Musawy, Georg Mascolo und Christian Baars: Auf der Spur des IS-Anführerp.In: tagesschau.de, 18. 2. 2015.

492 Wilfried Buchta: *Terror vor Europas Toren*, P.316.

493 Volkmar Kabisch, Amir Musawy, Georg Mascolo und Christian Baars: *Auf der Spur des IS-Anführerp.*In: tagesschau.de, 18. Februar 2015.

494 Martin Chulov: *Isis: the inside story*. In: The Guardian, 11. Dezember 2014 (englisch).

495 Charles Lister: *Profiling the Islamic State*, p.13.

496 https://de.wikipedia.org/wiki/Abu_Bakr_al-Baghdadi.

When the states in the Middle East were founded after the end of the Ottoman Empire, Kurds were not granted an independent Kurdistan after the First World War. Since then, many Kurds have been fighting for their own state or at least more autonomy in their areas. Especially against the respective security forces of the governments and often against each other too. '

'Until the time of the First World War, Kurdish consciousness was shaped on the one hand by tribal affiliation, and on the other hand by Sunni Islam. Under the influence of European ideas, they then developed their own national feeling. After the defeat of the Ottoman Empire against the Allies, the Kurds were promised an autonomous region in the Treaty of Sèvres.'[497] 'However, in the Treaty of Lausanne Kurdistan after the dissolution of the Ottoman Empire, the territory was divided by the Allies and Turkey into the four states of Iran, Iraq, Turkey and Syria.'[498]

'The Kurds in the newly founded states of Turkey, Iraq, Iran and later also in Syria more or less faced severe reprisals. They were not allowed to be politically active, and attempts were made to suppress their culture by, for example, banning their language or typical forms of clothing. Again and again, military action was taken against them. Militant Kurds responded to the suppression with terrorist attacks and acts of sabotage, so that, especially in Turkey, some war-like conditions arose.'[499]

We are dealing with four Kurdish areas.

2.7.1 Kurds in Iran

' In Shiite-dominated Iran, the Kurds were persecuted for their Sunni beliefs.'[500] 'At the beginning of the 20th century, there were repeated insurgencies led by Simko Aga. He was then shot in 1930 in an ambush. On January 22, 1946, after the Anglo-Soviet invasion of Iran under the auspices of the Soviet Union, in Mahabad, the Republic of Mahabad was founded. But this state collapsed again a year later. Until the Islamic revolution in 1979, a deathly silence prevailed in the Kurdish areas. However, the Kurds quarreled with Khomeini, who promised them no autonomy in the constitution. According to the new government, there were no ethnic groups, only the Islamic faith community. In August 1979, the Iranian army bombed Kurdish towns and villages, killing many civilians. In July 2005, an uprising against the Iranian government broke out after the killing of Kurdish Shuaneh Ghaderi in Mahabad City. This spread to about ten Kurdish cities. It killed about 20 people. The Iranian government described the insurgents as hooligans and transferred 100,000 troops to the Kurdish areas.'[501]

2.7.2 Kurds in Iraq

' In Iraq, the Kurds were sometimes given more freedom, but when the call for independence became too loud, the centrally-organized state struck back so as not to lose its access to natural resources. For example, Saddam Hussein [in the Mosul area] forcibly resettled the population and even used poison gas against Kurdish civilians. After the Gulf War in 1991, a security zone was built in Northern Iraq for the Kurds, who have since enjoyed extensive autonomy.'[502]

Since the Kurds in the Mosul region had a majority, they also participated in the fighting against the IS, which had conquered Mosul and been expelled again. They are in competition with the Iraqi troops of the national government.

But also the Kurds close to the PKK fought against the IS in northern Iraq. For example, the Yazidis, a special sect affiliated with Islam, owe them their liberation from the oppression of the IS. In the

---

[497] https://de.wikipedia.org/wiki/Kurden#Siedlungsgebiet.

[498] Ibid.

[499] http://www.planet-wissen.de/kultur/voelker/kurden_volk_ohne_staat/.

[500] Ibid.

[501] https://de.wikipedia.org/wiki/Kurden.

[502] http://www.planet-wissen.de/kultur/voelker/kurden_volk_ohne_staat/.

fighting against the IS, the Kurds of the autonomous region in Iraq were experiencing a certain tension with the Kurds of the PKK.

In respect of how complex the relationship between the Kurds themselves is, *Die Zeit* writes: 'Syrian Kurds, weapons brothers of the PKK, on the battlefield of the civil war in the north, have secured a quasi-autonomous area under the name "Rojava", to which Kobane also belongs. This outrages the government in Ankara, which does not want to tolerate a Kurdish semi-state under PKK control on its border. That is one of the reasons why Ankara has resumed the war against the Marxist guerrillas. It bothers Massoud Barzani, because Rojava competes with his Iraqi Kurdistan, which he and his clan have been dominating for years. That is why the autonomous government in Erbil only half-heartedly protests whenever Turkish bombers bombard the PKK on northern Iraqi soil.

All this does not make the fight against the "Islamic State" any easier - not even for the Western allies. The German government helps the Peshmerga with good intentions, but at the same time, has to take care that German weapons do not end up with the PKK at some point. After all, because the PKK itself used suicide bombers in the past against Turkish targets, it is still internationally classified as a terrorist organization. At the same time, the PKK in Syria, where it operates under the name "Democratic Union Party", is providing an effective ground force against IS terrorist militia. It is supported by the USA. '[503]

2.7.3 Kurds in Syria

' The Kurdish minority in Syria has been discriminated against under the Baathist Arab-nationalist regime for decades. [504][505] Over the course of the civil war in Syria towards the end of 2013, the Syrian government ceded control of the northern border regions. Local Kurdish forces took control in many places. On November 12, 2013, the Party of Democratic Union (Partiya Yekitîya Demokrat, PYD), along with the Christian Suryoye Unity Party (an Assyrian / Aramaic party) and other small parties in northern Syria decided to establish an interim administration to deal with the abuses caused by the war relating to the administration and supply of the population.[506] On January 21, 2014, the administration was established in Cizirê, on January 27 in Kobanê and a few days later in Efrîn.'[507]

The *PYD Party of the Democratic Union* 'was founded in 2003 by the decision of the PKK, and has no legal organizational structure in Syria. Its ideology corresponds to Democratic Confederalism and thus to the PKK line. The main concern is the solution of the Kurdish question. Its main demands, according to the party program, include respect for human rights, the release of political prisoners, freedom of expression and the abolition of the death penalty. [508]

After improving relations between Turkey and Syria, it initially shifted its focus from combating Turkey to nationalist agitation among the Syrian Kurds. In return, they paid a heavy price: in 2009, two-thirds of all convictions for illegal party activity among Syrian Kurds were against members of the PYD; and three quarters of all Kurdish torture victims were PYD sympathizers. '[509]

---

[503]http://www.zeit.de/politik/ausland/2015-12/kurden-islamischer-staat-kobane-widerstand-peschmerga-mossul/ seite-2.

[504] Syria: The silenced kurds, Bericht der HRW , Oktober 2006.

[505] Syria: End persecution of human rights defenders and human rights activists article 7. 12. 2004 from amnestyusa.org.

[506] "Kurds declare an interim administration in Syria", report on www.reuters.com 12. 11. 2013.

[507] https://de.wikipedia.org/wiki/Rojava.

[508] Programm in arabischer Sprache (PDF).

[509] https://de.wikipedia.org/wiki/Partiya_Yekit%C3%AEya_Demokrat.

'On March 17, 2016, a gathering of Kurdish, Assyrian, Arab and Turkmen delegates in Rumaylan decided to name an autonomous Federation of Northern Syria - Rojava. [510][511]' 512 'Rojava is divided into 4 cantons. The cantons are (from west to east): Efrîn, Şehba, Kobanê and Cizîrê (the Syrian province of al-Hasakah with Qamishli as the main town). The canton of Cizîrê is directly adjacent to the Kurdistan Autonomous Region in Iraq'513 'Neither the USA and Russia, nor the Assad regime and the Syrian opposition support their aspirations for autonomy[514].

The Federation of Northern Syria, Rojava, has diplomatic missions in Moscow, [515] in Stockholm[516] and, since May 2016, also in Berlin. [517] The purpose of representation is to establish diplomatic relations with the German state and to inform the public about developments in Rojava, said the representative of this autonomous region, Sipan Ibrahim. "We want to make it clear to people in Germany that in Rojava Kurds, Arabs and other population groups live together as brothers and sisters." [518] Also, in May 2016, a representative office opened in Paris. [519] There is also a representation of the YPG Self-Defense Force in Prague.[520]'521

'The administration is supposed to reflect the multi-ethnic and religious situation in northern Syria and consists of one Kurdish, one Arab and one Christian-Assyrian minister per department. Overall, the plan is pursued to build a democratic system in the sense of self-governing democratic confederalism, according to works by Abdullah Öcalan, so, for example, a quota of 40% of women in the administration is targeted. [522] According to the PYD, the longer-term plan is to unify all three cantons under one administration. [523]

With this step, however, the PYD came under criticism both within Syria and internationally. One point of criticism is that the PYD claims that the targeted contiguous stretch of land, called "Rojava", in northern Syria, is also a predominantly non-Kurdish populated area, which, above all, meets resistance from the Arab Sunni majority in these areas. [524][525]' 526

'The economic system in Rojava is based on the principles of democratic confederalism according to works by Abdullah Öcalan. Private property and entrepreneurship are protected by the principle of "ownership by use". Dara Kurdaxi, an economist from Rojava, formulated the principle: "The method in Rojava is less directed against private property, but has the goal of putting private property at the service of all citizens of Rojava." [527] The focus of economic policy is on an expansion of public services and

---

510 "Kurdische Autonomiepläne", Neue Zürcher Zeitung, 17. 3. 2016.
511 Rojava: Ausrufung einer kurdisch-syrischen "Demokratischen Föderation", Telepolis, 20. 3. 2016.
512 https://de.wikipedia.org/wiki/Rojava.
513 Ibid.
514 "Autonomiepläne isolieren Kurden", tagesschau.de, 17. 3. 2016.
515 "Syrian Kurds open diplomatic mission in Moscow", The Telegraph, 10. 2. 2016.
516 Syrian Kurds inaugurate representation office in Sweden, Ara News, 18. 4.2016.
517 Evrensel, 7. 5. 2016.
518 "Rojava-Vertretung in Deutschland", Junge Welt, 9. 5. 2016.
519 Syrian Kurds open unofficial representative mission in Parip.Al Arabiya. 24. 5. 2016.
520 Prague Monitor, 3. April 2016.
521 https://de.wikipedia.org/wiki/Rojava.
522 Onur Burçak Belli: *Traurige Gewinner. Zeit Online* vom 22. 3. 2014, abgerufen am 22. 3 2014.
523 *Rojava artık özerk*, Artikel der Radikal vom 31. 1. 2014 (turque).
524 *The Siege Of Kobani: Obama's Syrian Fiasco In Motion*, Analyse von US-Politologe David Stockman 11. 10.2014 (english).
525 *Will Syria's Kurds benefit from the crisis?*, BBC-Analysis of diplomatic correspondent Jonathan Marcus 10. 8.2012 (english).
526 https://de.wikipedia.org/wiki/Rojava.
527 Michael Knapp: *'Rojava – the formation of an economic alternative: Private property in the service of all'*.

cooperative economic activity; several hundred cooperatives, mostly with between 20 and 35 members, have been established since 2012.[528]

According to information from the Ministry of Economic Affairs, around three-quarters of the land was under public service management at the beginning of 2015 and one-third of industrial production was provided by companies managed by workers' councils. [529] No taxes are levied in Rojava; the revenue of the administration comes from customs duties as well as the sale of extracted oil and other natural resources. [530] Employees of the public administration are partly paid by the central government of Syria. [531][532]

The economy in Rojava has experienced comparatively less destruction in the civil war than other parts of Syria, and has mastered the circumstances comparatively well. In May 2016, Ahmed Yousef, Economics Minister and President of the University of Afrin, estimated Rojava's economic output at that time as 55 percent of Syria's gross national product.[533]' 534

'Armed Forces Rojavas are the PYD-affiliated People's Defense Units (YPG / YPJ). In the social contract, they are referred to as the national institution of all three cantons. Their relationship with the army of the central government of Syria is therefore to be determined by the laws of Rojava. They are closely supported by the allied Christian Syrian-Aramaic Sutoro militias and FSA brigades, among others. Liwa Thuwwar al-Raqqa, as part of the Burkān al-Furāt Alliance and the PKK and MLCP. The most important civil war opponent is the Islamic State (IS) terrorist organization. Since Kobanê's defense in September 2014, the YPG has been supported by air strikes by the American-led international coalition and by Peshmerga of the Kurdistan Region of Iraq.

On October 10, 2015, the YPG formed a military alliance with the Sunni Arab Army of Revolutionaries (Jachah ath-Thuwwar), the Sunni Arab Shammar tribal militia Quwat as-Sanadid and the Assyrian-Aramaic Military Council of the Suryoye (MFS) under the name of Syrian Democratic Forces (SDF),which together with the American-led international coalition, took action against the IS in Syria.[535][536]' 537

2.7.4 Kurds in Turkey

The extent to which the Ottoman Empire was weakening, giving up territories to Russia, coming under European influence and also as a reaction to the nationalist aspirations of the subjugated people, also led to the rise of nationalism in Turkey. This increased the repression against other ethnic groups up to pogroms. 'On the basis of the Lausanne Treaty, the Republic of Turkey, proclaimed by Mustafa Kemal Atatürk on October 29, 1923, did not recognize the Kurds as an ethnic minority. A number of revolts, such as the 1920 Koçgiri Rebellion, the Sheikh Said Uprising led by Sheikh Said in 1925, the Ararat Uprising of 1926-1930 and the Dersim Uprising in 1938 were defeated by the Turkish army.' 538

---

528 http://sange.fi/kvsolidaarisuustyo/wp-content/uploads/Dr.-Ahmad-Yousef-Social-economy-in-Rojava.pdf.
529 A Small Key Can Open a Large Door: The Rojava Revolution, 1st, Strangers In A Tangled Wilderness, 4. 3. 2015: „According to Dr. Ahmad Yousef, an economic co-minister, three-quarters of traditional private property is being used as commons and one quarter is still being owned by use of individuals...According to the Ministry of Economics, worker councils have only been set up for about one third of the enterprises in Rojava so far."
530 Efrîn Economy Minister Yousef: Rojava challenging norms of class, gender and power. downloaded 18. 2.2015.
531 Flight of Icarus? The PYD's Precarious Rise in Syria (PDF) International Crisis Group.
532 Zamana LWSL.
533 Will Syria's Kurds succeed at self-sufficiency?. downloaded 9. 5.2016.
534 https://de.wikipedia.org/wiki/Rojava.
535 Declaration of Establishment by Democratic Syria Forcep.15. 10. 2015, downloaded 4. 11. 2015.
536 Kampf gegen Terrormiliz: Syrische Kurden und Araber verbünden sich gegen IP.In: Die Welt. 12. 10. 2015, downloaded 4. 11. 2015.
537 https://de.wikipedia.org/wiki/Rojava.
538 https://de.wikipedia.org/wiki/Kurden.

The largest non-Turkish ethnic group in the heartland of today's Turkey, the Kurds, have been declared "Mountain Turks". Turkey operated an assimilation policy against them, denying cultural and ethnic differences. The attempt was made to portray the Kurds as Turkish people immigrating from Central Asia. Due to state restrictions, Kurdish culture could not be carried out freely. As late as 1979, the official dictionary (Türkçe Sözlük) of the Turkish Dil Kurumu explained the word "Kurd" as: *The name of a community or member of this community of Turkish origin who has lost their language, speaks a degenerate form of Persian and lives in Turkey, Iraq or Iran.* [539]'540

'In response, the Kurdistan Workers' Party (PKK) led by Abdullah Öcalan, came to power in 1978. '541 The Kurdistan Workers' Party (Kurdish: Partiya Karkerên Kurdistanê, Abkhaz PKK) is a Kurdish, socialist militant underground organization originating from the Kurdish settlement areas within Turkey.

Markus C. Schulte of Drach writes: 'After the military coup in 1980, the PKK was expelled from Turkey, and many members fled to Lebanon. Since 1984, the PKK has fought, with armed violence, against Turkish security forces with the aim of enforcing, if not its own state, then at least more autonomy. Tens of thousands of people died, including many civilians, in battles with the police and the army, as well as through attacks. In 1999, Abdullah Öcalan was caught and sentenced to death and in 2002, the verdict was turned into life imprisonment.' 542

In 2007, Abdullah Öcalan writes from his one-person prison İmralı to the international conference "EU, Turkey and the Kurds": 'The spirit of the founding of the Republic was a strategic alliance between Turks and Kurds. The inability to renew this alliance in the current phase of democratic construction underlines the Kurdish question in Turkey. The story is full of examples of Turkish-Kurdish alliances. Sultan Alp Arslan was only able to penetrate into Anatolia through a Kurdish-Turkish alliance. Through this alliance, Sultan Selim I raised his empire to the rank of world empire. Mustafa Kemal founded the republic through this alliance. Why should not we adapt the essence of these three alliances to today? Kurds and Turks should forge this millennial alliance today. If we recognize that neither chauvinistic Turkish nationalism nor primitive Kurdish nationalism can provide a solution, then building on democracy we will build a basis for the democratic development of the entire Middle East. However, a strategic partnership can only come about if the meeting between Kurds and Turks takes place on an equal footing. Therefore, relations must be reorganized in a democratic way.'543

' The solution that I offer to the society of Turkey and to all those who are sensitive and responsible is very simple. We want a democratic nation. We have nothing against the unitary state and the republic. We accept the Republic, its unitary state structure and secularism. But we believe that one has to redefine the democratic state in terms of its respect for people, cultures and rights. This definition should allow the Kurds a democratic organization through which they can develop, inter alia, in the fields of culture, language, economy and environment. Kurds, Turks and other cultures then all make up the Democratic Nation of Turkey. This is only possible through a democratic concept of nations, a democratic constitution and an advanced, multicultural legal system. Flags and borders are not a problem for our understanding of a democratic nation. Our democratic nation's conception includes the model of a democracy-based nation as opposed to a state-based nation. The nation of Turkey must be defined as encompassing all ethnic groups. What is meant is a model of nations that is not based on Turks, not on

539 Stephan Conermann, Geoffrey Haig (Hrsg.): *Asien und Afrika*, Bd. 8. p.135.
540 https://de.wikipedia.org/wiki/Kurden_in_der_T%C3%BCrkei.
541 https://de.wikipedia.org/wiki/T%C3%BCrkei.
542 Markus C. Schulte von Drach: *Volk ohne Staat. Ein Traum von Kurdistan*, http://www.sueddeutsche.de/politik/volk-ohne-staat-ein-traum-von-kurdistan-1.2585734, 28. 7. 2015,
543Abdullah Öcalan: *Lösungsvorschläge für die kurdische Frage in der Türkei*, 2007, http://freedom-for-ocalan.com/deutsch/download/vorschlaege-fuer-eine-politische-loesung.pdf.

religion or race, but on human rights. We start from the concept of a democratic nation that gathers all ethnicities and cultures.'[544]

As a solution, Abdullah Öcalan makes the following suggestions: '

1. The Kurdish question should be treated as a fundamental question of democratization, the Kurdish identity should be guaranteed by law and constitution. A mere article in the new constitution with the wording "The Constitution of the Turkish Republic recognizes the existence and expression of all cultures in a democratic way" would already fulfill this demand.

2. Linguistic and cultural rights should be protected by law. There should be no restriction for radio, television and press. Kurdish and other language programs should be subject to the same rules and institutions as Turkish radio and television broadcasts. Also, for cultural activities, the same laws and procedures should apply.

3. Kurdish should be used as a school language in primary schools. Anyone who wants this should be able to train their child in such schools. In grammar schools, sub-units on Kurdish culture, language and literature should be offered as optional subjects. At universities, however, institutes for Kurdish language, literature, culture and history should be set up.

4. All obstacles to freedom of expression and organization should be removed and all conditions for free political activity should be created. Even with issues that touch on the Kurdish question, these freedoms must apply without restrictions.

5. The party and electoral laws should be democratized and guaranteed so that the Kurdish people and all democratic forces can participate in their own free will in the formation of democratic will.

6. By adopting a democratic local government law, democracy should be deepened and broadened.

7. The village protection system and the illegitimate gangs that have settled in the state must be dissolved.

8. The return of the inhabitants forced out of their villages under duress during the war should be allowed. For this, the necessary administrative, legal, economic and social measures must be taken. In addition, a campaign for economic development should be launched and the prosperity level of the Kurds should be raised through incentives and other measures.

9. A law for social peace and democratic participation should be adopted. It was intended to allow guerrilla fighters, detainees and those who had to go into exile to participate in a democratic, political life without preconditions.'[545]

The proposals of Öcalan initially remained unheard. For 'the battles between the Turkish armed forces and the armed wing of the PKK, the HPG have increased in severity since 2007. The HPG has repeatedly carried out direct attacks on gendarmerie guards. Actions were reported not only from the "Kurdish heartland" but also up to the Black Sea region (the provinces of Erzincan and Giresun). [546]

On February 21, 2008, the Turkish army launched the 25th offensive in Northern Iraq since 1983, involving an estimated 10,000 troops.'[547] Only 'since 2012 have peace negotiations taken place between the Turkish government and the PKK, and in 2013, Öcalan announced a ceasefire and the withdrawal of PKK fighters from Turkey.'[548]

Obviously, as a result of these negotiations, the Erdogan government fulfilled Öcalan's main demands. 'The Erdoğan government's democracy package, passed in 2013, completely lifted the ban on

---

[544] Abdullah Öcalan: loc. cit.

[545] Öcalan: loc. cit.

[546] Siehe Bericht der Schweiz. Flüchtlingshilfe (SFH) Türkei Update: Aktuelle Entwicklungen vom 8. 10. 2008.

[547] https://de.wikipedia.org/wiki/Konflikt_zwischen_der_Republik_T%C3%BCrkei_und_der_PKK.

[548] Markus C. Schulte von Drach: *Volk ohne Staat. Ein Traum von Kurdistan,* loc. cit

Kurdish letters. [549] The Kurdish language is also offered as an optional subject in state schools and universities, and thus, for the first time, receives state support. Furthermore, this reform package also made possible the election campaign in the Kurdish language and the renaming of previously Turkish place names.[550]'551

'The obstruction of the practice of religion is also punishable. The prison term can be between one and three years.

For the first time, hate crimes and offenses are criminalized. Anyone who discriminates against a person based on his or her native language, race, nationality, skin color, gender, disability, political affil-iation, religion or denomination may be sentenced to one to three years in prison. This new law does not only refer to everyday life, but also to the labor and economic markets.

In election campaigns, non-Turkish languages may also be used. In addition, villages and other local-ities can reproduce their old names at the request of the municipalities. In this context, it is also allowed to use non-Turkish letters from now on.'552

Oliver Ernst: 'How positive the development of Kurdish political integration was, as a result of the desegregation of the Kurdish question and the high level of acceptance for the Kurdish political milieu, was made clear the 2014 presidential elections, when the pronounced Kurdish nationalist candidate, Se-lahattin Demirtas, won around ten percent of the vote. This success in the first presidential election, where the people could directly elect the president, then encouraged the strongly Kurdish Democratic Party of Peoples (HDP) in 2015 to compete for parliamentary elections on June 7, 2015, not only with individual candidates but as a as a Left-Wing Gathering Party with various political forces, including the Turkish Greens Left Party. Two parties from Germany also supported the HDP officially in their election campaign: The Left and Alliance 90 / The Greens.

Also, in these elections, the result of around 13 percent for the HDP confirmed that a strong political force of the Kurdish national movement was in conformity with the democratic development in Turkey.'553

Unfortunately, the peace negotiations between the Turkish government and Abdullah Öcalan were not completed. Turkish President Erdogan sought a presidential constitution that gave the president all the crucial powers. Since the Kurdish parliamentarians do not support him, he could not reach the nec-essary two-thirds majority for a constitutional amendment. That`s why he considered the Kurds to be opponents again.

Added to this is Erdogan's perceived danger that the part of Syria known as *Rojava* will form a Kurdish state beyond the Turkish border, which in turn will strengthen the Turkish Kurds. In order to prevent this formation of states, Turkey secretly supported ISIS as an opponent of the Kurds.

Rising tensions with the Kurds have been exacerbated by the Kurds' accusation that after the ter-rorist attack 'on Suruç, the most Kurd-inhabited city, on July 20, 2015,' the Turkish authorities in Ankara 'let the IS terrorist militias act or secretly support them. The PKK killed two Turkish policemen allegedly working with ISIS. In Turkey, several Kurds were arrested as sympathizers of the PKK and bases of

[549] See the report of the newspaper "Radikal" September 2013. 17. 7 2015 fouind under http://www.radikal.com.tr/.turkiye/q_w_xin _85_yillik_yasagi_bitiyor-1152737.

[550] See the report of the German Turkish News (DTN) of March 2014 titled „*Minderheiten freuen sich: Türkei verabschiedet Demokratie-Paket*". Am 17. 7. 2015 found under http://www.deutsch-tuerki-sche-na-chrichtn.de/2014/03/499187/minderheit%E2%80%8Ben-freuen-sich-tuerkei-verab-schie%E2%80%8Bdet-demokratie%E2%80%8B-pakt/.

[551] https://de.wikipedia.org/wiki/Kurden_in_der_T%C3%BCrkei#Legale_kurdische_Parteien.

[552]http://www.deutsch-tuerkische-nachrichten.de/2014/03/499187/minderheit%E2%80%8Ben-freuen-sich-tu-erkei-verabschie%E2%80%8B det-demokratie%E2%80%8B-paket/.

[553] Oliver Ernst: *Die Kurdenfrage in der Türkei und der Krieg in Syrien*, p.2, http://www.bpb.de/apuz/221174/die-kurdenfrage-in-der-tuerkei- und- der-krieg-in-syrien?p=all.

Kurdish fighters in northern Iraq were bombed by the Turkish Air Force. The PKK has canceled the cease-fire with Turkey ...

President Recep Tayyip Erdoğan has also officially canceled the peace process with the Kurds, following his announcement that politicians linked to terrorist groups should be prosecuted.'[554] So the Turkish parliament, as Hasnain Kazim writes, at the behest of Erdogan, 'repealed the immunity of a total of 138 politicians, against whom the prosecutor investigated. Above all, the members of the pro-Kurdish left-wing HDP are affected, as many as 50 out of 59. Almost the entire political group could no longer fulfill its mandate in the event of a conviction.'[555]

Instead of disturbing peace not only in Turkey, but also in the region, with his furious narrow-minded Turkish nationalism and his greed for sole rule, Turkish President, Recep Tayyip Erdoğan, should instead follow his neo-Ottoman ideas on the basis of the quoted Öcalan proposals *Aspiring to the Confederation*, which also includes the Syrian and Iraqi Kurdish areas. Because Oliver Ernst correctly writes: 'Since the territorial demarcations that prevented the emergence of a Kurdish state after the First World War in the Middle East, [556] the Kurdish conflict "is one of the most lasting causes of instability and cross-border conflicts in the country Region".[557] Even though it is sometimes referred to as "the Palestinian conflict of the 21st century",[558] Kurdish players, such as former Iraqi Kurdish Education Minister, Olawer Ala'Aldeen, are currently drawing surprisingly positive results, at least for Kurdish aspirations in Iraq: "For the first time, our neighbors can actually imagine an independent Kurdistan without spilt blood. (...) Yes, the overall order in the Middle East is changing - never before in history has the Kurdish constellation been so good."[559]'[560]

2.8 Egypt

Klaus Kreiser writes: Napoleon Bonaparte, 'In 1798, the young French Revolutionary General tried, with an expeditionary army, to wrest the land of the pyramids from the Ottomans and displace the English from the region.'[561]

' After the French capitulation, Istanbul uses the originally reform-oriented Hüsrev Pasha as its new governor in Cairo. But despite brutal measures, he does not manage to bring the province under control.' His successor, Mehmed Ali, succeeded. Mehmed Ali was born in 1770 or 1771 'in the Balkans, in the Macedonian Kavala, in modest circumstances, and grew up without a formal education.'[562]. He rose through the ranks of the Ottoman army and was eventually appointed Pasha and Viceroy of Egypt. 'Brutally he turns off the Mamluk elite, which, until then, had dominated Egypt.

In order to maintain the army, the modernized and expanded bureaucracy and the growing number of foreign advisers, resources needed to be expanded. Mehmed Ali replaced the traditional tax lease system with a centralized taxation policy. He quickly monopolizes the purchase and sale of wheat, rice

---

[554] Markus C. Schulte von Drach: *Volk ohne Staat*, Loc. cit.

[555] Hasnain Kazim: *Türkisches Parlament: Kniefall vor Erdogan*, http://www.spiegel.de/politik/ausland/tuerkei-par-lament-hebt-immunitae auf-kniefall-vor-recep-tayyip-erdogan-a-1093325.html.

[556] Vgl. Oliver Ernst: *Menschenrechte und Demokratie in den deutsch-türkischen Beziehungen. Die Menschenrechts-politikder Bundesrepublik Deutschland im Spannungsfeld der inneren und äußeren Sicherheit*, Münster 2002.

[557] Awat Asadi: *Der Kurdistan-Irak-Konflikt. Der Weg zur Autonomie seit dem Ersten Weltkrieg*, p.14.

[558] Oliver Ernst: *Erdogan kämpft gegen die PKK. Ein neuer Kurdenkrieg in der Türkei würde auch Deutschland erfas-sen*, 28.7.2015 »http://www.focus.de/politik/experten/ernst/tuerkei-kaempft-gegen-pkk-ein-neuer-kurdenkrieg-in-der-tuerkei-wuerde-auch- deutschland-erfassen_id_4842580.html« (16.1.2016).

[559] cit. after Hans-Joachim Löwer: *Die Stunde der Kurden. Wie sie den Nahen Osten verändern*, p.173f.

[560] Oliver Ernst: *Die Kurdenfrage in der Türkei und der Krieg in Syrien*, p.2, http://www.bpb.de/apuz/221174/die-kurdenfrage-in-der-tuerkei-und-der-krieg-in-syrien?p=all.

[561]Klaus Kreiser: *Das neue Ägypten*, p.2, http://www.zeit.de/2011/09/Osman-Mehmed-Ali-Pasch.

[562] Kreiser: loc. cit, p.1.

and sugarcane. ... In 1837, 95% of domestic trade was controlled by the state. In 1820, the canal between the Nile and Alexandria is completed. However, the first attempts at industrialization did not produce any resounding successes.' [563] He tried 'to set up his own industry in the province of Egypt by means of protective tariffs and state investment. The government revenue of his power range increased more than fivefold from the beginning of his reign until 1821.[564]

Although the attempt to industrialize the country and implement land reform was not as successful as it was thought, a new middle class emerged in the cotton production and trade sectors. The lack of success is due not least to the interventions of European powers. [565]' 566

Under Khedive (Viceroy) Ismail, the grandson of Mehmed Ali, 'arose the Suez Canal, which was opened in 1869.' [567] However, the construction of the Suez Canal (1859-1869) 'made the country so dependent on foreign borrowings that the sovereign debt administration established by Great Britain and France became the actual government of the country. To secure a route to India, Britain acquired the Egyptian Canal Shares, occupied the country in 1882, and formally made it a protectorate in 1914.' [568] The last ruler of the House, Muhammad Ali, was 'overthrown by the Free Officers around Nagib and Nasser only in 1952.'[569]

After the Second World War, the history of the young republic of Egypt was 'first determined by General Muhammad Nagib, then by the leader of the revolution, Colonel Gamal Abdel Nasser (1954-1970). Nasser's socialist regime maintained close ties with the Soviet Union. The nationalization of the Suez Canal Society in 1956 led to the military intervention of Israel, Britain and France. The Suez crisis was resolved by UN intervention. '[570]

Gamal Abdel Nasser considered himself an Arab nationalist and pursued 'a policy of merging all Arab countries (pan-Arabism). The aim of this policy was to push back American, British and French influence in the Near East and North Africa. This was countered by the conservative monarchies of Saudi Arabia, Iraq and Jordan.'[571]

' In 1958, Egypt merged with Syria and northern Yemen into the United Arab Republic (VAR), which in fact existed only until 1961.'[572] Because, 'in the Union, there were soon arose a number of differences. The Egyptians nationalized all companies and banks operating in Syria and designated Cairo as their capital. Almost the entire government were Egyptians. In Syria, people felt cheated and betrayed. On September 27, 1961, the army in Syria took power and declared the union dissolved on the following day.'[573]

As in other Muslim states, secularization in Egypt was thus pursued by the military and supported by European-trained intellectuals and business leaders. But a military rule that loses its national momentum is usually only about privileges and power, and is prone to corruption.

In order to secure their economic security, the military also founded business enterprises. However, in their hierarchical military structure, they were more in line with a centralized planned economy with monopolies that could not compete with private companies. Lack of cost-effectiveness was compensated

[563] Kreiser: p.2.
[564] Khaled Fahmy: *All The Pasha's Men – Mehmed Ali, his army and the making of modern Egypt*, p.9-11 , p.72.
[565] Immanuel Wallerstein: *Unthinking Social Science*, London, 1991, P.14 und Ismail Küpeli: *Was ging schief beim 'Untergang des Morgenlandes'?*, München, 2006, p.9.
[566] https://de.wikipedia.org/wiki/Muhammad_Ali_Pascha.
[567] Klaus Kreiser: *Das neue Ägypten*, p.2, http://www.zeit.de/2011/09/Osman-Mehmed-Ali-Pasch
[568] Kreiser: p.3.
[569] Kreiser: p.3.
[570] https://de.wikipedia.org/wiki/%C3%84gypten#.C3.84gypten_als_Republik.
[571] https://de.wikipedia.org/wiki/Vereinigte_Arabische_Republik.
[572] https://de.wikipedia.org/wiki/%C3%84gypten#.C3.84gypten_als_Republik.
[573] https://de.wikipedia.org/wiki/Vereinigte_Arabische_Republik.

if necessary by state security guarantees, in particular against foreign competition. So the economic development of the whole country still lagged behind.

Against the military dictatorships, on the one hand formed a liberal-thinking democratic, and on the other hand, an Islamic opposition. Both demanded a codetermination of the people through democratic elections and parties. But for the Islamic clergy and the masses, they chose democratic elections only to secure passage to a more or less reactionary Islamic state of God. They pushed aside all social ills on the secular social constitution and promised salvation through the reintroduction of Sharia. As a result, Islamic groups emerged that also operated socio-ethically and offered themselves as a salvific alternative to a military dictatorship. The resistance of religious fundamentalists also allowed the further development of Egypt.

In 1977, Sadat, the successor of Nasser, initiated a dialogue with Israel 'through a surprising peace initiative, which, in 1979, led to the peace treaty and withdrawal of Israeli troops from the Sinai Peninsula, but isolated the country within the Arab world and provoked the resistance of Islamic fundamentalists. In 1981, Sadat, who had been awarded the Nobel Peace Prize in 1978, along with Israeli Prime Minister Menachem Begin, was the victim of an assassination attempt.

His successor, the acting Vice President, Husni Mubarak, succeeded in restoring Egypt as a fully respected member of the Arab League. Critics noted, however, that he ruled as an authoritarian since the 1982 Emergency Act was passed, up until the 2011 Revolution. He therefore ruled over a pseudo-democratic system. They say that elections were partly falsified or postponed and some members of the opposition were jailed for fictitious causes. In Egypt, there was only the amount of public opposition that Mubarak allowed.'[574]

' Against the background of the Tunisian Jasmine revolution, the Arab Spring in Egypt began on January 25, 2011, focusing, above all, on the demand for the rule of law, freedom and democracy. In the wake of the revolution, which killed around 850 protesters in Egypt, Mubarak resigned. [575] From the three-round People's Council elections, held between November 28, 2011 and January 10, 2012, the Democratic Alliance for Egypt, headed by the Liberty and Justice Party (Muslim Brotherhood), was the strongest force for Egypt, accounting for some 45% of the total 498 seats. The Salafist Party of Light was the second largest fraction with about 25% of the seats. The successor parties of the once ruling National Democratic Party (NDP) lost a lot and only achieved 18 seats (2010: 420). This was followed by the liberal New Wafd party with 39 (6) seats and the left Egyptian block with 35 seats. 40 seats (70) were taken by independents and members of smaller parties.

From the sub-elections to the Shura Council, the Egyptian House of Lords, in January / February 2012, the Muslim Brotherhood also emerged as the strongest force, followed by the Salafists of the Party of Light and liberal forces. Then, for the first time, it came to free presidential elections. The first ballot was held on May 23 and 24, 2012, and the second ballot on June 16 and 17, 2012. On June 24, 2012, the result was announced: Mohammed Morsi was therefore elected with 51.7% of the valid votes for president[576] and with his swearing-in was on June 30, 2012, to becoming the acting head of state.[577]

But on June 15, 2012 the parliament was formally dissolved by the Supreme Military Council and subsequently denied access to parliament after the Supreme Court, the day before, declared the formation of parliament to be unconstitutional, since it was not allowed for one third of the seats to be filled by so-called "Independent" parties. [578]

---

[574] https://de.wikipedia.org/wiki/%C3%84gypten#.C3.84gypten_als_Republik.

[575] Neue ägyptische Regierung im März 2011, downloaded 23. 3. 2011.

[576] vgl. Homepage des U.P.Committee of the Blue Shield, downloaded 26. 10. 2016; Isabelle-Constance v. Opalinski: *Schüsse auf die Zivilisation*, FAZ vom 20. 8. 2014; Hans Haider: *Missbrauch von Kulturgütern ist strafbar*, Wiener Zeitung 29. 6. 2012.

[577] *Morsi wins Egypt's presidential election*, Bericht bei al-Dschasira vom 24. 6. 2012, downloaded 24. 6. 2012.

[578] *Mohamed Morsi sworn in as Egypt's president*, Bericht bei al-Dschasira vom 30. 6.2012, downloaded 30. 6.2012.

Since June 2012, the Constituent Assembly, in which Muslim Brothers and Salafists had a majority of 100 seats, drafted a new constitution. Over 60 percent voted in the referendum for the new constitution. In November 2012, newly-elected President Mohammed Morsi withdrew his decisions and decrees from control by the judiciary and declared them sacrosanct. He effectively overruled the separation of power. [579]

On July 3, 2013, at around 9:00 p.m., CEST, Colonel-General Abd al-Fattah as-Sisi announced that Mursi had been deposed by the military following massive public protests. The constitutional judge, Adli Mansur, was sworn in on July 4, 2013, after this military coup as interim president of the country. [580][581]'582 . On June 8, 2014, the non-party military as-Sisi became the new president. Thus, Egypt again had a military dictatorship as in the days of Mubarak. But without this dictatorship, Egypt would most likely have been transformed into a Muslim Sharia society, against which the secular and Coptic Christians would have resisted, so that social chaos could not be ruled out.

2.9. Libya

Italy had annexed Libya after the Italian-Turkish War (1911-1912). But in 1932, after a nearly ten-year colonial war, only the fascist, Benito Mussolini, could, according to Wikipedia, use 'bombs, poison gas and concentration camps, in which about 100,000 Libyans were killed, which corresponded to about 15% of the total population'583, and make Libya an Italian colony.

After the Italian and German units were forced to surrender at Tunis in May 1943, Libya was occupied by Great Britain and France until 1949. By a resolution of the United Nations, 1951 'Libya was given independence. Idris I, the head of the Senussi, became the king of the constitutional monarchy. The discovery of rich oil deposits in 1959 has made Libya one of the most important oil-exporting countries in the world.

On the other hand, however, the internal social tensions intensified, which, in addition to growing nationalist sentiment, finally led to the overthrow of the monarchy by the military on September 1, 1969 (...) and the proclamation of the Arab Republic of Libya. King Idris and Queen Fatima went into exile in Cairo.' 584

Libya was dictatorially ruled by Colonel Muammar al-Gaddafi, first in his role as "Chairman of the Revolutionary Command Council", then, after Libya was proclaimed a People's Democracy in 1977, as "Supreme Commander of the Armed Forces" and, from 1979, as "Revolutionary Leader".

Gaddafi operated a relatively secular policy. The free exercise of religion was 'guaranteed, as far as it was not contrary to traditions. State and religion were ... separate, with the clergy being confined to religion.'585

Libya had one of the highest per capita incomes of the African continent. The social security of the residents included free medical care as well as widow, orphan and retirement pensions. There was compulsory schooling, with free lessons for six to fifteen year olds. [586] Nevertheless, the illiteracy rate of women is still 29%, and for men, it is 8%; so this rate was very low in comparison to 17% in Africa as a whole. [587] 'There are universities in Tripoli, Benghazi and other larger places.

579 *SCAF formally disbands Egypt parliament*, report of al Jazeera vom 15. 6. 2012.
580 *Mursi macht sich zu Ägyptens „neuem Pharao"*. In: welt.de. 22. 11. 2012, downloaded 2. 2. 2015.
581 *Ägypten: Militär verhaftet Präsident Mursi, Jubelfeiern auf dem Tahrir-Platz* downloaded 3. Juli 2013.
582 https://de.wikipedia.org/wiki/%C3%84gypten#.C3.84gypten_als_Republik.
583 https://de.wikipedia.org/wiki/Libyen.
584 https://de.wikipedia.org/wiki/Libyen.
585 https://de.wikipedia.org/wiki/Libyen.
586 Literacy Rates of the World. downloaded 9. 8. 2011.
587 Literacy Rates of the World. downloaded 9. 8. 2011.

Although Gaddafi, in striking contrast to other Arab socialists, had conservative-Islamic views on the role of women, [588] women under his rule in Libya had a higher education compared to in other Arab countries. In the case of a divorce, they were allowed to keep the common house or apartment. There were day-care centers for working women as well as women in classical "male occupations" such as police officers or female pilots [589]. In 1979, Gaddafi set up a military academy for women. However, most educated women worked in health care and as teachers and the female employment rate fell below 10% in the mid-1990s. Polygamy was allowed in Libya, unlike in neighboring Tunisia, where men could get married to a second wife only with the approval of the other wife. Also, the spouse was, in most cases, selected by the family.[590]' 591

' After public protests in February 2011, which sought to stifle the security forces, there was a split in the country's political leadership. In Benghazi, armed opposition took control. Following a coordinated military intervention by NATO and a number of Arab states to enforce the no-fly zone established by UN Resolution 1973, the militia members of the Libyan National Liberation Army managed to defeat Libyan regular forces. The number of war dead is estimated to be between 10,000 and 50,000.[592]' 593

'After the war and international military intervention, the country was shaken by fighting rival militias. At first, the democratic process in Libya seemed to be progressing, because in 2012, the first fair and free elections in the history of Libya were held. In this election to the 2012 Libyan National Congress, the Secular Alliance of National Forces (ANK) was by far the strongest party. However, the rival Islamist Justice and Construction Party succeeded in forming a parliamentary majority against the ANK. In the aftermath, the Islamist governments have neither been able nor seem willing to dissolve the independent militia in Libya or to integrate them into the state. Terrorist groups and militias ... were able to move freely in the new Libya. Under the presidency of Nuri Busahmein, the situation finally escalated when the new head of state of Libya did not support the government in the fight against independent militias, but founded and promoted its own Islamist private army with the "Operation Room of Libyan Revolutionaries."' 594

'General Chalifa Haftar formed a secular alliance called "Dignity", which, in May 2014, attempted to seize power in a military coup. In contrast to the military coup in Egypt in 2013, this failed because the Muslim Brothers expected such action and in turn had their own militia founded. After the forces around Haftar won the election with an 18%, turnout the Islamist camp in Tripoli called "Dawn" returned to power and drove the new official government to the east of the country.

In this civil war, the two alliances, "Dignity" (which is the official government) and "Dawn" and the terrorist organization "the IS" are fighting for power in the country. It goes hand in hand with a dramatic increase in refugee numbers and serious human rights violations. '595

'On December 17, 2015, a peace agreement was signed between the rival camps of Tobruk and Tripoli, which provides for the rebuilding of the state and its institutions by 2018 as well as a unity government under Fayiz as-Sarradsch. On March 30, 2016, the unity government in Tripoli began its work. However, even after the peace treaty, Libya continued to be divided. The west of the country supports as-Sarradsch, while Chalifa Haftar has great influence in the eastern part [596] [597]. On February 16, 2017, the

---

588 Gerrit Hoekmann: *Zwischen Ölzweig und Kalaschnikow, Geschichte und Politik der palästinensischen Linken*, p.39.
589 Karin El Minawi, *Emanzipation über den Wolken*, Süddeutsche Zeitung, 28. 10. 2010.
590 Andreas Vrabl: *„Libyen: Eine Dritte Welt - Revolution in der Transition"*, p.68-71.
591 https://de.wikipedia.org/wiki/Libyen.
592 Seumas Milne: *If the Libyan war was about saving lives, it was a catastrophic failure*, The Guardian, 26. 10. 2011.
593 https://de.wikipedia.org/wiki/Libyen.
594 Ibid..
595 Ibid.
596 *Welche Rolle spielt Russland im libyschen Chaos?* FAZ 4.2.2017.
597 *Wettlauf ohne Ziel*, Süddeutsche 15.2.2017.

two power blocs agreed to conduct all-Libyan parliamentary elections in 2018, which should be organized jointly by the Eastern Council of Deputies and the Western High Council of State. [598] Between the power struggle of the two halves of the state, the militias of the self-proclaimed 3rd Government under Chalifa al-Ghweil [599] and the terrorist organizations Islamic State [600] and Al-Qaeda act through the resulting power vacuum [601].[602]

The political and social problems of Libya are not only due to the relatively advanced secularization of Libya by the former colonial administration, or because under Gaddafi, Islamic reactionaries are quashed, but there is also the fact that the society still lives with traditional tribal associations, and because of the shattered state structures, many militias have formed, which could even take over the plentiful supply possession of weapons in the country. In addition, the economy and living standards were largely supported by oil revenues and the economy has largely collapsed as a result of the turmoil.

2.10 Somalia

Sixty percent of all Somalians live partly or fully as nomads. Twenty-five percent of the people live as peasants who have settled in the most fertile region of the country between the Shabeelle and Jubba rivers. The rest of the population (15 to 20 percent) live in urban areas.' [603]

Somalia is an extreme example of the survival of an archaic clan system, which, as Wikipedia writes, 'was probably influenced by the tribal society of the Arabs. Every Somali belongs to a tribe or clan through his paternal lineage. ...

The traditional nomadic people: Dir, Darod, Isaaq and Hawiye are considered "Real Somali" or Samaal, while the sedentary peasant Rahanweyn are referred to as "unreal Somali" or as Sab. Like some ethnic minorities, they are not regarded as equal from the point of view of a part of Samaal and are traditionally subject to social disadvantage.

Each of these clan families is divided into a large number of subclans and "genders" (Somali: reer, which means "people of", "descendants of"). These each include a few hundred to a thousand men who pay or receive crime money for carrying out crime together (diya, mag). This system traditionally provides the individual Somalian with protection for life and property, but it also leads to blood feuds that not only relate to individual crimes, but also include disputes over water and grazing rights and political power.'[604]

After the proselytizing of Somalis to Muslims 'Muslim sultanates and city-states emerged. In the 16th century, the cities on the north coast under Turkish or Egyptian rule, those on the southern Benadirküste in the 17th century came under the sovereignty of Oman, or, in the 19th century, Zanzibar. '

However, the traditional practice of Islam in Somalia 'is rather temperate in villages and among nomads and mixed with the customary law of the clans.' However, the ancient tribal culture also includes archaic customs such as genital mutilation.

In these archaic structures, Somalia would probably have continued to live as if it had not been captured by European colonization, because 'at the end of the 19th century, the area inhabited by Somalians experienced its distribution, which is still effective today. The north of present-day Somalia was colonized by Britain as British Somaliland, and the south and east by Italy as Italian Somaliland. On July 1, 1960, the two colonies became independent as Somalia.'[605]

---

598 *Deal ohne Handschlag,* Sürddeutsche Zeitung 16.2.2017.
599 *Putschversuch in Libyen,* NZZ 16.10.2016.
600 *Was nach dem IS kommt,* Spiegel.online 14.9.2016.
601 *Tagebuch aus dem Fegefeuer,* Spiegel.online 20.8.2015.
602 https://de.wikipedia.org/wiki/Libyen.
603 https://de.wikipedia.org/wiki/Somalia#Geschichte.
604 Ibid.
605 Ibid.

However, the archaic potential for conflict was even extended by one further dimension, since the colonizers naturally influenced the economic and social system and nationalist liberation struggles emerged against the occupiers. Even after independence, this nationalism led to power struggles and conflicts with neighboring countries. In addition, these conflicts were again overshadowed by the East-West conflict.

'The relationship with neighboring states was strained because of territorial claims (...) made by Somalia, in particular on the Ethiopian region of Ogaden. Domestic tensions persisted between the north, the south and the east, between clans and parties. In 1969, President Sherkard was killed by a bodyguard, after which the pro-Soviet military took over under Siad Barre's power.

Barre initially leaned toward the Soviet Union, trying to introduce "scientific socialism" and limit the traditional influence of the clans. In 1977/78, he led the Ogaden war against Ethiopia, which Somalia lost. Because the Soviet Union supported the enemy communist Derg regime in Ethiopia in this war, Siad Barre economically and politically turned away from the Soviet Union and towards the United States. Inside the country, he was increasingly dictatorial, and different clans were subject to repression. Several rebel groups began an armed struggle against the Barre government, which led to its overthrow in 1991 ....

However, the victorious rebel groups could not agree on a successor government'[606], so that Somalia ended up in a mess and became a so-called failed state. In this chaos, the so-called Al Qaeda-affiliated al-Shabaab and other Islamic militias were able to spread all over the country with the exception of northern Somaliland (formerly a British colony). In addition, pirate groups emerged that endanger international shipping traffic on the coast. The fact that the internationally recognized Somali government was able to regain control of most of the country was, in particular, due to the military support of the AMI-SOM African Union, that is to say, the soldiers from Kenya, but also, to a lesser extent, from Ethiopia, Uganda and Burundi[607] and the financial and material support from the rest of the world. The piracy from Somalia is being combatted by international naval missions.

2.11 Eritrea

Another country that belonged to the Ottoman Empire for over 300 years and became an Italian colony in 1890 was Eritrea. The Italians had invaded Ethiopia in 1935 and created a common colony from Ethiopia, Somalia and Eritrea. [608] When Ethiopia became independent again, thanks to Allied forces in 1941, Eritrea's connection with Italy was also ended. 'The area was placed under the British military administration, and in 1947, after the formal release of Eritrea through Italy, became a British Mandate territory. After the Second World War, the United Nations opted for a federation of the Province of Eritrea with the Empire of Abyssinia.' [609]

'After the Ethiopian Emperor Haile Selassie systematically eroded the political rights of the Eritrean population from 1952 to 1961 and subsequently annexed Eritrea through the (self-) dissolution of the Eritrean parliament in 1961, Eritrean separatists took up arms. The War of Independence ended after thirty years in 1991 with the victory of the Eritrean People's Liberation Front (EPLF) and various other Ethiopian rebel groups. "Following a UN-supervised plebiscite, Eritrea became independent on May 24, 1993.

---

[606] https://de.wikipedia.org/wiki/Somalia#Geschichte.
[607] Siehe: https://de.wikipedia.org/wiki/Mission_der_Afrikanischen_Union_in_Somalia.
[608] Siehe: https://de.wikipedia.org/wiki/%C3%84thiopien.
[609] https://de.wikipedia.org/wiki/Eritrea.

"The population of Eritrea is divided almost equally [610]among Muslims (Sunnis) and Christians (Eritrean Orthodox Tewahedo Church, Protestants, Catholics, Orthodox).'[611] Unrecognized religious groups, especially Christian ones, are persecuted. 'Eritrea is ranked third in 2016 in the Open Doors annual World Tracing Index (WVI), which identifies and analyzes the countries with the highest amount of Christian persecution. ...[612]'[613]

'At the annual ranking of press freedom, published by the press freedom organization, Reporters Without Borders, in 2015, the country came 180th [614] and thus, repeatedly, in last place. According to Amnesty International, government critics, deserters and Eritreans who have sought asylum abroad are detained. [615] Overall, many international observers regard the political system in Eritrea as repressive or even a dictatorship. [616][617] The government argues that Eritrea is still in transition to democracy, harassed by Ethiopia and therefore is still at war. This would prevent the young government from collapsing.[618]'[619]

2.12 Turkish Republic

Wikipedia writes: 'After the defeat of the Central Powers, the Ottoman Empire lost its remaining territories outside of Anatolia and Thrace as a result of the peace treaty of Sèvres. In addition, the area of today's Turkey should be largely dismembered. Greece was awarded the city of Smyrna (Turkish Izmir) and parts of western Anatolia. The region around Antalya should become the possession of the Italians and the French, and should include Cilicia in addition to Syria. In the eastern parts of today's Turkey, with the cities of Kars, Ardahan and Erzurum, an Armenian state was to emerge. South of and east of the Euphrates, the Kurds were granted an autonomous region. These plans were not implemented.' [620]

' Mustafa Kemal Pasha organized the political and military resistance to these plans from May 19, 1919. The fights with Greece were especially intense from 1920 onwards. The war ended on September 9, 1922, with the recapture of Izmir. After the cessation of hostilities, ethnic cleansing took place in Greece and Turkey, expelling "Turks" from Greek territory and "Greeks" from Turkish territory, excluding the Greeks in Istanbul and the Muslims of western Thrace.

After the victory of Turkey, the provisions of the Treaty of Sèvres were revised on July 24, 1923, with the Treaty of Lausanne. The treaty recognized the limits of the new state that are still valid today under international law. At the same time, the mutual expulsion of minorities was legalized.' [621]

The secular but also nationalist ideal of society began in Turkey too with European-trained or inspired intellectuals and military men, the *Young Ottomans* and *Young Turks*.

---

[610] For 1936, the Small World Atlas of the German Book Club gave for the Italian colony 57 percent Mohammedans and only 39 percent Christians (...). The independence movement was also supported by Muslims in the 1970s (Meyers Enzyklopädisches Lexikon, Volume 8, P.119, Mannheim 1973/79)..

[611] https://de.wikipedia.org/wiki/Eritrea.

[612] Weltverfolgungsindex 2016. Open Doors.

[613] https://de.wikipedia.org/wiki/Eritrea.

[614] Ranking of Press Freedom Reporters Without Borders 2015.

[615] Amnesty International Report 2008: Eritrea.

[616] Bettina Rühl: *Vom Freiheitskampf in die Diktatur. Eritreas Abstieg.* Deutschlandfunk. 24. 5. 2011, downloaded 14.2.2015.

[617] Länderinformationen: *Eritrea – Innenpolitik.* Auswärtiges Amt. Oktober 2013, downloaded 14. 2. 2015.

[618] *Eritrea: Gute Nachrichten sind keine Nachrichten – Eritreas Entwicklung in der Diskussion,* in: Afrika-Bulletin 114: April/Mai 2004.

[619] https://de.wikipedia.org/wiki/Eritrea.

[620] https://de.wikipedia.org/wiki/T%C3%BCrkei#Atat.C3.BCrk_.E2.80.93_Republik_und_Reformen.

[621] Ibid.

Wikipedia writes: 'The Yuong or New Ottomans ... were founded in 1865 by a secret organization in the Ottoman Empire.'[622] 'The Young Turks followed the Young Ottomans' ideas a generation later. Like the Young Ottomans, the Young Turks wanted to save the Ottoman Empire from destruction. Both movements saw a solution in introducing constitutionalism and making all minorities legally equal. [623]'[624]

' Supporters of the Young Turk movement were modernist sections of the educated elite. The movement was founded in 1889 with the establishment of the secret organization, İttihad -ı Osmani Cemiyeti ("Association for the Unity of the Ottomans"), at the Military Medical School in Istanbul. [625] ...

The moderate faction of the Young Turks had connections at court and was led by Prince Sabahaddin, a relative of the imperial Ottoman house. More important, however, were the "little people" who had been promoted to the functional elites of the state (civil servants, teachers, officers) by modern education, and who were to set the tone very soon after the 1908 Young Turk Revolution. There developed, particularly after the second takeover of power of the Young Turks in 1913, an alliance between radical intellectuals (Ziya Gökalp, Nâzım) with civil bureaucrats (Talât Pasha) and ultimately decisive officers (Enver Pasha, Cemal Pasha).'[626]

Kemal Atatürk, emerging from the Young Turks but rising in the military hierarchy, succeeded in preventing the political and military disintegration of Turkey in the fight against foreign powers and thus became the most important political and military personality of Turkey. 'On October 29, 1923, the Republic of Turkey was founded by a major constitutional amendment, headed by a president as the head of the government and the sole head of the executive branch. There was an office tailored to the claim and position of Mustafa Kemal.'[627]

The principles of Kemalism: 'Republicanism in the sense of popular sovereignty, nationalism as a turn against the multi-ethnic state of Ottoman form, populism as an expression of a policy directed at the interests of the people, not a class, revolutionism in the sense of a steady continuation of reforms, secularism, i.e. the separation of state and religion, and statism with partial state economic control.

To secure the new state order and to enforce the model of a secular republic, however, not only the Ottoman Sultanate had to be broken, but also the Caliphate. As Caliphs, the Ottoman rulers saw themselves as "representatives of the Prophet of God" and as the religious leaders of all Muslims. [628]'[629]

In a diary entry of June 6, 1918, Kemal Atatürk 'had already formulated the basic motive of all later reform steps:

"Should one day I have great influence or power, I think it would be best to change our society abruptly - immediately and in the shortest possible time. For in contrast to others, I do not believe that this change can be achieved by only gradually leading the uneducated to a higher level. My heart balks at such a view. Why should I return to the lower levels of the general population after having trained for many years, studying civilization and social history and experiencing gratification through freedom at all stages of my life? I'll make sure they get there, too. I am not allowed to approach them, rather they have to approach me."[630]

[622] https://de.wikipedia.org/wiki/Jungosmanen.

[623] Feroz Ahmad: *İttihat ve Terakki 1908-1914*, p.42.

[624] https://de.wikipedia.org/wiki/Jungosmanen.

[625] Klaus Kreiser, Christoph K. Neumann: *Kleine Geschichte der Türkei*, p.351.

[626] https://de.wikipedia.org/wiki/Jungt%C3%BCrken.

[627] https://de.wikipedia.org/wiki/Mustafa_Kemal_Atat%C3%BCrk.

[628] Bernard Lewis: The Political Language of Islam. Chicago 1988, p.44-50.

[629] https://de.wikipedia.org/wiki/Mustafa_Kemal_Atat%C3%BCrk.

[630] Dietrich Gronau: Mustafa Kemal Atatürk oder die Geburt der Republik. Fischer, Frankfurt am Main 1994, p.125 f.

He realized this program step by step, after he had won and held the key position sought in the function of the President of the State. It was a multitude of profound changes in tradition and customs that he pretended to implement to his compatriots within a few years.'[631]

' In the following years, entire legal systems from European countries were adopted and adapted to Turkish conditions. In 1926, Swiss civil law, and thus, monogamy with equality between men and women, was adopted (gender equality only partially succeeded in everyday life). This was followed by German commercial law and Italian criminal law. In 1928, secularization was proclaimed, and in the same year Arabic script was replaced by Latin (...). In the wake of further reforms, women's suffrage was introduced in Turkey in 1930, and since 1934, women have been allowed to stand for election themselves (passive women's suffrage).'[632]

Secularism intends, to a large extent, to eliminate all religious influence on the public life and self-determination of the individual. In its most consistent form, secularization aims to make man a citizen of the world. Imperfect secularization and liberalization, however, bind self-understanding to the nation and demand unconditional commitment to one's own nation. This will fight anything that interferes with the unity of the nation. Secularization in Turkey is also linked to a strong downright morbid nationalism.

'Extreme manifestations of Turkish nationalism were expressed in the Turkish historical thesis (Türk Tarih Tezi) and in the so-called unspoken theory. Anatolia's early civilizations were regarded as the result of an early Turkish immigration and tried to prove that Turkish was the original language from which all other languages descended.

Moreover, geographically, place names and field names that were not Turkish, non-Muslim, disparaging or incomprehensible were changed, at first sporadically. But in 1956, a separate commission was established in the Ministry of the Interior. Harun Tunçel stated in a study that by 1968, 12,000 of 40,000 villages were renamed. Furthermore, a list of 2,000 changed field names was published in 1977. [633] The main aim was to eradicate the non-Turkish or non-Muslim character of the places by eradicating suffixes that are, for example, church-based or ethnonyms.'[634]

The enforcement of strict nationalism is most likely to be governed by a one-party government. Şahin Alpay wrote in 2009: 'The Kemalists' Republican People's Party (CHP), founded in 1923, proclaimed the one-party system and imposed reforms in 1925 to build a modern, secular nation-state instead of the defeated Ottoman Empire. The official policy of the authoritarian regime aimed to forge a homogenous nation out of the multi-ethnic and multi-religious population that speaks Turkish, adheres to Turkish culture and practices the state-sanctioned form of Sunni Islam, as it is represented (to this day) by the Presidium for Religious Affairs. Religious statements were banned in public life. The largest religious minority, the Alevites, was denied official recognition and ultimately the Sunni faith was imposed. All Muslim ethnic groups, including the Kurds' largest ethnic minority, were forced to assimilate and submit to "Turkification". Any expression of Kurdish identity was banned. Only in 1991 was the public use of the Kurdish language allowed. [635] The Turkish forces not only guaranteed the security of the state and its Kemalist ideology, but also took on the role of the main mediator in establishing a secular and homogeneous Turkish identity among citizens.

At the end of the Second World War, modernization was complemented by democratization from above. The transition to a multi-party system was initiated and controlled by the authoritarian rulers, most of whom belonged to the CHP. It was forbidden to question the Kemalist state ideology; communism,

---

https://de.wikipedia.org/wiki/Mustafa_Kemal_Atat%C3%BCrk.

[632] https://de.wikipedia.org/wiki/T%C3%BCrkei.

[633] AZINLIK OKULLARINA. In: http://www.cnnturk.com/. CNN Türk, 19. Juni 2009, downloaded 19. 6. 2009 (turque).

[634]https://de.wikipedia.org/wiki/Volksgruppen_in_der_T%C3%BCrkei.

[635] Vgl. Hugh Poulton, The Top Hat, the Grey Wolf, and the Crescent, London 1997.

fundamentalist religions (meaning Islam), ethnic nationalism (meaning Kurdish nationalism) and liberalism in politics were prohibited. [[636]] The Turkish democracy was heavily controlled right from the beginning, in which the military took on a leading role.[637]

The leading role of the military in the Turkish state was initially also guaranteed by the way the constitution was put together, favoring the military, who repeatedly tried to organize a coup and take over power for a time, even after the introduction of the multi-party system. However, they feared political chaos, especially when they saw endangered Turkey's strict national unity by the Kurds' demands for recognition of their own identity and, accordingly, a degree of autonomy.

The secularization enforced by the Kemalists was imperfect, because it only brought about a military dictatorship and did not reach the mass of faithful supporters in the countryside. Here, we have the same phenomenon - military dictatorships in the form of the Shah of Persia, Saddam Hussein in Iraq, Colonel Gaddafi in Libya, Assad in Syria and Al Sissi in Egypt. When Europeans push for countries to be democratized, Islamists routinely use them to vote to elect an Islamic state in which Islamic clerics have the last word and are bound by a more or less strictly-interpreted Sharia law.

If Islam remains the highest norm, then depending on whether Islam is believed to be Shiite or Sunni, it establishes either a caliphate encompassing all countries, such as ISIS, or an all-embracing mullah rule, as intended by Iran. By contrast, if the country is already secularized to the point that nationalism has become the dominant motive of political action and Islamic faith only a component of nationalism, then a state is aspired to, as in Erdogan's Turkey, for example, which could be described as the "Holy Ottoman Empire of the Turkish Nation".

Supported by demands from the EU to remove the military from the political process as a precondition for EU accession, the then Prime Minister and current President of Turkey, Recep Tayyip Erdoğan, was able to reduce the special position of the military. Since the Turks have always longed for a strong central order of power, Recep Tayyip Erdoğan could use the principles of the Kemalists and how Kemal Atatürk concentrated all the power in his hands. At the same time, he enforces a witch hunt against anyone who stands in the way of his goals or even those who pursue the corrupt activities of his family.

He is dreaming of a kind of revival of the Ottoman Empire. So Luise Sammann and Fatih Kanalici reported on July 9, 2016 on radio station Deutschlandfunk: '"We are moved by the spirit that founded the Ottoman Empire," Recep Tayyip Recep Tayyip Erdoğan, then prime minister, announced to his compatriots in November 2012.'[638]

'Another example of this historical trend was President Recep Tayyip Erdoğan's recent call for compulsory instruction in Ottoman Turkish in secondary schools. According to conservative politicians, Turkish students should be able to decipher the tombstones of their grandparents again in the future.' [639]

Thus, it is not surprising that such propaganda-making films about the Ottoman Empire are becoming a popular success. The film "Fetih 1453", about the conquest of Constantinople, using 500-year-old knight's armor, with endless battles on horseback, 'was, shortly after its theatrical release in February 2012, the most successful film ever in Turkey. The 17 million dollar production costs were recouped in no time, because on the Bosporus there is an Ottoman fever!'[640]

'Known as "Neo-Ottoman", the policy of the AKP is called such because of these speeches. It is only half true, however, believes the Istanbul historian, Aydin. The thoroughly positive Ottoman image, to which

---

[636] Vgl. Ilkay Sunar: *State, Society and Democracy in Turkey*, Istanbul 2004.

[637] Şahin Alpay: *Die politische Rolle des Militärs in der Türkei*, http://www.bpb.de/apuz/31728/die-politische-rolle-des-militaers-in-der-tu erkei?p=all.

[638] Luise Sammann und Fatih Kanalici: *Träume von der osmanischen Vergangenheit*, http://www.deutschlandfunk.de/tuerkei-traeume-von-der-osmanischen-vergangenheit.724.de.html?dram:article_id=312910.

[639] Ibid.

[640] Ibid.

conservative politicians in Ankara like to refer, has little to do with true history. "The Ottoman Empire is shown to people as a perfect constitutional state, but we historians know that reality looked different and if we look at history, we see a despotic government."

But the image of the Ottomans, which is already being taught to Turkish elementary school students in the classroom, avoids unpopular truths. Often, it is no less romantic than the life between the Sultan's Palace and Harem, which was shown to the viewers on television for years. No wonder Recep Tayyip Erdoğan, who, at that time, was prime minister, began to publicly rant against the series "Wonderful Century" when it no longer met his expectations.

"Such an ancestor, as this series shows, we do not have! The Sultan Süleyman, whom we know, spent 30 years on the back of a horse and not in the harem. I condemn the directors of this series and the owners of this station in front of the whole nation! '"[641]

'"He opposed anything in this series that could damage the image of the sultan. For example, he could not accept showing that the Sultan killed his son and oppressed those who claimed their rights. A dream is to be created on the example of the Ottomans and people should think that even if we unconditionally obey our ruler, Turkey will become as powerful as the Ottomans once were.'"[642]

When one considers the disgust that Islam has against Europeanism, it is understandable why there are many attempts in Turkey up to the present day to suppress secularization in favor of Islamic standards. Understandably, these aspirations come from the Islamic clergy, which, as we have already seen in Iran, can rely on the masses, especially the rural population. Because Western influence is primarily valid only in larger cities.

The Islamic clergy also achieved that after the introduction of the multi-party system, where Islam-based parties were founded and so was the ruling AKP. As a result, more and more religious laws were abolished over time. The head of the Turkish parliament, Ismail Karaman, even called for the introduction of Sharia law in Turkey in April 2016. He was jeered because of the upcoming protests. But, as it says in the *Deutschen Wirtschafts Nachrichten*: 'It is unlikely that the parliamentary leader, Karaman, has acted without the knowledge and will of Erdoğan. Karaman belongs to the closest circle of the Turkish head of state.'[643]

Obviously, Recep Tayyip Erdoğan sees himself as the reborn sultan of an "Ottoman Empire", who, in the sense of the Ottoman sultan's caliph function, also sees himself as the center of Sunni Islam. This is also reflected in his megalomania. Luise Sammann and Fatih Kanalici write: 'One example among many is the palace with more than 1,000 rooms, which Recep Tayyip Erdoğan consecrated in Ankara on August 28, 2014, shortly after he the won presidential election. Just one of the countless toilets in the magnificent building cost several thousand dollars, cried critical journalists. His followers, however, proudly accept this. After all, as many argue, the Ottoman sultans also lived in breathtaking palaces! ...

But Turkish society is divided like no other. What makes the voters of the AK party proud often makes their opponents angry. For weeks, they demonstrated against the palace, which was built in the middle of a protected forest. Hundreds of trees had to give way to the magnificent building. Trees that the founder of modern Turkey, Mustafa Kemal Atatürk, had personally put under natural reserve over 80 years ago. The fact that Recep Tayyip Erdoğan had cut them down was also like a demonstration of power against Atatürk's supporters, the Kemalists. For a long time, the heritage of the founder of the Republic was considered inviolable on the Bosporus. Recep Tayyip Erdoğan has ended this era, and he never misses an opportunity to emphasize that. For instance, if he wants to build a mosque on Istanbul's iconic Taksim Square, which is so symbolic of the republic, or replace Turkey's largest airport, Atatürk Airport,

---

[641] Ibid.
[642] Ibid.
[643] http://deutsche-wirtschafts-nachrichten.de/2016/04/27/nach-scharia-forderung-tuerkische-regierung-macht-rueckzieher/.

with an even larger one, under the name *Recep Tayyip Erdoğan Airport*, according to media rumors, then he can do so.

The scramble for supremacy between the secular, previously often wealthier, Kemalist elite and the Anatolian masses neglected by them as a minor people is an old struggle that underlies many conflicts in present-day Turkey. It also has its place in the enthusiasm of the Turkish government for its Ottoman past.

"The secular reforms that Atatürk enforced in the first years after the founding of the Republic made many people strangers in their own country," explains Ismail Caglar from the ACP-affiliated thinktank, SETA. Even then, right in the early days of modern Turkey, the longing of many conservative Turks for the Ottoman Empire, which had just perished, began.'[644]

Ottoman visions also determine the foreign policy of Recep Tayyip Erdoğan. In itself, a secular state community of former Ottoman countries is a fascinating idea and could be an important contribution to the pacification of the Muslim world and world peace as a whole.

A new Ottoman secular community of states should, if possible, also include the North African countries of Egypt to Morocco. Such a community of states would have a Sunni Muslim majority. But that was already the case in the Ottoman Empire. It should, however, also show the same tolerance towards other religious communities as in the Ottoman Empire. Of course, the non-Sunnis would have to be full citizens, as befits a secular state where religion and the State are separated.

For Muslims, especially Palestinians, this would mean that their feeling of inferiority towards Israel would be lost. They could face the Israelis at least as equals as a member of a major power, while at the same time pushing back the influence of the Israelis in the Palestinian territories and on the Golan Heights.

If the Turks are really concerned with a new Ottoman community, then they should

1. strengthen their secular society and not weaken it by relapsing into their people's religiously determined immaturity. In particular, they should avoid any form of religious discrimination. Only in this way can they eliminate fears and reservations from other people besides the Sunni population;

2. for the Turkish policy on Syria, this means that they take away the fears of the Alawites, Christians and other religious communities clinging to Assad, to be persecuted by Sunnis after the fall of the Assad regime. Turkey must no longer militarily support the IS and the Al Qaeda offshoot, the Al Nusra Front, militarily - only secular resistance groups;

3. The Turks should make peace with the Kurds and assure them the utmost autonomy in Turkey, and, in particular, not try to weaken or completely destroy the party of the Kurds. Turkey should offer the Kurds in Syria and Iraq an association with Turkey and its unconditional support in the fight against the so-called Islamic State;

The Turks would have to recognize that the autonomy of Kurdish areas as sovereign states can no longer be prevented, because the position of the Kurdish autonomous area in Iraq, but also the Kurdish dominated areas in Syria, are already too strong. In this sense, Oliver Ernst also says 'If Turkey would support the process of political integration of the Syrian Kurds, who have been oppressed and disenfranchised for decades by the Baathist regime, into a post-war Syria, then this would potentially promote the reconciliation process with those forces among the Turkish Kurds, who still see themselves today as a "liberation movement" and partly oppose the Turkish state with terrorist violence. The dictum of Atatürk, the founder of the Turkish Republic - "peace in the land - peace in the world" - would thereby receive a new radiance, and strengthen the role of Turkey as an anchor country in an unstable crisis region.'[645]

[644] Luise Sammann und Fatih Kanalici: *Träume von der osmanischen Vergangenheit.*
[645] Oliver Ernst: *Die Kurdenfrage in der Türkei und der Krieg in Syrien*, S.3; http://www.bpb.de/apuz/221174/die-kurdenfrage-in-der-tuerkei-und-der-krieg-in-syrien?p=2.

Instead, the Turks have so far done everything to make the Kurds an enemy. Apart from fighting against the Kurds in their own country and the PKK, it also fights against the Kurdish areas bordering Turkey, and therefore supports the IS. For the IS Turkey, was a retreat - a recruitment office for IS supporters from all over the world, who traveled to Syria via Turkey, selling oil and other foreign exchange and weapons transport.

Apart from the fact that the Turks, with the support of the IS, endangered their relations with Europe, the USA, other Islamic countries and finally also with Russia, and therefore their support of the IS could only be halfhearted, the IS's terror also does not stop in Turkey. So in the end, Turkey had to join the camp of opponents of the IS.

Nor will the Turks resist their rejection of the Assad regime. It is clear that the Assad clan in post-war Syria may no longer play a role. But the existing relatively secular Syrian state must continue to exist, possibly with separation of the areas inhabited by the Kurds. A pacification of Syria will only be possible - and thus the Russians are right - if the existing Syria continues and is reformed in such a way that the Sunni majority and other groups can confess to the state.

3. The failure of the Americanization of Russia, Eurasism and the ebirth of the East-West antagonism

After the collapse of the Soviet Union, the Western world, under the leadership of the United States, sought to extend its influence to the former Eastern-bloc countries and Russia. The Russians were also open to the Western economy and democracy because they recognized their superiority. Der Spiegel writes: 'In December 1991, the Soviet Union collapsed and Boris Yeltsin, Russia's first democratically-elected president, condemned communism as a misanthropic doctrine. The country now had an ideological vacuum and chaos erupted with the introduction of the market economy. For the Yeltsin team, there was only one direction to head toward: the USA.

The Kremlin and the White House worked almost hand in hand. The economist, Jeffrey Sachs, prescribed a shock therapy for the Russian economy. It forced the Russians to suddenly privatize the economy without pumping enough Western money into Russia. The result: much shock, but no therapy. The radical neo-liberal course, according to Joseph E. Stiglitz, once chief economist at the World Bank, contributed to the economic collapse. Millions of Russians were impoverished. From a Russian point of view, these were the years of humiliation by the West.'[646]

The fact that this shock therapy did not have the desired success is, of course, also attributable to the fact that capitalist behavior is repugnant to Russians. Thus, after the collapse of the Soviet Union, a member of the audience from my talk on the nature of the market economy in Vladimir summarized the content: "So, speculators - folk pests in the Soviet Union - are *businessmen* in the market economy!" Because of the lack of businessmen there, there were only few, as we would say, *dynamic entrepreneurs*. Unscrupulous people, from Russia's point of view, misappropriated the vouchers issued as part of the privatization of state enterprises as employee shares, and became, often with a certain amount of criminal impetus, the oligarchs of Russia and the rest of the former countries that comprised the Soviet Union.

---

[646] Sven Becker und andere: *Die russische Frage*, in Der Spiegel Nr. 10/4.3.2017 p.14.

At the same time, the Russians had to learn painfully that the countries connected with them were alienated from them or had to suffer from a dissolution too.

Russians have always felt connected to Serbia, as with all Slav people, especially since they belong to the Orthodox Church. The Russian alliance with Serbia was also the occasion for the outbreak of the First World War. Then after the Second World War Kosovo, perceived as an integral part of Serbia, was separated from Serbia with the help of the West, and the United States announced the bombing of Serbia to end the Kosovo conflict without consulting the Kremlin.

In the Iraq war, Americans 'forged their "coalition of the willing" and pushed forward their plans for missile defense in Europe.' [647] However, the USA declared that this missile defense was not directed against the Russians. But they were also unwilling to involve the Russians in building this missile defense, for example, in Russia. Sven Becker and others write 'This dramatically worsened relations, yet the Kremlin still hoped to be invited to NATO as a member.' [648]

'It went downhill. At the 2008 NATO summit, the West promised Georgia and Ukraine NATO membership, but shortly thereafter followed the Caucasus war between Russia and Georgia. Under Barack Obama, the relationship was even worse. Putin felt that the intervention of the West in the Libyan civil war a betrayal. He was convinced that only Gaddafi's initial concessions had led to his downfall.' [649]

The Kremlin had trusted that the West would not expand further to the East after reunification. But as long as Russia still hoped to become a fully-fledged partner of the European Union and NATO, the Kremlin tolerated more and more countries becoming members of the European Union and NATO. However, when the Kremlin realized that Russia was being excluded from these organizations and the enlargement of the European Union, and NATO had the effect of containing Russia's influence, Russia once again turned to itself and its own mission, which became more and more the so-called *Eurasism*.

In addition to Soviet Europeanism, the more religiously-motivated ideas behind the Russian mission of *Eurasism* are also alive. Eurasism has many representatives. Prince Nikolai Sergeyevich Trubetskoy (who was born in 1890 in Moscow and died in 1938 in Vienna) may be considered the first. He 'was a Russian linguist and ethnologist as well as the founder of phonology ' [650]

Wikipedia writes: The Eurasian worldview is based on the claim that 'there is a third continent between Europe and Asia, Eurasia (which largely coincides with the former territory of the Russian Tsarist empire), and there is an insurmountable antagonism between the Eurasian culture of the Russian Empire on the one hand and the "Romano-Germanic" civilization of Western Europe on the other hand.[651][652]'[653].

---

[647] Sven Becker und andere: loc. cit. p.14.

[648] Becker, p.14 f.

[649] Becker: p.15.

[650] https://de.wikipedia.org/wiki/Nikolai_Sergejewitsch_Trubetzkoy.

[651] Andreas Umland: *Der „Neoeurasismus" im außenpolitischen Denken Russlands* In: e-politik.de, 10. 3. 2009.

[652] Stefan Wiederkehr: *»Kontinent Evrasija« – Klassischer Eurasismus und Geopolitik in der Lesart Alexander Dugins*, p.127.

[653] https://de.wikipedia.org/wiki/Eurasismus.

Already in the Soviet Union, Lev Gumilev[654] championed *Eurasism*. He called the unconscious spiritual, cultural and civilizing impulses in people: "Passionarnost". Passionarnost contains passion in both senses of the word, that is, as a passionate drive, as well as in the execution of this passion, as in the Passion of Christ's suffering. In Russia "Passionarnost" is shown as Eurasian humanism. Evidently, in the spirit of this passion, Lev Gumilev has also endured arrests and yet remained faithful to his passion, because he was repeatedly arrested and had to spend many years in a camp (1930-1934 and 1938-1943). 'In autumn 1944, Gumilev volunteered in the Red Army and fought in the 1st Belorussian Front, which participated in the conquest of Berlin.' In 1949, he was again sentenced to ten years in a camp. 'It was not until 1956, three years after Stalin's death, that he was rehabilitated and released back home.'[655]

Charles Clover writes: 'In 2012, Vladimir Putin publicly confessed to Gumilev's theory of Passionarnost.'[656]

According to Otto Böss, Eurasia's goal is 'the unification of the major Christian churches under the leadership of the Russian Orthodox Church - Catholicism had falsified the original ideas of Christianity. The Jews should also be included, but the "Orthodox Jewish Church" would remain independent in its cult. A Tsar should govern this "State of Wisdom … in Christian love", in which all nationalities are equal. Ukraine too has its place in this Eurasian empire; the claim of Ukrainian nationalists to belong to Europe is historically unfounded. Eurasia's most important neighbor is China. The appropriate economic form is an advanced planned economy.[[657]]'[658]

On the occasion of Lew Gumilev's 112th birthday, Natalia Pavlova writes: '"Eurasians of the 20th century, such as Nikolai Trubetskoi and Lev Gumilev, have always maintained that our main idea is to be an alternative to the West and to have a more just order, to develop a nobler idea that could be offered to other

---

[654] >>Lew Nikolajewitsch Gumiljow (Russian Лев Николаевич Гумилёв; * … 1912 in Zarskoje Selo, Russian Empire; † … 1992 in Saint Petersburg) was a Russian historian and ethnologist, author of some new and controversial theories on ethnogenesis poetand translator from the Persian language. He was the son of the poet couple Anna Achmatova and Nikolai Gumilev.<< >>When he was just nine years old in 1921, his father Nikolai Gumilev was shot for alleged involvement in a counter-revolutionary conspiracy. << https://de.wikipedia.org/wiki/Lew_Nikolajewitsch_Gumiljow.

[655] https://de.wikipedia.org/wiki/Lew_Nikolajewitsch_Gumiljow.

[656] Charles Clover: Putin, power and „passionarnost", in: Financial Times, 12. 3. 2016, p.1, p.20: >>Putin's definition of "passionarity" (from the Latin word passio) was a slightly sanitised one. "Moving forward and embracing change" was one way of putting what Gumilev meant, though more accurate would be something like "capacity for suffering". It was a word with allusions to the New Testament and the crucifixion, that had been dreamt up by Gumilev during his 14 years in Siberian prison camp. In 1939, while digging the White Sea Canal and daily watching inmates die of exhaustion and hypothermia, Gumilev invented his theory of passionarnost. The defining trait of greatness, he would write in Ethnogenesis and the Biosphere, the book that established his ideas (written in 1979 and circulated in samizdat form until 1989), was sacrifice.<<

[657] Otto Böss: *Die Lehre der Eurasier. Ein Beitrag zur russischen Ideengeschichte des 20. Jahrhunderts*, p.72, 85-87, 98-104.

[658] https://de.wikipedia.org/wiki/Eurasismus.

people. The ideas of justice and truth are central to the Eurasian ideology. And while the West was always building on the aggression, conquest and colonization of new territories, Russia introduced another idea.

The Russians have always treated other nations at eye level, like their peers. That was also the reason why the small principality on the Moskva River took in a plethora of peoples from Alaska to the Balkans, from Afghans to the Baltics. All these peoples succeeded in peaceful coexistence, complementing each other and building an inimitable civilization based on ancient civilizations such as the Golden Horde, the Turkic Khanate and the Great Scythia. This was proved by Lev Gumilev, who described in his works the history of this great space.'"[659]

Andreas Umland writes: Since the early 1990s, the Russian political philosopher and journalist Alexander Dugin 'represents a Neo-Eurasism. However, classical Eurasism is only one of the sources of Dugin's eclectic ideology; it combines the more culturalist concepts of Trubetskoy and Sawizki (whom he casually mentions and even misleads in his works) with elements of geopolitics of a more recent Western character. For example, he refers to representatives of the Western European New Right, such as Jean-François Thiriart and Alain de Benoist, the traditionalists René Guénon and Julius Evola, representatives of the Conservative Revolution, such as Carl Schmitt, and geopoliticians such as Karl Haushofer. [660][661]

Contrary to the central thesis of classical Eurasism that there is a third continent, "Eurasia", between Europe and Asia, Dugin understands "Eurasia" to be Europe and Asia. Following on from Thiriarts idea of a Pax Eurasiatica, Dugin advocates a Eurasian Empire from Dublin to Vladivostok under the leadership of Russia, because according to Dugin, "the true, geopolitically-justified borders of Russia lie in Cadiz and Dublin and Europe is destined (…) to join the Soviet Union".[662]

Classic Eurasians and Neo-Eurasians like Dugin hold the common bipolar worldview that "Eurasia" faces a major enemy. The difference is that classic Eurasians saw "Romano-Germanic Europe" as an opponent, whereas Neo-Eurasians envisage a struggle between the hierarchically organized "Eurasian" land forces led by Russia and the liberal "Atlantic" maritime powers under the leadership of the United States. [663][664]Europe is occupied by the Americans, according to Dugin, and Russia must take on the role of the liberator. The success of "Eurasia" depends on the rebirth of the imperial Russian people. [665] In Dugin's apocalyptic worldview, this centuries-old antagonism between land and naval powers is heading for a "final battle". [666][667]

---

[659] Natalia Pavlova: *Eurasischer Humanismus als Alternative zum Westen*, https://de.sputniknews.com/german.ruvr.ru/2014_10_03/Eurasischer-Humanismus-als-Alternative-zudem-Westen-4959/.

[660] Andreas Umland: Alexander Dugin, loc. cit, p.2–5.

[661] Mark J. Sedgwick: *Neo-Eurasianism in Russia*, p.221–240.

[662] Zitiert in: Stefan Wiederkehr, »*Kontinent Evrasija*«, P.128 f

[663] Andreas Umland: *Alexander Dugin, the Issue of Post-Soviet Fascism*, p.2–5.

[664] Stefan Wiederkehr loc. cit., p.125–138.

[665] Ibid.

[666] Andreas Umland: loc. cit., p.2–5.

[667] https://de.wikipedia.org/wiki/Eurasismus#Neo-Eurasismus.

With that, Eurasism is catching up with the extreme Right in the USA. For example, Heinrich Vogel (Stiftung Wissenschaft und Politik Deutsches Institut für Internationale Politik und Sicherheit) supports the 'thesis that the Neoconservatives of the USA and Russia need reciprocal amplifiers of an imperial worldview. Even the Democrat presidential candidate, Hillary Clinton, is convinced: "The United States can, must and will lead in this new century". The Russian Conservatives are enthusiastic.'[668]

The Neoconservatives and Eurasians ultimately assume a bipolar world where both sides are antagonistic. Vladimir Putin certainly does not pursue such extreme politics beyond the Russian borders. The *Eurasian Economic Union* initiated by him however is supported by Eurasian ideas. Members of the Eurasian Economic Union are Russia, Belarus, Kazakhstan, Armenia and Kyrgyzstan. 'On the basis of different partnerships of the CIS countries and political statements a number of states are being considered as potential candidates for accession. These include Tajikistan, Mongolia and Uzbekistan.[[669]]'[670]

Eurasia also receives additional impetus from China's revival of the traditional Silk Road. The expected climate change, which is dangerous for many countries, is likely to favor Russia and possibly make Siberia far to the North a thriving garden. When the decadence of the USA as a world power progresses and the USA withdraws more and more from the rest of the world, especially from Asia and the Middle East, or *smashes so much porcelain* with its policies there that they are no longer recognized as a regulatory power, while, on the other hand, "the sleeping giant", Russia, awakens, then Eurasia as the new center of the world can take shape more and more. In the Far East, China is increasingly taking over the position of the United States and the Middle East is increasingly being ruled by Russia.

Given the Russian objectives, the West should have been warned. Nevertheless, the West supported the aspirations of Western Ukrainians to join the European Union and NATO. It was in Kiev that the first Russian Empire was founded, so therefore, Ukraine was, for the Russians, always an integral part of the Pan-Slav world. When, therefore, all of Putin's economic offerings to Ukraine could not prevent Ukraine's imminent integration into the West and anti-Russian aspirations in Ukraine even sought to ban the Russian language, it was understandable that, no doubt with the support of Russia, there was a rebellion of the predominantly Russian-speaking parts of Ukraine. Russia then annexed Crimea, supported by a referendum, which had formerly belonged to Russia and became Ukrainian through an administrative act of Nikita Khrushchev. Russia had to fear losing its naval base on the Black Sea, Sevastopol, which certainly also played a role.

Ukraine, though different in its founding, has roughly the same significance for Russia as Cuba has for the USA. Robin Brunold writes: 'The USA's special relationship with Cuba dates back to the 19th century. In 1889, in the Spanish-American War, the so-called "splendid little war", the Americans finally broke the influence of the Spanish crown on Cuba and castrated Cuba from Spain's Central

[668] Heinrich Vogel: *Putin, der Putinismus und Europa*, Vortrag beim Int.ernationalen Club La Redoute, Bonn e.V., Bonn, 16. 9. 2014, p.15.
[669] Astana gears up for Eurasian Economic Union 23. 5. 2014.
[670] https://de.wikipedia.org/wiki/Eurasische_Wirtschaftsunion.

and South American colonial empire. After that, the island gradually became totally economically dependent on the Americans, mainly due to its geographical proximity to the USA and its different relative size and power relations. At the height of American power, rumors even circulated among the Cuban elites that it was not the Cuban president that was the most powerful man in Cuba, but the American ambassador. Even the annexation of Cuba had been repeatedly considered by the United States. What is certain is that over time, Cuba has become almost totally dependent on its big neighbor, the USA. The Americans considered Cuba from now on to be in their sole and unconditional sphere of influence.'[671]

Not only American capital interests were hurt by the expropriations by Fidel Castro, but also American national pride. That's why America did its utmost to regain its influence. After the Bay of Pigs Invasion failed, Kennedy was more than ready to eliminate the Castro regime. Kennedy approved another CIA operation, codenamed "Mongoose", and had an annual budget of $50 million. It involved over 400 CIA agents. Since January, Miami has been upgraded to a CIA base. 3,000 Cuban exiles and their own fleet were subordinate to the CIA. At the same time, "emergency plans" were being drafted in the Pentagon, just as Cuba could, if necessary, be taken militarily.'[672]

In his distress, Fidel Castro turned to Nikita Khrushchev. 'The CPSU General Secretary did not miss the chance to take revenge for the American deployment of medium-range nuclear weapons in Italy and Turkey from 1959.'[673] That JF Kennedy did not immediately yield to the proponents of an air strike and an invasion of Cuba, apparently as an immediate answer to the Russian rockets, was obviously due to his fear that the Soviet Union would invade West Berlin as a reaction. It is well known that the Cuban crisis ended when the Soviet Union withdrew its nuclear missiles and the USA renounced an invasion of Cuba and removed its Jupiter missiles from Turkey. Nevertheless, the USA has blocked Cuba to this day. Accordingly, Russia will defend its influence on Ukraine.

4. The failure of Western and Eastern Europeanism, also as a result of the transition from bipolar to multipolar world politics

To the extent that as Eastern and Western Europeanism collapses, emerging economies gain economic and political importance and Russia and the United States lose control of themselves. This is because of the international problems they created themselves, and as they want to withdraw from international politics, East-West antagonism loses importance and multipolar power structures develop across the world.

This development has already begun with the merging of non-aligned developing countries.

Over the course of globalization, those states in particular have reached greater economic and political significance, which have opened up to Europeanism. Japan

---

[671] Robin Brunold: *Geschichte der Kuba-Krise – Als die Welt am atomaren Abgrund stand*, http://www.geschichte-lernen.net/kuba-krise/.
[672] Robin Brunold: loc. cit.
[673] loc. cit.

has caught up with European industrialized countries and the United States and can thus be regarded as part of the Western world.

China is the most important power besides Russia and the USA, outstripping Russia in terms of economic importance. China combines the centralist communist state form of the Eastern bloc with the Western capitalist economic system. China, in particular, then broke up bipolar East-West power relations in the world.

China and other emerging economies, as buyers of capital goods and mass-market suppliers, have made traditional industrialized countries as dependent on them as they depend on industrialized countries. Together with the oil-producing states and the corrupt elites from less dynamic developing countries, they spur on capital market games, finance government public spending and buy into industries in developed countries.

While the emerging economies owe their economic dynamism to the adaptation of Europeanism, Europeanism is rather opposed to the backward-looking Muslim countries, with the result that terror and destruction frequently occur in these countries. But since these conflicts are increasingly fed by the religious opposition between Shiites and Sunnis, the East-West antagonism plays only a minor role in these Muslim countries. When East and West intervene in the affairs of these states, as in the examples of Iran, Iraq, Afghanistan, Syria and Libya show, the conflicts are not only fueled but also carried to the industrialized countries themselves.

The missionary component, which also motivated Eastern and Western Europeanization, had to go down like this. For Russia and the United States, therefore, it is wiser to withdraw and engage only when new developments threatens them directly. The pro-Trump stance developing in the USA and in the European countries has its roots also in these world political upheavals.

IV. The blessing and curse of globalization

The globalization of Europeanism has brought a huge boost to development in non-European countries. This development spurt is greater, depending on how well-developed the culture of the countries was before and to what extent they were prepared to open themselves up to Europeanism.

Europeans' involvement in traditional social and economic systems, including colonization, has meant that non-European countries have suffered much.

The hardest-hit countries are those which have had no high culture and still live in archaic tribal cultures and / or in which the proportion of settled Europeans is low, as in many countries of the Black African region. But these countries, too, gained their independence because of the weakening of European industrial countries during the two world wars and the utilization of East-West antagonism during the Cold War.

While China, India, Brazil and South Africa were able to adapt Europeanism to emerge, and, in the case of China, even become a leading industrial power, many African countries have barely managed to build well-functioning state structures. If they have valuable reserves of raw materials, they are often unable to develop them and, if possible, process the raw materials in the country. As far as

169

these resources are tapped, the profits derived from them flow to foreign corporations and tribal elites. The tribal elites do not even invest their profits back in the country, but use them abroad.

Of course, it is not easy to build up your own industrial capacity against established companies from industrialized countries. But if countries had dynamic entrepreneurs, capitalists willing to invest and development-minded politicians, then they could get foreign companies to manufacture their products in the country and possibly even force them to employ local people, so that they could acquire modern industrial expertise.

Instead, politicians, if they earn enough by themselves, allow foreign traders to exploit natural resources, clear forests and put aside agricultural areas, from which often the local population is displaced, to grow natural resources for foreign countries. Foreign agrochemical companies are enabled to make domestic farmers dependent on them through licenses for the sale of seed, crop protection and fertilizers.

Insofar as academics and qualified specialists are actually trained in the country, they are forced to move abroad due to the lack of sufficient employment opportunities in their domestic territory. Because of undeveloped infrastructure and bureaucratic administration, in some countries, even contract manufacturing cannot be provided.

If the tribal leaders do not incite conflicts against each other by themselves, then often these unemployed people and their dissatisfaction result in militias emerging, who then attack the population, then plunder and destroy their livelihoods. The captured children are turned into child soldiers. In this way, the militias grow and live off robbery and destruction.

Chaos is further intensified if Islamists in Muslim populations are also able to fund terrorist movements, whose terror is then reciprocated by Christians and other religious groups.

In contrast to Africa and other countries with archaic societies, the countries of the Near and Middle East are based on the same cultures and civilizations as Europe. An essential part of the common Hellenistic heritage, which, at first, was not cultivated in Europe, was retransmitted to Europe by the Arabs through Spain.

Also, Muslims shared the belief in one god with Christians and Jews. But while the Christians, as it were, made themselves gods and went on to new shores in spiritual history, Muslims submit fatalistically to their Allah and still live largely in archaic tribal societies. Such a mental attitude, which only recognizes the Qur'an as the source of all knowledge, did not give rise to any European equivalent of scientific, economic and social dynamism.

But since Muslims consider their religion superior to Judaism and Christianity, they cannot bear being ruled by Christians and Europeanism derived from Christianity.

However, from the shared cultural and civilizing heritage, enlightened Muslims are open to Europeanism. It has been shown that it has captured the intellectuals, traders and military and made them nationalists. However, they could not show their nationalism if, like the Kurds, they were spread over many countries or had to represent states that, like Iraq, were patched together to other states by arbitrary demarcations with different ethnicities and religious groups.

As we have seen, a nationalist has emancipated himself from natural families and tribal relations and saw in his nation himself. At the same time, he sets himself apart from other nationalities and strives to establish appropriate empires, depending on how he defines his nationality, which in turn causes conflicts. The burgeoning nationalism in Turkey led to clashes between Kurds, Armenians and Turks, which then led to the genocide of the Armenians and the cultural oppression of the Kurds. Jewish and Arab nationalism erupted in several wars and caused Syria, Egypt and Northern Yemen to be temporary merged with the VAR United Arab Republic.

Saddam Hussein wanted to conquer the oil areas of Iran and Kuwait for nationalist reasons.

However, the rural population remained conservatively Islamic. In secular forms of societies, they also saw foreign bodies imported from the West. Although Muslims use the technical achievements of the West, the thinking that underlies these achievements must be the devil's work to a believing Muslim, for whom all wisdom is only found in the Koran. Consequently, there is an Islamic Nigerian terrorist group calling itself *Boko Haram*, which means: *Western education is a sin*.

To make matters worse, Islam is not a homogeneous faith. Between the two largest directions - the Sunnis with about 80% and the Shiites with about 15% of the Muslims, there is an almost mortal hostility, which overshadows everything else.

There have always been wars between Islamic countries, empires have been conquered and lapsed again. Within the Ottoman Empire, however, the people were largely pacified and all ethnic groups and faiths lived together relatively peacefully, of course, under the supremacy of the Turks.

However, the Ottoman Empire suffered from internal destruction accelerated by Western and Eastern Europeanism. Something similar can be said of Persia. Also, in response to Europeanism, the Shah was overthrown in Iran and Ayatollah Khomeini founded a Shiite mullah rule.

In the Near and Middle East, overlapping conflict potentials emerged, which are most blatant in Syria. In individual countries, of course, different conflicts are dominant. But ultimately, they all affect each other. The conflicts are either brutally suppressed, as in Egypt, or are discharged in tribal feuds and bloody conflicts and destruction, as in Syria and Iraq.

Growing industrialization and increased consumption, not least as a result of the extreme increase in the world population, endanger the environment. Due to the high fossil energy consumption, global warming is expected to bring drought and other floods to large areas of Africa and other countries. Due to the melting of the ice at the North and South Poles, sea levels rise, causing areas that are not protected by high dikes to sink.

I summarize:

The globalization of Europeanism has brought the world to a higher level of development. For most people, the standard of living increased. At the same time, the earth's population could grow to an unimaginable extent.

On the other hand, there is:

- the relative impoverishment of developing countries, exacerbated by tribal feuds,
- religious, especially Muslim, oppression through the establishment of archaic religious dictatorships or terror against dissenters and the fight against it,
- national conflicts between developing countries and
- growing environmental problems.

They threaten to plunge the world into chaos.

As a result of this development, huge numbers of refugees are emerging. Ulrike Scheffer and Christian Böhme write: 'War, terror, persecution and poverty are forcing more and more people to leave their homeland. 65.6 million people were fleeing at the end of 2016 - almost as many as France has citizens. Twenty years ago, the figure was only half as large, according to the UN report on World Refugee Day. 40.3 million people are displaced in their own country and 25.3 million seek protection elsewhere. Europe remains unreachable for most due to distance and high travel costs. The flight across the Mediterranean is the most dangerous - with more than 5,000 dead in 2016 alone.'.[674]

---

[674] Ulrike Scheffer und Christian Böhme: *Alles auf eine Karte*, in: Der Tagesspiegel Nr. 2349/20.6.2017, p. 2.

C. The crisis and the evolution of Europeanism in a globalized world

The economic, political, social and environmental problems presented are, to be sure, a consequence of the globalization of Europeanism. But without European science, technology, economics and social development and the image of man on which they are based, these problems cannot be solved, because from the ancient civilizations and cultures, people may still receive spiritual and artistic suggestions. For technical progress and the associated economic and social structures, however, these traditions cannot be used. Even Muslim zealots must recognize this. For by resorting to Sharia law, only individual oppression and chaos can arise, or, at best, as in Iran, paralysis of spiritual, economic and social development. But which Europeanism should the countries orient themselves to?

Eastern Europeanism, in the form of Soviet Communism, collapsed. Vladimir Putin has so far only succeeded in preventing the collapse of the Russian Empire, further developing infrastructure and stabilizing administrative structures, as long as revenue from the oil and gas wells gush in. Economically, however, Russia remains underdeveloped and dominated by the oligarchy, with rampant corruption.

Pavel Lokshin writes: 'Transparency International's Corruption Perception Index puts Russia in 136th place, surpassed in Europe only by Ukraine in 142nd place. Some economists, including Andrei Movchan, even go so far as to declare corruption the main pillar of the current Russian system. In state-dominated Russian "market feudalism", one could not carry out any other business. If there is no functioning legal system, corruption is the last remaining gap in the free market.' [675]

In terms of world politics, Russia is again present due to its military strength and size. Overall, however, Russia is like a sounding colossus, which can give other countries no impetus for their development.

Western Europeanism is economically perverted into *Casinocapitalism*, which, in the end, is only kept afloat by money flooding, where real economic demand needs are stabilized by government spending to avoid a global crisis. Western countries too suffer from high unemployment and / or more and more precarious work and relative poverty, especially among the less skilled workforce.

Politically, the USA are frustrated that they have failed to propagate their economic and social order and their economic and political policies, and in the Muslim countries of the Middle East and other countries, have only caused chaos, terrorism and refugee flows.

The original Europe had surrendered to Western and Eastern Europe, and after the collapse of the Eastern Bloc, only to Western Europeanism, thus only playing a minor role internationally. But Europe too has suffered the consequences of the perverseness of capitalism, the repercussions of chaos in the developing world and in the Muslim world, especially through terrorist acts and refugee flows.

---

[675] Pavel Lokshin: *Ohne Schmiergeld geht gar nichts*, in: ZeitOnline, http://www.zeit.de/politik/ausland/2016-01/russland-korruption-alexej-nawalny-kreml-wladimir-putin.

Social descent favors left-wing radicalism. If the actual or feared social decline is accompanied by terror and the fear of being alienated by refugees, then salvation is sought in national demarcation. People then demand: *USA, Great Britain* or even *Poland* or *Hungary first!*

Since they also assume their own selfish attitude toward other countries, even higher-level communities of states, such as the European Union, are also considered to be complicit in the problem. Yes, even the political system itself with its establishment is called into question. Unfortunately, this is not completely unjustified, because it caused these problems or did not prevent them. If you ask for a strong leader, *Trumpism* is born.

I. Trumpism as a crisis of Europeanism

In a broader sense, I call Trumpism the result of a society reached crisis point, in the narrower sense, the crisis of Europeanism and in the narrowest sense, the failure of Anglo-Saxon American West Europeanism. Characteristics of Trumpism are lack of security, economic and social problems, inequalities between countries and the resulting frustrations and fears and the loss of faith in the ideals and principles of organization that underlie society.

From these frustrations and fears, confidence in the ruling class disappears. There is a perceived split between the people and the establishment. The establishment continues to live in good conditions, even profiting from the relative impoverishment of the lower classes, because it lowers the wage level. Because of this, and of course, because it fears drawbacks to changes, the establishment maintains and propagates the existing order for *no alternative*.

Since the statements of the establishment do not correspond with the reality felt by the excluded lower class, those living in precarious circumstances perceive them as lying and the media propagating the theses of the establishment as "lying press".

If rationalization increases the income gap more and more between the wealthy few and the masses of workers, or even the unemployed, but economic development is nevertheless interpreted as positive on the basis of ever-increasing stock prices, then the mass of workers must find this interpretation to be false.

Because what do the constant rising stock prices mean? They are the result of:
1. speculation and unhealthy investment pressure due to lack of alternative investment opportunities or
2. the consequence of rationalization and thereby conversion of labor income into capital income and
3. only partly from product innovations.

Only in the latter case are they economically viable. In the other two cases, they do not necessarily show healthy economic development.

The feeling of being deceived also sets in when entire sectors of industry are relocated to emerging economies, industrial brownfields emerge in developed countries and industrial workers become unemployed or settle for precarious jobs.

As far as Germany is concerned, the apologists for free trade celebrate the successes of the Agenda 2010 - that there is almost full employment in Germany. However, they do not take into account that this near-total employment is also paid for by reducing tariff barriers to the extent that ordinary workers have to compete with wage laborers in developing countries. For this reason, the economy is also fighting against minimum wages, arguing that even more jobs will be shifted abroad.

In Germany, economic poverty is being mitigated with Hartz subsidies. But it does not take into account how a worker, who works in indefinite and often multiple part-time jobs and then still needs additional social assistance, feels.

Marie Rövekamp reports: The number of mini-jobs in Germany has risen from 5,600,000 to 7,800,000 between 2003 and last summer. 'the model is generally open to criticism: According to studies, mini-jobs rarely lead to a solid full-time job. It is also criticized that they can replace regular full-time jobs, especially in the retail and catering sectors.'[676]

The apologists of any lower wage level do not even have a guilty conscience when it comes to the interest of people in precarious employment. So, the head of the Ifo-Institute in Munich, Clemens Fuest, supports Hartz laws, because they force workers to accept less-skilled jobs as quickly as possible, even if, as a result, wages for low-skilled jobs will stagnate. But for him it is crucial 'that unemployment as a whole has fallen sharply.'[677] In this sense, the Secretary General of the CDU, Peter Tauber, tweeted the following in response to the electoral campaign of the SPD to burden the rich more: '"Full employment is better than justice". At the request of a user, enquiring whether this would mean three mini-jobs for him, Tauber replied: "If you have learned something decent, then you do not need mini-jobs."'[678] However, according to the latest figures from the Federal Employment Agency (BA), "mini jobs are not a phenomenon among people with only low-level education ... 19.2% of marginally employed people do not have a vocational qualification, but a good half have already graduated and around 7% even have a degree.'[679]

Again and again, it is argued that the employability of the unemployed decreases with each month of unemployment and it is therefore good for unemployed people to be forced to accept precarious employment as quickly as possible.

Morally, these arguments are shameful, as it was said before that black people would be *forced* to work, if necessary, with the whip. It is even true that other people have a different attitude to work compared to Germans. But even with this other attitude to work, the affected feel that such a "scientific" pronouncement is *false*.

The proponents of supply-side economic policy also do not realize that rising government spending is necessary to balance economic demand. In order to reduce the high national debt, they insist on limiting government spending rather than financing the necessary government spending through higher taxes on the wealthy. These measures are also propagated as reasonable and just contrary to what the masses of the population perceive as just.

---

[676] Marie Rövekamp: *Nichts gelernt*, in: Der Tagesspiegel Nr. 23 164/3.7.2017, p.14.

[677] Spiegel-Streitgespräch mit den Ökonomen Peter Bofinger und Clemens Fuest in: Der Spiegel 13/2017 p.72.

[678] Marie Rövekamp: loc. cit.

[679] Marie Rövekamp: loc. cit.

The frustration of the unemployed and those living in precarious working conditions is intensified when refugees arrive in large numbers and are cared for than themselves. Previously, when it was argued that there was not enough money for better health care, education and old-age insurance and then billions are made available to refugees, their foreclosure and development aid, so they do not keep coming, all these previous announcements also appear to be *lies*. Threatened by the refugees' crime and terror, or even their unusual behavior, protests and riots begin to arise.

By the way, how long has it been expected in economic statements that inflation will be generated by increasing the amount of money in the economy, and how desperately is the European Central Bank trying to achieve a 2% increase in price levels by flooding the market with €80 billion a month and a current total of €60 billion? The authoritative teachings in today's secular stagnation no longer correspond to reality. Of course, as these doctrines are also represented and printed by the press, this also contributes to denigrating them as a "lying press".

As long-standing staff of the NDR, Uli Gellermann, Friedhelm Klinkhammer and Volker Bräutigam describe in their book *Die Macht um acht. Der Faktor Tagesschau*, documenting it by means of protest notes, and the ARD takes on the government ratings in its Tagesschau and political broadcasts. Thus, among other things, when rebels report against the Assad regime in Syria, it is regularly concealed that most of them are Islamist radicals similar to ISIS. In Ukraine, reporting is made rather unilaterally in the sense of the Poroshenko government. For the presentation of pension problems, common report templates that the pension level must fall because fewer and fewer workers must finance more pensioners are presented as self-evident and barely any alternatives are considered.

Of course, the election results needed for change are also so difficult because the less qualified sections of the population feel overwhelmed by prevailing public opinion and the established parties hardly differ because of these general convictions. Therefore, these population groups, which are not among the most dynamic in society anyway, but expect salvation from the state, do not believe in being able to change anything through their turnout. But when somebody comes along who, like Donald Trump, articulates what they perceive to be true and what also corresponds to the naked reality, namely, that

1. they have lost their industrial jobs because the production plants have been relocated abroad,
2. with general tariff reductions and free trade agreements, their wages have stagnated or even declined,
3. Wall Street is perverted into a capital market swamp,
4. Muslims endanger their lives and their safety,

they follow this political demagogue.

For "reasonable" factual thinking also means not understanding why socially disadvantaged Americans hoped that a billionaire would just solve their economic problems. But as far as defamation and lies are concerned, Donald Trump's acclaimed followers can identify with him because they cannot derive their position from theoretical considerations, but can instead vent their anger by ranting. This ranting is not theoretically correct, but that the insults are bad.

Americans also see their social misery as a betrayal of the American dream, which promises them the opportunity to become successful and rich. So, they expect the billionaire, Donald Trump, to make the American dream again possible due to his experience.

Rather than realizing that a degenerating society itself is prone to lies, interestingly, the lies are viewed by the American historian, Timothy Snyder, as an import from Russia. In an interview with Claudia von Salzen, he expresses his disappointment that the West has failed to westernize Russia as well. He said: 'Russia's war against Ukraine has always been about the West. The key question was whether the EU could hold together and welcome new members and whether states that develop into constitutional states could join. The Russian President knows that under his rule, Russia will not become such a constitutional state. Therefore, the rule of law in Ukraine should be prevented.'[680]

Instead of allowing the West to transfer its form of society to the East, the East has succeeded in infecting and destabilizing the West with disinformation and lies. Timothy Snyder writes: 'Americans and Europeans still believe that history is made in the West and moves from there to the East. But it's been the other way round for about ten years. The kleptocracy, the media manipulation and the cyberwar all came from the East to the West. We were too vain and complacent to understand that. ... The Russians had a preferred candidate and supported him with information and hacker attacks. ... Russia has won a cyberwar in the USA. ... The weapon was Donald Trump.'[681]

To counter this view, disinformation and lies have been used in all wars, including by the USA. Note, for example, the reports of Wikileaks or the statement of the then US Secretary of State, Colin Powell, that Iraq was building a nuclear bomb, which then justified the attack on Iraq.

Only the methods of the respective intelligence services are used as a means of defense or attack in the interest of their respective people. But in the USA, slipping into lies and disinformation has already affected parts of civil society, according to the report by Philipp Oehmke on the *Alt Right*.

'The Alt Right has everything a movement needs: its own reference world, which is mainly staged on the Internet, its own symbols, myths, martyrs, stories and even its own vocabulary. It is the first protest movement that makes full use of the possibilities of the digital and would be inconceivable without the internet. "Internet trolling" is one of its favorite techniques. It means insulting and provoking the political opponent on websites until he loses his composure.'[682] '"The ideal troll," Yiannopoulos writes in his book "Dangerous", "lures his victim into a trap from which there is no way out without public exposure. It is an art form beyond the capacity of ordinary mortals. It is partly trickery, partly malice. "'[683]

---

[680] Timothy Snyder: *Russland hat einen Cyberkrieg gewonnen*, Interview mit Claudia Salzmann, in. Der Tagesspiegel Nr. 21 157, v. 28.6.2017.
[681] Timothy Snyder: *Russland hat einen Cyberkrieg gewonnen*, loc. cit.
[682] Philipp Oehmke: *Im Geiste des Gorillas*, in: Der Spiegel Nr. 26/ 22.6.2017, p.68.
[683] Oehmke: p.69.

An example of this is Mikle Cernovich. His 'tweets are read more than three million times a month. During the election campaign, he virtually single-handedly spread the rumors about Hillary Clinton's allegedly covered-up nervous disease.'[684]

'So far, Yiannopoulos had derived his political outlook from a quasi-pop-cultural argument: if the left-wing establishment set the tone in the Western world, it was suddenly cool to be right-wing, just as it was cool in the 1970s to be left-wing.'[685]

The dynamic people are anxious to succeed and rise to the establishment. The masses of people, however, tended more to be led rather more. As a rule, these sections of the population do not even think about social and political issues and for that reason are less likely to vote. Therefore, even parties that would stand up for them, cannot attain strength.

From a certain sense of powerlessness and lack of risk-taking, but also because less qualified people have to fight for their livelihood, lower classes usually endure considerable economic and social adversity. Only when conditions become unbearable and then a clever demagogue declares their commonplace wisdom about the solution of the problems to his political program, can this reach larger actions of protest, social unrest and new party foundations. This brings us to the actual Trumpists, but, and this must be considered, can only succeed if the social conditions are as described.

Of course, *Trumpism* is named after the current American President. However, Trumpists already existed before him, such as Vladimir Putin in Russia, Victor Orbán in Hungary, Jarosław Kaczyński in Poland, Geert Wilders in Holland, Marine le Pen in France, Beppe Grillo in Italy, Necip Erdogan in Turkey and the leaders of the AfD in Germany. They are all trying to seize or abuse the pillars of democratic governance, such as justice, free press and media. All of them are more or less megalomaniac and often corrupt, or mingle politics with their own business interests. They lie and defame in order to incite the masses and weaken their opponents.

Deviating from Donald Trump, however, the other Trumpists are politically experienced and act tactically and deliberately with the view of enforcing their political goals, so they are therefore calculable for other politicians. Donald Trump, on the other hand, is politically inexperienced and allows himself to be guided by spontaneous ideas in his political actions, which he then disseminates via Twitter, but can also change in the short term. It means that the USA, which for many was the protector and guardian of European values, becomes unpredictable.

Since Donald Trump is only influenced by his ideas, he takes no account of what other members of the government think or have already said on behalf of the government. In doing so, he not only destroys the credibility of his employees, but also the government apparatus itself, because the employees will not tolerate this behavior in the long run or support him.

All Trumpists are more or less narcissistic. With Donald Trump, however, his narcissism seems to have pathological features, so that even in political decisions,

---

[684] Oehmke: p.68.
[685] Oehmke: p.71.

he can essentially be determined by the extent to which others court him and recognize him as a great statesman.

Other Trumpists use lies and defamation on a calculated basis and, if possible, they should not be recognized as lies and defamation. For Donald Trump, lying and defamation are common means of communication to express that others have *called him evil* and do not recognize its importance. Therefore, defamation and lies can be recognized as such, and need not be corrected. If the relationship with those affected changes, then they are no longer defamed and lied to, but referred to as friends and praised.

Since Trumpism is in Donald Trump's character traits, his narcissism and his political actions are self-evident, and in him, as President of the United States, manifests the disintegration of Western Europeanism. Other remarks on Trumpism refer, in particular, to his policies and their consequences.

Trumpists come to power as the result of

1. perverting the capitalist economy into *casinocapitalism*
2. secular stagnation caused by the increasingly unequal distribution of wealth and income, as well as
3. problems that have arisen from the globalization of Europeanism, including the influx of refugees and terror.

Established society calls the behavior of Donald Trump and the other Trumps such as Victor Orbán, Jarosław Kaczyński, Geert Wilders, Marine le Pen and Beppe Grillo and the leaders of the AfD *post-factional*, because it is not fact-based. Accordingly, Trump's ideas question prevalent economic convictions and the worldwide protest of established economic institutes rise against them, including governments, parties, well-established press organizations and there is even intra-party resistance within the Republican Party of the United States. It is, of course, assumed that in a rational society, the facts must be as they are. However, *post-factional* reasoning wants to make the faulty aspect of economic and social conditions tangible. It evaluates the arguments of the establishment as an interest-related, and therefore lying, representation of social reality.

For the establishment, in the broadest sense, the proclaimed political goals of Trumpists are *populism*. Populism is to defend the opposite position to that which the less skilled generally perceive as *lying*. According to prevailing opinion, the demands of the populists are unrealistic because

1. higher taxes jeopardize investment and business activity,
2. protective tariffs hinder economic development,
3. minimum wages reduce employment opportunities for the less qualified,
4. refugees enjoy protection according to international standards and all people have equal rights etc.

But as far as current economic theories are concerned, we have already explained why they do not apply in times of secular stagnation. Also, it must have become clear from the previous statements

1. that smaller countries must join together to form a larger market in order to be of interest as a production location,
2. that economic unions must also have such high import barriers for certain products, so that in Europe and the USA, the less qualified and less industrialized regions can earn sufficient income for a decent life in Europe

179

and are protected against sickness and old-age poverty. Accordingly, less developed countries must have protective tariffs, so that know-how-intensive manufacturing in the country is possible and can develop and engineers and professionals find employment,

3. that in all countries, public expenditure rather than public debt has to be financed by higher taxes for wealthy people. In Germany, an additional public debt to compensate for the lack of demand is not necessary, because the demand is made by export surpluses abroad. But this creates international inequalities. For this reason, government spending and private demand must also be increased so much in Germany by higher taxes for wealthy people that increase additional domestic imports, thereby offsetting the external trade balance.

A policy of "*as it was!*", which, ultimately, is only possible by creating money, speculation support and, if necessary, public bank rescue, scrapping premiums for basic industries and wage compensation in production restrictions, increases tensions around the world and in the world economy, and sooner or later will lead to ever-greater financial and global economic crises. In this respect, Trump's claims are fatally legitimate.

On the other hand, Donald Trump acquired his economic success as a real estate speculator. So, of course, it seems natural that he sees the economic recovery of the country in terms of supply-side economic policy that also means the deregulation of the capital market and thus, the repealing of banking regulation and tax cuts. Accordingly, he appoints many billionaires and successful capital market players to government offices.

Of course, the high-achievers who make a lot of money realize that Donald Trump must first break his promise to drain the Wall Street mire. In fact, it increases the fragility of the economy and the danger of financial and economic crises and, to avert these dangers, he is forced to increase government spending and finance it with even higher debts. Donald Trump wants to redevelop the desolate infrastructure of America and build a wall along the Mexican border. To finance these additional expenditures, he is thinking of burdening imports, which are supposed to be raised anyway, to force companies to produce in the USA again.

So, for Donald Trump, the circle of mutually supporting measures closes. However, these measures are not calculated and contain a wealth of wrong decisions. In particular, many implementation difficulties are to be expected because they will affect the entire international economic relations system and the other countries affected will also take countermeasures, which in turn will harm the American economy.

Among other things, it remains unclear how Donald Trump wants to accomplish the restructuring and stabilization of international trade relations without capital market controls. Because despite huge import surpluses, the US dollar exchange rate is still relatively high. Otherwise, foreign products for Americans would not be too cheap and cut off competition in the USA. If import barriers reduced import surpluses, stray capital from all over the world would continue to flow into the USA and push the price even higher. Thus, imports would become cheaper again, or the import duty would be compensated to a certain extent.

One of the dogmas of neo-liberal economic policy is that tax cuts stimulate the economy. Accordingly, Donald Trump celebrates that he has launched the "biggest tax cut in the US". The reduction of corporate taxes from 35% to 21% will provide the US with a return of tax evasion from tax havens, and the US will become more attractive as a location for capital market players and disposals. For example, capital is expected to flow into the US on a large scale, and the resulting taxes will reduce tax losses due to tax cuts.

As a result of these capital flows, the dollar should rise and at the same time reduce the expectations that more will be made in the USA itself. For in the global economy, the demand of consumer goods will increase substantially only insofar as the tax cuts increase the purchasing power of the lower income strata and this demand will hardly lead to real economic investments in the USA, since the products can also be imported more cheaply due to the expected rising dollar.

Thus, only the rich will profit, and also primarily only due to capital market games, as far as they increase the prices of equities and other investments. As government spending tends to continue to increase as a result of the planned construction of the wall on the Mexican border and for infrastructure measures and armaments, government debt is expected to grow at a very high rate. The risk of a crisis is thereby further increased, as well as the danger that the ever-increasing share prices and investment prices will collapse.

In the global economy, one can only hope that the tax cuts will not lead to another tax reduction race and that too much capital will be withdrawn from developing countries.

Through his economic policy and his policy of "America first"

1. Donald Trump increases the worldwide risk of crisis,
2. the US are losing their position as an anchor of security and social values in Europe and the United States-friendly countries in Asia, Africa and the Middle East and
3. it hinders global efforts to avoid a climate change catastrophe.

But factual thinking tends to perceive salvation in a "go on as before!" policy and not recognize necessary changes. For example, without the marriage-loving King Henry VIII., England would not have become Protestant and a world power, without Hitler there would be no *UN*, no *European Union*, no *International Court of Human Rights*, and then perhaps a Donald Trump would also be needed to save the world from dangerous aberrations. Of course, I know that this statement is cynical.

In response to his policy, there is a possibility to

1. strengthen European integration and Europe's responsibility for the world,
2. foster the development of China in East Asia and Russia in the Near and Middle East into order powers,
3. reduce the confrontation between the Sunnis and Shiites as a reaction to Trump recognizing Jerusalem as the Jewish capital and moving the American embassy there, because both will see their common enemy as the USA and so the tolerance between religions in the Middle East might grow and thus peace might be promoted,

4. even accelerate global efforts to prevent a climate catastrophe, even by private American initiatives and American states themselves.

II. The unification of Europe as a condition for overcoming the crisis of Europeanism

As a result of the devastating world war, the realization had prevailed that nationalism in Europe had to be overcome and the countries of Europe united. The Western victorious powers were initially anxious to keep Germany weak and there were even tendencies to de-industrialize Germany. However, the worsening East-West opposition prompted the Western powers to reconstitute Germany as a *Federal Republic of Germany* and to include it in the Western Defense Community. Thus, the insight of a necessary overcoming of nationalism was combined with the need for defense against Eastern ideology and politics.

1. The division of Germany and Europe and Europe's degradation into parts of the USA-led Western and Soviet Union-led Eastern Europeanism

As a reaction to the founding of the *Federal Republic of Germany*, the *GDR German Democratic Republic* emerged in East Germany. The Federal Republic of Germany became part of the *European Economic Community* after the *Treaty of Rome*, together with the countries of France, Italy and the Benelux, which later evolved into the *European Union*, and militarily, the Federal Republic became part of *NATO*. In response, the *Warsaw Pact* and the *Mutual Economic Assistance Council* were established in the East.

This is how two European unions came into being. Germany as a nation, its capital Berlin and the whole of Europe were split. The potential for conflict was taken to extremes because both East and West had nuclear weapons.

But the two halves of Europe were ideologically as well as militarily dependent on the very centers of Western and Eastern Europeanism, that is, dependent on the USA and the Soviet Union, that an independent European policy was only partially possible. Yes, European governments even feared that they would be sacrificed as bargaining chips in political poker between the USA and the Soviet Union.

'American President, Ronald Reagan, elected in November 1980, increased American arms spending enormously and rejected the unratified SALT II Treaty. [686] He tripled the production of medium-range missiles and talked of destroying the East by armament competition. [687] In August 1981, he ordered a neutron weapon to be built, against Carter's refusal. In March 1983, he called the Soviet Union a realm of evil, called for a worldwide crusade against communism and announced the Strategic Defense Initiative (SDI) about two weeks later. He signaled a departure from the ABM Treaty of 1972. [688]The aim of this policy was

---

[686] Josef Holik: *Die Rüstungskontrolle: Rückblick auf eine kurze Ära*, P.20 und 104.
[687] Ulrike Poppe, Rainer Eckert, Ilko-Sascha Kowalczuk: *Zwischen Selbstbehauptung und Anpassung: Formen des Widerstandes und der Opposition in der DDR,* P.275.
[688] Michael Ploetz, Hans-Peter Müller: *Ferngelenkte Friedensbewegung?,* P.125.

to secure the United States' unassailable technological superiority and invulnerability [689] and to render the Soviet second-strike capability, on which the strategic balance was based, ineffective. [690]' 691

This policy was highly dangerous, especially for Europe at the interface between the blocs. Usually a cornered opponent, who still has such a great power and can totally destroy the opponent with a preemptive strike, will not allow itself to be disempowered.

Thus, even though the Eastern bloc lagged behind the West in its economic development and showed signs of disintegration in Eastern Europe, the Soviet Union had always reacted with violence to threats to its sphere of influence and defeated revolts, as on June 17, 1951, in the GDR, in 1965 in Hungary and in 1968 in Prague. The construction of the Wall in 1961 on the GDR's western border was also a defensive measure. The defection of skilled workers to West Germany should be prevented so that the economy does not collapse.

The fact that the East gave in was ultimately also due to the preceding policy of detente initiated by Willy Brandt and Dietrich Genscher, which was then continued by Helmut Kohl.

2. The development of the European Union

In the East, Eastern European countries were so strongly related to the Soviet Union that they could not speak of an independent Eastern European Union. Western European countries, on the other hand, joined together more and more and founded the *European Union* with the *Treaty of Rome*. The European Union was then also the basis for the integration of Eastern European countries after the Cold War.

Nevertheless, Europe has remained a fantastical notion to this day. European unification mainly benefited from the war generation and the adolescent youth. Germans were most willing to give up sovereign rights in favor of Europe. However, there was also a degree of openness to European integration in other countries. The masses of the population in these countries remained relatively nationalistic. When, as a result of the *German Economic Miracle*, the international importance of the Federal Republic rose again, nationalist sentiment also reappeared in Germany.

The United Kingdom and Northern European countries initially remained outside the European Union for national reasons and formed only a Free Trade Area, the EFTA. Only when the economic benefits of the common market became apparent did they, with the exception of Norway, join the European Union. However, Britain, as the original leader of Western Europeanism, still maintained closer ties to the USA than to Central European countries. The United Kingdom was therefore always a brake on the close bind of European countries and voted in 2016 to leave the European Union.

---

689 Philipp Gassert und andere (Hrsg.): *Zweiter Kalter Krieg und Friedensbewegung*, P.58.
690 Franz Josef Meiers: *Von der Entspannung zur Konfrontation: die amerikanische Sowjetpolitik im Widerstreit von Innen- und Außenpolitik 1969–1980*. P.313.
691 https://de.wikipedia.org/wiki/NATO-Doppelbeschluss.

Spain, Portugal and Greece could become members of the European Union only after they had overcome their authoritarian regimes. After the end of the Cold War, Eastern European countries joined the European Union, and, to some extent, the Eurozone. However, the more countries that belonged to the European Union, the more difficult the voting process and the agreement on further necessary integration steps became. Because of national reservations, the European agreement was only made in small steps, at the same time creating practical constraints that would further the unification.

Russia and the United States of America also determined the respective half of the block in terms of economic policy. Eastern European countries introduced Central Administration Economies, which were linked in the *RGW Council for Mutual Economic Assistance* for production specializations in individual countries.

In the West, and because of the ultimate economic importance of the USA for the whole world, the US dollar became the world currency. At the same time, Western European countries adopted the liberal market economy, and as they recovered economically after the Second World War, they opened their customs frontiers and made their currencies convertible.

After the economic and political collapse of the Eastern Bloc, the weaknesses of uncontrolled market development and the perverted Western-style economy of *Casino Capitalism* became apparent in the following years.

Economically, however, Europe tried to counteract pure capitalism. In the Federal Republic, for example, there was the ideal of the "Social Market Economy" and Article 14 (2) of the Basic Law were "Property obligates. Its use should also serve the public good."

Companies with a certain number of employees can set up a works council, which is particularly involved in personnel decisions, and in companies with more than 2,000 employees, the employees are also represented in the supervisory board. There is also employee participation in companies in other European countries.

The participation of workers in company decisions and the extensive social cushioning of workers and the socially disadvantaged Americans do not know. Resistance to the health care reform introduced by Barack Obama is correspondingly high.

Despite the European social-oriented market economy, American economic principles are increasingly gaining ground in Europe as well. The *Supply-sided Economic Policy* introduced in Anglo-Saxon countries by former American President, Ronald Reagan, and the then British Prime Minister, Margaret Thatcher, also became the leading economic policy maxim of European countries. The same applies to the so-called *Shareholder Value Principle*, which allows the company's success to be geared exclusively toward the interests of the capital and the unbridled growth of executive salaries.

The problems of perverted capitalism have become so unbearable in the United States that Donald Trump was able to win the election with theses that contradicted the classic economic principles of the United States. Naturally, Donald Trump as an entrepreneur and real estate mogul is an inveterate capitalist and now he seeks to solve the economic problems through a mixture of the further liberalization of *markets* and protectionist measures.

2.1 Errors in the founding of the European Union and its consequences

It is believed that it goes without saying that international trade is equally advantageous for all partners. Because this is an international division of labor in which each partner specializes in the services that he or she can do best. It is therefore never or only imperfectly taken into account that this same advantage only arises if the partners have the same starting point, i.e. if the same level of economic development exists, and, for example, bananas from tropical areas are exchanged for Bernstein from Baltic countries. On the other hand, if we are dealing with differences in manufacturing methods, in trade organizations, in banking systems and in available assets, then all international trade relations tend to have an increasingly unequal advantage for trading partners.

Just as an unequal distribution of wealth under otherwise equal conditions becomes more and more unequal over time, because the rich can save more than the poor, big companies have greater rationalization possibilities than small ones and retail chains have lower purchase prices and much lower costs per sold product than smaller ones, so in international trade, the advantages of the more developed countries are greater than those of less developed ones. Similarly developing countries are becoming relatively depressed in respect to developed economies if this depletion is not compensated or overcompensated by other factors, such as specific raw material resources or difficult import conditions for industrialized goods. Let's take a look at better opportunities for the industrialized world to trade with developing countries:

1. The highest profit in the economy is not with the manufacturer, but with the dealer. As industrial trading companies reside in industrialized countries, their profits flow into industrialized countries. The same applies to the transport companies, insurance companies and banks, all of which not only make money on imports into developing countries, but also on exports.
2. Using advanced reproductive conditions, developed countries are even able to export goods to developing countries, which they could also produce themselves. Example: cereals and meat from America, poultry and dairy products from Europe. This can destroy local manufacturing operations.
3. Investing in developing countries increases the social product of these countries. However, foreign owners and / or capital and know-how givers make money as well.

4. Developing countries can become rich through deposits of raw materials, as the oil-exporting countries in particular show. First, however, the sources of raw materials are usually developed and exploited by companies in industrialized countries, and from this wealth, developing countries themselves can earn only in the amount of the royalties.

Experience has shown that the relative impoverishment of countries which are lagging behind can only be avoided if protective tariffs take into account the different stages of development of the partners and the backward country pushes research and development and the training of skilled workers.

185

In Europe, Britain was known to be the most developed industrial country. Germany was only able to catch up with England and overtake it as an industrial power by means of protective tariffs for its industries and state-supported research and development.

In 1911, Kaiser-Willem-Gesellschaft, today known as the Max Planck Society, was founded in the German Empire, creating 30 research and development institutes until 1943: for chemistry, physical chemistry and electrochemistry, biology, coal research, industrial psychology, physics, iron research, pulp chemistry, metalworking, etc. The is the same way that Japan gained its industrial importance, and the same goes for emerging economies such as China.

What applies as a general trend of development between economies of varying degrees of development also applies to relations between European countries. The abolition of customs barriers within the European Union has primarily benefited industrially developed countries, in particular, Germany. Graduated according to the level of industrial development, companies from industrialized countries also dominate enterprises in less industrialized countries, provided that the latter has any industry to speak of.

When developing countries had fewer skilled workers and their emerging economies were less developed, it was worthwhile to set up manufacturing operations in southern European countries for lower labor costs. The more developed-market companies could be forced by emerging economies to set up manufacturing operations in emerging markets to prevent loss of access to the huge markets of emerging economies and in the wake of global tariff reductions under the GATT and the WTO, the European market could be supplied from outside the EU as well, without major tariff barriers. However, this made the southern European countries less attractive as an investment location.

Nevertheless, the less industrialized countries in the European Union also experienced accelerated economic development. They were able to deliver their goods preferably to other countries in the European Union and received the most diverse subsidies for infrastructure and economic development, research, etc., without having to make corresponding payments to the EU Commission due to their low economic power.

As in all countries, economic demands by the countries of the European Union has been stimulated by debt-financed public expenditure, which has led to a constant increase in the countries' debt burden.

Because of the growing investment pressure of savings that could not be invested lucratively in the real economy, real estate speculation has repeatedly surfaced, even in the southern European countries, which additionally fueled the economy. With the bursting of Real Estate Bubbles in 2008, the global economy fell into a deep financial and economic crisis. The resulting unemployment or underemployment required further public expenditure to cushion the consequences of this crisis. In addition, public money was used to rescue banks, stimulate demand for sensitive industries (the scrapping premium) and set up economic stimulus programs.

Government debt therefore rose dramatically in all countries, resulting in smaller countries such as Greece, Portugal and other debt repayments not being refinanced and threatened with national bankruptcy. Since the creditors of these countries were European banks, which would have been endangered by bank-ruptcy as well, these countries were granted financial aid by industrialized countries, the *IMF International Monetary Fund*, the *European Central Bank* and other central banks, but under conditions that stifled the economic activity of these countries, leading to unemployment and social hardship.

Because of the worldwide excess of public debt and the resulting risk of sovereign default in European countries, European Union countries imposed a debt brake on themselves. As a result, the gaps in demand caused by secular stagnation could no longer be offset by additional debt-financed government spending. Unemployment and hardship rose correspondingly in European countries, with the exception of Germany, which was able to offset its demand gap with export surpluses.

2.2 The Eurozone and the consequences of errors in its creation

The advantages of a monetary union are:

1. fixed price relations within the monetary union. There are no exchange rate fluctuations between the countries of the monetary union, because every citizen calculates in the same currency. In the case of different currencies, additional hedging transactions would have to be concluded in trade agreements between different countries in order to avoid price risks.
2. For transactions with trading partners outside the monetary union, the sellers and buyers from the monetary union can more easily enforce transactions in their own currency. Since currencies of a strong monetary union fluctuate less in price and their central banks are strong enough to cushion even price fluctuations by buying and selling their own currency, even the foreign exchange risk for the foreign seller is lower.
3. Economic partners from a monetary union can also borrow more easily and with less risk internationally. Business partners from smaller countries are usually denied credit in their own currency or at a higher interest rate. For the borrower from a smaller country, there is a significant risk that if his own currency is devaluated, he will have to repay more than he has received. For example, before the financial crisis of 2008, as *Die Presse* writes, 'around one million Hungarian households borrowed foreign currencies, around 90 percent of it in Swiss francs. ... many have taken over. They not only built houses and apartments with these loans, but also bought automobiles, refrigerators and financed travel. But due to the massive decline of the national currency, credit rates exploded. In 2012, the owners of more than 100,000 properties were so late with their installment payments that banks demanded eviction.'[692]
4. In the case of uncertainty over the performance of a currency or economic crises, the resulting breakdown of a country's economy is also a smaller risk for countries in a strong monetary union. The very words of the President of the European Central Bank, Mario Draghi, that in case of doubt,

---

[692]   http://diepresse.com/home/wirtschaft/international/5061215/Frankenkredite-als-soziale-Zeitbombe-in-Ungarn.

the ECB would buy all the endangered government bonds of eurozone countries, was enough to end speculation against the euro.

These advantages, however, are offset by considerable disadvantages if, as in the euro area, countries of different levels of development are tied together in a monetary union.

Despite the relative falling behind of less industrialized countries without a monetary union, they can better maintain the competitiveness of their products, as they can devalue their currency to maintain a foreign trade balance. This would make their products cheaper on the international market, but their imports would be more expensive. In a monetary union, they are unable to do so with the result that if they cannot increase their efficiency, they lose competitiveness over countries outside the monetary union. Since a devaluation of their national currency makes imports more expensive, as in a monetary union, they do not tend to import more than they can according to their exports and possibly even import products that they have produced themselves so far.

The price of a currency is determined by the strongest economic partners. If the strongest economic partners, in particular Germany in the eurozone, have chronic export surpluses, then the price of the euro will be boosted. This means that the lagging countries have to sell their products more expensively than if they were outside the currency union. If the less industrialized countries lose their competitiveness or import more than they should, given their economic performance with corresponding debt, then the exchange rate will not rise as high as it would rise without the weaker euro countries. Germany and the other industrialized countries can therefore offer cheaper rates and increase their export surplus even further. In other words, in the Eurozone, Germany benefits to the same degree that the other European countries are lagging behind.

Because of these disadvantages, either

- the eurozone should not been founded, or the southern European countries should not have been admitted into the Eurozone. Greece only gained entrance due to false figures. However, the other members, and especially the then German Chancellor Helmut Kohl, did not want to know it either. Critics of the Eurozone are right in this respect. Or
- a solidarity community should have been created immediately, so that the weaker countries, such as Germany's Schleswig-Holstein, the Sauerland, Bremen and the eastern states, could have been supported by the stronger countries. Of course, all countries would have to submit to an enforceable discipline and carry out reforms. But in order to maintain a common minimum standard of living in the European Union, the weaker countries should be helped with financial equalization beyond the European Commission's infrastructure and economic support.

Since more industrialized countries benefit most from customs and monetary unions, their contribution to offsetting economic deficits in less industrialized countries would be justified and in their own interest. What would Germany be without the Eurozone and the European Union? The DM price would most likely rise further and exports would shrink. In addition, as the Marshall Plan teaches, every economy thrives on partners.

It is also in the interest of the stronger countries to belong to a larger market and a strong Eurozone. Especially in view of the ever-increasing risk of a global economic crisis, a strong Europe must be in everyone's interest.

2.3 Germany's endangerment of the European Union and, in particular, the Eurozone, through Agenda 2010

Until the introduction of Agenda 2010 in years 2003-2005, Germany was considered, for a long time, to be the sick man of Europe. However, R. von Heusinger and W. Uchatius in their article *The Myth of Descent: Germany - the "Sick Man of Europe"?* in: DIE ZEIT 15.04.2004, have made clear the questionable element of this statement. They write: 'The fact is: The German economy has grown weaker in the past ten years than any other in the European Union. In the meantime, per capita economic output in Germany is below the EU average. So far, the story is true. The only question is, what are the true reasons for the growth weakness?

"Germany's competitiveness is sinking." (from an investigation by the Institute for Management Development in Lausanne)

"In terms of unit labor costs, we do not look good in an international comparison." (said BDI boss, Michael Rogowski, in the "Berliner Zeitung")

The site. Grundig, Voigtländer, silk stickers. Television from Nuremberg, cameras from Brunswick, shirts from Bielefeld. The fifties were good times. At that time, a factory worker cost only a few marks an hour and German companies supplied half the world.

Then came the Japanese. The Koreans. Later the Chinese. And of course, the Poles and Czechs. Today, labor costs in West German industry are around €26 per hour, whereas in Eastern Europe they are €5 and even lower in East Asia. So, it's no surprise that local companies are losing out on world markets.

Or perhaps it is a surprise, because they were not left empty-handed. On the contrary - "Germany dominates all others," says Andreas Cors of the German Institute for Economic Research (DIW). In fact, in no major industrialized country have exports grown so much in recent years (...).

On closer inspection, German labor costs are among the highest in the world, but since 1995, according to the OECD, wages have hardly increased - in contrast to in other industrialized countries. What rose was the productivity of German companies. The innovation offensive, announced by the chancellor, has long been reality in many companies. "We are the technological leader of the world," says Olaf Wortmann from the VDMA engineering association. As a result, unit labor costs have developed far more favorably than in almost all competing countries. "Competitiveness is no longer a problem in Germany," says Harald Joerg, economist at Dresdner Bank.

The surprising quality of Germany as a location is also reflected in a second number: foreign direct investment. Local politicians and officials may have lost confidence in the German economy, but American and Asian CEOs think otherwise. Since 1998, statisticians have registered a large influx of foreign capital into

Germany. Lastly, no industrialized country except France could attract so many investments from the rest of the world.' [693]

Another argument for the bad situation of Germany is: *'"This state hangs us like a lead ball on the leg."* (according to DIHK boss, Ludwig Georg Braun, in the "Welt am Sonntag")

"The increase in the government ratio must be gradually reduced." (says CDU fraction vice, Friedrich Merz, before entrepreneurs)

The State. For six months they go to work and get no money for it. They sit in the office, they toil in the factory, but the salary is collected by the treasury. That's what happens to German citizens year after year, at least to those who have a job. The taxpayers' federation has calculated that the Germans are working only for the state for the first half of the year. For taxes and social security contributions, unemployment insurance, pension and health insurance. Perhaps economic performance in Germany is weaker than elsewhere because performance is not worthwhile.

A look at the facts shows that it pays off more than in most European countries. The Federal Republic of Germany is in the middle of the tax ratio (the ratio of taxes and social contributions to economic output). However, in high-growth countries such as Finland, Sweden or France, the state takes its citizens far deeper into its pockets (...). That reminds us of earlier times. "Even in the Sixties, the German social service rate and then also the tax and duty rate were among the best in Europe," says Stephan Leibfried, head of the Center for Social Policy at the University of Bremen. At that time, Germany was the leader in growth.

Since then, the social and fiscal state has grown much faster in most European countries than in Germany.

In Germany, by contrast, the share of the state sector in economic output is no higher than in 1975. In the west it even fell slightly. However, not to the level of Japan with its internationally small state sector. "Nevertheless, the Japanese did not emerge from the crisis for ten years," says Peter Bofinger, Member of the Council of Economic Experts. He adds: "A relationship between government ratio and growth rates is extremely doubtful."'[694]

At that time, it was much less was seen that government spending was needed to compensate little private demand, so the economy slid into depression.

How has Agenda 2010 caused unemployment in Germany to shrink? In Germany, it has lowered benefits for the unemployed to a large extent, thereby increasing the pressure on the unemployed to return to work as quickly as possible. Labor costs for employers have been reduced considerably, because employees increasingly had to accept precarious jobs and temporary fixed-term contracts. If wages fell below the subsistence level, then the income of the workers were increased by so-called Hartz IV subsidies. Companies were indirectly subsidized for their labor costs.

Why should the wage level of the less qualified be lowered? The wage level of the less qualified should be lowered so that companies in the globalized world can compete with companies in developing countries.

---

[693] W. Uchatius und R. von Heusinger: loc. cit. p.1f.
[694] W. Uchatius and R. von Heusinger, p.3f.

If the tariff rates and import barriers were high enough, then less qualified people could be employed for wages appropriate to more developed countries. It is true that prices in industrialized countries would be higher because of higher labor costs. But the purchasing power of the masses would be higher as well, and economic purchasing power is likely to rise more sharply than is saved by cheaper pricing from abroad. Because, as already stated, it is through globalization that the profits of companies primarily increase, as can be seen in the share price performance of globally-operating companies, unless this price development is driven up by investment pressure and speculation. On the other hand, mass income could hardly grow or did not grow.

As the tariff reduction rounds progressed, the 2010 Agenda has brought Germany closer to developing countries in terms of labor costs. But Germany is out of step with other European countries and has become more competitive with its partner countries.

Harald Schumann writes: 'The instability of the Euro system stems from the uneven development of wages and inflation. This is confirmed by a new study by the EU think-tank. In it, the authors show that it is the Germans who constantly break the central rule of the monetary union in Euroland by adhering to the common inflation target. In order to maintain this, wages would have to increase as productivity increases, i.e., the output per hour worked, plus the ECBs aimed at just under 2% depreciation.

That's what the French have done. In Germany, by contrast, wages and salaries have consistently risen more slowly than productivity since the Euro started. The flight of the enterprises from collective agreements and the Hartz reforms reduced the wage structure enormously.'[695]

Accordingly, export surpluses have increased even further. What has been gained by this? A sick Europe!

It is true that Agenda 2010 has also improved the bureaucratic administration of the unemployed, the needy and the need for retraining and reduced social abuse. But as a model for the rest of Europe, it can only be recommended to a limited extent. It is not about reducing mass income and disproportionately increasing entrepreneurial profits and salaries for special forces, but about a well-balanced income structure in which not only highly qualified, but also low-skilled workers have a decent income. There are no countries where only top-level workers live and others where only unqualified wage-earners live. Just as it must be acknowledged that developing countries are doing everything in their power to bring know-how and capital into the country and to establish import barriers to this end, industrialized countries must also be allowed to protect themselves against cheap imports of such products that low-skilled workers in the country can produce in order to remain employed. In that regard, the policy of the new American President, Donald Trump, is understandable if he wants to reverse the de-industrialization of the United States by import barriers.

We should bear in mind that last year's economic development (2016) was largely driven by higher consumer spending in Germany, and higher consumption

---

[695] Harald Schumann: *Emanuel Macron und die deutsche Krankheit*, in: Der Tagesspiegel Nr. 23 124, v. 24.5.2017, p.8.

also led to higher imports, benefiting other European countries. These imports would rise much more if the public sector in Germany no longer retained tax revenues, but instead spent them

lowered throughout Europe? To the extent that all workers can be employed, the wage level cannot fall, in any case, in relation to developing countries. Also imagine that all European countries would have export surpluses like Germany has, so who then should have the import surpluses?

3. The threat to social peace and European unity by refugee flows

The result of the distress and turmoil of war are flows of refugees into economically prosperous or even politically and militarily secure countries. Economically backward countries which want to develop, or, if skilled workers are absent, can be open-minded toward taking in refugees. Refugees were recruited by the Great Elector from France and Holland, because the population in Brandenburg was largely decimated by the plague, and the Huguenots from France and the Flemings brought special skills.

When workers in Germany became scarce after the reconstruction phase, Germany also wooed guest workers in southern Europe and Turkey.

Refugees bring with them their own traditions, habitual social relationships and their beliefs and attitudes. The more they differ from those of the host country, the less easily they can integrate. They then team up with compatriots with the result that ghettos form in the host country.

Refugees, unless they are special personalities who, as such, have outgrown their particular ancestry, are often perceived as alien or even rejected by the host population, and therefore find themselves in a stronger reflection on their inherited nation. That is why Germans in Chile, in Russia and in other countries are often more nationalistic than Germans living in their home country, and this applies, for example, to many Turks in Germany as well.

If refugees enter the country in large numbers, they can be perceived by the host country's population as a threat to their own culture and way of life and therefore be combated.

As the economic problems and conflicts in the world increase, more and more refugees are moving to industrialized countries. Understandably, resistance is rising against them. Refugee flows therefore favor right-wing parties and populists.

The USA has always been a country with immigration at the forefront. Individualism is realized there in such an extreme way that it can also integrate immigrants from other cultures. The free development of the individual as a social ideal makes traditional social ties to public and economic life take a back seat, so that social and private life can coexist.

The connecting factor is the *American Dream*, which offers everyone free individual development. On the one hand, America is certainly the most secular country, which can be home to all races and religions and is therefore regarded as a melting pot in which all human differences are melted down. This does not mean that religions have disappeared in the United States. On the contrary: religion is generally far more intensively cultivated in the respective religious groups than in many European countries. But religion is a private matter.

Nevertheless, as the center of Western Europeanism, the United States is, of course, deeply influenced by Christianity, Antiquity and European settlers. And since Europeanism itself is a secularized form of the antique and Christian heritage, the Americans of other religions and civilizations are being Europeanized to this extent.

Of course, there are white Americans, especially those who are socially and economically lagging behind - that is, especially today, the Donald Trump voters who reject non-whites. There has always been racial prejudice in the lower American strata. Since the USA, has tensions with the Islamic world, which has already started with the fall of the Shah's regime in Iran, and the USA also has to fear terrorist attacks, Muslims are also becoming increasingly marginalized.

However, the secular stagnation and relative impoverishment of mass workers, which are also suffering from the immigration of less skilled workers from Latin America and the relocation of manufacturing facilities abroad has created an increasing potential for conflict in American society that has enabled Donald Trump to become President of the USA.

4. Left protesters as serious critics of social undesirable developments and as rioters

There has always been opposition to one-sidedness in Western and Eastern Europeanism. As early as the 1950s, peace movements began to protest against rearmament and the division of Germany and Europe. In the sixties, there were student revolts:

- in the West, they were against capitalist inequality, crusted social structures and imperialist wars, for independence efforts in Vietnam and Algeria and against the destruction of nature,
- in the East, they were against party dictatorship and for a *socialism with a human face*.

These revolts have given rise to the Green Parties and the Green Initiatives, which have more or less entered the programs of all established parties today.

Since the 1980s and 1990s, opposition to Neoliberalism and the decline of the economy into Casino-Capitalism has risen, as well as the decline of the working class in unemployment and precarious jobs.

In order to prevent the development of globalization through international cooperation and to prevent world problems such as those of a climate catastrophe, the leading economic states come together in the so-called G7 or G20 conferences or meet with business leaders for talks in Davos.

Since the conference participants are representatives of the establishment, who benefit from the given social and economic structures and therefore they also ideologically support the best of knowledge and therefore think in the criteria of the dominant *supply-sided economic policy.* It is of course not excluded that the real problems are not properly seen or treated wrongly.

The real problem to be addressed by the G-20 states, in whose emergence these states are significantly involved, because they 'represent 2/3 of the world's population, a good ¾ of global economic output and 4/5 of greenhouse gas emissions 'summarizes Alexander Jung as follows: 'Every ten seconds a child starves to death on Earth - although there is food for 10-12 billion people and 7.5 billion live on Earth. Almost 800 million are considered extremely poor, while there more money in the world than ever before. 81% of energy is produced by burning coal, gas and oil, although this practice warms the earth. There are alternatives, however, such as solar and wind power.

When the powerful G20 countries meet ... they have the power to resolve some of the contradictions, or at least defuse them, but it is they who have caused the problems for the most part.' From this, it is understandable that the G20 countries are the enemy of globalization critics, '"The G20 are part of the problem and not the solution," says Werner Reitz, co-founder of Attac in Germany, the globalization critical network'[696]

These protests and revolts are leftist because they oppose established power structures. They advocate tolerance of other ethnicities and cultures and oppose national isolation. In this way, leftists stand, in particular, in opposition to all right-wing nationalist movements, eternal reactionaries, but also to those who are afraid of alienation by refugees.

The members of these left-wing movements, unlike the right-wing members, are enlightened and intellectual, advocating active democratic participation in societal decisions, while the rightists tend to long for a leader who tells them what to do.

In democratic states, the established elites defend their position against the left, although they also put the extreme right in their place. They can point to a social order, albeit not a necessarily ideal one, that functions well and in which all institutions and processes are interrelated and which are endangered by changes. Therefore, the established order usually turns against any change and advocates quicker military intervention. Under normal circumstances, they can rely on the masses of the population, who, in case of doubt, want to preserve the given conditions and shy away from the risk of change.

For those who are established, only such measures make sense in terms of *realpolitik*, which strengthen the established powers, because economic prosperity depends on them. Typical of this is the Supply-sided Economic Policy, which sees the true key to economic progress only in the promotion of enterprises. In contrast, leftists are more inclined to promote the weak, increase public spending on infrastructure investment, increase development aid, protect nature and adopt a peace policy.

As for the "real politics" of the established, it has brought infinite military destruction and death, as can be seen in Vietnam, Iraq and other countries. And the problems of enforcing economic power in developing countries have already been explained.

As the essence of Europeanism over traditional cultures, individual and social development has been elaborated. Because leftists fight against social encrustations and undesirable developments and strive for an all-round development of man, society, culture and nature, they are inherently more European than the established and, of course, backward-looking right.

---

[696] Alexander Jung: *Selbstbetrug mit System*, in: Der Spiegel, Nr. 27/1.7.2017, p.14.

Nevertheless, it cannot be assumed that all social problems can be solved with unreflective ideals and especially the methods of the left. Left theses are mostly abstract ideals that cannot be implemented in practice. Also, leftists are mostly intellectual individualists, who usually have endless discussions with regard to the realization of their goals, until someone stifles the discussions, becomes the spokesman or even the dictator and defames the others as deviants. Then a left-wing rule can very quickly turn into a regime of terror in which the abstract ideals are enforced forcibly. Typical examples of this are the Jacobin rule after the French Revolution, the Socialist Revolution in Russia and the RAF Red Army Faction, which terrorized Germany in particular.

In terms of refugee flows, leftists tend to fall from their cosmopolitanism into multiculturalism and overstrain established societies. Of course, a tolerant coexistence of different ethnic groups and religions should be sought. But for that, the host countries, as well as the refugees, have to be ready.

However, quite legitimate arguments of the protesters are happily hushed up or dismissed as unrealistic. This creates frustrations for those who care for the interests not only of their person and family, but of humanity as well, who then are utilized by radicals to commit acts of violence. Tragically, they believe they attract attention for their arguments, but are perceived by the population only as rioters.

It would be right to make the voice of the protesters heard at international conferences and to include them in international talks. It could also reduce the frustration of those involved in society and possibly reduce the high costs of securing conferences.

III. The tasks for the further development of Europe and Europe's responsibility for the harmonization of the East-West Contrast and the further development of the globalized world

Europeanism is based on the common antique and Christian heritage of European countries. Nevertheless, this heritage manifests itself in many different forms, depending on which traditions have a stronger effect and which ethnic groups still have a say in the respective popular culture.

Tolerating diversity has made the formation of the European Union difficult and could make it even more difficult in the future. The transfer of national competences to the European Commission has even sparked anti-European feelings and actions, and, if and insofar as this impairs living conditions or even environmental standards, or even, as in international free trade agreements, globally operating companies can escape the jurisdiction of the Länder, protests occur.

Also standardization rage of supraregional authorities, such as standards for cucumber curvature and bananas, can hurt the feelings of the citizens.

World political issues often call for Europe to speak with one voice. If this demand were to be realized, all European states would have to be deprived of their foreign policy and military competence and transferred to the European Commission. Europe would become a world power like the USA and Russia. But would that be desirable?

As we have tried to show, the USA and Russia each have their own Europeanism, with which they want to make the world happy. The collectivist Marxist social ideal of the East has failed. Russian President Vladimir Putin has to make do with stabilizing and economically developing his huge empire, fueling Russian nationalism and Eurasian ideas.

In the United States, the liberal individualistic ideal of man has increasingly been reduced to Darwinist-capitalist money-*making*, money-*owning* and *spending* money. The economy has become perverted into *Casino Capitalism*, the state order has become a *Plutocracy* and the politics has become *Trumpism*.

The Darwinist-capitalist image of man and its social order are regarded by the Americans as finished and as the last state of social development anyway. Therefore, they assume their image of humanity and their social order as a self-evident ideal of all other peoples. Only in technical progress and constant economic growth is further development seen.

The American Dream that everyone can be the creator of his wealth and it's all about that, is deeply rooted in American society, so deep that the economically dependent just elected a billionaire president of the United States, because they expect from him the revive this dream for all.

In Europe, on the other hand, social conditions and the effects of growth and progress on society and nature are repeatedly discussed and made political programs. The European party landscape is correspondingly diverse. The sense of responsibility underlying these motives also determines the European relationship to the world and other peoples. A *"Europe first"* according to the *"America first!"* or even *"Britain first!"* cannot and should not be possible for Europe because that runs counter to the European mentality.

It is true that since the United States took over the world's position of power from Great Britain after the World War II, the United States has been massively interfering in the affairs of other states when it seemed opportune. However, they were usually only concerned with the enforcement of American interests and at best with the proselytizing on the "American way of life". The failure of the United States to propagate its social system in Iran, Vietnam, Iraq and Afghanistan has contributed to the *America first!* attitude. In terms of power politics, however, the USA will continue to pursue its goals in world politics, and Russia will try to do the same.

The spiritual vitality of Europe is favored by its diversity. In addition, from their colonial past, individual countries have different relationships with Third World countries and, accordingly, have a special understanding and sense of responsibility for these countries. We have dealt with the thoroughly self-serving relationship of France to its former African colonies. However, the special relations cause France to intervene again and again in order to stabilize the political conditions of these countries.

As far as the solution of social and economic problems is concerned, Germany, France, the Netherlands, Poland and the Scandinavian countries sometimes take different paths. Their successes, however, also stimulate other countries. So, when it comes to international conflicts, it does not always have to be beneficial for Europe, as it is called, *to speak with one voice*. Depending on the experiences and ties of individual countries, it may be better for individual European countries to engage in individual conflicts, while others can listen to the other side and mediate in the conflicts.

Let us take the Ukraine conflict as an example. How fast could it escalate into a proper war if there were not Europeans who

- understand that Russia feels threatened by the constant expansion of NATO to its limits,
- look reservedly at the narrow-minded Western Ukrainian nationalism and
- do not believe in Russians intentions of aggression against the Baltic States and Poland and therefore consider the sabre-rattling of NATO to be dangerous.

Only with Anglo-Saxon power logic, as the experiences in the Near and Middle East show, peaceful relations between people cannot be achieved. That's why a Europe that always speaks with one voice and acts on the world stage, like the USA and Russia, will probably foster less peace.

This is not to say that European countries should not cooperate more closely in terms of defense and foreign policy. Especially given the view of the confused attitude of Donald Trump toward NATO, the European national armies should be closely interlinked, so that common European military actions are possible. However, joint action should not be mandatory. In other words, apart from a European foreign minister trying to coordinate European foreign policy, individual countries should also retain their own national foreign and defense ministers.

However, while maintaining as much autonomy as possible, it must be an obligation for all European countries to respect fundamental democratic rights. Therefore, the erosion of these rights in Hungary and Poland cannot be tolerated. However, the fears and social concerns of Eastern Europeans must also be addressed. Their stubborn attitude, as shown by the containment of the incoming refugees on the Balkan Route, may also make sense.

What is important for Europe's international position is the common market, the Euro as a common currency and a solid economic policy.

As the origin and unity of Europeanism, Europe has the task of balancing the one-sidedness of Americanism and Eurasism and to act in a manner of individualizing the East and fostering solidarity in the West.

Since the economy must secure the living conditions of the world's population while protecting nature from destruction, because American turbo-capitalism sooner or later destroys the economy and nature, it is necessary, first of all, to reconsider the economic order and its principles. Any order will be respected only insofar as the relevant parties feel committed to certain ethical principles. Therefore, the outcome must be taken from working out the necessary ethical principles of economic behavior and making them aware of the population.

Europe must also be an anchor for Third World countries if they are not forced to become dependent on the USA, Russia or other power constellations or become victims of military and / or religious conflicts.

The significance of Europeanization for the development of the Third World, and that it was also responsible for their economic and social problems, has been explained in detail. That is why, apart from the fact that Europeanism also includes a mission to develop the entire world, Europe is also forced to engage in the rest of the world in order to prevent conflicts in other countries from becoming a world conflagration and to counteract a flood of refugees into Europe.

In their own interest, but also in order to do justice to world political tasks, European integration must be intensified. The need for a European Economic Community is likely to be evident in the face of Britain's foreseeable problems after *BREXIT*.

Investing is only possible in a sufficiently large market. No foreign company would invest more in a European country outside the European Union. Such a country could thus only import products that it does not produce itself. Yes, globally-operating companies of such a country would probably also relocate their own production to an emerging market with great market potential or to the European Union or the USA, and would supply their own country from there.

To the extent that larger markets isolate themselves further to protect young industries against competition from developed countries, or, like the USA and / or the European Union, to preserve or recover companies of certain industries that would otherwise be relocated to low-wage countries, primarily it is the smaller countries that do not belong to any economic community that will be affected. Because within the big markets, there is enough sales potential for larger companies. Therefore, if Donald Trump can realize his foreclosure of the American market, although there will be major conversion difficulties, the USA can also ultimately live without global trade.

1. Principles of new business ethics

Social life requires ethical behavior. Ethics need not be codified in the form of rules and behavior. It can instinctively control people's behavior. Seen in this way, ethical behavior that not only determines their coexistence, but also makes it possible, can already be assumed for animals.

However, such quasi-natural behavior does not allow any further development of social conditions. Over the course of history, conquerors, prophets or other creative personalities were needed – those who emerged from the path of accepted behaviors and initiated new ones. Through them, the previous conditions were more or less revolutionized until people had inhaled the new ones as they were and connected it with the traditional. Each new society formed its own rules and behaviors anew, and they were then transferred from parents to children.

Until the industrial revolution, the "income according to one's rank" was considered as a guide to craft activity and the rationalization of production for profit accumulation was even considered dishonorable. Peter Borscheid writes: '"No craftsman should conceive or invent or use something new, but everyone should follow his neighbor out of civic and brotherly love and do his work without damage for his neighbor," says the Thorner guild order of 1523. [697] By the end of the 17th century, the Kaiser and the Reichstag tried to prevent the use of water mills

---

[697] Karlheinz A. Geißler: *Die Zeiten ändern sich. Vom Umgang mit der Zeit in unterschiedlichen Epochen, in: Aus Politik und Zeitgeschichte*, p.5.

for faster production of strings, because the use of hydropower would make thousands of people and families into beggars. [698] This thinking continued, despite, or even because of, liberal economic claims, even in the 18th century. In Amiens, France, two manufacturers are prosecuted in 1742 because they want to innovate and better monitor and accelerate their work by setting up a factory with 200 looms. [699]'700

It was only under capitalism that the indefinite profit-seeking of individuals gained intrinsic value, but not initially to lead a life of luxury. Rather, profits were to be reinvested to increase aggregate output, so remained product-driven.

The company founders also usually identified with their companies, that is, with the employees and the manufactured products. Entrepreneurs, employees and workers gained their self-confidence from this activity and their contribution to economic production. Even with family businesses, heirs often do not lend themselves to running the business, so outsiders are often appointed as directors. As a result, the emotional ties between entrepreneurs and their businesses naturally diminishes.

In Anglo-Saxon countries, and, in particular, the USA, the interest of the entrepreneur changed from the products themselves very early on. They understood themselves more and more as capitalists, who were concerned only with the financial result of their activity. Of course, this attitude was favored in the USA by the huge market, which could quickly make a resourceful entrepreneur rich. The more money was accumulated, the more the entrepreneurs could devote themselves to the profitable reinvestment of free funds.

Because of their high capital requirements, companies seeking to grow had to acquire loan capital as well. Equities and corporate bonds were created, in which a capital owner could invest his free funds. Money was not only made through skillful buying and selling stocks and entire companies, but also through speculation in commodities, currencies and financial derivatives.

Over the course of globalization, not only did investment opportunities grow beyond national borders. The American money-oriented economic concept also became the economic philosophy of the rest of the world.

The guiding principle for corporations was the so-called *Shareholder Value Principle*, which, as economic activity, prescribed the optimization of the short-term profit of the shareholders.

In the past, corporate executives recognized their social recognition as leading a company that provided valuable products, while today, only the monetary gains made in relation to others count. Employees are expected to keep an eye on the company's maximum profit. Identification with the company, work colleagues and manufactured products is lost. The actual work is devalued and must also be given up if the management closes branches of production or relocates them to low-wage countries.

---

[698] Rudolf Wendorff (1980): *Zeit und Kultur. Geschichte des Zeitbewusstseins in Europa*, P.130.

[699] Bernard Lepetit: *Frankreich 1750-1850*, p.503.

[700] Peter Borscheid: *Das Tempo-Virup.Eine Kulturgeschichte der Beschleunigung*, p.22.

Even capitalists, at least in Europe, felt connected in the early days of capitalism with the companies they held shares in. One thought also in the long-term - short-term price fluctuations were ignored. *An entrepreneur did not speculate.* Of course, stocks were sold or bought when confidence in a company dwindled or rose.

In the past, companies were valued more by their intrinsic value, that is, their ownership of real estate and other tangible assets, while today it is a question of divesting all non-essential assets and only valuing companies by the value of their earnings. The income value depends on the expected profit. Thus, the shares of the companies rise and fall compared to other investment options, depending on what kind of profit is expected.

By extracting inventory values, companies' creditworthiness naturally falls in respect of the loans available and can go bankrupt more quickly and then their know-how is cheaply bought up by other firms and employees are laid off. Deindustrialization can deplete entire regions.

In order for the boards of corporations to follow the *Shareholder Value Principle*, they are involved in the profits through bonuses. The salaries of board members and other senior executives have skyrocketed worldwide. The CEO of Daimler-Benz is said to have earned €15[701] million in 2015.

Why does a person need so much money in a year? Ultimately, it is just a status symbol that compares one board member to another and to which he sets his self-confidence. And because they are status symbols, of course everyone is anxious to earn a little more, so we have to deal with board salaries with an *open-topped Richter scale.*

Such high salaries corrupt business morals. Any sense of decency and adequacy is destroyed. Such extreme income and wealth differences are ethically unjustifiable and any sense of the adequacy of a job will also be lost.

Over the course of globalization, globally-operating companies and capitalists can also be less and less restricted by state laws, because they can play states off against each other and make their profit where they are taxed the least. Financial power becomes medial and political power that can lead states to shape laws in a way that favors global companies.

We have also seen that the increasingly unequal distribution of wealth and income is generating an increasing gap of private demand, leading to secular stagnation and self-destruction of the economy.

The only justification for accumulating wealth that is no longer needed for one's livelihood, including luxury needs, is the somewhat legitimate belief that the market controls the creativity of companies so that production meets the demand for money and one consistent market economy causes large income differences. But then at least it should be noted that the economic equality of the people in the market is only guaranteed if all people have the same starting chances. In order to approximate these, individuals should only be allowed to accumulate wealth until their deaths. After that, the assets would have to go back to the company, because

---

[701]http://www.faz.net/aktuell/finanzen/aktien/daimler-chef-dieter-zetsche-verdiente-2015-am-meisten-14151530.html.

inheritance is not a principle of the market economy, with basically equal economic partners, but a relic of feudalism.

Biological and traditional forms of life have survived into our time, so it is justifiable to inherit personal property. However, it is probably only about items with personal reference, including personal apartments and possibly castles.

Insofar as a family identifies with its company, like, for example, in craft enterprises or medium-sized companies, where the children want to continue the operation of the parents, an inheritance can also be justified in a socio-ethical manner. In addition, parents will be allowed to leave their children with good starting conditions and reserves for crisis situations. But anything beyond that would have to revert to society, which would then be able to support public concerns, general education, culture and business start-ups. If these principles were followed, excesses of current wealth and income distribution could be tolerated.

What also corrupts by narrowing economic motivation to *making money* is the impression of work itself.

While man used to understand himself more as a user of the fruits of the earth and work as a necessary evil, which was imposed on slaves as much as possible, work in Christianity became the actual content of life, to realize one's self.

The attitude of seeing work as an essential human activity, in which man finds fulfillment, is lost in capitalism, which is only concerned with increasing capital, the more it dissolves from the real economy. Since man works most of his life, work in the capitalist economy is reduced to hardship for him and he finds satisfaction only in consumption as a result of his work.

For the capitalists themselves, on the other hand, work becomes a game, which, as such, grants the satisfaction of a player regardless of the profit and in addition to being able to live a luxurious life.

The capitalist economic conception incites egoism. As long as egoism is still bound by natural economic motivation, that is, people's work, cooperation with peers and customer satisfaction remain important, it can serve the well-being of all. Then, progress and economic growth can benefit everyone involved in the work process. However, the more only rationalization takes place and wages stagnate, the more the rate of growth falls with the risk that the economy may turn into a recession and only the profits of entrepreneurs and capitalists grow.

To the extent that the fellow human being is only seen as a tool for their own increase in profits, the tendency to commit fraud and overreach also increases. Aggressive advertising is used to bring dubious benefits, product and environmental standards are violated, banks give scrap papers to unsuspecting investors or even falsify the Libor ('the interest rate that banks are charged on the euro money market in London for short-term borrowing from other banks.'[702]) and more and more are trying to avoid taxes, ignoring the fact that they are needed to finance macroeconomic concerns.

Since economic behavior is significantly influenced by the theories of economics, it becomes particularly difficult to change the behaviors that used to be virtues. Saving was previously considered a virtue. The prevailing economic theory went

---

[702]https://www.google.de/search?q=Libor&ie=utf-8&oe=utf-8&client=firefox-b-ab&gfe_rd=cr&ei=XG8ZWfG 4DKXi8AfmmprIBg

without saying that capital is scarce and as a result of saving the capital supply, investment opportunities increase. But if, as at present, so much capital does not find real economic investment opportunities, then it is better not to save it. Because every saved Euro not spent on investment is poison for the economy. It follows the norm: *Try to earn only as much as you need for consumer spending (including luxury consumption), real economic investment, charitable spending and retirement savings!*

Those participating in a business life must know and pay attention to what is economically meaningful, and thus allowed, and what is not. Most of the rules regarding customers and suppliers are already observed out of self-interest. Otherwise suppliers are no longer willing to sell to customers and customers are no longer willing to buy from suppliers who are not respecting existing standards. Nevertheless, this insight can be promoted by strict declaration obligations, quality seals and, of course, by increasing publicity work of consumer associations and the media.

It becomes more difficult to enforce norms, such as the prohibition of mass animal husbandry, if goods can be sourced alternatively from abroad, where these standards do not apply. It is therefore important to ensure that common standards apply in an economic community or customs union. Companies that meet higher standards must be accordingly favored by VAT benefits or other measures. Non-compliant imports must be blocked or burdened with higher import sales taxes.

But rules are of no use if they are not understood and accepted by people. For example, how do you want to fight corruption in government and business when all employees are corrupt?

Therefore, it is necessary to reflect more on the spiritual roots of our society and to develop and formulate ethical principles for all areas of life and, in particular, for business people. All graduates should be tested in ethics, just as the *Hippocratic Oath* guides doctors in their work.

It would also be desirable if companies such as Amazon, Facebook, Windows, as well as the other global companies, would take on role models in ethical behavior. In general, they earn very well and, of course, they are particularly displeased when they try to avoid taxes, are negligent in meeting environmental standards and / or practice wage dumping. The standard of living of its shareholders would not be affected. However, the role model function could be a signal to which other economic operators are guided, apart from the fact that reservations about them would disappear.

Multicultural representatives often take offense at Europeanism. They forget, however, that Europeanism has enabled economic and social development and its global networking and thus also multiculturalism itself. Also, the development of society and the earth is not to be expected from Islam, nor from Hinduism, nor Taoism. From these religions, moral impulses, from Buddhism and Taoism also suggestions for a deeper spiritual development may come, but all on the basis of European tolerance.

Modern science and research and the further development of society can only be expected from a deeper Europeanism. Since Europe is itself the true bearer of Europeanism, the continuation of the unification of Europe should be understood as necessary for the harmonious development, not only of Europe itself, but of the world as a whole.

2. Stabilization and further development of the European Union

2.1 Economic stabilization and further development of the European Union
The tasks to be solved for the stabilization and further development of the European Union are:
1. overcoming secular stagnation,
2. the elimination of economic imbalances between European countries and regions,
3. the protection of the European market against the emigration of companies and enterprises,
4. the coordination of tax policy and the fight against tax fraud, tax avoidance and evasion in tax havens,
5. the elimination of letterbox companies,
6. capital transfer taxes and
7. the strengthening of the Eurozone.

2.1.1 Overcoming secular stagnation
The biggest economic problem, as was explained, is secular stagnation, mainly caused by the uneven distribution of income.

The incomes are derived from working income, which includes entrepreneurial profits and income from capital, including all forms of rent and retirement income.

Rapid salary growth for executives was criticized as economically and ethically alarming, since remuneration has no traceable relation to work performance. The discussion on how to tackle this development has already been opened and the first rules of limitation have already been introduced. For example, it is no longer the directors of large companies who fix the salaries of managers, but the shareholders themselves. Individual companies have already set themselves limits on a maximum salary.

As a tax measure, the restriction on the tax deductibility of manager salaries was brought into play. Salaries above a certain limit should not be able to be claimed by companies as costs. Such a restriction would give the state somewhat higher revenue. However, companies would hardly be affected by such a tax deduction limit. The additional taxes to be paid would be, as they say, only peanuts.

Now it should not be forgotten in this discussion that high executive salaries only mean lower profits for the shareholders, even if they are unlikely to make a big impact on the individual share of large companies. High managerial salaries are therefore essentially only a redistribution within the super income recipients themselves. Therefore, this question should not be given too great an economic policy role. The recommended measure against super salaries would thus be a sharply progressive increase in wealth tax for all salaries above a certain limit.

The second major source of unequal income distribution results from capital income. In order to reduce the extremely unequal distribution of wealth, progressive inheritance taxes are recommended, whereby generous allowances should be generally granted for small craft businesses and small and medium-sized enterprises that are continued as a family business.

But social injustice is not the main problem for the functioning of the economy. What is more important in times of secular stagnation is that every euro not issued is poison to the economy, because it causes the economy to shrink if the state does not then carry over this euro to government debt and in turn returns it to government spending. It was also pointed out that the increasing government securities (without real value) and the savings that are not used for the real economy can foster capital market games and speculation, making the world economy more fragile and triggering economic crises.

Progressive inheritance taxes of course only melt away super-assets slowly, as long as the loss of wealth through inheritance taxes is not earned again soon. If this inequality is to be remedied more quickly, also in view of the fact that government bonds can be redeemed and the capital market is thus relieved, a capital levy would be a possibility, as it was in Germany at that time charged to wealthy people who were not affected by the war, in favor of those who had lost their assets during the last World War.

Taking into account that repayments of government debt from contributions of the wealthy must be made anyway because the lower classes cannot be burdened with it, - it would also increase the economic demand gap even further - then it would be a zero-sum game so far, because those who are charged, essentially also receive the repayments. Of course, that is just a rough calculation, because those who have invested their money in companies are charged as much as those who hold stocks, bonds and government bonds. For the latter, only their security holdings are reduced. For the former, if they do not also have securities, may have to sell shares or take out loans, or they cannot invest in a given amount.

Property tax should be designed so that the business operation is not burdened. Therefore, the capital charge would have to be paid off over a longer period of time or by issuing additional shares and liable debt of the companies to the state, which could later be repurchased.

Although a wealth recovery tax would be best, it is the hardest to realize because it affects the powerful people in society, who will fight against this redistribution against capital levies as well as a wealth tax or higher inheritance taxes. It is repeatedly claimed that this harms craft businesses and small businesses in the family estate. The arguments against this are:
1. It only hits high assets. That means crafts and small businesses are not subject to the tax.
2. If the company owners also have financial titles and real estate, they can assign them or burden them with the levies.

Also, in our time, one should not overestimate the romantic conceptions of a continuation of a company by the next generation. Which children of company owners still want to continue the paternal inheritance and which heirs are willing to renounce their inheritance? If the next-generation owner inherits more so that it falls under the wealth tax, then a state participation that can be repatriated would facilitate the continuation. But if no suitable heir exists, then, with state aid, the operation could be handed over to another craftsman or competent successor.

2.1.2 Economic promotion measures to overcome the inequality in the economic development of countries and regions

In order to overcome the imbalances in economic development in individual European countries, the solidarity of the richer states must be strengthened in favor of the less industrialized. Germany, as the largest industrial power in Europe, plays a special role.

We have shown how Germany itself has contributed to the problems of Europe with its large export surpluses and rigorous austerity policies, which it also expected from the weaker European countries and made it a condition for financial aid. The German export surpluses are constantly criticized by the USA, the European countries and the IMF International Monetary Fund.

In order to reduce export surpluses, the fiscal space available to the public should be used "for initiatives to improve growth potential as well as investment in infrastructure and digitization, childcare, refugee integration and reducing the tax burden on labor", as was mentioned in the recommendations [of the International Monetary Fund] on Monday [15.05.2017] in Berlin.' [703] These recommendations, which have long been part of the party program of the SPD, the Greens and even more of the Left, are obviously being taken more seriously by the CDU. But with higher taxes for the 2017 election program, the CDU does not even want to burden the super-rich. Both the CDU and the FDP seem to have failed to grasp the necessities caused by secular stagnation.

The demand, in particular of Germany, for economic reforms in the European deficit countries, is largely justified and necessary. However, to comply with the "debt brake", government spending should not be limited, but should only be diverted into projects of social and economic development. If the European Union does not provide assistance through grants, financing should only have to be funded by higher taxes and public charges of the super-rich. The unequal distribution of wealth and income in the economically lagging countries with high unemployment tends to be higher than in Germany.

However, Germany would have to set a good example by cutting high profits and wealth taxation, at least with inheritance tax, in order not to have such low taxes, in relation to the other European countries, so that there would still be an influx of companies and investors from these countries.

Increasing public spending and relieving lower income earners in Germany should go beyond the additional tax revenues and be financed by a higher burden on the wealthy and high income earners.

2.1.3 Protection of sensitive industries of the European market and prevention from their emigration

2.1.3.1 Import barriers to protect sensitive industries

Economies have their own level of development. This also is reflected in the general cost level and the amount of rent. Accordingly, the income of the workers must be so high that they can cover the need for life. But if they are compelled to compete with workers in low-wage countries because the tariff barriers are set too

---

[703] Der Tagesspiegel: *IWF liest Deutschland die Leviten*, Nr. 23 116, 16.5.3017, p.8.

low, then the wages fall and they can still earn something in precarious jobs. But they cannot pay for their living. What is earned in low-wage countries will be more in line with the need for living there than equal pay in developed industrialized countries.

Low tariffs in developed countries shift jobs to low-wage countries, unless they agree with wage cuts and high-skilled workers in developing countries do not find jobs there, because the know-how-intensive workplaces are in industrialized countries.

As a result, lower-skilled workers in industrialized countries are losing their pay. In Germany, this development was accelerated by the *Hartz laws*. Harald Schumann writes: 'The hardest hit was the bottom 40% of wage earners. Their real hourly wages in 2015 were lower than 20 years earlier. A significant part of the population has no share in economic progress.'[704]

Conditions in an economy can only satisfy everyone if there are job opportunities for all people, that is, for people of the most varied qualifications and the less qualified do not have to work in precarious conditions and still have to rely on social assistance. However, such a situation can only be achieved if the domestic market is adequately shielded from low-wage countries and yet large enough that a large degree of self-sufficiency is possible and companies already invest in the economic area because of the size of the market.

With tariffs falling, industrialized countries also have to fear that even high-quality production and service companies will be relocated to other countries. That is why adequate tariff barriers are important to national economies, so that they do not lose important industries that are necessary for good economic structure.

For example, Apple's iPhones and other devices 'and by far the most electronic products' are mainly produced in China, 'because in Asia, large parts of the supply chain and also large reserves rely on cheap labor.' 'The group is producing smartphones only in countries where otherwise there would be sales restrictions. For example, production in Brazil was set up with the Asian production partner Foxconn in order to avoid an import duty of 30%. In India, it should have been a requirement for the opening of Apple stores.'[705]

The arguments against customs barriers are, as claimed by neoliberal economics theorists, that this would eliminate rationalization opportunities. In view of the possibility of rationing through digitization and robotization, and the possible resulting adaptation to different standards, the disadvantage, if any, should remain manageable. This also makes it possible to *produce as necessary*, for example, *print on demand*, which means smaller batch sizes and fast conversion of production. Only the undisturbed utilization of low wages and the international tax optimization is restricted, along with the associated further conversion of wages into capital income.

A result of globalization and, in particular, digitalization and robotization, is that the power of globally operating companies is still increasing. They are less

---

[704] Harald Schumann: *Emanuel Macron und die deutsche Krankheit*, in: Der Tagesspiegel Nr. 23 124, v. 24.5.2017, p.8.
[705] dpa: *Traumfabriken*, in: Der Tagesspiegel, Nr. 23 186/27.7.2017.

and less dependent on manpower and can optimize their location decisions all the more for financial and tax avoidance reasons.

Of course, protectionism is not intended to be favored here in general, but only a differentiated economic policy should be called for. Incidentally, higher tariffs would not mean the end of global economic activity. After all, if all companies in all markets had to be present in order to supply these markets, then international networking is guaranteed.

Insofar as it is not a question of maintaining or expanding a healthy economic structure, but merely of ensuring decent employment for the workforce, an alternative to higher tariffs could be the provision of a general basic income. As a result, people would no longer be dependent on living primarily on precarious jobs, but their earned income, even in precarious jobs, would be earned in addition to a basic income.

As a solution to the economic problems in other countries, the German side recommends introducing Hartz laws in their respective countries. Harald Schumann correctly writes: 'Everyone else should do it like the Germans, so that they can become "competitive", but that is economically ineffective. Businesses should be in competition, not states, and certainly not in a monetary union.

... Macron is right: a monetary union cannot exist if it forces everyone into a race to the bottom. This aggravates inequality and strengthens the nationalists' position. On the other hand, a common budget for Euroland would, if anything, be a consolation. Much more important would be to fight the German disease of the eurozone itself. The key to this is German public investment. Since 2003, it has not even been enough to compensate for the decline of the existing infrastructure. Since then, state-owned capital stock is shrinking. Roads, bridges, railways, schools and universities are rotting nationwide. If the federal and state governments took advantage of the opportunity to stop decaying with loans at zero cost, then that would be a blessing for the entire Eurozone. With such an investment offensive, as the Macroeconomic Policy Institute (IMK) recently suggested, the incomes and thus the demand for foreign goods and services could rise enough to balance the current account.

If, by contrast, it remains the same course, it would also force Macron's France into the downward spiral of falling wages and declining government spending. The victory of the Front National at the next election would then be guaranteed.'[706] Better than taking on more debt and even the lowest interest rates, it would be to raise more money from the wealthy and super rich so that public debt does not rise any further.

2.1.3.2 Participation of employees or of the state in the important companies of the national economy

Each state is responsible for ensuring that the domestic economy functions and is so diversified that it provides jobs for all segments of the population and also allows for synergies between different sectors of the economy.

---

[706] Harald Schumann: loc. cit., p.8.

Companies operating globally have no inhibitions about changing owners, relocating their permanent establishments or even relocating the company headquarters. On the other hand, the states and the employees concerned must be able to defend themselves. That's why companies sensitive to the economy should
1. allow codetermination laws be strengthened,
2. ensure employees are entitled to certain profit sharing,
3. make sure that states hold a qualified blocking minority in important companies, like Niedersachsen at the Volkswagen plant.

For all these proposals, there are already examples in individual states. However, it is not enough for companies to set the level of profit sharing for employees. It is better to issue legal provisions for how to regulate the ratio of premiums for board members, officers and ordinary workers.

This would then also make the socially poisonous discussion about excessive participation in executives superfluous. After all, if the profit-sharing arrangements for members of the Executive Board are too opulent, the premiums for the other employees would increase accordingly, which would soon result in a size that is no longer acceptable to the owners of the capital. High profit sharing for top executives only is not overly significant, but it also does bind executives too much to the interests of capital owners.

A qualified blocking minority of the public sector can prevent companies from becoming the plaything of "grasshoppers" who buy companies with borrowed money and smash them if necessary. For example, the state of Lower Saxony was able to prevent the Volkswagen plant from being taken over by other companies and banks, and that the small Porsche AG, in relation to Volkswagen AG, wanted to buy the Volkswagen plant with borrowed money and repay the loan from the cash reserves of the Volkswagen factory.

For example, if the German State would have held a qualified blocking minority at Deutsche Bank, then CEO Josef Ackermann would not have been forced to seek a 25% return on capital, otherwise the Deutsche Bank share would have dropped so far that Deutsche Bank would have been taken over by foreigners. Then the equity could have been higher and would not have burdened the staff so much, which has led to all the scams from which Deutsche Bank suffers today.

It would also make sense to stipulate by law that in the case of a relocation of production, production facilities, including facilities, fall to the state, which makes it easier to locate other companies for the production site and the employees.

Of course, a state can only legislate if it has a large enough economic area and if necessary, it can set up import barriers high enough for companies to accept these regulations if they want to sell their goods competitively in the country.

2.1.4 Capital transfer taxes, the coordination of tax policy and the fight against tax fraud, tax avoidance and dodging it in tax havens

Tax policy is the most crucial instrument for reducing the excesses of the extremely unequal distribution of wealth and income and also to bring back surplus savings, which are unable to find real investment and therefore fail as economic demand, through government spending, into the economic cycle. Because individual governments are attracting investors with low taxes, thereby hindering the collection of higher taxes for all, the coordination of individual countries' tax policies is a priority. Significantly, Donald Trump violates this principle again with his latest tax reform.

Internationally-developed tax principles

1. ensure that taxes accrue according to value added in each country. In addition, it would be appropriate to levy corporate taxes in accordance with the principles of German trade tax. According to this, long-term interest and license fees would no longer be deductible as costs, thus increasing the company's profit.

    With appropriate design it would no longer be advantageous to deduct profits in tax havens with letterbox companies by lending or licensing and to have them taxed there.

    Profits from independent trading companies, of which the investors of producers have more than 40%, and which have their headquarters abroad and through which the goods are sold, should only be entitled to distribute the profits according to the proportional wage and salary costs.

2. Minimum tax rates would have to be set for income, wealth, inheritance and gift tax.

    With low taxes, less industrialized countries could be allowed to levy lower corporate taxes to favor the establishment of entrepreneurs, but the profits have only to be calculated on the basis of added value, not in respect of transferred capital and royalties.

Of course, in particular, tax havens are resisting such measures. Therefore, efforts to do so will be made in a piecemeal fashion, if at all. It will probably become necessary for the states in which the actual value added takes place to act amicably and, if necessary, Germany will have to modify its tax legislation alone, which will then exert pressure on others to do so as well.

2.1.5 Stabilization of the euro zone and new monetary policy principles

The fact that the CEO of the European Central Bank, Mario Draghi, has been able to calm the markets by declaring that he is buying up all the troubled sovereign debts of the Eurozone if necessary, particularly highlights the financialization of the economy. The traditional concept of monetary policy has become dull, but new opportunities for economic control have opened up.

Traditional economics assume that money is automatically used to either consume or invest. John Maynard Keynes and others have brought the possibility of additional liquidity into play. But either it was not believed, or this possibility was only considered temporary to await better investment opportunities.

In times of secular stagnation, we have completely different conditions. The savings do not find lucrative real investment opportunities and consumption stagnates due to saturation phenomena or because the state or large sections of the population cannot spend enough due to low revenues. In earlier times, when central banks pumped money into the economy, it stimulated investment. With additional employment, wages and thus also consumption then increased.

In times of secular stagnation, however, increasing the money supply no longer works. The European Central Bank desperately tries to stimulate investment by flooding the economy with €60-80bn per month to achieve inflation of 2%, because it believes that such inflation is necessary for positive economic development. In fact, it has done almost nothing with this measure. The cheap money has essentially only stimulated speculation, even in real estate, and otherwise flowed into the capital market and increased the prices, and that produces economic mockery profits.

On the other hand, as illustrated, the ECB was able to calm speculation by buying up distressed government bonds, and did not need to fear that it would trigger galloping inflation.

However, this flood of money is not without danger. It contributes to the fact that the mass of small savers and medium-sized companies no longer participate in the economic profits of companies. These profits then flow only to the already wealthy, who can use the savings of the small people for almost 0% interest on their investments and speculation. In addition, the exchange rate is also affected and alienates international trade relations. If interest rates are raised again, this can lead to harmful countermeasures for international economic relations and especially for developing countries.

Since the equivalent of the money thrown on the market is government paper, which has already been set out above, that they have no real value and are therefore classified as scrap papers, the states bear for their central banks the risk of loss of value of securities from bankrupt states. In other words, by repurchasing distressed government bonds by the European Central Bank, the risk of loss of the government securities in question is transferred from private individuals and banks to taxpayers. Seen in this light, this monetary policy, can at the same time, be regarded as a promotion of those who are already wealthy, and it also promotes the unjust distribution of wealth and income, and thus secular stagnation.

According to classical economic theory, it was taken for granted that increasing the money supply meant inflation. It was assumed that every new mark pumped into the market automatically becomes a demand. However, according to the experience of recent years, this view is wrong. Extra money will only increase demand if the one who receives the money spends it.

For example, if the central bank lends money to the state and thus increases spending, then of course the demand for the economy increases. But if the money supply only increases the liquidity needs of the economy or is needed for capital market transactions, and those who receive the money do not spend it on real economic investments, then the ECB cannot expect 2 percent inflation by increasing its money supply. Even a lowering of the interest rate level to almost 0%, as is well known, did not sufficiently stimulate investment activity. The excess economic savings have been invested almost exclusively in liquidity.

The experience of flooding the economy with liquidity to combat secular stagnation should be a reason to rethink the meaning and value of money to the economy.

***What is money and what would be the overcoming of the illusionary idea of
money as a promissory note of the central bank in favor of recognition of
money as a product of the state mean?***

Money is a product that is used as a means of payment. In ancient times, goods
were paid for with cattle and sheep, then later more and more with precious metals,
which were then later monetized to state coins.

So far, central bank money was considered to be the equivalent of any real
goods, originally gold and silver. Some money theorists still dream of returning to
the gold standard today. They do not realize that the value of money will depend
on the amount of available gold and that then the value of money will automatically increase as the economy grows or capital transactions increase, unless the
recovery of gold increases by the same percentage. If not, the lack of liquidity
would stifle the economy, and hoarding gold would deprive the economy of liquidity and paralyze the economy. Given today's demand for money, the return in
the gold standard would very quickly turn out to be an impossibility.

Even if the equivalent of a certain amount of money is no longer covered by
gold, the central banks are expected to accept the equivalent in the form of securities, including government bonds, for issuing banknotes. As we have already seen,
government debt is not based on real value and can usually only be prolonged.

What value should government bonds have if they amount up to 100% and
more of the gross domestic product? Besides, nobody asks what real value a bank-
note has. It is valued solely for the authority of the state issuing it and because it
has a certain value in relation to the demand for money.

Already with coinage, the state authority was associated with the value of the
precious metal, that is: in a coin, not only the metal value, but also the state authority was counted. With the issuance of paper money, the metal value represented by it has become more and more obsolete and plays almost no role in the
valuation of currencies today. A paper money note is just as much a product as an
insurance policy, a building permit or a vehicle registration certificate.

Central bank money should therefore be considered as a product or a payment
license, that is, as a product of a subsidiary of the state. The state gives the economy a means to exchange goods more easily. Just as a product or license must be
purchased, the money must be bought as well. Money printing would then be a
production process like any other economic activity and the additional amount of
money given into the economic cycle would be part of the national product.

The value of money depends, on the one hand, on the importance and power
of the state making the money available, and, on the other hand, as with all commodities, on its relative scarcity. The latter was true even for pure metal currencies.
Thus, especially at the time of the Spanish precious metal imports from South
America, there were also inflations due to the large circulation of gold money.

In money and economic theory, however, they are adhering to the fiction of
a net value of money, that is, the money must be covered by a material value and
the product character of the money is not recognized. Money is treated like a promissory note. The consequence of this is that states that make money available
through their central banks have to lend it themselves and they must not even lend
it directly from the central bank, but have to go through the capital market, with
the abstruse consequence that the central banks have to buy the public debt to

increase the amount of money, so states are thus indirectly indebted to themselves. The interest due on the government debt then also flows back to them through the distributions of the central banks. It would make more sense if, in the context of growing basic money requirements, this money would be made available to states directly.

The previous view of money was also supported by the fact that money creation was almost equated with additional economic demand. The result then is the theory that money creation, if it goes beyond the real economic payment needs, is automatically additional demand and thus means inflation.

Underrated is:
1. how much the extra money will be used by lower income strata, who prefer consumer spending, and how far it goes to wealthy people who largely save it,
2. the liquidity requirement for capital market games, which is a multiple of the real economic liquidity requirement,
3. liquidity preference, in particular of capital market players and
4. the fact that it is also invested in currency, the more recognized the currency is, the more so.

Money as a state product was already recognized by the Campaign for Monetary Reform. They call it Sovereign Money, and it shall be implemented by a referendum in Switzerland. I refer to the detailed discussion of the pros and cons mentioned under: https://www.vollgeld-initiative.ch/english/.

If money is a product of the state, then the normal process of how money flows into the economy is that the state can use its money to finance government spending.

That is harmless, as long as the state does not pump more money into the economy than the economy needs. But that is true for all products. Therefore, of course, it still requires an independent central bank, which provides the state only with as much additional money as the economic cycle needs.

The European Central Bank strives to stimulate the economy to invest and spend by increasing the amount of money in huge quantities without much success. The real economic effect fails to materialize, because no additional demand is generated by this money allocation. If money were understood as a product of the state and used by the state for additional government spending, then the increase in money would directly stimulate the economic cycle. Then the ECB would have to pump less money into the market as a monthly €60-80 billion.

Of course, the central banks will continue to buy and sell stocks and other securities, even in order to control the circulating money supply in this way.

On the central bank balance sheet, money would then not be shown as a liability and on the active side of the balance sheet as assets, but issued money would be posted as revenue. The offsetting entry would be cash. As far as the money is provided to the state, the booking would be profit distribution against cash.

In practice, this is the way that the economy was stimulated in the thirties by the increase of government spending in Nazi Germany and in the New Deal in the USA. This recovery in public demand is still carried out by the USA today, as the money supply is expanded and lent to the state. But because the fiction is maintained that money is to be covered by securities, the public debts are increasing permanently and, as far as the central bank holds the sovereign debt, the interest payments to the central bank as well, which then let their profits refloat back to the state.

It is also based on the illusion that government debt can eventually be repaid. The fact that the repayment of public debt is an impossibility and would plunge the economy into a depression, because the creditors cannot do anything with the repaid money, has already been explained. Repayment of debts to the central bank would also deprive the economy of liquidity. It is therefore simpler to make the net proceeds from additional money directly available to the state and to avoid, to that extent, rising public debt.

Because of the high national debt of European countries and their bankruptcy risk national bonds are purchased, to a huge extent, from the European Central Bank. The fear then arises that if these securities lose value, all European countries, and especially Germany, as the largest shareholder in the European Central Bank, will have to pay for these losses. Upon these fears, election campaigns are also structured.

In a practical sense, however, such a claim will never occur. It would only make sense if its deposits were to reduce the circulating money supply. But the central bank could also sell held promissory notes on the capital market, as it now buys billions of euros of debt every month to expand the money supply.

If the ECB were to extinguish debt to European countries in the amount of bought-up government securities, worthless government securities, which cannot be repaid anyway, would disappear from the capital market and, accordingly, reduce the risk of sovereign default.

But a better understanding of the importance of money and its role in the economy would eliminate nonsensical debt-restructuring problems. Such a derecognition of sovereign debt or its depreciation could reduce public debt. In that regard, there would be no need for Greece and other countries to provide assistance in the payment of their debts when they are due. All the measures hindering the Greek economy could be eliminated.

Of course, one would continue to insist on reforms and prevent countries from getting into debt again. This is because endless debt cannot be canceled, but only to the extent of the circulating money supply, because it is needed as liquidity, as well as vehicles that, if they are provided by a public truck manufacturer, would not be shown as liabilities in the balance sheet as before money creation and their purchase price will also be determined by how many vehicles are needed.

The Greek public debt of approximately €315 billion would correspond to the money creation of 6 months of the European Central Bank. This means that within 6 months, the European Central Bank could buy all Greek bonds and thus make the country debt free.

Of course, the European Central Bank cannot just settle Greek debt in this way. It also needs assets to be able to limit the money supply again. Nevertheless, if the ECB only partially destroys promissory notes, according to the importance of the individual economies, this would be of great help without interfering with any real economic relations.

However, they would do a disservice to the countries if, on the basis of these debt reliefs, they in turn absorb new debts and finance government expenditures not through additional revenue from the super-rich, but through debt. It is also important to encourage countries to reduce bureaucracy and economic reforms. However, I do not understand by this the lowering of the wage level to precarious employment. On the other hand, the different levels of industrial development of individual countries require fiscal equalization within Europe.

To understand money as a product, in this case of a community of states, and to spend proportionally to each state, the International Monetary Fund also practices in increasing SDR Special Drawing Rights.

The so-called "book money" of commercial banks, which is also used for payments, is only derived money, because it can only be made available in relation to a given amount of central bank money. Book money is only a multiple use of central bank money. The more cashless amounts, i.e. by bank transfers are paid, the more book money can be created in relation to the cash reserves. However, as practiced by the commercial banks, sufficient cash reserves must be maintained.

In summary it can be stated that sovereign money overcomes the illusionary equalization of money with government bonds and allows:

1. an enormous debt relief of states, whereby only government bonds bought up by the central banks would have to be canceled,

2. the possibility to sell the gold resting in the cellars of the central bank as far as possible and to make the equivalent available to the states. – It is actually a scandal that gold is not used for jewelry and consumer goods, but pressed into bars and locked away in basements! – and

3. better steering of the economy cycles.

3. Principles for a European refugee and immigration policy

How should the industrialized countries react to the real and potential flows of refugees?

From their fundamental attitude, Europeans cannot do anything else but tolerate and openly face the people of all ethnic groups and all cultures and recognize them as equal people. In particular the Germans feel responsible for refugees. They have gained refugee experience themselves in fleeing Nazi Germany and at the end of World War II from the former eastern territories.

However, the positive attitude of German Chancellor, Angela Merkel, to refugees was understood as an invitation and as a political presumption by the other European countries to speak for the whole of Europe, and this harmed European unification.

Also, such a sense of responsibility for the problems of the world must not obscure the mind emotionally. As sympathetic as the openness to foreign cultures and warmth toward refugees is, it can also be so harmful and dangerous for Europe and as well for the rest of the world, because Europe can no longer adequately fulfill its mission in and for the world.

Multicultural devotees often do not realize that the majority of refugees are usually so deeply rooted in their native culture and religion that these refugees are not at all open to the European mentality and social structure and therefore, at least latently, suffer from being inferior to Europeanism, from which terrorist acts then arise. Thus, the multicultural swarmers, who want to bring all refugees into the country and provide them, can even promote the terrorism and the opportunity for it.

From such fears, writers have written books on Islam, such as Michel Houellebecq's "Subjugation" or Hans-Peter Raddatz's "Iran," and others who even go so far as prophesizing the fall of the Occident due to this multi-cultural attitude.

Thankfully or unfortunately, social reality has shaken the European population so much that today, radical Muslims are largely marginalized and right-wing terrorism has emerged, which also endangers social peace. This is because the refugee flows and the resulting problems have overstrained the cosmopolitan liberal attitude, especially those of the less individualized population groups. It is also evident in England, Holland, Denmark and Sweden today, as it is usually called, "The boat is full". Europe threatens to break with the large number of refugees. Because, as is said, the European as an individual is also related to his respective national community. That's why European unification is such a lengthy process.

If Europeans also have to defend their national identity against the strangeness of refugees who do not want to become Germans, Austrians, and certainly not Hungarians, except in dual citizenship to enjoy the social benefits, there is little European solidarity and the European unification itself is endangered.

That's why Europe can only accept a limited number of refugees. The problems of the refugee movements in the countries of origin cannot be solved by accepting refugees. Europe can only integrate qualified people, but because of their qualifications, they have absorbed so much *Europeanism* that they realize that integration also makes them spiritually richer and that they also gain a more reflective understanding of their home nations.

As far as the problems of the country of origin are concerned, they can ultimately only be solved with the people of the countries. That is, anyone who runs away to save themselves leaves their fellow human beings to their fate instead of contributing to the solution itself. It must come to the realization that apart from natural disasters, the problems of a country and a people do not fall from the sky, but are founded in the people themselves, and everyone may not only enjoy the traditions and strengths of a people, but are also responsible for its sins - a truth that is difficult to understand for individualists.

It is true that Europeans are forced to do everything they can to solve economic and political conditions and social hardship in the refugees' home countries. But at the same time, social peace in Europe must be safeguarded and further developed. Refugee flows must therefore be limited to the extent that the host countries can cope without endangering social peace. The refugees must not be granted higher benefits than the poorest in their own country. That is why the living and working conditions of the local population must be improved.

This means, especially in times of secular stagnation, that the wealthy are more heavily burdened with the rehabilitation and development of infrastructure, social issues, education and research and giving aid to disadvantaged countries, even to avoid social envy.

Refugees are only considered worthy of protection if they are subjected to political, religious or ethnic persecution or have to fear for their lives in war zones or due to natural disasters. For these reasons, however, people usually do not flee far, because when the danger is over, they do not want to lose their home and their land. Also, if they flee far away, they usually want to return as soon as possible.

Something else is the case with refugees for economic reasons, as they flow from Africa to Europe in large numbers today. The faster the population in Africa rises and the further the economic and social development falls behind Europe, the more people will embark on the march to Europe despite great dangers. The only long-term safety, on the other hand, is the stabilization and development of the developing countries themselves.

The prerequisite for economic development, however, is that the country has not become incapable of governing itself through tribal feuds and / or militias, as is evident in South Sudan at present. Then, the country would have to be placed under a UN administration until national administrative structures are possible again.

Therefore, in order to prevent economic refugees, Europe should acquire extraterritorial areas from African countries in which asylum applications can be examined and to which all refugees arriving in Europe are repatriated, until their application is decided. It must be avoided for economic refugees to arrive at all in Europe and even have to be rescued in the Mediterranean.

European solidarity also requires that excessive burdens on refugees, such as in Italy and Greece, should be solved together.

4. The need for an enhanced development policy

We have seen emerging economies owe their partly rapid economic development to the adaptation of European education, technology and Western entrepreneurship. They were capable of doing so, because either they already lived in a high culture and / or enough Europeans settled in their country, who then promoted the development. In the economically backward African countries, on the other hand, we are largely dealing with tribal cultures and with regard to European archaic attitudes to life. Also, generally, they are too small for emerging markets to be worthwhile as an industrial location for foreign investors.

These countries are mostly void of any protection against global players of industrialized countries. As mentioned earlier, GATT's customs rounds are forcing them to lower their tariff rates. Because of these tariff reductions, but also due to the more developed agricultural economy in the industrialized countries, which is also subsidized, they are then flooded with cheaper food and other products and even products that they can produce themselves.

Here, it is necessary to discourage imports with sufficiently high barriers, so that the domestic economy can stabilize. Farmers need to be trained on how to increase their yields and not necessarily use pesticides, fertilizers and seeds purchased from international agribusinesses and chemical companies, but as ecologically as possible. Unfortunately, environmental damage and dependency on globally-operating agricultural and pharmaceutical companies are still favored by the development policies of the industrialized countries, as the following example shows:

Concerning Mozambique, Veronika Frenzel writes: 'The Mozambican politicians ... have implemented ... sooner than anywhere else, the conditions attached to international development assistance, such as investment under the G7 program "New Alliance for Food Security ". The Mozambicans have immediately transposed the guidelines of seed protection companies into laws. Only certified traders have been allowed to sell the certified seeds since then, as traditional trade is prohibited. The fact that the farmers are criminalized by this does not bother anyone.

The international private sector is getting a lot of power in the current programs of development policy, which is also the Marshall Plan by German Development Minister, Gerd Müller. The Deal: The international politicians are winning global corporations for investment, the "reform-oriented African politicians" are doing everything they can to make it easy for investors to invest in their countries.

Alberto, a 21-year-old Mozambican agronomist ..., is one of the winners of the development policy. He has a well-paid job with a large international seed company. Now he drives to the farmers and their fields every day explaining that improved seed doubles harvests, that peasants earn a lot of money from it, and that they can send their children to school. He does not say that the seed makes them dependent. It is expensive because they have to buy new seed every year because they cannot trade it. It is also because the seedlings from the new seed grow only with a lot of fertilizer and pesticides, and because they too do not give off anything if there is too much rain or too much drought. Alberto is convinced that he is doing everything right. He says he does business and that his goal is to get as much profit as possible. The common good is secondary.

Whether the farmers with the new seed and other investments really earn more money, neither Alberto nor the politicians, nor the companies are checking. Mozambicans already participating in the programs claim that they have less income since international companies have been in the country [707]

In developing countries, as with the Raiffeisenverband, a cooperation for joint purchasing, sales and use of agricultural machinery should be promoted. Information about market conditions, weather conditions and plants to be grown can already be accessed via smartphone. There are also organizations offering small loans, electronic payment and credit brokerage.

With the help of modern media knowledge, this should be communicated to the broad masses on the broadest front possible, and thus a working and economic attitude can be formed, on which industrial development can build. Only through the transfer of knowledge can a willingness develop to co-create social life.

However, this requires that industrialized countries change their development and agricultural policy from foreign trade promotion to a real development policy. Because, and I quote Horand Knaup et al., "'Our agricultural and food policy and also trade policy have a direct and indirect negative impact on many developing countries and especially on the poor population there," criticizes Klaus Töpfer, who has led the UN environmental program in Nairobi for many years. ... "Do we want to promote the African economy or our own?" asks the green expert, Uwe Kekeritz. ... "As long as Europe and the USA subsidize their agriculture so heavily, African farmers have no chance in Europe's markets," says Africa expert Kappel, "apart from the products that are not produced here."

---

[707] Veronika Frenzel: *Afrika kann die Welt retten*, in: Der Tagesspiegel, Nr. 23 161/ 2.7.2017, p.7.

For the African scientist, Helmut Asche, a professor at the University of Mainz, the key to a solid development of the continent lies in a comprehensive reform of European trade, as well as agricultural and fishing policies. Brussels protects and subsidizes European farmers and fishermen in a unique worldwide dimension". Fighting the causes of flight that were meant to be serious would end this one-sided help," says Asche.'[708]

5. Germany's responsibility for Europe and the world

If one traces the history of Europeanism, Germany played an important role in its geographical position. From Charlemagne, in 800 AD, until the abdication of the Habsburg Emperor Franz II on August 6, 1806, about 1000 years later, Germany understood itself to be the *Holy Roman Empire of the German Nation* and thus, at the same time, the guardian of the antique heritage and Christianity.

Certainly, the importance of the Emperor has steadily decreased over the centuries. The rulers, who originally ruled only as lords, emancipated themselves into sovereign kings, dukes and counts. The empire experienced an additional weakening through the Reformation, in which the Protestant princes deprived those faithful of the pope and made themselves masters of their regional church.

In the fifteenth century, with the rise of Spain and Portugal and later, the Netherlands, becoming the first naval powers, and their expansion into overseas territories, Western Europeanism developed, drawing its strength first from individual adventure, commerce and the domination of the seas.

In the wake of secularization and the emergence of political absolutism, France then became the leading European power, albeit in competition with the ever-growing Britain. With the French Revolution and the expansion of its ideals on continental Europe by Napoleon, the European emperorship also passed from the Habsburgs to Napoleon.

After the demise of Napoleon, England rose to become the bearer of Western Europeanism and retained this post until after the First World War. From then on, the leadership of the Western world passed to the United States.

The origin of East-West antagonism, however, already began with the division of the Roman Empire and Christianity into a Catholic and an Orthodox Church.

The Western European states and Russia gained political and military world power. In Western European countries, this dynamic was determined by individualistic intellectual development: statist, military and intellectual prowess in France and Darwinian, pragmatic, technical and economic competence in England. In Russia, on the other hand, the motivation for political action was Caesarean and personal motivation was a collective, mystical, Christian striving for salvation, the latter represented by Russian poets, thinkers and composers.

In German thinking, feeling and willing, the antique and Christian heritage and thus, the original Europeanism, was best preserved in its versatility, deepened and developed further. This is what the German composers, poets and thinkers stand

---

[708] Horand Knaup, Peter Müller, Jonas Weyrosta: *Das große Missverständnis*, in: Der Spiegel, Nr.28/8.7.2017, p.59.

for. Goethe, Schiller and the idealistic philosophy from Kant to Hegel are particularly representative of the motivation of German spirituality. In that regard, the Germans were world citizens and " the German essence should recover ~~of~~ the world".

But after the founding of the Empire at the end of the German-French War of 1870/71 and the abdication of the French Emperor, Napoleon III., but Germany also wanted to be a world power economically, militarily and politically and, as it was said, the other states had "a place in the sun". After the accession to the throne of Emperor Willem II, Germany also moved onto the political scene in a cocky and clumsy way, and provoked the states both to the West and to the East.

Just as France carried out the *French Revolution* not only for France, but for the world as a whole, so that *being French* was synonymous with *being a citizen of the world*, the French then fell back into narrow-minded nationalism, thus Germany pursued nationalistic aims after the founding of the Reich in 1871,

Now the confession of the nation is an advance insofar as the individual emancipates himself from his tribal and family relations as well as from foreign rule. Also, the awareness of national culture and its identification with its cultural heritage make people richer. But just as material wealth obliges us to work for our fellow human beings and the world according to its wealth, and as though the economy and society were going to be destroyed, when wealth becomes an end in itself, so too should the citizen consider his national cultural heritage a blessing to humanity. Otherwise, there will be an attempt to dominate and oppress other people and to start wars.

Historically, under the political circumstances of the nineteenth century, it was probably only possible to politically unite Germany, as Bismarck did and only the foundation of the Second German Kaiserreich could realize the economic and scientific potencies of Germany. The associated nationalism was, however, precisely because Germany had its value as a cultural nation, an even greater betrayal of German ideals.

If history had any meaning, then it was only logical that in the two world wars, Germans nationalism was most consistently destroyed, and that Germany should today be guided least, out of all European countries, by national interests alone.

The Germans were then in danger of sacrificing their own identity to Western capitalist, self-centered Americanism, or, as before the turn of the GDR, to Sovietism.

Sovietism has collapsed economically, politically and socially. Americanism has meanwhile perverted into Casino Capitalism and Trumpism. Europe must be the driving force for the harmonious economic and social development of the world, and Germany, as the center of Europe and leading European economic power, must take on a special responsibility for this. An economic guide should be followed to the principles of *Social Market Economy* and the constitutional principle *Property obliges*.

What is necessary for the recovery of the economy has already been presented and is publicly discussed in many aspects. It has also been outlined how Germany's export surpluses and narrow-minded austerity policies aggravated economic problems inside and outside Europe.

As is said, reducing budgetary surpluses and, moreover, the unequal distribution of income and wealth in favor of higher government spending could help to increase imports and thus reduce export surpluses.

With regard to the distribution of income and wealth, it has been emphasized that income and wealth are the merit of the current generation only to the extent that the inventors and entrepreneurs living in it have acquired income and wealth themselves. Everything inherited is the work of earlier generations, and according to the general understanding of society, should belong to the community of human beings again at the latest when people have died.

Also, as far as inherited culture and economic development are concerned, they are the merit of previous generations. If the inhabitants of industrialized countries build on this, they should be aware of it and feel the obligation all the more strongly to share in the inheritance, even those non-beneficiaries.

The primary principle of the economy is not, as capitalist Darwinism suggests, only struggle and competition, but the division of labor and mutual dependence. Even entrepreneurs are only successful to the extent that others supply them with the necessary precursors and with what they need for their lives, and are prepared to buy their products.

Competition will continue to develop the economy, but only so long as the reciprocity of economic relations does not suffer. If economic relations dry up, it is because all resources and assets are now left in the hands of the few, and the others fall out of the economic process, so economic demand is reduced. All people are affected, including the wealthy. That is why every economic operator must be interested in the fact that everyone else can live, work and develop optimally. An illustrative example of this was the Marshall Plan after World War II, which revitalized the European economy, and also made the USA a strong economic partner.

This principle should be a guide to German foreign policy and foreign trade policy. First and foremost, it will be about developing Europe as a whole so that it is not crushed by the USA and Russia, and it can help developing countries as well.

Germany, as the economically strongest European country, should lead by example in the implementation of the described economic policy tasks. Only then can it insist that other countries tackle their economic deficits, especially since reforms always mean painful interventions for the former beneficiaries.

The narrow-minded Supply-sided Economic Policy must be overcome. The economic objective should not be primarily aimed at increasing entrepreneurial profits, but rather at meeting national and global economic needs and steering purchasing power there. Moreover, it is only by stimulating demand that sufficient investment can be stimulated and in case of doubt, entrepreneurial profits increase more than in an economy slowed down by secular stagnation.

Germany can learn economic and social policy from Scandinavian countries. The most important intra-European partners should be France and Poland. Everything should be done so that the new French President, Emmanuel Macron, succeeds in revitalizing the French economy and thus setting an example for Southern European countries.

In order to ease the strained political relationship with Russia, the fears of Eastern European countries vis-à-vis Russia would have to be overcome, and they should play a bridging role to the huge Russian market and Russian goods. Poland, as the largest Eastern European country, plays an exemplary role here. For this, however, fascist tendencies in Poland must be overcome.

D. Summary

Without the special intellectual, economic and social development of the antique and Christian heritage and its globalization, humanity would not have developed as before. Europeanism caused:

- the emancipation of the free, self-confident and self-responsible individual from tribal societies and family hierarchies and thus science and technology, a liberal economy and a democratic state form and
- the return of the individual to society, and thus, a social relationship with his fellow human beings and responsibility for the earth.

What in Europe is more or less just two components of Europeanism is diverging in the West and the East. It becomes an extremely individualistic capitalist Western European in the West and a more collective, socialist attitude in the East.

Western and Eastern Europeanism develop antagonistically. Accordingly, Western European globalization is taking place in the form of the colonization of overseas territories and finally becomes an American-dominated capitalist world, while in the East, there is Russia's expansion to Vladivostok and the Black Sea and finally, the Soviet-dominated Eastern Bloc.

The globalization of Europeanism and especially the individualization and secularization of society, which developed in Europe over a thousand years, tore non-Europeans out of their traditional references in a relatively short period of time and created greater social crises in these countries, the extent of which depended on how archaic the social structures were before.

Advanced Asian cultures have been able to adapt to Europeanism more easily, and so Japan, South Korea and, more recently, China, have been economically aligned with industrialized countries. African countries, especially if there are few settlers from Europe or were deprived there, are still relatively underdeveloped. These countries suffer in part from internal conflicts and corrupt elites. Nevertheless, the level of development is, of course, much higher than before colonization. But with this progress, new social problems have arisen.

In the Muslim states, religious resistance also developed over the course of the globalization of Europeanism. Islam, like Christianity, in contrast to ethnically-based religions, is a faith that applies, in principle, to all people. Therefore, Christianity and Islam competed with each other and stood for "the souls of the people".

Since Islam considers itself to be the last divine revelation, there are reservations in Islam against Christian or even secular forms of rule, because secularism is rightly regarded as the outflow of Europeanism. Then add the fundamental enmity between Sunnis and Shiites to this.

The propensity for violence, built up in the early days of Islam, had largely declined over the centuries, but was then stirred up again with the globalization of Europeanism, the collapse of the Ottoman Empire and the founding of Israel.

In addition, Europeanism was globalized in the western capitalist and eastern socialist one-sidedness and Europeans did not appear as world citizens but as nationalists. Therefore, globalization was experienced as colonization, oppression and exploitation.

Besides, countries were divided by the European countries and arbitrary borders were drawn through ethnic groups, or different ethnic groups were tied together in a state. Also, the emancipation of people from their tribe did also not make them world citizens, but nationalists.

The development of the economy, and thus also of prosperity and society, the individual's creativity, aroused by Western Europeanism, proved to be a driving force. However, over the decades entrepreneurship has increasingly become perverted to capitalist money making and turned the economy into Casino Capitalism.

In addition, the acquired assets were inherited - a relic of the feudal society and so, in a society related to the individual, were deemed absurd. Thus, with each generation, wealth and income distribution changed in favor of less and less wealthy people and had poorer people worse starting conditions for entry into professional life.

As long as the rising savings were reinvested in the real economy, the economy was able to develop all the more dynamically. But from the sixties onwards, when profitable investment opportunities lagged behind growing savings volume, the economy fell into a *secular stagnation*. The emergence of crises due to insufficient demand could only be prevented by increasing government spending. But since these were financed not by higher taxes and levies, but by borrowing, national debt grew and dumped more and more worthless government securities into the capital market.

While the masses of the population emancipated themselves from tribal and family hierarchies, but have themselves in their nation, scientists and entrepreneurs go beyond national boundaries and feel rather like a world citizen. As capitalists, and even more as capital market players who indulge in egoistic profit-making are also expanding beyond national borders with more and more global companies and becoming powers that evade state order. Since the economies of the states depend on them, states vie for them, offering low taxes and other perks to bring them into the country. In doing so, the states themselves are contributing to the intensification of secular stagnation and the destruction of the global economy.

In order to reduce labor costs, manufacturing from industrialized countries is relocated to low-wage countries, leaving unemployment or precarious employment conditions for the less skilled workers in industrialized countries. On the other hand, large companies from industrialized countries flood developing countries with their agricultural products, causing their domestic operations to perish there. The open land and more and more virgin forest are being bought and used for the mass production of raw materials for industrialized countries. This in turn will primarily benefit industrialized countries and corrupt elites in developing countries.

Digitization and robotization will mean that more and more jobs will be lost worldwide. Rationalization also means that labor income will fall in favor of higher profits and capital market returns, i.e., an increase in unequal wealth and income distribution and thus, in turn, an increase in Secular Stagnation and Casino Capitalism.

Due to already-achieved and still growing international interdependence, more and more all states are affected by abuse from other countries. Manifold problems from the perverted economy, social need in developing countries, refugees and nationally and religiously-motivated conflicts create international chaos.

This chaos causes more and more people to doubt the meaning of globalization and its responsibilities, and to demand a retreat to national concerns. For these motives, Britain left the European Union and the new American President, Donald Trump, with the motto "America first", pursues a purely national foreign trade policy. Trumpism is also threatening to divide and weaken Europe.

The USA is big enough as an economic area and an industrial power and can afford isolation policies, even if they harm themselves, at least during the transition to it. Smaller countries, however, become the plaything of international corporations if they cannot join forces with other countries to form a larger economic area and exert an influence on entrepreneurial behavior solely through the size of their market.

With the emergence of emerging economies such as China, and, in particular, the world's superpowers, the USA and Russia, Western and Eastern Europeanism are losing their importance. But that does not mean that Europeanism would become obsolete as a catalyst for further economic and social development. On the contrary, it is important to remember the true ideals of Europeanism. That can only come from the European center - in both senses of the word. That is why Europe needs to consolidate and strengthen, but should remain as cosmopolitan as possible.

The ideals of the French Revolution, "Freedom, equality, brotherhood", must be given equal weight, and what has to be done and what particular responsibility Germany has to shoulder, is worked out. But perhaps it needs such an erratic American president, like Donald Trump, to recollect and overcome *keep-it-coming politics*.

Literaturverzeichnis

Abrahamian, Ervand: *A History of Modern Iran*. Cambridge Univ. Press, 2008, ISBN 978-0-521-52891-7.

Al-Marashi, Ibrahim, Sammy Salama: *Iraq's Armed Forces: An Analytical History*, New York, 2008.

Al-Massad Joseph: *Colonial Effects. The Making of National Jordan*. New York City 2001.

Ansprenger, Franz: *Auflösung der Kolonialreiche* München, 4. Aufl. 1981.

Asadi, Awat: *Der Kurdistan-Irak-Konflikt. Der Weg zur Autonomie seit dem Ersten Weltkrieg*, Berlin 2007.

Axworthy, Michael: *Revolutionary Iran: A History of the Islamic Republic*. 1. Aufl. Penguin Books, London 2013, ISBN 978-1-84614-291-8, S. 28.

Baba, Masao/Tatemoto, Masahiro: *Foreign Trade and Economic Growth in Japan: 1858-1937*. in: Klein, Lawrence/ Ohkawa, Kazushi: *Economic Growth. The Japanese Experience since the Meiji Era*. Richard D. Irwin Inc. Illinois, 1968.

Balaghi, Shiva: *Saddam Hussein* - A Biography, Westport, 2006.

Barker, A. J.: *The First Iraq War, 1914-1918: Britain's Mesopotamian Campaign* (New York: Enigma Books, 2009). ISBN 978-1-929631-86-5

Barth, Boris: *Die Zäsur des Ersten Weltkriegs. Hochzeit und Dekolonisation der Kolonialreiche*. In: Ders. et al.: Das Zeitalter des Kolonialismus. Stuttgart 2007.

Benz, Ernst: *Die russische Kirche und das abendländische Christentum*, München 1966.

Bierling, Stephan: *Geschichte des Irakkrieges. Der Sturz Saddams und Amerikas Albtraum im Mittleren Osten*. Beck, München 2010.

Black, George: *Genocide in Iraq: The Anfal Campaign Against the Kurds*. Human Rights Watch, 1993, ISBN 978-1-56432-108-4.

Borscheid, Peter: *Das Tempo-Virus. Eine Kulturgeschichte der Beschleunigung*, Campus Verlag Frankfurt/New York 2004.

Böss Otto: *Die Lehre der Eurasier. Ein Beitrag zur russischen Ideengeschichte des 20. Jahrhunderts*. Harrassowitz, Wiesbaden 1961.

Brechna, Habibo: *Die Geschichte Afghanistans*. 2. Auflage. vdf Hochschulverlag AG, Zürich 2012, ISBN 3-7281-3391-4.

Bringen, Dieter, Krzysztof Ruchniewicz (Hrsg.): *Länderbericht Polen*. Bundeszentrale für politische Bildung, Bonn 2009, ISBN 978-3-593-38991-2, S. 373.

Buchta, Wilfried: *Terror vor Europas Toren. Der Islamische Staat, Iraks Zerfall und Amerikas Ohnmacht*. Campus Verlag, Frankfurt am Main, 2015, ISBN 978-3-593-50290-8.

Clausen, Markus: *Am Ursprung des Arbeitsethos*, Schweizer Monatshefte : Zeitschrift für Politik, Wirtschaft, Kultur, Band (Jahr): 75 (1995), Heft 3, S.23, PDF erstellt am: 30.05.2016. Persistenter Link: http://dx.doi.org/10.5169/seals-165423 .

Clements, Frank: *Conflict in Afghanistan: A Hist. Encyclopedia*. ABC-CLIO, 2003, ISBN 1-85109-402-4.

Collins, Joseph J.: *Understanding War in Afghanistan.* National Defense University Press, Washington, D.C. 2011. ISBN 978-1-78039-924-9.

Conermann, Stephan und Geoffrey Haig (Hrsg.): Asien und Afrika: Beiträge des Zentrums für Asiat. und Afrik. Studien (ZAAS) der Christian-Albrechts-Universität zu Kiel. Bd. 8. Die Kurden. Schenefeld 2004.

Cooper, J. P.: *The New Cambridge Modern History*, Volume IV: The Decline of Spain and the Thirty Years War, 1609–48/59. CUP Archive, 1979, ISBN 0521297134.

Drews, Peter: Herder und die Slawen. Mat. zur Wirkungsgeschichte bis zur Mitte des 19. Jahrhunderts. München 1990. Und auch das Kapitel 1.3.2 Die Spezifika der poln. Geschichte und ihre Mythologisierung.

Eckelt, Markus: *Syrien im internationalen System. Die Politische Ökonomie des Ba'th-Regimes vor und nach der doppellten Zäsur 1990, Demokratie und Entwicklung* Bd.64, LIT Verlag.

Edlinger, Fritz (Hg.): *Libyen. Hintergründe, Analysen, Berichte*, Wien 2011.

Esmeray: *"Das Reich der Osmanen"*, Diplomarbeit, http://meissoun.ch/i-harem.html.

Fahmy, Khaled: *All The Pasha's Men – Mehmed Ali, his army and the making of modern Egypt*, Kairo, New York, 1997.

Finkel, Caroline: *Osman's Dream: The Story of the Ottoman Empire 1300–1923.* John Murray, London 2006, ISBN 978-0-7195-6112-2.

Gassert, Philipp und andere (Hrsg.): *Zweiter Kalter Krieg und Friedensbewegung.* München 2011.

Geißler, Karlheinz A.: *Die Zeiten ändern sich. Vom Umgang mit der Zeit in unterschiedlichen Epochen*, in: Aus Politik und Zeitgeschichte. Beilage zu Wochenzeitung Das Parlament vom 30.07.1999.

Gellermann, Uli/Friedhelm Klinkhammer /Volker Bräutigam: *Die Macht um acht. Der Faktor Tagesschau* , Papa Rossa Verlag Köln 2017.

Ghani, Cyrus: *Iran and the Rise of Reza Shah. From Qajar Collapse to Pahlavi Rule.* I. B. Tauris, London u. a. 2000, ISBN 1-86064-629-8.

Ghirshman, R.: *Afghanistan*, (ii) ethnography, in The Encyclopaedia of Islam. New Edition, CD-ROM Edition v. 1.0 ed., Leiden, Niederlande

Glatzer, Bernt: *Afghanistan: Ethnic and tribal disintegration?* In: William Maley (Hrsg.): Fundamentalism Reborn?: Afghanistan And The Taliban. New York Univ. Press, New York 1998, ISBN 0-8147-5585-2.

Goerdt, Wilhelm: *Russische Philosophie*, Verlag Karl Alber Freiburg/München 1984.

Gronau, Dietrich: *Mustafa Kemal Atatürk oder die Geburt der Republik.* Fischer, Frankfurt am Main 1994.

Gronke, Monika: *Geschichte Irans, Von der Islamisierung bis zur Gegenwart.* 3. Aufl. C.H. Beck Verlag, 2009, ISBN 978-3-406-48021-8.

Gründer, Horst: *Geschichte der deutschen Kolonien*, Schöningh UTB.

Guthrie, Alice: *Decoding Daesh: Why is the new name for ISIS so hard to understand?*, Free Word Centre vom 19. Februar 2015.

Hoekmann, Gerrit: *Zwischen Ölzweig und Kalaschnikow, Geschichte und Politik der palästinensischen Linken*, Münster 1999, ISBN 3-928300-88-1.

Hofmann, Tessa: *Annäherung an Armenien. Geschichte und Gegenwart*. München: Beck, 1997.

Holik, Josef: *Die Rüstungskontrolle: Rückblick auf eine kurze Ära*. Duncker & Humblot, 2008, ISBN 978-3-428-12928-7.

Hottinger, Arnold: *7mal Naher Osten*. München 1972.

İnalçık, Halil und Donald Quataert (Hrsg.): *An economic and social history of the Ottoman Empire*. 1. Auflage. Cambridge University Press, Cambridge, New York 1997, ©1994, ISBN 0-521-34315-1.

Isam, Salem Kamel: *Islam und Völkerrecht. Das Völkerrecht der islamischen Weltanschauung*. Berlin 1984.

Karsh, Efraim, Inari Rautsi: *Saddam Hussein - A political biography*, New York, 1991.

Kazimierzewicz, Kasimierz: *Europa wird es kosakisch oder republikanisch? Eine auf die Memoiren Napoleons, das Testament Peter des Großen und viele andere gewichtsvolle Dokumente gestützte Abhandlung über die unserem Welttheil drohenden Gefahren und die Mittel zu deren Abwendung als Vorlage für einen europäi-schen Kongress*. 2. Aufl. Leipzig 1866

Küpeli, Ismail: *Was ging schief beim 'Untergang des Morgenlandes'?*, München, 2006.

Kreiser, Klaus, Christoph K. Neumann: *Kleine Geschichte der Türkei*, Stuttgart 2009.

Kruhöffer, Gerald: *Was heißt christliche Freiheit heute?,* Text erschienen im Loccumer Pelikan 3/2003.

Landgrebe, Alix: „Wenn es Polen nicht gäbe, dann müsste es erfunden werden" Die Entwicklung des polnischen Nationalbewusstseins im europäischen Kontext, Studien der Forschungsstelle Ostmitteleuropa an der Univer-sität Dortmund, Bd. 35, Harrassowitz Verlag 2003.

Leo, M.: *Patriotische Färbung und Wirklichkeit in der russ. Literatur im ersten Drittel des XVIII. Jahrhunderts*. Diss./Münster 1969, ungedr.

Lepetit, Bernard: *Frankreich 1750-1850*, in: Mieck, Ilja (Hg.) (1993): Hdb. der europäischen Wirtschafts- und Sozialgeschichte, Bd. 4, Stuttgart.

Lewis, Bernard: *The Political Language of Islam*. Chicago 1988.

Lister, Charles: *Profling the Islamic State*, Brookings Doha Center, 2014.

Löwer, Hans-Joachim: *Die Stunde der Kurden. Wie sie den Nahen Osten verändern*, Wien–Graz–Klagenfurt 2015.

Marr, Phebe: *The Modern History of Iraq*, Boulder, 2012.

Mehmet, Özay: *Fundamentalismus und Nationalstaat*. Europ. Verlagsanstalt 2002. ISBN 3-434-46104-3.

Meier, Andreas: *Der politische Auftrag des Islam*, Wuppertal 1994.

Meiers, Franz Josef: *Von der Entspannung zur Konfrontation: die amerikanische Sowjetpolitik im Widerstreit von Innen- und Außenpolitik 1969–1980*. Brockmeyer, 1987, ISBN 3-88339-630-3.

Meyer, Henrik: *Hamas und Hizbollah. Eine Analyse ihres Politischen Denkens*. LIT Verlag, 2009, ISBN 978-3-8258-1836-4.

Milton-Edwards, Beverley, Farrell, Stephen: *Hamas: The Islamic Resistance Movement*. John Wiley & Sons, 2010, ISBN 978-0-7456-4296-3.

Mittelsten Scheid Jörg: *Pulverfass Pakistan*. Nikolaische Verlagsbuchhandlung GMBH,Berlin, ISBN 978-3-89479-808-6.

Morris, Benny: *1948 – A History of the First Arab-Israeli War*. New Haven 2008.

Mustafa Nazdar (Pseud.): *Die Kurden in Syrien*, in: Gérard Chaliand (Hrg.), Kurdistan und die Kurden, Bd. 1, Göttingen 1988, ISBN 3-922197-24-8.

Naimark, Norman M.: *Flammender Haß. Ethnische Säuberungen im 20. Jahrhundert*. Fischer Taschenbuch, Stuttgart 2008, (Originaltitel: Fires of Hatred: Ethnic Cleansing in Twentieth-Century Europe, 2001)

Oehring, Otmar: *Zur gegenwärtigen Situation der Christen im Nahen Osten*, KAS-Auslandsinfo., 4/2010.

Oğuzlu, H. Tarık: *The Turkomans of Iraq as A Factor in Turkish Foreign Policy: Socio-Political and Demo-graphic Perspectives*. Turkish Foreign Policy Institute, 2001, abg. am 6. 1. 2012.

Oliver Ernst: *Menschenrechte und Demokratie in den deutsch-türkischen Beziehungen. Die Menschenrechtspolitik der Bundesrepublik Deutschland im Spannungsfeld der inneren und äußeren Sicherheit*, Münster 2002.

Osterhammel, Jürgen: *Vom Umgang mit dem „Anderen". Zivilisierungsmissionen – in Europa und darüber hinaus*. In: Boris Barth et al.: Das Zeitalter des Kolonialismus. Stuttgart 2007.

Patterson, David: *Denial, Evasion, and Antihistorical Antisemitism: The Continuing Assault on Memory*. In Alvin H. Rosenfeld (Hrsg.): Deciphering the New Antisemitism. Indiana University Press, Bloomington (IN) 2015, ISBN 978-0-253-01865-6.

Petersen, Uwe: *Das Böse in uns. Phänomenologie und Genealogie des Bösen*, Novum Verlag 2005.

Petersen, Uwe: *Im Anfang war die Tat I. Die Geburt des Willens in der europäischen Philosophie*, Verlag Dr. Kovac Hamburg 2012.

Petersen, Uwe: Philosophie der Psychologie, Psychogenealogie und Psychotherapie. Ein Leitfaden für Philosophische Praxis, Verlag Dr. Kovac Hamburg 2010, S. 360ff.

Petersen, Uwe: *Raum, Zeit Fortschritt. Kategorien des Handelns und der Globalisierung*, Novum Verlag 2006.

Petersen, Uwe: *Säkulare Stagnation unser Schicksal. Grenzen der Angebotsorientierten Wirtschaftspolitik*, „. Aktual. Aufl. 2016.

Petersen, Uwe: *Sprache als wissenschaftlicher er Gegenstand, philosophisches Phänomen und Tat*, Königshausen @Neumann 2008.

Petersen, Uwe: Wirtschaftsethik und Wirtschaftspolitik, Verlag Dr. Kovac Hamburg 2010.

Ploetz, Michael, Hans-Peter Müller: *Ferngelenkte Friedensbewegung?* Münster 2004.

Poppe, Ulrike, Rainer Eckert, Ilko-Sascha Kowalczuk: *Zwischen Selbstbehauptung und Anpassung: Formen des Widerstandes und der Opposition in der DDR*. Christoph Links, Berlin 1995, ISBN 3-86153-097-X.

Radischtschew, A.N.: Ausgew. Werke …, Berlin 1959, „*Wer ist ein Sohn des Vaterlandes?*";

Rasanayagam, Angelo: *Afghanistan: A Modern History*. I.B. Tauris, 2005 ISBN 1-85043-857-9.

Raschid, Achmed: *Taliban: Islam, Oil and the New Great Game in Central Asia*. I.B. Tauris, 2002 ISBN 1-86064-830-4 S.57.

Roemer, H. R.: *The Safavid Period*. In: The Cambridge History of Iran, Vol. 6: The Timurid and Safavid Periods. Cambridge University Press, Cambridge 1986, ISBN 0521200946, S. 189–350.

Schetter, Conrad: *II. Strukturen und Lebenswelten – Stammesstrukturen und ethnische Gruppen.*

Schimmel, Annemarie: *Das islamische Jahr. Zeiten und Feste*. C.H.Beck, München 2002, ISBN 3406475671.

Sedgwick, Mark J.: *Neo-Eurasianism in Russia*. In: Against the Modern World. Traditionalism and the Secret Intellectual History of the Twentieth Century. Oxford University Press, New York 2004, ISBN 0-19-515297-2, S. 221–240.

Segev, Tom: *Es war einmal ein Palästina – Juden und Araber vor der Staatsgründung Israels*. 4. Auflage, München 2005.

Sezgin, Fuat: *Geschichte des arabischen Schrifttums*. Brill, 1967. Band 1.

Shirali Mahnaz: *The Mystery of Contemporary Iran*. 1. Aufl. Transaction Publishers, New Brunswick 2015, ISBN 978-1-4128-5462-7.

Simonyi, K.: *Kulturgeschichte der Physik*, Wiss.Verlag Harry Deutsch 2001, ISBN 3-8171-1651-9.

Solowjew, Wl.: Deutsche Gesamtausgabe der Werke, Freiburg i.Br. 1957.

Ternon, Yves: *Tabu Armenien: Geschichte eines Völkermordes*. Frankfurt am Main Berlin 1988.

Umland, Andreas: *Alexander Dugin, the Issue of Post-Soviet Fascism, and Russian Political Discourse Today*. In: Russian Analystical Digest. 14, Nr. 7, 2007.

Utermark, Sören: *„Schwarzer Untertan versus schwarzer Bruder". Bernhard Dernburgs Reformen in den Kolonien Deutsch-Ostafrika, Deutsch-Südwestafrika, Togo und Kamerun*, Dissertation, Uni. Kassel 2012.

Vrabl, Andreas: *„Libyen: Eine Dritte Welt - Revolution in der Transition"*, Diplomarbeit, Wien 2008.

Wallerstein, Immanuel: Unthinking Social Science, London, 1991.

Wendorff, Rudolf (1980): *Zeit und Kultur. Geschichte des Zeitbewusstseins in Europa*, Opladen.

Wiedemann, Erich: *DAS ZEITALTER DER KOLONIEN ZWIESPÄLTIGES ERBE*, in: SPIEGEL SPECIAL Geschichte 2/2007.

Wiederkehr, Stefan: *»Kontinent Evrasija« – Klassischer Eurasismus und Geopolitik in der Lesart Alexander Dugins*, in: Markus Kaiser (Hrsg.): Auf der Suche nach Eurasien. Politik, Religion und Alltagskultur zwischen Russland und Europa. Transcript, Bielefeld 2004, ISBN 3-89942-131-0.

Wiederkehr, Stefan: *»Kontinent Evrasija« – Klassischer Eurasismus und Geopolitik in der Lesart Alexander Dugins*. In Markus Kaiser (Hrsg.): Auf der Suche nach Eurasien. Politik, Religion und Alltagskultur zwischen Russland und Europa. Transcript, Bielefeld 2004, ISBN 3-89942-131-0, S. 125–138.

Wilke, Boris: *Governance und Gewalt. Eine Untersuchung zur Krise des Regierens in Pakistan am Fall Belutschistan.* (Memento vom 22. Dezember 2009 im Internet Archive) (PDF; 731 kB) SFB – Governance Working Paper

Author

Uwe Petersen born August 2.1932 in Rendsburg Germany, 1956 Diploma in Economics in Heidelberg, 1964 Doctor of Philosophy in Heidelberg (supervisor Hans-Georg Gadamer, co-supervisor Jürgen Habermas) with the thesis "The Relation of Theory and Practise in the Transcendental Phenomenology of Edmund Husserl". From 1965 in different economic groups and in the economic promotion and strategical management consultancy. Since 1998 he deals mainly with philosophy of action.

Previous Publications

Das Verhältnis von Theorie und Praxis in der Transzendentalen Phänomenologie Edmund Husserls, Dissertation Heidelberg 1964

Ost-West-Kooperation- Möglichkeiten und Grenzen, Rissener Studien, Eigenverlag HAUS RISSEN, Institut für Politik und Wirtschaft 1974

Arbeitslosigkeit unser Schicksal - Wirtschaftspolitik in der Stagflation Peter Lang Verlag, Frankfurt/M. 1985

Finanzmittelplanung in: "Unternehmensgründung, Handbuch des Gründungsmanagements", Verlag Franz Vahlen, München 1990

Finanzmittelplanung, in "Gründungsplanung und Gründungsfinanzierung", Beck-Wirtschaftsberater im dtv, 1991, 2. völlig überarb. Auflage 1995, Finanzbedarfs- und Finanzierungsplanung in 3. Aufl. 2000.

Das Böse in uns. Phänomenologie und Genealogie des Bösen novum Verlag Horitschon-Wien-München 2005.

The Evil in us Phenomenology an Genealogy of Evil, novum pro Verlag 2014.

Raum, Zeit, Fortschritt. Kategorien des Handelns und der Globalisierung novum Verlag, Horitschon-Wien-München 2006.

Das Verhältnis von Theorie und Praxis in der Transzendentalen Phänomenologie Edmund Husserls, Neudruck der Heidelberger Dissertation mit einem Nachtrag: *Husserl als Handlungsphilosoph*, Philosophische Reihe Hg. J. Heil, Turnshare Ltd. London 2007.

Kreativität und Willensfreiheit im Zwielicht sinnlicher Erfahrung und theoretische Leugnung, Königshausen& Neumann, Würzburg 2007.

Religionsphilosophie der Naturwissenschaften, Philosophische Reihe Hg. J. Heil, Turnshare Ltd. London 2007.

Sprache als wissenschaftlicher Gegenstand, philosophisches Phänomen und Tat, Königshausen& Neumann, Würzburg 2008.

Philosophie der Psychologie, Psychogenealogie und Psychotherapie. Ein Leitfaden für Philosophische Praxis, Verlag Dr. Kovač 2010.

Wirtschaftsethik und Wirtschaftspolitik. Zur Lösung der globalen Wirtschaftskrise.

Von der liberalen zur sozialliberalen Wirtschaftsordnung, Verlag Dr. Kovač 2010.

Anthropologie und Handlungsphilosophie, Verlag Dr. Kovač 2011

Unkonventionelle Betrachtungsweisen zur Wirtschaftskrise.
> *Von Haien, Heuschrecken und anderem Getier*, Peter Lang Verlag 2011.

Unkonventionelle Betrachtungsweisen zur Wirtschaftskrise II.
> *Krankheiten des Wirtschaftssystems und Möglichkeiten und Grenzen ihrer Heilung.* Peter Lang Verlag 2011.

Unkonventionelle Betrachtungsweisen zur Wirtschaftskrise III.
> *Was ist zur Lösung der Krise zu tun?* Peter Lang Verlag 2012.

Unconventional Consideration Manners of the Economic Crisis III.
> *What is to be done for the solution of the crisis?* Peter Lang Verlag 2013

Im Anfang war die Tat I. Die Geburt des Willens in der Europäischen Philosophie

Im Anfang war die Tat II. Vom Willen zur Tat Verlag Dr. Kovač 2012.

*Are we Doomed to Secular Stagnation? Limitations of Supply-Side Economic Policies.*2014,
> *ISBN -13: 978-1503319103.*

Säkulare Stagnation unser Schicksal? Grenzen der Angebotsorientierten Wirtschaftspolitik.
> 2. aktual. Aufl. 2016, ISBN 978-3-00-054939-7.

Zeitfracht Medien GmbH
Ferdinand-Jühlke-Straße 7
99095 Erfurt, Deutschland
produktsicherheit@kolibri360.de